READING COMPREHENSION:
FROM RESEARCH TO PRACTICE

READING COMPREHENSION:
FROM RESEARCH TO PRACTICE

Edited by

Judith Orasanu
U.S. Army Research Institute for the
Behavioral and Social Sciences

LEA LAWRENCE ERLBAUM ASSOCIATES, PUBLISHERS
1986   Hillsdale, New Jersey   London

Lawrence Erlbaum Associates, Inc., Publishers
365 Broadway
Hillsdale, New Jersey 07642

Library of Congress Cataloging in Publication Data
Main entry under title:

Reading comprehension.

Bibliography: p.
Includes index.
1. Reading comprehension — Addresses, essays,
lectures.   2. Language arts — Addresses, essays,
lectures.   3. Reading — Research — United States — Case
studies.   I. Orasanu, Judith.
LB1050.45.R425   1986   428.4′3   85-12956
ISBN 0-89859-528-2
ISBN 0-89859-798-6 (pbk.)

Printed in the United States of America
10   9   8   7   6   5   4   3   2   1

To my parents, who read to me.

Contents

Part III   Instructional Implications

Part IV   From Research to Practice: Case Studies

Preface

When the National Institute of Education (NIE) was created in 1972, a planning group was commissioned to lay out a research agenda on reading. After listening to the views of reading researchers and educators, the group produced a report entitled *Linguistic Communication: Perspectives for Research* (Miller, 1973). It identified the two most pressing national literacy problems as: imparting basic literacy to those who most need it, and raising language comprehension in the entire population.

By then, the Office of Education had already committed substantial resources to the first of these two problems, mainly through support for research on curriculum development and improvement of reading instruction at the elementary school level, which focused mainly on teaching decoding skills. The new agenda primarily addressed the second issue.

Specifically, the study group's major recommendation was that high priority be given to research to develop an explicit theory of how people communicate:

> Comprehension is the purpose of reading, yet we know far too little about the knowledge and conceptual organization needed for advanced reading competence. Although we have learned much about the legibility of type, patterns of eye movements, rates of information processing, and the like, these facts have not been put together in a coherent scientific theory of reading. We must understand better the higher mental processes that control the intentional act of reading. Because principled improvements in current practice will depend on sound theory of the skills to be taught, recommendation V deserves high priority.

Recommendation V was that the NIE should support efforts to understand: (a) the cognitive processes involved in acquiring basic reading skills, and (b) the cognitive processes involved in comprehending linguistic messages.

Spurred on by national statistics concerning literacy achievement in schools, functional literacy problems in the workplace, and rising literacy demands of a technological society, the NIE accepted the challenge and supported research that addressed those needs.

This book summarizes what has been learned about reading comprehension in the decade since the NIE planning group made its recommendations. Many of the individual chapters are based on a workshop held in Washington, DC, in September, 1982, to assess progress toward the report's goals and to identify remaining problems. The first section of the book summarizes fundamental new knowledge about the comprehension process. This includes the psychological processes involved in reading and understanding text, the role of background knowledge in comprehension and making inferences, the contributions of discourse and communication analysis to comprehension, the purposeful, strategic and self-monitoring aspects of comprehension, and the relation between oral language development and reading. These topics represent the major lines of research that have emerged over the past decade, steps toward developing the sound theory on which to base instruction called for by the planning group. These chapters serve as the foundation for the next two sections.

A new concept of what reading comprehension is carries with it implications for how and what to teach, for writing and selecting instructional materials, and for assessment procedures. These practical implications are described in the second section of this book.

While researchers were piecing together a theory of comprehension, educators had to get on with the business of teaching reading. The third section of the book presents case studies of several local school districts' efforts to apply the new research findings and concept of comprehension to classroom instruction. The cases describe both the substance of the changes and the process of making those changes.

Beyond the researchers and practitioners whose efforts are evident in these chapters, a virtual army of people has contributed to this project. I wish to express my gratitude to them for their insights, sense of history and purpose, and personal encouragement. Most significant were my colleagues at NIE who supported this work from the beginning. Credit for initiating the 10-year retrospective and synthesis rests with Lois-ellin Datta and Ned Chalker, then of the Teaching and Learning Program at NIE, which supported much of the research reported in this volume. Monte Penney must be credited not only with helping to organize the synthesis effort, but for the direction of NIE's reading research program while he was Team Leader for Reading. Thanks go also to Shirley Jackson and Ramsay Selden for keeping the project on track when it was in danger of falling off. More recently, support for completing this volume has come from Vernetta Stevenson and Jeff Schiller, of NIE, and from Diane Vines and her staff in the Education Department. Special thanks go to Marilyn Binkley for her help in editing and completing the references and index.

E. H. White and Company, under contract with NIE, provided support for the synthesis project. They managed the 1982 workshop and assisted in preparing the final manuscript. Staff who deserve special thanks include Ted Allen, Barbara Dutchak, Regina Kyle, Margaret Charles, who typed and re-typed chapters, and Eileen Vedral.

Editorial work on this book began while I was on the staff of NIE; it was completed after I moved to the Army Research Institute (ARI). Special appreciation goes to Robert M. Sasmor, Director of Basic Research at ARI, for his support during the final stages. Finally, I want to thank my husband, Ernest, for his patience, encouragement and ever present good humor.

The opinions expressed in this volume are solely those of the editor and authors and do not represent official policy of the Department of Education or Department of the Army.

Judith Orasanu
U.S. Army Research Institute for
the Behavioral and Social Sciences

I   Introduction

1 Introduction: Comprehension Theory and How It Grew

Judith Orasanu

Monte Penney

This book documents some of the most significant advances made in explaining how people understand what they read. Although people have read, and have taught other people to read for over 5,000 years, serious scientific research on the reading process has been conducted only during the last 100 years. While the history of reading, reading instruction, and reading research is a fascinating one, characterized most notably by the keen intellectual insights of E. B. Huey (1908/1968), it is also one of little practical progress. Throughout history, most reading instruction in the Western world has been based on the alphabetic principle: Letters stand for sounds; sounds can be combined into words. From Gedike (1754-1803) onward, there have been flurries of experimentation with methods purported to emphasize "meaning" (See Mathews, 1966). Of these, only the "look–say" method, prominent in the 1930s, 40s, and 50s, reached a large number of students. Viewed from the vantage point of modern research, the look–say method merely offered another way of recognizing individual words without making the meaning of the text one whit more accessible. Its role in instruction today is to aid in recognizing irregularly spelled words, while the alphabetic and phonetic aspects of language remain dominant. The basic assumptions the ancient Greeks held about reading are the same ones that guide most instruction today.

Research conducted over the past fifteen years has shaken those assumptions to their foundations and has fashioned new ones that replace them. The old view of reading says that we proceed letter by letter to unlock sounds and combine them into words, then string the words into sentences; once the sentences are in oral form, comprehension automatically takes place. According to this view, the major instructional task is to teach readers to break the

1

letter-sound code. Lots of practice with various letter combinations was recommended to build fluent decoding, a major assumption being that decoding skills need to be highly practiced before they can be put to work in reading real text, much like practicing scales on an instrument. Scant attention was paid to understanding a text beyond identifying the main idea from a paragraph. Reading comprehension difficulties were usually treated with more practice in decoding.

The new view is quite different. While it does not deny the importance of fluent decoding, it emphasizes active construction of meaning from text, with decoding being a means to that goal rather than the end in itself. In the new view, we first establish a purpose for reading the text, and then activate, or bring to mind, anything we know about the topic based on the title and headings. As we begin reading, we recognize words, familiar ones almost instantaneously, less familiar ones by recognizing common letter clusters. This recognition is influenced by our expectations that certain words will occur, based on our knowledge of language, communication, and what we have already read. Drawing on our background knowledge, we begin actively constructing a sensible interpretation of what is written on the page. A critical difference between the old and new views is the status of meaning: in the old view the meaning resides in the text, the reader's task being to ferret it out; in the new view, the reader creates meaning based on the text, and her or his existing knowledge about its content, language and structure.

Such a view does not imply an "anything goes" approach to comprehension, in which a text can mean "anything I choose it to mean," in Humpty Dumpty fashion. Rather, authors use certain conventions of writing, leaving out information they know the reader will provide, based on shared knowledge of language, culture and communication. Obviously, if the shared knowledge assumption is not met, the author's message may be misunderstood. Ample evidence, mostly from memory tests, supports this point. Readers from different cultural backgrounds interpret and remember the same story differently (Bartlett, 1932; Steffensen, Joag-dev & Anderson, 1979). In addition, people tend to "remember" more than is explicitly presented in the text, and have difficulty remembering much of anything at all if they are not already familiar with the content or structure of the text (Spiro, 1980; Bransford & Johnson, 1973). These findings highlight the fact that comprehension goes beyond simple recognition of words and sentences, although these are clearly necessary components.

The instructional implication of this view is that readers need to acquire strategies for inferring the author's message, using the information written on the page in conjunction with their existing knowledge. This represents a shift of emphasis from decoding to developing language and communication skills. It is important to recognize that the emerging view does not disregard the need for skill in decoding or the need to teach it. Rather, it reflects the emergence of an "interactive" rather than a sequential view of reading processes. The older sequential view, already described, assumes that readers work their way up the scale of units—first recognizing letters, then words, then sentences, then passage meaning, with a requirement that lower level skills be highly mastered before being applied to higher level tasks. The interactive view maintains that higher order and lower order knowledge are both brought to bear and influence each other. While it is obvious that interpretation is based on the printed words, a so-called "bottom up" process, the reverse influence is not so obvious, the "top down" aspect. Our recognition and interpretation of what is written on the page is also influenced by what is already in our heads. Letters in words can be "seen" faster than if they occur in isolation; likewise, words in sentences are recognized faster than out of context. This implies that reading ability may be enhanced by training readers to use the knowledge they already have about language, communication and the content rather than by giving them more extensive drill on letters, letter clusters or words outside of any meaningful context.

In skilled readers decoding processes appear "automatic," that is, little effort is required for recognizing individual words. However, we do not yet fully understand how this automaticity is achieved (see Beck & McKeown, this volume, for a thorough treatment of this issue). Automaticity is desirable because when lower level processes are efficient, more mental effort can be applied to higher level processes that require more conscious attention. These include monitoring one's comprehension and applying strategies to achieve one's reading goal. For example, good readers ask themselves questions such as, "Do I understand this? If not, have I ever seen similar material? What did I do then? Should I go to the chapter summary for some clues?" and so on.

In short, the act of reading and the skills that need to be taught have been reconceptualized. Reading is now seen as an active search for meaning instead of a mechanical translation from written to oral code. Once considered a content free process applicable to any written material, reading is now seen as a flexible set of interacting processes. In the old view, readers had one strategy, to plod letter-by-letter and word-by-word through a text. Now we see good readers using many strategies depending on their purpose, the nature and organization of the material, and their moment to moment success in understanding it.

Theoretical Ancestors

The reconceptualization of reading just described did not come about only through research in the field of reading. Rather, it was embedded in and reflected shifts in many fields, including psychology, linguistics, anthropology, computer science, and education.

The shift in psychology from a behaviorist to a cognitive orientation had a significant impact on the study of language and thereby on reading comprehension. That shift was marked by a few distinguished events, the first being

Chomsky's (1959) critique of Skinner's *Verbal Behavior* (1957). The behaviorist view of language is that it consists of associations between words or classes of words that form "legal" strings. These associations are thought to be established through reinforced practice. In contrast, Chomsky proposed that linguistic competence is characterized by an underlying knowledge of syntax, that there are deep structural relations among the words in a sentence, and that these relations can be described by a set of formal rules.

In 1965, George Miller propelled psychologists into the study of psycholinguistics, or the psychology of language (as defined by Chomsky, 1959). First, Miller pointed out that the meaning of a sentence is not equivalent to the sum of the meanings of its constituent words: for example, a venetian blind is not the same as a blind Venetian. Thus, a simple associationist account is inadequate. Second, a principled basis for grouping words is needed to account for multiple accepted readings of sentences like, "They are hunting dogs," where the dogs may be either the hunters or the hunted. Third, he pointed out that it would be impossible for people to acquire language on the basis of reinforced practice because of the infinite number of allowable word sequences in any language. In short, behavior theory cannot account for the creativity of language or for the comprehension of novel utterances. These and related observations radically altered the kinds of studies that were done on language processing, including reading comprehension.

Miller (1956) also provided a second landmark for the theoretical shift, one dealing with an increased appreciation of the limits of the human information processing system. In his paper "The magical number seven plus or minus two," Miller pointed out that people appear to be able to hold only seven (give or take two) "units" of information in immediate memory at one time. The corollary of this observation is that a unit can actually consist of a large amount of information. This idea led to the investigation of how information is organized in memory, allowing one to retain enormous bodies of knowledge in long-term storage with little apparent difficulty, despite the limits on working memory.

A third and related event was Jerome Bruner's work on "going beyond the information given." Bruner (1957) characterized the mind as essentially an inference machine using knowledge it already possesses to interpret and organize new information in abstract terms or relations not directly given by the stimuli. Though his major concern was the development of the mind, his observations have served as the foundation for understanding reading as an inferential process.

Meanwhile, in the computer lab, Newell, Shaw, Simon, Minsky, Feigenbaum, and other scientists were building machines that could "think" (Feigenbaum & Feldman, 1963). In developing computer programs to play chess and solve problems, they were both building models of human cognitive processes and generating metaphors for human information processing. The computer revolution of the late 50s and early 60s opened the way for the study of parallel, sequential, and interactive processes, buffers and working memory, and knowledge representations.

These events marked the beginning of a new generation of research. Studies began to appear on knowledge structures underlying regular behavior, as in the early psycholinguistic work on sentence comprehension and memory of Fodor, Bever, and Garrett (1974). These studies examined the information loads associated with various numbers and types of mental operations predicted by linguistic theory, mainly by assessing their interference with performance on concomitant tasks. Studies that compared perception and memory for word strings of varied linguistic and semantic structure tested the contribution of prior knowledge to the perception and organization of new information in memory (Miller & Selfridge, 1950). Efforts to determine where these effects took place, i.e., in immediate perception and organization of information units or in their transfer to long-term memory, led to the investigation of the interactive nature of the reading process. The earlier sequential view was consistent with behaviorist-associationist learning theories that took a building block approach to learning and teaching: break down a task into its smallest elements, then establish associations between appropriate elements to form larger units until a complex behavior is assembled. Though this approach worked fine for teaching pigeons to play ping pong, it failed to account for people's specialized language abilities, their need for larger functional units of meaningful information, and for generating hypotheses about regularities in linguistic input.

Other linguists studied semantics (the meaning component of language), noting that meaning of certain elements of sentences (e.g., pronouns) frequently depends on information beyond the confines of the individual sentence—either within the discourse or in the nonlinquistic context. This observation was an impetus for studying language in units larger than single sentences, a trend that led to research on discourse structures, information integration, inferencing, cohesion devices, and schema theory (see Carroll & Freedle, 1972).

Study of texts longer than single sentences brought research on the "constructive" approach (e.g., Bransford, Barclay, & Franks, 1972). Derived in part from Bruner's work in the 1960s, this research demonstrated that people: (a) integrate related information into a unified representation, thereby reducing their memory load; and (b) spontaneously draw inferences that are consistent with, but go beyond, the information actually presented. In parallel with these research findings, Ausubel (1968) extended these ideas to reading instruction, recommending the use of advance organizers to facilitate the organization and integration of new text information into the reader's existing knowledge structures. Readers will recognize here the influence of Piaget, whose notions of assimilation and accommodation laid the groundwork for present day "schema theory" (Wilson & Anderson, this volume; Rumelhart, 1980). This theory emphasized the crucial role of existing knowledge as the basis for organizing new input and drawing inferences.

Finally, it became respectable once again for scientists to consider people's thoughts about their own thinking, or metacognition. Flavell (1981) and Brown (1975) found that even children can recognize whether they understand something or know it well enough to be tested on it, and can learn to apply specific strategies to satisfy their learning goals. This work showed that people can establish their own internal criteria for learning, monitor their own progress according to those criteria, and take appropriate actions to satisfy goals. Scientific study along these lines would have been difficult within the behaviorist-associationist framework.

Meanwhile, anthropologists and sociolinguists had begun studying people using language in everyday settings. This work yielded new insights into: (a) variations in the way people use language depending on the social context and the cultural meanings ascribed to language (Labov, 1966; Shuy, Wolfram & Riley, 1967); (b) the significance of verbal "genre" (Hymes, 1972); (c) recent analyses of typical spoken and written forms of language (Tannen, 1982); (d) the complexity of nonstandard dialects; and, (e) the understanding that much more is involved in comprehending written text than simply decoding the words.

One should not conclude that the theoretical revolution has produced a finished theory of reading comprehension. On the contrary, there is much we do not yet know. Many of the papers in this volume identify these gaps in our knowledge waiting to be filled by future research. However, we now know what many of the ingredients of this theory are and have a pretty good idea of what the finished product should look like.

Our knowledge about the process of learning to read and how instruction can best facilitate it, both in young children who are simultaneously learning their language, developing cognitively, and amassing knowledge about their world, and in adults, who bring to the learning task highly developed communication skills, strategies, metacognitive capabilities, and organized knowledge not available to the child, is incomplete at best. How fundamental knowledge about comprehension can help explain what has gone wrong when children do not learn to read at the usual age or in the usual manner is a research problem that still needs the attention of our nation's best minds.

Changing Views of Learning and Teaching

The conceptual shift in basic research has been accompanied by a shift in assumptions about learning and teaching in classrooms that will make possible a new kind of applied research. Shifting views of the learner and of teaching and learning create a context for new approaches to teaching reading comprehension. The characterization of the learner as an "empty vessel" has shifted to that of a "spontaneous apprentice" (Miller, 1977). The empty vessel model assumes that the teacher has the knowledge, the student does not, and somehow the knowledge must be "poured" from one repository to another. As spontaneous apprentice, the learner is an active participant, a hypothesis generator and tester, a model builder, and a seeker of sense.

The instructional implications of this shift are major. In the new view, the teacher is a model for intellectual activity and a guide of the child's activities. The teacher–student relationship shifts from active teacher/passive student to one based on teacher/student interaction. Rather than trying to transmit knowledge directly or build it up piecemeal, the teacher strives to develop the knowledge within the student by directing the student's thinking via questions and activity prompts. This approach, derived from Vygotsky (1978), emphasizes that the child's developing knowledge is organized through the child's interactions with others who are knowledgeable about the activities and can mediate the purpose and means of achieving goals in a functional context. Thus, the shift is away from building up discrete skills in no particular context to helping the child develop skills in a purposeful context, with an emphasis on communication.

Instructional Implications

The new conception of reading provides a basis for creating a new scenario for teaching reading. More classroom time will be spent preparing children to comprehend by helping them call to mind, or activate, their existing knowledge on the topic of each reading assignment. Teachers will ask more open-ended or inferential questions, as opposed to literal, short answer ones. Students will receive direct instruction in techniques for avoiding distraction, monitoring their own comprehension, and changing their reading strategies as necessary. The organizing features of texts—headings, summaries, topic paragraphs, and story plots—will be taught explicitly, as aids to comprehension. And children will learn how to study—making their own study guides, identifying important material, and self-testing. Because both readers and writers construct meaning, it is likely the schools will see the qualitative advantages, as well as the efficiency, of teaching reading and writing together. More recognition will be given to the functional contexts of reading and writing so that fewer classroom assignments will take place in the hum drum vacuum of "My Summer Vacation."

As teachers become more familiar with recent research findings, especially those concerning text analysis and instruction, they are likely to place new demands on the textbook publishing industry for improved teaching materials. Research by Anderson, Armbruster, and Kantor (1980), among others, has shown that the effort to make textbooks "easy," by keeping words and sentences short, removes connective language that promotes coherence. Because of current demands for tight control of readability levels, the language of many basal reader stories has been simplified, resulting in "colorless artificial prose" (Green-Morgan, 1984) when compared to the trade book stories on which they are based. Beck and her colleagues have already shown that theoretically motivated changes in the teachers' manuals that accompany basal readers can significantly improve the teacher's effectiveness (see Beck & McKeown, this volume).

The future scenario also is likely to include new ways of assessing reading skills and progress in acquiring those skills. Process-based models that are sensitive to distinctions in knowledge about decoding, inferencing, text structures and conventions, language, reading purposes, strategies and self-monitoring are on the horizon (see Farr, Tone, & Carey, this volume).

Whereas a theoretical framework for such extensions presently exists, the applied research has not yet been done in more than a piecemeal fashion. As the study group on linguistic communication (Miller, 1973) noted when it set the agenda for NIE's comprehension research, "Principled improvements in practice will depend on a sound theory of the skills to be taught." Those words are equally true today.

Practical Advances

What we see in practice testifies to the value of the new conceptions of reading comprehension. School administrators, teachers, reading specialists, curriculum developers, and teacher trainers are searching for better ways to teach children to read. They are demonstrating how a new conceptual understanding of what it means to comprehend can change their roles as teachers, the goal of their instruction, and what they do in the classroom.

The case studies reported in the final section of this book show how staff in different school districts across the country have taken hold of essentially the same basic research findings and extracted from them principles, goals, and guidelines for instruction. These efforts should not be viewed as either simple application of someone else's ideas, or miraculous or heroic (and hence, unreproducible) efforts. Rather, sensitive people in schools recognized that something was wrong, that too many students were not learning to read flexibly, fluently, and independently, and were determined to do something about it. They brought their knowledge, their concern for children, and their willpower to the task of improving instruction.

Each case represents a collaboration among researchers and school-based practitioners, bringing together the latest research and classroom-based knowledge. In each case, there was a person with strong, substantive leadership abilities, either within the school system or invited from a university, who evoked instructional strategies and techniques from the teachers themselves, rather than impose procedures upon them. Despite the independence of the cases, many of the solutions and practices developed in the various districts are similar. The differences reflect the special concerns of each district, such as developing the principal's instructional leadership, or developing instructional practices that incorporate the students' cultural backgrounds.

One common element across all the case studies is the leadership provided by the district superintendents and school principals. In all cases commitment from the top created a favorable climate for the staff to undertake and complete the arduous task of developing these new instructional approaches. In all cases the district leaders appreciated that the commitment was long-term; no one expected quick fixes. Such development efforts seem to take a minimum of four years to work out the basic approaches; full curriculum development, teacher training, and implementation can take as long again. It is interesting to note that in 1972 the Study Group on Linguistic Communication, convened by NIE to develop a research agenda on reading comprehension, cautioned that 7–10 years would be required to develop a new basal reader series. That six case studies were found in such an advanced state of development in 1982 testifies to the schools' sensitivity both to the problems and to potential solutions available in new research findings. The ink was hardly dry when these pioneers first began trying to apply the results.

This volume offers a summary of research findings from several major lines of research on reading comprehension, some suggestions for how that body of knowledge can be usefully applied, and examples where this has already been done. This information is offered as a slice of history, a single frame from a growing, living body of knowledge. These are not the last words on comprehension and instruction, but souvenirs of a journey that may entice future travelers to explore the territory themselves.

II   The Comprehension Process

2 Cognitive Processes in Reading

Patricia A. Carpenter
Marcel Adam Just
Carnegie-Mellon University

This paper describes basic research on the cognitive processes in reading—what occurs in the mind of the reader—focusing on four areas of research: perceptual processes, comprehension processes, theoretical models of reading, and individual differences. In each of these areas, we present a few research issues to convey something of the nature of the research enterprise, summarize the main themes, and present suggestions for future directions.

The research primarily has been concerned with normal and skilled readers, and to a lesser extent, poor and beginning readers. Skilled readers were studied in order to understand how the normal mechanisms work, and to provide a baseline for analyzing and understanding nonskilled readers, or those with particular reading problems. Such research may eventually suggest better ways of preventing or remediating reading difficulties. Since reading involves mental processes and structures that are learned and can be modified, an understanding of skilled reading should indicate the end point of the learning process and provide some clues as to how to attain it.

PERCEPTUAL PROCESSES

Reading research attempts to explain how the printed symbols on a page are transformed into a meaningful mental representation. The fact that print is visual and must be sensed through the eyes is the most easily observable aspect of reading. Correspondingly, perceptual issues, such as control of eye fixations, the width of the perceptual span, and word decoding, have been a major focus of research, some of which is described in this section.

Eye Fixations

Since the turn of the century, it has been known that during reading a reader's eyes do not move smoothly along the lines of print. Rather, they make discrete pauses (fixations) on the words. The purpose of pointing the eyes at a particular word of a text is to make it project onto the retina (called the fovea), since acuity markedly decreases with distance from the fovea. Fixations constitute between 90–95% of reading time. Consequently, reading research has focused on what occurs during fixations, rather than on the movements (saccades) between fixations. Eye fixations are a useful tool for studying reading processes because their locus and duration can indicate the relative difficulty of different parts of a text. From the reader's allocation of processing time across a text we can infer the nature of the underlying perceptual and conceptual processes.

A small sample of eye fixation behavior can illustrate several important points. Fig. 2.1 shows the time a college student spent on each word while reading a passage from *Time* magazine. When more than one fixation occurred on a single word, we added their durations. We will refer to these as gaze durations. There are two major features to notice about the gazes. First, this reader looks at most of the important words. Typically, a reader fixates on approximately 80% of the content words, such as nouns, verbs, adjectives, and approximately 40% of the short, inferable function words, such as the, etc. Second, the time that the reader spends on a word varies considerably and systematically from word to word. These variations largely reflect properties of the underlying perceptual and conceptual processes.

Between the early 1900s and the 1930s, a number of important facts were discovered about eye fixations and reading: (1) poor readers made many more fixations than good readers; (2) harder texts elicited more fixations than easier text; and (3) beginning readers made more and longer fixations than advanced readers. Although these findings are interesting, they fail to tell us why a more difficult text degrades a reader's performance or why some readers have more difficulty than others.

Current research differs from earlier work by using eye fixations to trace the moment–by–moment processing of readers. Rather than counting the number of fixations a reader makes, researchers have begun to examine how much time is spent on individual words and what determines whether a word is fixated. Technological advances have made it possible to determine uninvasively and automatically the location and duration of the eye fixations of a sizeable group of readers reading ordinary texts. These measures are then related to perceptual and cognitive processes occurring at each point. For instance, the research has shown that less familiar words are looked at longer (up to a fifth of a second longer) than familiar words of the same length (Carpenter & Just, 1983). The finding that the gaze duration increases as the logarithm of the word frequency

384   267   184   300   333   333   517
Another answer to the ever-intriguing questions of pyramid construction has been suggested.

267   283   200 350 283 283 733   333 266   183   467   200
The Egyptian Engineer of 5,000 years ago may have used a simple wooden device called a

1201   333   367 1151   583   568   417   267 183   217
weightarm for handling the 2½-to-7 ton pyramid blocks. The weightarm is like a lever or beam

600   167 200 617   383   300   550 234 217   200   650   117
pivoting on a fulcrum. Hundreds of weightarms may have been needed for each pyramid.

267   367   250 283   234   384   216 350   267 250   433
Weightarms may have been used to lift the blocks off the barges which came from the upriver

899   300   400   217   613 83 383   634   350   333
quarries. Also, they would be needed to transfer the blocks to skid roads leading to the base and

333   267   267   550   317   350 100 350   317   367
for lifting the blocks onto sledges. The sledges were hauled up greased tracks to the working

333   267   766   350   350 217   333   300   333   333 350
levels. Again, weightarms were used to pick up the blocks from the sledges and put them on

400   316   467   2150
skidways where workers pulled them to their placements.

FIG. 2.1   The gaze durations of a typical reader.

decreases provides us with a large clue to the nature of the underlying process that accesses the word meaning.

Another finding is that words are generally interpreted while they are being fixated. Readers do not wait to see what words are coming next before making an interpretation, except in unusual circumstances. If the immediate interpretation occasionally proves to be incorrect, then efficient recovery procedures help pinpoint the source of error. Readers may look back to the problem word or phrase and choose an alternative interpretation.

Eye fixations are not the cause of good or poor reading; rather, they are an indication of the ongoing perceptual and comprehension processes. Only by analyzing these processes can we better understand what is responsible for good or poor reading.

Perceptual Span

Since the turn of the century, a classic question has been how far into the periphery a reader can see during reading. Many readers believe they need to look at only a couple of places on a line to see all the words. However, as seen in Fig. 2.1, a normal reader directly fixates on most of the important words. Consequently, the focus of research has been to determine the span over which a reader can visually encode and process information. Although there have been many attempts to study this, early efforts were generally unsatisfactory because they were not conducted in normal reading situations.

It was only recently that the research of Rayner and McConkie gave a firmer answer to the question of perceptual span. Using a reading task that approximates normal reading (McConkie & Rayner, 1974; Rayner, 1975), they showed that the span over which information is semantically processed is quite small, although some information about word and letter shape is available in the periphery.

To estimate the perceptual span during reading, Rayner used a computer-controlled screen to present a short text that contained a nonword, such as:

The two factions were at a standstill.

The rebels guarded the pyctce with their guns.

How close to the nonword *pyctce* would readers have to fixate before they noticed its strangeness? The noticing of the strangeness would be indicated by an increase in a fixation duration on a preceding word like *the* or *guarded*. The increase can be measured by a comparison to the fixation durations of a control group of subjects who had no strangeness to notice, because their text contained the word *palace* instead of *pyctce*. The surprising and seldom-quoted result was that readers never gave any indication of having noticed the strangeness until they fixated within three character spaces of the nonword. That is, they noticed the strangeness only if they fixated no further left than the *h* or *e* of the immediately preceding *the*. If they fixated the *t* of *the*, they did not notice the strangeness of *pyctce*. This finding indicates that the perceptual span within which we encode words during reading is rather narrow.

Rayner's experiment estimated the perceptual span in a second way, namely by making a change in the critical word just as the reader's eyes were making a saccade to that word. In the example above, *pyctce* was changed to *palace* during the saccade to *palace*, when acuity is low. If the reader had picked up any information about that word before fixating it, then he should be "surprised" by the change that had surreptitiously been made in the word. The surprise would be indicated by a longer fixation on the word when the eyes arrived there. The experiment measured the degree of surprise as a function of the distance of the previous fixation. How close to the critical word would the previous fixation have to be in order to enable the reader to acquire enough information about it to be surprised by a change? This measurement would indicate the span within which information was being picked up. The finding was that the size of the span depended on the nature of the change. The span extended about 6 character spaces to the right of the point of regard if the change constituted a change in meaning (e.g. from *police* to *palace*), but about 14 characters if the change was a large change in the word shape. Thus we have different spans for different kinds of information, and the span for semantic information as indicated by this experiment probably lies somewhere between 6 and 12 character spaces.

Current research on issues related to eye fixations include: (1) determining where fixations are placed; (2) how information is integrated across fixations; and (3) how long into a fixation a decision is made about where and when to move the eye (see Rayner, 1978; McConkie, 1983). The important point here is that considerable progress is being made in understanding the nature of perceptual processes in reading.

Decoding

The first step in reading is to register the printed text and decode words, identifying the orthographic form and accessing the corresponding word in the mental lexicon. The decoding process has received a great deal of attention from researchers, constituting the bulk of the early reading research (see Gibson & Levin, 1975). Three central issues have been raised in this research.

One question was whether a reader must retrieve the sound of a printed word in order to access its meaning. Many readers report "hearing" the words as they read, suggesting that there is a phonological component in reading. The advantage of such phonological mediation is that processes used in speech understanding could be used directly in reading. However, it is possible that the sound is retrieved after or along with the meaning, rather than being the route to the meaning. Indeed, most of the evidence suggests that skilled readers generally do not use a phonological code to access a word's meaning (Banks, Oka & Sugarman, 1981; Bradshaw, 1975). Some evidence against simple phonological recoding is the difficulty we have in reading phonologically correct but orthographically anomalous sentences such as: "Eye Do Knot No What You Herd" (Baron, 1977).

However, children or adults dealing with difficult words may, in fact, rely on a phonological code. If the material is very difficult, or if the reader is not very skilled, he or she may even make lip movements. The skilled reader, on the other hand, may use an intervening phonological code to access meaning only if the word is unfamiliar, or if the material is particularly difficult. Phonological codes may also be used to retain information in short-term memory (Kleiman, 1975; Perfetti & Lesgold, 1977).

A second issue is the unit of word decoding—letters, letter clusters (such as *ch*), syllables, or whole words (Gibson & Levin, 1975). One very simple model of word perception holds that the reader identifies each letter and combines them to identify the resulting word. However, it has been found that it is easier to identify a letter that is embedded in a word (such as the letter *a* in *cat*) than when it is embedded in a nonword (as in *tac*) or presented alone (Baron & Thurston, 1973; Wheeler, 1970), suggesting that a word is psychologically more than just the sum of its parts. This result is called the word superiority effect.

An alternative model suggests that word recognition may not depend exclusively on serially identifying individual letters. Rather, the reader may identify several letters at once, using information about one letter to help identify other letters (McClelland & Rumelhart, 1981). It is probable that there are several routes to recognizing words, depending on the word's familiarity and the context.

A third issue is that words themselves are easier to identify if preceded by a semantically related context. It is easier, for example, to process the word *doctor* if one has very recently processed the word *nurse* (Meyer & Schvaneveldt, 1971). The general explanation for this phenomenon is that accessing a given concept also activates some semantically related concepts. The results of such laboratory studies suggest that a rich knowledge of the relations among words may facilitate decoding, lexical access and, perhaps, other levels of processing during reading.

COMPREHENSION PROCESSES

During the last 10 years, considerable progress has been made in delineating the cognitive processes that take the results of the perceptual process and combine the information into an understanding of the text. This research has focused on language-understanding processes and on the role of general knowledge of the world in understanding a text. It may be that comprehension processes are not specific to understanding print and may in fact, be similar in listening and reading. There is some scientific support for this assumption, namely that for adults, listening and reading skills are highly correlated, suggesting that they are not two distinct sets of skills (Daneman & Carpenter, 1980; Sticht, 1972). Consequently, studies of the way people understand spoken speech can be useful in understanding what occurs in reading.

Language Processes: Syntax and Semantics

In the late 1950s, the field of linguistics (and several related disciplines) was jolted by Chomsky's (1957) study of English syntax. While Chomsky's particular theory is probably of less direct relevance to psychological models than was originally thought, his work did contribute to the current basic research in reading in two important ways. First, his and subsequent linguistic analyses have shown the importance of the structural characteristics of language. This may have been the major contribution of linguistic research, perhaps more than any specific formal model. For example, renewed attention is now given to the structure of texts given to young readers, to the relation between written and oral languages, and to how spoken dialects may differ from the language expressed in a text. Second, Chomsky shifted the focus of language research from lower units, like morphemes and words, to the level of sentences, by initiating the large-scale study of syntax (grammar).

Linguistics-oriented research examined how a reader extracts and uses syntactic information within a sentence to determine the subject of the sentence, what he is doing, in what manner, where, when, and so on. These relations are presumably determined by a set of strategies sensitive to grammatical and semantic structure. For example, consider the strategy readers use to determine which clause is being modified by *yesterday* in the sentence:

John was angry when Herb said Mary left yesterday.

Most readers (and listeners) will interpret the sentence to mean that *Mary left yesterday,* rather than other logical possibilities, such as *Herb said it yesterday* or *John was angry yesterday.* The general strategy is to assume that a word or phrase modifies the immediately preceding phrase. Hence, *yesterday* is mentally connected to the clause *Mary left* because it is the immediately preceding clause (Kimball, 1973). Of course, this is only a heuristic strategy and sentences can be constructed for which it won't work:

John was angry when Herb said Mary will leave yesterday.

Although some research still focuses on purely syntactic aspects of text, the emphasis has shifted to meaning and the influence of pragmatic factors, such as context. Consequently, there has been a shift from the analysis of isolated sentences to extended texts, such as paragraphs and short stories.

Understanding Texts

Major progress has been made in analyzing the structure and content of extended texts. Many analyses characterize the structures in terms of a hierarchy (Meyer, 1975), while others distinguish between low-level propositions (units approximately the size of a simple clause) and higher order abstractions, sometimes referred to as micro structure and macro structure, respectively (Kintsch & vanDijk, 1978). The ordering derived from these structural analyses correlates with the way texts are recalled by readers; information high in a hierarchy is recalled more often than information low in the hierarchy. These analyses have permitted experimenters to investigate reading tasks that are much closer to what occurs in natural settings.

A related development has been the construction of "story grammars" that describe the formal structure of narratives in terms of plot components such as setting, conflict, and resolution. The analysis has been useful in analyzing story recall as certain kinds of information are more likely to be recalled than others (Mandler & Johnson, 1977; Rumelhart, 1975). Even young children seem to use such plot outlines in generating stories of their own (Stein & Trabasso, 1982).

Considerable research also has been initiated on specific linguistic structures, such as pronouns, repeated references, and connectives (Carpenter & Just, 1977; Halliday & Hasan, 1976; Kintsch & vanDijk, 1978), that establish relations among the parts of a text. The goal has been to see what processes are triggered by a particular linguistic construction. For example, consider the difference between *the* and *a*. The definite article *the* usually marks a concept as already known or easily inferred. By contrast, an author uses *a* in order to introduce a concept to the reader. *The* appears to trigger a memory search to find a known referent to relate new information to what is already known (Haviland & Clark, 1974). Other research has shown that various syntactic devices can facilitate reading by directing the reader's attention to a text's major themes (Carpenter & Just, 1977). A related approach is to determine which cues readers use to distinguish between important and unimportant information (Kieras, 1981). For example, the opening sentence of a paragraph is often interpreted as the theme, even when it is not. Knowledge of the significance of these linguistic structures appears to be one factor that differentiates good and poor readers.

Knowledge

When we read, or listen, we rely on previous knowledge to guide our comprehension. It has been shown that if the reader has no clue to the topic of a text, it may be difficult to understand or remember, even if all the words are simple to understand (Bransford & Johnson, 1973). Conversely, experts on a topic understand new information about that topic more easily and remember it better (Spilich, Vesonder, Chiesi & Voss, 1979).

Knowledge affects comprehension in several ways. For example, it provides the vocabulary needed to understand the passage. Yet, its influence can be at once more subtle and more dramatic. Knowledge is internally organized, providing a preexisting framework that the reader can use to assimilate new information. The reader already has some idea about what is or is not important, and about what is or is not likely to happen.

Several of the theoretical and empirical advances in describing how knowledge is represented and used are based on *schema* theory. Schemas are stereotyped notions of typical events or situations. For example, Schank and Abelson (1977) propose a schema for organizing knowledge about what occurs in restaurants. Possible occurrences described in a text deal with entering, ordering, eating, paying, and exiting, and each of these, in turn, can be further decomposed.

Knowledge-driven comprehension appears to be an important construct necessary in explaining how readers process texts that deal with familiar topics. What is needed now is to go beyond demonstrations that knowledge improves comprehension and specify how the appropriate knowledge is evoked to organize new information and to provide a basis for inference making.

Processing of Text

The analysis of text structure has gone hand in hand with concern for the processes by which a reader interrelates parts of a text. For example, what processes occur when the reader encounters a pronoun that refers to an earlier referent? What cues does a reader use to interrelate the phrases, clauses, and sentences of a text?

One analysis of integrative processes focusing on text structure is provided by Kintsch and vanDijk (1978). They were interested in characterizing the inference processes that permit a reader to summarize a passage. Their basic assumption was that these processes are triggered by coreference; that is, if one sentence refers to some person, object or concept that has been referred to before, the reader will try to interrelate the information. If the previous information is not in short-term memory, the process will take longer or be less likely to succeed. Kintsch and vanDijk assumed that the information in short-term memory includes very recent information, such as the last part of the preceding sentence, and important information, like the theme. Consequently, tests are less readable if the reader must frequently search long-term memory to relate currently read information to earlier text (Kintsch & Vipond, 1979; Miller & Kintsch, 1980).

Applications of this hypothesis have met with some preliminary success. By analyzing a text, it is possible to determine how distant various concepts are in the text, and whether the connection can be made based on information presumed to be in short-term memory or whether the reader must infer or search long-term memory. These analyses have successfully predicted which passages were more readable according to various comprehension measures, such as reading time and recall.

Beyond this, Kintsch and vanDijk suggest several specific inference processes. If a piece of information (a proposition, roughly corresponding to a simple clause) is irrelevant, then it is not retained and does not appear in the summary. If several propositions allow for a generalization, the reader will attempt to make one (e.g., *John played with his toys,* may be a generalization of the separate clauses *John turned on his electric train, put together a puzzle, and colored with his crayons).*

While much of the research has involved analyzing what people know after they have read a text, large strides have been made in studying the comprehension processes as they occur, by seeing how long a reader takes to understand a particular part of a text. For example, we know that when readers encounter a word that requires an indirect inference, they pause longer on that very word (Just & Carpenter, 1978). Consider the sentences:

The millionaire was found dead in his room on a dark and stormy night.
The killer left no clues for the police to trace.

The time a reader pauses on the word *killer* is longer than if the sentences are:

The millionaire was found murdered in his room on a dark and stormy night. The killer left no clues for the police to trace.

The longer pause in the first instance reflects the fact that the inference relating *dead* to *killer* is more difficult than the inference relating *murdered* to *killer.* The longer pause on *killer* is evidence that readers compute inferences as they encounter a need for coherence in the text. Moreover, by determining where readers pause and how long, it is possible to estimate the difficulty of particular inferences.

Eye fixation analyses have been used to construct a detailed model of encoding, parsing and inferential processes, as well as their interaction (Just & Carpenter, 1980). As previously mentioned, the time a reader spends on a word decreases as a logarithmic function of its frequency. This may result from a recognition process in which readers require less perceptual evidence to recognize frequently occurring words.

A second finding indicates that readers often attempt to interpret a word while directly fixating it, rather than holding several words in memory and delaying interpetation. This strategy is most evident in the processing of "garden-path" sentences (Carpenter & Daneman, 1981). These are sentences that mislead readers in their initial interpretation of an ambiguous word, and then provide later information that causes a reinterpretation. Eye fixations illustrate how readers often detect the misinterpretation as soon as they fixate the disambiguating information. Consider the following passage:

The young man turned his back on the rock concert stage and looked across the resort lake. Tomorrow was the annual one day fishing contest and fishermen would invade the place. Some of the best bass guitarists in the country would come to this spot. The usual routine of the fishing resort would be disrupted by the festivities.

Most readers initially interpret the word *bass* in line 3 to mean "a kind of fish" because this interpretation is primed by the prior sentence. However, "a kind of fish" is incompatible with the subsequent disambiguating word *guitarists*, and the resolution requires a reinterpretation of *bass* to mean "a low music note."

An example of one reader's protocol in Fig. 2.2 indicates how the eye fixations reflect the duration and sequence of comprehension processes. The figure indicates both the sequence of eye fixations and the reader's verbal protocol as he read aloud. The sequence of gazes is denoted by the successive numbers above and below the word being fixated. The reader made a series of forward fixations from left to right until the disambiguating word *guitarists* (gazes 1–5), at which point he regressed back to *bass* to reread the phrase (gazes 6–7) and then finished the sentence (gazes 8–12). The duration of each gaze (in milliseconds) is shown below the associated gaze.

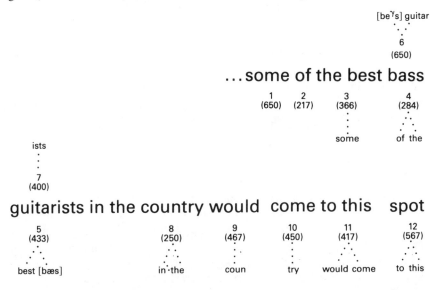

FIG. 2.2   The *bass* target sentence with a reader's eye fixations and read-aloud protocol in small print. The numbers 1–12 indicate the sequence of fixations; the forward fixations are indicated by the numbers below the fixated word, and the regressive fixations are indicated by the numbers above the fixated word. The numbers in parentheses indicate the gaze duration (in milliseconds). The read-aloud protocol shows that *bass* was initially interpreted as [b(æ)s], meaning "fish," and then revised to [beᵞs], meaning "music note." (From Carpenter, P. A., & Daneman, M. [1981]. Lexical retrieval and error recovery in reading: A model based on eye fixations. *Journal of Verbal Learning and Verbal Behavior, 20,* 137–160).

The model that explains these data assumes that the gaze duration on a word reflects the reading processes initiated by that word. The duration of the initial fixation on the ambiguous word *bass* reflects the time it takes to encode the visual stimulus, retrieve its interpretation from semantic memory, and integrate it with the representation of the text that has been read up to that point. This duration depends on the prior context and the frequency or familiarity of the word. The long duration on the disambiguating word (gaze 5) reflects the attempt to integrate the word *guitarists* and the detection of an inconsistency with the preceding text. The long regressive fixation on *bass* reflects the error-recovery process that reinterprets *bass*. The oral reading protocol (indicated by the small type in Fig. 2.2 and connected to the associated fixation by dots) indicates that this reader successfully recovered from the inconsistency by reinterpreting *bass*.

This protocol also demonstrates an interesting point about the relation between eye fixations and the voice in oral reading. The voice lags behind the eye, giving rise to the well known eye-voice span. However, the locus of the eye fixation and not the voice is the index of what the reader is currently comprehending. As the figure shows, the reader typically detects the inconsistency when he fixates the disambiguating words; he does not have to verbalize the inconsistency in order to detect it.

By making detailed analyses of the eye fixations for other kinds of text, including scientific text, texts with syntactically difficult constructions, and texts that require difficult inferences, it has been possible to construct a very detailed model of the time course of the individual processes, from lexical access to inference making. Moreover, we have made some progress in understanding how these processes are coordinated in the skilled reader.

MODELS AND SIMULATIONS

One approach that encompasses much of the current research on reading is information processing—an analysis of the psychological processes and structures involved in comprehension. This approach attempts to understand how previous knowledge is represented in memory, how new information is acquired from text, how various processes are invoked, how long they take, and how they are acquired. An important contribution of this approach is its acknowledgement of the role of the environment in explaining human behavior. The direction and content of thought processes can be shaped by current circumstances, as well as previously acquired knowledge and thought patterns. Strategic behavior is adaptive, so that variations in a task evoke corresponding changes in a person's strategies. As applied to reading, this means that how a person reads and what he understands and remembers depends not only on knowledge and reading skill, but also on the text that he or she is reading and on the particular reading situation.

The information processing approach analyzes reading in terms of its component processes, such as word decoding, syntactic analysis, semantic analysis, and analysis of the situation referred to by the text. This decomposition has obvious benefits for research and instructional purposes. However, the parts are not always easily reconstituted into the act of reading.

Representing how various subprocesses in a complex task work together is difficult. One solution has come from the field of computer science. When expressed as a computer simulation model, each component process is specified in detail, and the many component processes must function collaboratively to perform some complex task.

A number of computer simulation models of natural language understanding provide insight into human reading. These programs are invariably large and complex and have certain properties in common with human readers. One commonality is the need for a great deal of knowledge about words and language structure. Many programs have vocabularies of only a few hundred words, while a few have more than 1,000 words. The word-related knowledge necessary for comprehension increases exponentially with vocabulary size. For each new word, information must be added indicating its relation to all relevant previous entries.

Successful programs also have a considerable knowledge of the text's topic. This was first made clear in Winograd's (1972) program, which understands questions and instructions about a restricted world made of toy blocks. But the lesson was even more impressive when programs turned to more naturalistic text. Charniak (1972) illustrated the point by detailing the specific knowledge a reader must provide to understand a simple child's story describing a little girl going to her piggy bank after hearing the ice cream man's bell. The moral is that good comprehension depends on familiarity with the subject matter, a result that has been consistently documented with human readers as well.

A third commonality is that all successful computer understanding programs analyze several aspects of the text, including its vocabulary, syntax, semantics, pragmatics, and morphology. No program relying exclusively on syntax or semantics is successful; different kinds of analyses and knowledge are necessary to achieve comprehension. Moreover, the use of these various levels of analysis must be effectively coordinated, so that they can collaborate on comprehending a given piece of text.

Current simulation research is attempting to match computer models to human performance data, such as eye fixations (Thibadeau, Just & Carpenter, 1982). We have developed a computer model that can understand a scientific passage well enough to produce a summary similar to the kind given by human readers. Moreover, the amount of time that the computer model spends on each word of a text in order to interpret it closely corresponds to the time human readers spend. The correspondence suggests that similar processes are operating in the two instances. This detailed model provides a more precise specification of what it means to understand, and it can tell us why some texts are more difficult than others and why some readers are poorer than others.

INDIVIDUAL DIFFERENCES

The analysis of individual differences is at the heart of the educational process. It is particularly important in reading, since reading is a fundamental component of the educational system. While individual differences have long been of interest to educators and psychometricians, only recently have they received the attention of basic researchers. This section will discuss some of the findings on good and poor readers, and on dyslexia, a specific disability.

Relation between Reading and Listening

One important research finding is the high correlation between reading and listening skills in adults. "Reading" problems may not be specific to the visual modality, because reading and listening share many cognitive processes. Therefore, some theoretical generalizations about comprehension can be made from either listening or reading research. At a practical level, listening and reading skills may facilitate each other, although research is needed to study this possibility.

Sticht (1972) initially documented this correlation in a series of studies comparing how well Army recruits of varying levels of verbal ability comprehended texts that they read and texts that were read to them. The texts varied in levels of difficulty. Irrespective of the recruits' assessed verbal ability, there was a close relation between how well they understood what they read and what they heard. Harder texts were not just harder to read; they were also harder to understand when they were heard.

Other studies using nonmilitary adult populations (usually college students) tend to confirm these findings (Jackson & McClelland, 1979; Daneman & Carpenter, 1980). In contrast to the research with adults, Curtis (1981) found that in the early grades, comprehension scores correlated highly with measures of decoding ability rather than listening ability. Beyond grade three, however, this correlation decreases and reading is more highly correlated with listening comprehension.

These results mean that for a variety of adult readers, "reading" problems are not specific to reading—they also apply to listening comprehension. The correlation between reading and listening comprehension is not perfect, however; some individuals do have problems in reading, but not in listening.

We have studied a few dyslexics who have high college grades and good listening comprehension performance, but have severe reading difficulties. In these unusual cases, only reading performance is weak, probably because of a visual decoding difficulty.

Lexical Access

Recent attempts to determine which processes differentiate good and poor readers can be traced to a stimulating set of studies by Hunt and his colleagues (Hunt, Lunneborg & Lewis, 1975). Hunt divided a population of freshmen at the University of Washington into high and low skill groups based on a verbal comprehension test. He then administered a variety of cognitive tests and examined what differentiated those students at the high end of the distribution (high verbal skills) from those at the lower end (medium verbal skills). He found that high verbals take less time to access name codes for letters in long-term memory. A similar finding from Perfetti and Lesgold (1977) is that good and poor readers are differentiated by the time needed to access the mental representation of a word.

However, Jackson and McClelland (1979) have shown the variation in time to access names, as indexed by the letter judgment task, accounts for only 10% of the variance among college student readers. That is, while poorer readers take longer in a letter-comparison task, the correlation between how long they take and their overall comprehension scores is not high. Thus, access time is only one process that differentiates readers, accounting for a statistically significant but relatively small amount of the variation among readers.

Functional Memory Span

More recently, Daneman and Carpenter (1980) have argued that the speed of many different processes may differentiate readers. The reading span test was devised to measure functional ability to execute a number of key processes efficiently. In this test, subjects read a list of two to five sentences and then are asked to recall the last word of each sentence. Sample sentences would look like this:

When at last his eyes opened, there was no gleam of triumph, no shade of anger.

The taxi turned up Michigan Avenue where they had a clear view of the lake.

After reading these two sentences, subjects would have to recall *anger* and *lake*. College students typically perform perfectly, i.e., recall all final words, in lists of 2–5 sentences. However, poorer readers devote so many resources to the mechanics of reading the sentences that they have fewer resources for storing and remembering the final words. The maximum number of final words a reader can recall correlates with verbal SAT scores. This contrasts with typical word and digit span tests of short-term memory capacity, which generally do not correlate with reading or verbal ability.

Verbal ability measures, however, consist of many subskills, and we sought to determine if the reading span measure correlated with any specific reading subskill. The span measure was highly correlated with readers' ability to answer questions about passages they had read. It also correlated with the reader's ability to compute pronominal references over various distances. For example, consider the following passage:

> Sitting with Richie, Archie, Walter and the rest of my gang in the Grill yesterday, I began to feel uneasy. Robbie had put a dime in the juke box. It was blaring one of the latest "Rock and Roll" favorites. I was studying, in horror, the reactions of my friends to the music. I was especially perturbed by the expression on my best friend's face. Wayne looked intense and was pounding the table furiously to the beat. Now, I like most of the things other teenage boys like. I like girls with soft blond hair, girls with dark curly hair, in fact, all girls. I like milkshakes, football games and beach parties. I like denim jeans, fancy T-shirts and sneakers. It is not that I dislike rock music but I think it is supposed to be fun and not taken too seriously. And here he was, "all shook up" and serious over the crazy music.

After such a passage, the reader was asked questions like: Who was "all shook up" and serious over the music? The referent had occurred six sentences before the pronoun. Only readers with large functional reading spans were able to retrieve the referent over such a long distance. Indeed, once the number of intervening sentences between a prior referent and a pronoun exceeded the reader's span, the probability of successfully retrieving the referent dropped very rapidly. This research suggests that the concept of functional memory span may be a fruitful tool for future research on individual differences.

Vocabulary

Researchers have also focused on the robust correlation between comprehension and vocabulary scores. Such a correlation may seem uninteresting because it is obvious that a reader must understand the vocabulary in order to read a passage successfully. However, teaching readers relevant vocabulary does not necessarily raise their comprehension (Tuinman & Brady, 1973). Marshalek (1981) suggests that the inferential abilities necessary to comprehend a passage are the same as those used to infer the meanings of novel words.

While this explanation needs further research, it suggests that a large vocabulary is a correlate but not a cause of good reading ability. It also requires further exploration of the skill of constructing inferences.

While this beginning work on individual differences is promising, there are two important limitations to this particular type of correlational research. First, one cannot unambiguously determine the causal direction of a correlation. The difference between good and poor readers in lexical access time, for example, could be the *result* of their reading difficulties, rather than the cause of them. Alternatively, some third factor may be responsible for the correlation. For example, poorer readers could be slower simply because they read less than good readers.

A second limitation concerns the interpretation of the numerical size of the correlation; the percentage of variance accounted for by a factor does not reflect its conceptual importance. The size of a correlation is always specific to the particular set of conditions in which it was measured—including the specific population and the specific materials. For example, the usually high correlation between reading and listening would not be found with a group of dyslexics. The degree of correlation depends upon how much other factors vary. For example, suppose that one is interested in determining the relative contribution of background knowledge and reading skill to reading performance. If background knowledge varies widely, and reading skill varies across a relatively small range, then background knowledge might appear to be the most important determinant of reading. By contrast, if reading skill varies widely and background knowledge is kept more homogeneous, then reading skill would appear to be the most important determinant of reading performance. Thus, one cannot describe the importance of particular factors independently of the population and situation being studied.

Thus far, most basic research has described the processes that differentiate good and poor readers as a necessary first step. However, this research must ultimately specify how low-level coding skills or the higher-level inference skills are acquired or modified. For example, can faster lexical access times be acquired through training? If so, do poor readers then become more similar to good readers in terms of their higher-level skills as well? Another issue is the optimal training schedule. However, training studies are sometimes not feasible or appropriate if the skills can only be acquired over several years. In that case, it might be better to adopt quasi-experimental techniques to take advantage of naturally-occurring reading programs to determine how to improve and change reading skills.

Specific Reading Disability

A population of children and adults who have inordinate difficulty in reading, compared with their performance in other areas, are classified as *dyslexic* or as having a *specific reading disability,* to distinguish their problem from general intellectual difficulties. The latter term is something of a misnomer, because the disability may not be specific to reading, but may reflect a more general language comprehension problem. Although specific reading disability has attracted research attention from educational, medical, and psychological circles (see Benton & Pearl, 1978; Vellutino, 1977), it has not benefited from recent cognitive research.

One major difficulty with research in this area is that there is no general consensus about the definition of dyslexia (Rutter, 1978). Consequently, children are selected by excluding those who have "good reasons" for their reading problems—general intellectual deficits, obvious visual or hearing problems, or marked emotional problems. If a person does not fall into these categories but still lags two years or more behind peers in reading, he or she may be classified as having a specific reading disability. However, definition by exclusion does not necessarily result in a homogeneous population.

Some dyslexic children and adults may have difficulty not only with reading but also with some basic language functions. Initially, a rather popular hypothesis was that reading disability was visual and there were reports of confusions between letters such as *b* and *d,* or between words such as *saw* and *was.* Such reversals tend to be infrequent, accounting for only 25% of the errors in lists constructed to allow maximally for such errors (Liberman, Shankweiler, Orlando, Harris & Berti, 1971). In addition, the confusion may not be visual in origin, since dyslexic readers "see" such letters and words in an unreversed order, as they demonstrate when asked to copy them (Vellutino, Smith, Steger & Kamin, 1975).

That the children may reverse the words in naming but not in copying suggests that the limitation is not in their graphic encoding. Similarly, normal and dyslexic readers may not differ with respect to reproducing geometric designs (Vellutino et al., 1975). Rather, the observed inaccuracies of some poor readers may reflect linguistic problems rather than perceptual distortions.

One early theory suggested that dyslexic readers have particular difficulty in associating visual and verbal elements (Birch, 1962). Subsequently, however, it has been shown that poor readers have a great deal of difficulty coding information verbally and that such problems could explain problems with visual-verbal association (Bryant, 1968; Vellutino, 1977).

Another unlikely hypothesis is that poor readers suffer from an inability to maintain information about the sequence in which a group of items occurs. Currently there is little support for this hypothesis. Rather, it appears that poor readers have difficulty with labelling the items (Vellutino, 1977).

A more recent hypothesis is that poor readers have difficulty with some specifically auditory-linguistic aspects of either reading or learning to read. Studies have suggested that dyslexics have difficulty in retrieving words. For example, Denckla and Rudel (1976a, 1976b) found that dyslexics take longer than normal readers to name common objects, colors, words, and letters. This suggests a connection to the finding that poor (but not necessarily dyslexic) readers have been found to take longer on other word-naming tasks.

Researchers cannot assume that specific reading disability refers to a single characteristic. Some evidence suggests that there are several distinct kinds of reading disability. There is also a confusion of cause and effect. Researchers may be studying an effect or a corollary of reading dysfunction, rather than a cause. Research policy on specific reading disability might encourage more joint efforts by psychologists and educators to examine individuals in detail and to encourage more longitudinal research.

Evaluation of Reading Skills

A final suggestion from the research on individual differences is that the evaluation of reading skill should distinguish between reading and listening skills. While reading is a form of language understanding that shares many elements with the understanding of spoken language, it consists of some psychological processes that are specific to the visual processing of language. Because the contributions of the comprehension processes to reading performance have generally been underestimated and sometimes entirely ignored, reading comprehension has often been considered as something apart from listening comprehension. Consequently, reading problems have been assumed to reflect something very specific about extracting meaning from *print*.

The inherent problems in confusing these issues is most apparent in reading assessment. In determining reading skills, there is often an interchangeable use of the terms *reading* and *literacy*. However, literacy sometimes involves much more than reading comprehension, including writing, problem solving, broader language skills, and functional uses of print. At a simple level, reading problems may be distinguished from more general language or knowledge deficits by testing whether someone can understand oral material. If not, then the problem should not be construed as strictly a reading difficulty. At a practical level, it makes sense to distinguish between general language skills, reading skills, attention management, comprehension strategies and background knowledge. All are used in reading, but they point to different approaches to remediation, such as teaching more general language skills, problem-solving skills and perhaps more specific knowledge relevant to the various kinds of texts to be read.

What They Don't Know Will Hurt Them: The Role of Prior Knowledge in Comprehension

3

Paul T. Wilson
Richard C. Anderson
University of Illinois at Urbana-Champaign

In summarizing almost a decade of research on the role of the reader's prior knowledge in comprehension, we must emphasize that the fundamental ideas are not new. Analyses of the role of background knowledge can be traced to the very origins of educational, psychological, and philosophical thought. Plato's explanation of how we know was based on recollection; the Socratic dialogue was a method of generating new ideas through novel combinations of what was already known.

In the early 19th century, Herbart thought each new sensation caused the memory of previous similar sensations to rise to consciousness, followed by other less similar sensations. Binet, though better known for developing the individual intelligence test, was also concerned with how world knowledge affects memory for text (Binet & Henri, 1894/1978). Piaget believed that children grasp concepts such as conservation only after a series of crucial developmental experiences. For each of these thinkers, mature cognition depended on prerequisite knowledge.

Bartlett's work (1932) is usually credited with being the seminal influence on recent comprehension and memory research. While accepting that past experiences and reactions are used when something is comprehended or remembered, he discounted the idea that memory is primarily a matter of retrieving information from a vast storehouse of traces of particular past events. Instead, he maintained that specific memories are reconstructed at the occasion of recollection on the basis of schemata.

There are two important aspects of schemata—activity and organization. In the 1960's, Bruner (1960) and Ausubel (1963) stressed the significance of these different aspects. For Bruner, the key to knowledge was active integration of old and new information. A reader, for example, could fill information gaps by drawing on previous experience. Ausubel believed that knowledge is structured in a hierarchical fashion, with the most abstract and inclusive ideas at the apex. His main contribution was the "advance organizer," a short introduction to a text that provides the abstract structure needed to assimilate the more detailed information that follows. In Ausubel's words, an advance organizer provides the "ideational scaffolding" that bridges the gap from the student's prior knowledge to the new information.

Most reading scholars have acknowledged the function of background knowledge in reading. For example, Huey (1908) thought comprehension resulted from recollected "meaning feelings" called up by the sequence of words, phrases, and sentences. Subvocalization—the inner voice that readers hear—was a result of the meanings they read into the words. Gray, founder of the basal reading program, observed that mature readers had the "capacity and the habit of making use of all that [they] know . . . in construing the meaning of ideas read" (Gray & Rogers, 1956, p. 54). Betts (1946) devised the Directed Reading Activity in which the teacher helped students relate past experiences to new concepts they encountered in reading. This is still the model for most basal reader lessons. More recently, Stauffer (1969b, 1970) refined Betts' ideas into the Directed Reading-Thinking Activity. In this approach, the teacher guides students to make predictions about the text based on what they already know, and then to evaluate and refine these predictions during reading based on information provided in the text.

During the last decade significant progress has been made in explicating the role of prior knowledge. We now possess more subtle and precise evidence that the knowledge a reader brings to a text is a principal determiner of how that text will be comprehended, and what may be learned and remembered.

One way to gauge the importance of a factor is to compare its influence to factors whose effects are well-established. Freebody and Anderson (1983) had sixth graders read descriptions of a familiar and an unfamiliar game. One description, familiar to Midwestern youngsters, was of horseshoes; the unfamiliar description was of a North American Indian game called "huta." The texts were constructed so that there was a point-by-point correspondence in the topics covered. The syntax and wording were virtually identical. So the manipulation was primarily of knowledge of the two games.

Freebody and Anderson also manipulated the difficulty of the words. In the easy version, all the words were familiar to sixth graders, while in the difficult version low frequency synonyms were substituted for one-third of the content words. The results with free recall, summarization, and sentence verification measures indicated that topic familiarity accounted for almost three times as much variance as vocabulary difficulty and even slightly more variance than a measure of verbal ability. Compared to word difficulty (and hence readability) and verbal ability, then, prior knowledge of the topic must be ranked as a potent determiner of performance.

SCHEMA THEORY

Schema theory explains how people's existing knowledge affects comprehension. A schema is an abstract structure of knowledge. It is *structured* in the sense that it indicates relations among constituent concepts. It is *abstract* in the sense that one schema has the potential to cover a number of texts that differ in particulars.

The concepts that constitute a schema are said to provide *slots* that can be *instantiated* with specific information from a text. There are specifications for the kind of information that can instantiate each slot. For instance, an important concept in one's dining-at-a-fancy-restaurant schema (Schank & Abelson, 1977; Anderson, Spiro, & Anderson, 1978) is the main entree. Upon reading, "John ordered the sirloin medium-rare, a baked potato, and apple pie à la mode," a reader will instantiate the main entree slot with the sirloin because the knowledge incorporated in his schema specifies the sort of food that can be a main entree.

A reader comprehends a message when she is able to activate or construct a schema that gives a good account of the objects and events described. An account is "good" in the same sense that the solution to a jigsaw puzzle is satisfactory: all of the pieces are used; the pieces have been fit into place without forcing; there are no empty places; and the completed puzzle makes a coherent overall picture. Similarly, a reader has the sense that a text has been satisfactorily comprehended when a schema has been invoked that meets these conditions: every piece of information can be placed into a slot; the information can be fit into the slots without violating specifications; all of the important slots contain information; and there is a coherent overall interpretation of the message. However, at one point, the analogy breaks down. Whereas a puzzle that is not defective contains a piece for every space, a well-formed text does not typically contain information for every slot in a schema. These slots must be instantiated by inference, a process in which the conceptual machinery of the schema plays a major role.

Comprehension usually proceeds so smoothly that we are not aware of the operation of our own schemata. We remain unaware of the process of fitting information into a schema in order to achieve a satisfactory account of a message. It is instructive, therefore, to try to understand examples of material that frustrate normal comprehension processes. In a now classic study by Bransford and Johnson (1972), subjects were unable to understand or remember short paragraphs without special help. They were unable to construct an overall representation of what seemed to be a simple description of everyday objects and phenomena such as balloons, electricity, a musical instrument, and the transmission of sound. A cartoon drawing, containing all the relevant objects without clarifying their relationships, was not helpful to comprehension. But when readers were shown a similar cartoon of a guitar player standing on a city street serenading his lady love many floors above him by means of a speaker suspended in the air near her with balloons, the passage as a whole made sense.

This experiment demonstrates that what is critical for comprehension is being able to elaborate a schema accounting for the *relations* among the various elements. It is not enough for the elements to be concrete, imageable, and easily identifiable.

Schemata, therefore, are necessary for comprehension. But every reader does not come to a given text with the same background or schemata. Schema theory highlights the fact that more than one interpretation of a text is possible. The schema that will be brought to bear on a text depends on the reader's age, sex, race, religion, nationality, occupation. In short, it depends upon the reader's primary cultural reference group. This point was illustrated in an experiment completed by Anderson, Reynolds, Schallert, and Goetz (1977), who asked people to read the following passage:

> Tony slowly got up from the mat, planning his escape. He hesitated a moment and thought. Things were not going well. What bothered him most was being held, especially since the charge against him had been weak. He considered his present situation. The lock that held him was strong but he thought he could break it. He knew, however, that his timing would have to be perfect. Tony was aware that it was because of his early roughness that he had been penalized so severely—much too severely from his point of view. This situation was becoming frustrating; the pressure had been grinding on him for too long. He was being ridden unmercifully. Tony was getting angry now. He felt he was ready to make his move. He knew that his success or failure would depend on what he did in the next few seconds.

Most people think the foregoing passage is about a convict planning his escape from prison. Men who have been involved in the sport of wrestling, however, think the passage is about a wrestler caught in the hold (or "lock") of an opponent. As expected, interpretations of the passage showed striking relations to the subjects' backgrounds.

Similarly, when subjects were asked to recall the passage, theme-revealing distortions appeared, even though instructions emphasized reproducing the exact words of the original text. A physical education student stated, "Tony was penalized early in the match for roughness or a dangerous hold," while a music student wrote, "He was angry that he had been caught and arrested." Not only do these results support the idea that different interpretations are due to different schemata; they also underscore the more fundamental tenet of schema theory that the knowledge a reader brings to the text is a potent determiner of how that text will be comprehended.

How Schemata Operate

According to schema theory, comprehension is a matter of activating or constructing a schema that provides a coherent explanation of the relations between the objects and events mentioned in a discourse. In contrast, the conventional view has been that comprehension proceeds by aggregating the meanings of words to form the meanings of clauses, aggregating clauses to form sentences, sentences to form paragraphs, and so on. In this view, comprehension is a linear, text-driven process. The illustrations provided above were intended to show the insufficiency of this conventional view. The meanings of the words in a text cannot be "added up" to give the meaning of the text as a whole. The click of comprehension occurs only when the reader is able to evolve a schema that explains the whole message.

According to schema theory, reading involves more or less simultaneous analysis at many different levels—from the textual levels of graphophonemic, morphemic, semantic, and syntactic features, to the experience-based levels of knowledge of specific content, pragmatics, and interpretive thinking. Reading is conceived to be an interactive process, which means that it does not proceed in a strict order from the visual information in letters to the overall interpretation of a text. Instead, as a person reads, the interpretation of what a segment of a text might mean depends both on analysis of the print and on hypotheses in the person's mind.

Processes that flow from the print are called bottom-up or *data driven*, whereas processes that flow in the other direction are called top-down or *hypothesis driven* (Bobrow & Norman, 1975). In the passage about Tony, who is either a wrestler or a prisoner, the word *lock* has the potential to activate either a hardware or a wrestling hold interpretation. The hypothesis the reader has already formulated will tip the scales in the direction of one, usually without the reader's awareness that an alternative meaning is possible.

Functions of Schemata

The role of organized knowledge (schemata) in comprehension is now beyond dispute. Schemata are accessed, and often elaborated, during comprehension. Different schemata give rise to different interpretations, so that one person's interpretation of a text may differ from somebody else's. So far we have been concerned with comprehension at a general level. We turn now to specific functions schemata may serve (see Anderson, 1983; Anderson & Pichert, 1978; Anderson, Spiro, & Anderson, 1978).

A schema provides ideational scaffolding.   A schema embodies structural organization of the information it represents. Important text information fits into places called slots within the schema. For instance, there is a slot for the murder weapon in a who-done-it schema. Information that fits slots in the reader's schema is readily learned, perhaps with little mental effort.

A schema directs allocation of attention.   A schema can help a reader determine the important aspects of a text, thus serving as a guide for allocating cognitive resources. Skilled readers may use their schemata to judge how important and how familiar information is, and then pay more attention to what is more important or less familiar.

A schema enables inferential elaboration.   No text is completely explicit. Facts necessary to comprehension are often omitted. The reader's schema provides the basis for making inferences that go beyond the literally stated information to complete the meaning of the text, thus ensuring comprehension.

A schema allows orderly searches of memory.   A schema has slots for certain types of information. Thus it can guide the reader to the kinds of information that need to be recalled. Of particular importance may be the order in which the slots occur. For example, a person attempting to recall the dinner he ate at a fine restaurant can review the categories of food typically included in such a restaurant meal—the kind of wine, appetizer, soup, salad, and so on. By tracing through the schema used to structure the text, the reader gains access to the particular information learned when the text was read.

A schema facilitates editing and summarizing.   A schema contains criteria for the relative importance of different information. A reader can draw on these criteria in order to compose summaries that include significant propositions and omit trivial ones.

A schema permits inferential reconstruction.   When there are gaps in memory for a text, the reader's schema—coupled with the specific text information that can be recalled—helps to generate hypotheses about the missing information. Suppose that a person cannot remember the beverage she ordered when she was eating at a restaurant. If she can recall that her entree was fish, she will be able to infer from her schema that the beverage might have been a white wine.

The six functions taken together provide the broadest possible interpretation of the available data regarding prior knowledge effects on learning and remembering. Further research will be necessary in order to determine the precise nature of the functions of schemata.

Text Structure

With respect to reading, there are two types of prior knowledge that have concerned researchers in recent times—knowledge of text structure and knowledge of text content. Literary critics and theoreticians have always supposed that there are text genres with formal characteristics such as the sonnet, the elegy, or the romance. For centuries, authors have attempted to compose according to the constraints of a genre. Readers could then judge the author's artfulness in terms of his or her success in working within the genre.

Literary texts are not the only ones with definite structures. Personal letters and menus, for instance, have typical structures. The texts that have received the most research attention have been simple stories. In his seminal paper, "Notes on a schema for stories," Rumelhart outlined a "grammar" that could be used to represent the structure of simple stories (Rumelhart, 1975). Since then many researchers have contributed to a now substantial body of literature (see Stein & Trabasso, 1981, for comprehensive documentation). Mandler and Johnson (1977) and Stein and Glenn (1979), in particular, have developed alternative representations of story structure. Table 3.1, drawn from Stein and Glenn (1979), is typical of the structure for stories which the various grammars specify.

TABLE 3.1
Categories and Types of Causal Relations
Occurring in a Simple Story

1.	SETTING Allow Episode	Introduction of the protagonist; contains information about the social, physical, or temporal context in which the story events occur.
2.	INITIATING EVENT Cause	An action, an internal event, or a physical event that serves to initiate the story-line or cause the protagonist to respond emotionally and to formulate a goal.
3.	INTERNAL RESPONSE Cause	An emotional reaction and a goal, often incorporating the thought of the protagonist, that cause him to initiate action.
4.	ATTEMPT Cause or Enable	An overt action or series of actions, carried out in the service of attaining a goal.
5.	CONSEQUENCE Cause	An event, action, or endstate, marking the attainment or nonattainment of the protagonist's goal.
6.	REACTION	An internal response expressing the protagonist's feelings about the outcome of his actions, or the occurrence of broader, general consequences resulting from the goal attainment or nonattainment of the protagonist.

(From Stein & Glenn, 1979)

According to the grammars, it is possible to analyze simple stories as episodes centered around attempts to resolve some kind of problem. The story schema represents a temporally ordered sequence of events that, in a well-formed story, are linked in a causal chain. The schema enables a reader to interpret the events and make sense of the relations among them. Thus the schema makes available an integrally-structured ideational scaffold for comprehending and remembering story events.

Theorists such as Black and Bower (1980), and Omanson (1982a), have attributed a hierarchical structure to the story schema. Stories, in general, are about people who experience problems and attempt to solve them. Events or information closely related to the problem, the protagonist's goal, and the eventual solution are highest in the hierarchy. Consistent with the theory, Black (1977) found that college students rated as more important statements that contained information on the causal path of the protagonist's attempt to solve his problem. The same statements were also better recalled. Similarly, Nezworski, Stein, and Trabasso (1979) and Omanson (1982b) have found that children recall goal-related information better than peripheral information.

It is well-established that the story schema enables inferential elaboration and/or inferential reconstruction of information. For instance, Stein and Glenn (1979) found that six-year-olds can answer "why?" questions about successive events in a story, giving the same kinds of answers as older children, though fewer of them. Other studies show that children as young as four can infer the motives and feelings of the characters in well formed stories (Day, Stein, Trabasso, & Shirey, 1979; Stein, Trabasso, & Garfin, 1979). The story schema evidently enables even young children to inferentially elaborate their internal representations of a story.

Quite young children make use of the story schema in recalling or reconstructing story events, and this ability improves with age. Mandler and Johnson (1977), Nezworski, Stein and Trabasso (1979), Stein and Glenn (1979), and Day et al. (1979) have found that four-year-olds do very well recalling story events in correct order as long as the story is written according to story grammar rules. The correct order is theorized to help youngsters construct causal links in the narrative, which then aid subsequent recall.

McClure, Mason, and Barnitz (1979) carried out an interesting study on the ordering of story information. Third-, sixth-, and ninth-graders were asked to put jumbled sentences from six-sentence basal reader stories into correct order. Each story had three almost identical versions, differing only in the most appropriate first sentence.

In one version, that sentence was written to include information about the conclusion of the story. In a second version, that sentence was written as a question about whether the protagonist's goal would be achieved. For the third version, the sentence contained "normal" setting information. Not surprisingly, the older children did better reordering all versions. The setting version of the story led to the best performance, particularly for the younger children.

Though the third-graders had difficulty with the conclusion and question versions, they did well with the setting version. Presumably this was because they were able to find a sentence that started them off on the right track. With the other versions, they were not able to find a sensible place to begin. It also seems that the older students had acquired more flexibility in the use of their story schemata. Apparently they were not so dependent on getting started into the canonical order with the help of a typical setting statement, but rather could accommodate the material to what they knew should be the underlying order.

In keeping with this interpretation are the age-related effects on recall of the order of story events. When stories are written in the order expected on the basis of the story schema, the events are recalled in that order. But when stories are written so that the temporal order of events is altered or distorted, the "listener or reader constructs a representation of events corresponding to the real time order of occurrence rather than to the narrative time sequence" (Stein & Trabasso, 1981).

For experimental purposes, stories have been written so that they do not conform strictly to an event schema. It also is true that many real stories, both in basal readers and in literature at large, do not conform to the expected schema. Authors do not always *intend* to write their stories in the expected order. They modify that order for aesthetic purposes or psychological effect.

With a murder mystery, for example, the facts about the murder are only very gradually revealed, and almost never in their "proper" order of occurrence. If the entire sequence of events were simply recounted in temporal order, there would be no mystery, no surprise or suspense.

Brewer and Lichtenstein (1982) distinguish between *event schemata* and *story schemata* in order to explain systematic deviations from natural temporal order that authors use in some types of stories to achieve surprise, suspense, or humor. An event schema embodies knowledge about the temporal and causal relationships among events in the real or imaginary world in which a story is situated. A story schema embodies knowledge about conventions for ordering events within the narrative to produce an emotional response.

Understanding a story requires knowing an event schema. *Appreciating* the story requires knowing a story schema. For a reader to differentiate story schemata from event schemata probably depends on both cognitive development and considerable exposure to different literary genres. Stories that deviate significantly from the event schema to produce suspense or surprise may be less well comprehended by younger readers than simpler stories with more obvious structures and clearly defined character types.

In just a few short years, rather rapid progress has been made in understanding how readers use their story schemata as an aid for comprehending simple narratives. Some progress also has been made with longer, more complex stories and expository texts. Armbruster and Anderson (1982a) have done promising research on how students work with expository texts, and how comprehension can be improved through training in expository text structure. A recent paper by Meyer (1982) summarizes most of the work on exposition. The major analytical tool has been a "text grammar" characterizing the propositions underlying the text (Deese, 1983; Frederiksen, 1977b; Kintsch, 1974). These grammars represent the ideas in the text at a fine level of detail. Also represented are the relations among the ideas.

Usually a hierarchical relationship is postulated among the propositions of a text. Meyer (1977), for example, has been able to show that most of the relations between serial position of propositions in a text and recall of these propositions, and between ratings of the importance of the propositions and recall, can be explained by how those variables relate to the hierarchical structure of the ideas in the text. Other researchers have demonstrated that a hierarchical analysis gives a good account of studying and recall data (Estes & Wetmore, 1983).

Overall, research on text structure during the last decade has been very productive. More work is needed, particularly in the comparison of expository and narrative text structures. It may be helpful to draw on the longstanding traditions of literary criticism, stylistics, and rhetorical theory, as well as the contemporary field of composition teaching. One of the main emphases in rhetoric, for example, has been on persuasion, which highlights the author's or speaker's intentions towards the reader. This is important because comprehending the author's intent often involves making inferences, which the present school curriculum, with its emphasis on word drills (see Duffy, 1982) and literal interpretation, probably fails to develop in many children.

Text Content

We turn now to representative studies of prior knowledge of text content. Whereas text structure schemata represent knowledge about discourse-level forms, content schemata represent knowledge of the substance conveyed in the text.

Studies of the role of content knowledge fall into three categories. In the first, individuals are selected because there are qualitative differences in the knowledge they possess. Cross-cultural studies fall in this category. In the second, readers possess more or less knowledge about a particular topic. Expert-novice contrasts fall in this category. In the third, readers are induced to bring different knowledge to bear on the same or similar texts through different introductions or different instructions prior to reading.

Cross-cultural studies.   In an experiment by Steffensen, Joag-dev, and Anderson (1979), Americans and natives of India read two letters—one about an American wedding, the other about the analogous Indian ceremony. Most every adult member of a society has attended weddings and can be assumed to have well developed knowledge about how they are conducted. Since American and Indian weddings are very different, the two groups were expected to have very different schemata for marriage rituals and customs, differences that should affect learning and recall.

In fact, subjects spent less time reading the letter that was culturally appropriate for them. It is hypothesized that they already had slots available in their schema to match and easily assimilate the information in the letter. With the non-native letter, on the other hand, they had to piece together somewhat puzzling material so that it would fit their schema. This took more time. Although subjects spent less time reading about their native ceremony, they remembered more about it. The theory is that not only was the ideational scaffolding helpful in learning, but it also enabled a memory search in which the newly learned information was more readily accessed.

Steffensen, Joag-dev, and Anderson observed interesting elaborations and distortions which, ever since Bartlett's day, have provided compelling evidence for the role of schemata. Both groups made more culturally appropriate elaborations of their native passage, and more culturally inappropriate distortions of the non-native passage. For instance, the letter about the American wedding noted that the bride would wear her grandmother's wedding dress, which was old as well as borrowed, and described how charming she looked in it. An Indian reader, though, recalled that the bride looked "alright except the dress was too old and out of fashion." This subject missed the several cues in the text indicating the acceptability of an heirloom wedding dress. Instead she interpreted the information in terms of the Indian notion that it is important to demonstrate social status by wearing up-to-date, fashionable garb.

In another facet of this same study, additional groups of Indian and American subjects read the letters and rated the importance of each proposition. With both letters, Americans rated as important those propositions containing information about the ritual and ceremony. The Indians saw as important the propositions that dealt with financial and social status. Schema theory would predict that propositions which are rated as important in light of the schema are more likely to be learned and remembered. The prediction was confirmed: Whichever the text, native or non-native, subjects recalled more of the propositions rated important by their cultural group.

A more educationally relevant study that explored differential effects of culturally sensitive schemata was done by Reynolds, Taylor, Steffensen, Shirey, and Anderson (1981). They wrote a passage about an incident involving "sounding." As described by Labov (1972), sounding is an activity characteristic of the Black community in which the participants try to outdo each other in an exchange of witty insults.

Black and white teenagers were presented with the passage in two group experiments, and in an individual interview situation. Black teenagers understood the passage for what it was—a description of friendly, competitive, give and take. White teenagers, on the other hand, tended to interpret it as an ugly confrontation, sometimes involving physical violence. The contrast in the two views is made clear by the following examples. One Black male recalled the incident in this way: "Then everybody tried to get on the person side that joke were the best." A White male wrote, "Soon there was a riot. All the kids were fighting." Different schemata caused readers to interpret the same text differently.

The suggestion from this experiment is that cultural variation within the United States could be a significant factor in differential reading achievement. The extent to which school reading material is culturally loaded ought to be researched over the next ten years.

Expert-novice studies.   The second category of schema function studies involved subjects who had different amounts of knowledge about the same topic. Chiesi, Spilich, and Voss (1979) and Spilich, Vesonder, Chiesi, and Voss (1979) used questionnaires about baseball and a reading comprehension test to identify subjects who were high or low in their knowledge of baseball but equivalent in verbal ability. Chiesi, Spilich, and Voss (1979) did a series of experiments with three-sentence descriptions of baseball situations. High-knowledge subjects were better able to recognize previously presented descriptions from among distractors and to detect changes from the initial wording. A more elaborated schema seems to have more slots available so that the relevant information is more easily learned and retrieved. Interestingly, high-knowledge subjects were also able to generate more appropriate continuations for incomplete descriptions, which illustrates the inferential elaboration function of schemata as well.

The investigators concluded that when someone already has considerable knowledge of a particular domain, the acquisition of new information is facilitated, because it is mapped onto the existing knowledge structure. They argued that the schema of the high-knowledge individual embodies more information about (1) the goal structure of the game, (2) how to relate actions to the goal structure, and (3) how to relate successive actions to each other as well.

Spilich, Vesonder, Chiesi, and Voss (1979) asked high- and low-knowledge subjects to listen to a 750-word text describing a half-inning from a baseball game. High-knowledge subjects were more likely to recall and embellish points of strategic significance to the game. In contrast, low-knowledge subjects were more likely to include information that was incidental to the game. These findings suggest that the more elaborated and articulated a schema is the better developed are its internal criteria for what is important.

While most studies of this type use college students for subjects, Pearson, Hansen, and Gordon (1979) had average second graders read a grade-appropriate selection about spiders. Using an oral pretest, these researchers identified second graders who were high and low in knowledge of spiders but who were otherwise equal in ability. A week later the children read the story about spiders and gave oral responses to a posttest. There were two types of questions on the posttest. Half could be answered through direct reference to the text. The other half, though derived from and related to the text, could be answered only if the reader also utilized prior knowledge. Children with greater knowledge of spiders answered more questions correctly, especially ones that required integrating prior knowledge.

Manipulated purposes and texts.   In this category of studies, people are induced to bring to bear certain schemata through manipulations of the text or the instructions. Bransford and Johnson (1972) provided titles or illustrations prior to the reading of vague passages. Owens, Bower, and Black (1979) wrote different introductions to a narrative causing readers to identify with one character or another. In a series of studies, beginning with Pichert and Anderson (1977), people were asked to pretend they were either burglars or homebuyers before reading about what two boys did at one of the boys' homes while skipping school. This is an interesting approach because neither perspective is directly related to the ostensible topic of the passage—the two boys playing hooky. However, the main activity the boys engage in is a protracted tour of the house, punctuated by appropriate idle chatter. Underlying this surface level plot, there is a description of the house and grounds.

This study found that people learned more of the information relevant to their assigned perspective. For instance, pretend burglars were more likely to learn that three 10-speed bikes were locked in the garage, the side door was always open for the little sister to get in after school, or there were collections of coins and paintings. Pretend homebuyers were more likely to learn about the wall-to-wall carpeting and spiral staircase, or the leaky roof over one bedroom.

Anderson and Pichert (1978) carried this research further by asking readers to switch perspectives after their first attempt to recall. Subjects were able to recall additional, previously unrecalled information important to their new perspective, but unimportant to their old perspective. Anderson, Pichert, and Shirey (1983) replicated these findings and discovered there was still an effect for the persepctive shift even when it was carried out two weeks after the initial reading. Anderson et al. (1983) concluded that a schema influences learning and memory when activated before reading, and retrieval when accessed after reading.

The studies cited in this section illustrate strong and varied effects of content schemata. Evidence differentiating the specific functions served by schemata is scant, however. Exceptions are the experiments by Anderson and Pichert suggesting independent effects of schemata on learning and memory and experiments in several laboratories showing that schemata are one mechanism for selective allocation of attention during reading (Haberlandt, Berian, & Sandson, 1980; Cirilo & Foss, 1980; Just & Carpenter, 1980; Anderson, 1982). The era when demonstration experiments could serve a useful purpose has drawn to a close. The time has come for the harder work of formulating and testing alternative realizations of schema theory.

Another shortcoming of the existing body of research has been the use of contrived, even whimsical texts involving such matters as fictitious baseball games, pretend burglars, characters who may be either wrestlers or convicts, or a modern day Romeo who sings to his Juliet through a loud speaker suspended from a bunch of balloons. There are exceptions, of course, notably the classroom-typical and age-appropriate text on spiders employed by Pearson, Hansen, and Gordon (1979). Nonetheless, we know very little about the structure of knowledge within various domains nor the organization of typical texts about these domains. These ought to be high priority areas for future research. The frame for historical narrative proposed by Armbruster and Anderson (1982b) is a good illustration of the kind of scholarship that is needed.

IMPLICATIONS

For basic and instructional research on schemata to advance, attention should be focused on at least one new area: the growth of schemata embodying knowledge of school subjects. Such research will have significant implications for curriculum designers. This, however, is a concern for the future. Our concern here is with educational applications of already completed work. We will point out three areas for applications that aid comprehension: (1) how to help students use text structures; (2) how to provide instruction that builds or activates knowledge of content; and (3) how to promote an active effort after meaning.

The Use of Structure

Research on stories demonstrates that children develop and use a schema for the structure of events in stories that aids comprehension. It is also clear that as children get older, they acquire greater flexibility in applying the event/story schema to generate comprehensible interpretations of texts that do not conform to the schema's canonical order. This development apparently occurs largely in the absence of formal instruction, though it is probably fair to state that substantial exposure to well-structured texts is important. We believe, with Strickland (1985), that children should have a steady diet of good stories from the earliest stage of kindergarten, where the teacher should read to them every day. In addition, they probably should receive direct instruction regarding the story schema so they will be able to recognize elements in a story and more rapidly develop their ability to apply the schema flexibly.

Curiously, there has been little research on training students to use the story schema (though see Santa and Schuder, this volume). In contrast, good results have been achieved by researchers working with expository text structures. Two related techniques are "mapping" (Anderson & Armbruster, 1982b) and "networking" (Dansereau, 1978). Students are explicitly taught simple relations, such as compare-contrast, often used in exposition. With knowledge of these relations and graphic symbols to represent them, students can create their own representation of the content. These contemporary versions of outlining apparently lead to more effective studying and learning.

The most impressive results have been obtained by Meyer and her colleagues (e.g., Meyer, Brandt, & Bluth, 1980), who have taught students to discern and use the overall organization of texts when studying. Bartlett (1978), for example, gave ninth-graders a week of instruction on several types of text structure. Not only were the students better able to recognize these structures, but they also recalled almost twice as much information from studied passages as students who had not received the instruction.

More text-structure training studies are needed, as well as more systematic application of instruction in text structures in American classrooms. We suspect that learning text structures will proceed more efficiently when integrated with writing exercises, particularly in the early stages of training. Children can enjoy discovering how text structures can be used to organize and represent what they know already, which can then serve as a basis for elaboration to new, less familiar content.

One crucial assumption underlying these recommendations is that all texts American students work with have clear structures. Regrettably, too many texts do not have optimal structures (Anderson, Armbruster, & Kantor, 1980). They often consist of little more than lists of loosely related facts where the real point is not clear, or stories without problems for the characters to resolve— just sequences of events in temporal order. With less than optimally structured texts, only students already familiar with the content have a chance of comprehending. The others spend their time contending with the text. Educators must demand effectively structured texts from textbook publishers, and must provide training so that students can use the structure.

Instruction and Knowledge of Content

As illustrated in the cultural differences research of Reynolds, Taylor, Steffensen, Shirey, and Anderson (1981), it is obvious that if students do not already know something about the content, they often misinterpret or fail to comprehend. Ensuring that students possess the required knowledge of the content must be the first priority in every classroom.

Building knowledge can be as simple as telling students things they don't know, but more subtle teaching tactics may be required if the topic is abstract or completely unfamiliar. One such tactic is the use of analogy. Hayes and Tierney (1982) showed that an introduction to the game of cricket, particularly one drawing correspondences with baseball, helped American students understand newspaper reports of cricket matches. Similarly, Royer and Cable (1976) found that reading a concrete passage about the flow of water along a creek bed helped students understand an abstract passage about the flow of electricity. One might happily recommend that teachers introduce new selections with appropriate analogies, but this is more easily said than done. Good analogies are not in abundant supply. However, it may be possible to engage students in providing their own analogies.

In a significant demonstration, Paris and Lindauer (1976) showed that young students were not very good at activating their own prior knowledge. They might know something relevant, yet not bring it to bear. Hansen and her associates have used pre-reading discussions to assist children in bringing to mind relevant ideas. First, the class discusses previous experiences the children have had relevant to the assigned passage. Doing this teaches them to think about and to compare information that is old with what is new. It also allows the children to provide each other with analogies for the new material. As the children repeat this kind of discussion over a period of time, they achieve a second goal. They learn *why* they should relate what they read to what they already know: it makes the reading easier to understand (Hansen & Pearson, 1983).

Pre-reading discussions have been recommended by educators for years. Unfortunately the impact on teaching has been insignificant so far. Several studies show that pre-reading discussions are the exception rather than the rule. Mason (1983) found, for example, that in only 16 of 130 third-grade reading lessons observed were there any pre-reading discussions. Such discussions should be the norm, not the exception.

Durkin's (1979, 1985) investigations of teaching practices have shown poorly organized lessons based primarily on manuals and accompanying workbooks. According to Durkin, teacher's manuals that are part of basal reading programs contain a smorgasbord of suggestions which promote "flitting" from topic to topic and the mere "mentioning" (as opposed to teaching) of ideas important for comprehension. Most manuals do suggest pre-reading discussion, or other techniques to help activate relevant knowledge, but this is one suggestion teachers tend to ignore. They say they do not have enough time. That they might feel they do not have enough time is perfectly understandable in light of Mason's (1982) finding that 75-80% of the instructional events in reading lessons involve assigning, explaining, and checking worksheets.

The diversity of subject matter in children's reading selections makes great demands on prior knowledge, so teachers may be correct in their assessment of how long it would take to build and activate appropriate knowledge for each new lesson. Beck (1985) has made the useful suggestion that selections in basal readers ought to be organized into topical units. With this kind of grouping, teachers could do a good job of building prior knowledge for the entire unit, and thus prepare children for several weeks of work. Each new assigned reading would not require an elaborate new introduction, but could be treated in relation to what had gone before.

The knowledge we furnish for children, or help them to access and use, must be precise, accurate, and relevant to the text at hand. Basal reading lessons can be much better than they are now, as demonstrated recently by Beck, Omanson, and McKeown (1982). They revised the lessons for two basal reader stories to emphasize precisely relevant knowledge in pre-reading discussions and to focus later questions on the central story events. They even re-did the illustrations to draw attention to important aspects of the story. As expected, their revisions enhanced comprehension, particularly of central events.

The concepts Beck, Omanson, and McKeown used for carrying out their revisions could easily be adopted, and ought to be, by basal publishers. Many of the implications of such research for the publishing industry are already clear. Published materials account for a considerable portion of what passes for instruction in our classrooms (L. Anderson, 1984). Thus, it is important that they be designed better. Textbook selections should have more obvious, usable structures. In basal readers, selections should be grouped into topical units. Finally, teachers' manuals should provide systematic help in building/activating students' prior knowledge, and in helping students use what they know and evaluate how their knowledge has changed as a consequence of reading.

The Active Effort After Meaning

Readers must be able to reason about text material during reading. If they are taught only that reading is decoding (Duffy, 1982), or if they are given new information about a text but without training in how to use it, they may not reason about the text, nor learn any new information. In other words, children will comprehend and learn more if they make an active effort to get the meaning (Anderson, Mason, & Shirey, 1983).

There is evidence that self-questioning strategies (e.g., Andre & Anderson, 1978) promote an active effort after meaning. Predicting what a text may be about (Stauffer, 1969b) is also a good way of leading students to make judgments about how new information relates to what they know, so that they can fit new pieces into the partially assembled puzzle already in their heads.

Research indicates that direct instruction in techniques that involve students in actively reasoning about texts improves comprehension. Paris, Lipson, et al (1982) have shown that training students in metacognitive problem solving strategies that ensure a high level of involvement in the learning task has a strong facilitative effect on comprehension even a year later. Palincsar and Brown (1985) have developed a technique called "reciprocal teaching," in which teacher and students take turns asking and answering good questions about sections of text. The students learn to think about what the important questions are as they read and to check themselves to be sure they can answer the questions. Reciprocal teaching has produced excellent results with middle school students whose word identification skills are satisfactory but who lag behind in comprehension. Especially noteworthy is that these students do better in science and social studies classes when no longer under the guidance of the special teacher. The key point is that there are now proven, data-based techniques to be adopted in American classrooms.

We close with an important general implication that cannot be over-emphasized. Becoming a superior reader requires a curriculum that is rich with concepts from history, geography, science, art, and literature. Any knowledge a child acquires will eventually help that child understand written material. A curriculum that is empty of anything but drill on words is likely to produce empty, noncomprehending readers. What they don't know *will* hurt them.

4

The Role of Metacognition in Reading and Studying

Ann L. Brown
Bonnie B. Armbruster
University of Illinois

Linda Baker
University of Maryland Baltimore County

INTRODUCTION

Metacognition plays a vital role in reading. The term, which literally means transcending knowledge, refers to one's understanding of any cognitive process. Understanding in the context of reading can be revealed in two ways: first, in one's *knowledge* of strategies for learning from texts, differing demands of various reading chores, textual structures, and one's own strengths and weaknesses as a learner; second, in the *control* readers have of their own actions while reading for different purposes. Successful readers monitor their state of learning; they plan strategies, adjust effort appropriately, and evaluate the success of their on-going efforts to understand.

Novice readers experience a great deal of difficulty reading intelligently because their understanding of what reading means is only partially accurate. For example, third-grade students feel there is no way to predict how well they have done on a test before getting it back from the teacher (Forrest & Waller, 1979). Second graders believe it is as easy to read a list of random words as it is to read the same words presented as a coherent text. These same second graders also decided that the purpose of reading was to sound out words, not to understand (Canney & Winograd, 1979). They also believe that skimming means reading all the easy words rather than obtaining the gist, or finding a particular sought-after piece of information (Myers & Paris, 1978). Even high school poor readers claim that they would use the same strategy when reading to glean details as when reading to obtain a general impression (Smith, 1967).

Given these misapprehensions, it is not surprising that poor readers' control of their actions while reading seems somewhat sporadic. They behave the same if told to read for fun or to learn, remembering no more in the second case than in the first (Forrest & Waller, 1979). Poor readers, instructed to learn material, read the passage through once, without looking back or checking difficult sections, claiming they are ready for a test well before they are (Brown, Campione, & Barclay, 1979). They read statements that are incoherent, inconsistent, or just plain untrue without indication that they have detected a problem (Paris & Myers, 1981). When reading aloud, they make errors they fail to correct. Even when they do make corrections, their substitutions are rarely plausible (Beebe, 1980; Clay, 1973; Isakson & Miller, 1976). In short, novice readers often act inappropriately because they do not yet have the necessary understanding of the reading process to control their own activities when reading for different purposes.

The term *metacognition* is new, the concept is not. Although the term has only been in general use since the middle 1970s, the sheer volume of theoretical discussions and experimentation since then has shown it to be a popular theme in reading research (for reviews see Armbruster, Echols, & Brown, 1982; Baker, in press; Baker & Brown, 1984a, 1984b; Brown, 1980, Flavell, 1981; Markman, 1981). Educators since the turn of the century (e.g., Dewey, 1910; Huey, 1908; Thorndike, 1917) have recognized that reading involves understanding and monitoring activities. Furthermore, many early educators, notably Binet (1909) and Dewey (1910), prescribed exercises or mental orthopedics (Binet, 1909) to help overcome metacognitive problems of reading.

Of interest is how the new wave of research contributes to our understanding of reading. Is the renewed interest in such problems a classic case of academic old wine in not such new bottles? Is this generation of educational psychologists recapitulating tried and true findings from the past? We would like to argue that although many of the ideas currently under scrutiny have a long and honorable history, today's approach differs from past research in certain important ways.

Inspired to a great extent by funding and encouragement from the National Institute of Education, research in the last decade has taken the topic of metacognition out of the realm of educational truisms and has provided a firm empirical base for understanding children's problems. The new wave of research has delineated students' metacognitive difficulties in a wide range of ages. The pervasiveness of these problems has been documented for readers of all ability levels, but notably for children at risk for academic failure. We believe that the most important educational implications of this work are that we now have a better understanding of the pervasiveness of children's ignorance concerning active learning from texts and, even more important, that this understanding has led to effective intervention, remediation that works both under laboratory conditions and in the classroom.

DEVELOPMENTAL DIFFERENCES IN METACOGNITION

Metacognition in reading to learn involves knowledge of four major variables and how they interact to affect learning outcomes (Brown, Bransford, Ferrara, & Campione, 1983; Brown, Campione, & Day, 1981; Flavell & Wellman, 1977). These are (1) *text*—the features of reading materials that influence comprehension and memory (for example, difficulty, clarity, structure); (2) *task*—the requirements of various tasks and purposes of reading that learners commonly encounter in school; (3) *strategies*—the activities learners engage in to understand and remember information from the text; and (4) *learner characteristics*—such as ability, familiarity with the material, motivation, and other personal attributes and states that influence learning. Metacognition in reading also involves *control* or self-regulation; the effective learner must coordinate the complex interaction of these four variables.

Texts

Many text features influence students' learning, and one essential form of metacognition is the knowledge readers have about salient aspects of the material they read. Vocabulary, syntax, the clarity of presentation (style, coherence, etc.), the structure (i.e., the rhetorical and logical organization), and the topic itself (familiarity, interest, compatibility with prior knowledge, etc.) are all factors contributing to text difficulty. To what extent are young readers aware of such factors, and does such awareness, or lack of it, influence their reading proficiency? We will consider evidence indicating that novice readers have difficulty identifying (1) the difference between easy and difficult texts; (2) important elements versus trivia; (3) contextual constraints on meaning; (4) textual structure; and (5) anomalies and confusions present in the texts.

Sensitivity to Text Difficulty.   Many factors render texts easy or hard to read, so sensitivity to this factor can be a subtle form of knowledge. Young children, however, have difficulty with even such basic distinctions as whether a text is readable or not. For example, Canney and Winograd (1979) presented children in grades 2 through 8 with passages that were intact, or disrupted at four levels of severity: correct syntax, but some semantically inappropriate words; semantic and syntactic violations, but some semblance to connected discourse; strings of random words; and strings of random letters. The children were asked if each type of passage could be read and why. Children in second and fourth grades, and even sixth graders identified as poor comprehenders, focused on the decoding aspect of reading, claiming that all but the letter strings could be read. In contrast, older and better readers, who know that understanding is the primary goal of reading, identified only the intact texts and those with correct syntax as readable. The poorer readers behaved as if reading involves merely saying words correctly; a passage of unrelated words was judged just as readable as an intact passage.

A more subtle distinction was required of second to sixth graders in a study by Danner (1976). Presented with texts with sentences arranged randomly or clustered into three topics, they were asked to recall the passages, determine which type was more difficult to learn, and justify their answers. For all students, organized passages were better recalled than disorganized ones. Although the majority of children reported that the disorganized passages were more difficult to remember, only older children attributed the difficulty to the difference in organization. The younger children did not appear to be aware of the text organization that had made the passage easy or hard to remember.

Sensitivity to Importance.   Readers must be able to distinguish between central ideas in a text versus those that are peripheral (Omanson, 1979). This is no easy matter. Even college students experience problems pinpointing important elements of college texts. But school children are commonly asked to concentrate on main ideas when reading and studying. To be responsive to this suggestion, they must be able to identify the main points of a passage. Although children as young as six can often indicate the main character and sequence of events in a simple well-structured narrative, they experience difficulty isolating central issues in more complex prose (Brown & Smiley, 1977; Smiley, Oakley, Worthen, Campione, & Brown, 1977; Yussen, Mathews, Buss, & Kane, 1980). For example, grade school children who were perfectly able to recall the main ideas of folk stories had much more difficulty rating sections of the stories in terms of importance to the theme (Brown & Smiley, 1977). The ability to distinguish relative importance was strongly related to age. Eighteen-year-olds could reliably discriminate across four levels of importance, whereas 8-year-olds made no reliable distinction between levels of importance. Even junior high school students had some difficulty deciding on the relative importance of text elements.

Young readers need help in focusing attention on relevant text information. For example, if provided with a particular perspective from which to interpret a passage, they are much better able to judge what is important. Told to read a description of a house from the perspective of a potential house owner or a burglar, children as young as third grade could identify what would be important information (to a burglar or home buyer) in the text (Pichert, 1978).

Sensitivity to Contextual Constraints.   Good comprehenders use context as much as possible in constructing a representation of text. They use context to make predictions about subsequent information and to organize words into higher order units. Because they are sensitive to the semantic and syntactic contraints of their language, they are quickly aware of contextual violations.

Several studies of oral reading have revealed differences in readers' sensitivity to contextual contraints. Good and poor readers differ in both the type of errors they make while reading aloud and in the likelihood of spontaneous corrections when what they read does not make sense. For example, Clay (1973) found that beginning readers in the upper half of their class spontaneously corrected 33% of their errors, whereas beginners in the lower half corrected only 5%. First-grade good readers were twice as likely as poor readers to correct errors that were grammatically inappropriate (Weber, 1970). Similarly, among fourth-grade boys, those identified as poor readers were less likely to correct their unacceptable substitutions than good readers (Beebe, 1980). The same pattern has been obtained for poorer readers in seventh grade (Kavale & Schreiner, 1979) and college students (Fairbanks, 1937) with texts of appropriate difficulty.

One explanation for these differences between readers is that poor readers have general difficulty decoding words; the resultant disruption in fluent reading means they are unable to process adequately the contextual information that signals meaning distortions. However, experiments by Isakson and Miller (1976) have shown that even when good and poor readers are matched on ability to decode text words in isolation, good readers still make fewer errors when reading them in context. In addition, the good readers in these studies were more likely to detect semantic and syntactic anomalies introduced into sentences than were poor readers. When the good readers encountered an anomalous word, they frequently tried to "fix up" the resulting comprehension difficulty by substituting a more sensible word. Poor readers, on the other hand, read the anomalous words without apparent awareness of the problem. Thus, good readers, in addition to tracking the success or failure of their comprehension, also take measures to deal with difficulties when they arise.

Sensitivity to Text Structure.   Mature readers are sensitive to various kinds of text structure and use this information to understand and remember what they are reading. An expert learner, designing a learning plan, might first examine the text itself and make decisions about the kind of material it is. Is it a story? An expository text? An instruction book? Major text forms have standard structures that can be identified by astute learners to help them set up expectations that guide the reading process. For instance, stories in general have a reliable structure (Stein & Glenn, 1979): a simple form would be that a main character reaches some desired goal after overcoming an obstacle. More complex forms include competition, conflict, or sharing between major characters (Bruce & Newman, 1978). Authors strive to provide cues to guide (or misguide) readers' expectations, as in the typical mystery story. Clues to the character of the main protagonist can be contained in his physical description or early behavior. General themes of surprise, danger, or villainy are created intentionally by the author and can be used by readers to help them understand the plot. The more the reader knows about such standard story characteristics, the easier it will be to read and understand stories.

Expository texts, although not as uniform in structure, take predictable forms, such as the compare and contrast mode described by Armbruster and Anderson (1980). Authors flag important statements by such devices as headings, subsections, topic sentences, summaries, redundancies, and just plain statements like "and now for something really important" (Meyer, in press). Expert learners know about such devices and use them as clues to help them concentrate on essential information.

It is sometimes necessary to train even college students to identify inherent text structure and to use this information as an aid to learning (Dansereau, in press). Therefore, it is encouraging to note that children also are responsive to explicit instruction. For example, Bartlett (quoted in Meyer, 1984) taught ninth graders to identify and use four common expository text structures when studying. Recall by the trained group both 1 day and 3 weeks after instruction was significantly greater than either their pre-instruction performance or the performance of an untrained control group. Increasing students' awareness of the inherent structure of text and relations among its parts is one of the main aims of techniques like mapping (Armbruster & Anderson, 1981) that are proving to be successful study aids.

Although text features may affect learning in the absence of awareness, awareness of the role of text features in learning *is* essential if the learner is to use the features consciously to enhance learning from text. The following studies demonstrate this point. Owings, Petersen, Bransford, Morris, and Stein (1980) varied the extent to which descriptions of characters were logically related to their behaviors. Successful and less successful fifth graders read and studied "arbitrary" and "nonarbitrary" versions of stories, rated them for difficulty and justified their responses, then recalled the stories. All children remembered the logically structured passage better than the arbitrary passage, but only the more successful students consistently recognized that the arbitrary passage was more difficult and justified their answers appropriately. Furthermore, the better students spent more time reading and studying the arbitrary passages, whereas the study times of less successful students were the same for the two types. Aware of the difference in text structure and the effect of this difference on learning, the better students were able to adjust their study strategies accordingly. The poorer students, on the other hand, were not aware of the structural differences and thus made no appropriate adjustment in their study behaviors.

Following the logic of the previous study, academically successful and less successful fifth graders were presented with passages describing two types of robots—a house painter and a gardener. In the arbitrary version of each passage, no justification was given for why a robot had various properties, such as a bucket on its head. In the nonarbitrary version the robots' specific features were explained. For example, the house painter robot had a bucket on its head *in order to carry paint;* and it carried a roll of tape *to put on windows to protect them from the paint,* and so forth. Students were required to read the passage in order to learn which properties went with which robot and to *understand why* a particular robot needed a particular property. Academically successful students performed well on both the arbitrary and nonarbitrary passages. They were able to provide justifications and elaborations even if such elaborations were not explicit in the text. However, the poor student performed well only if the passage was explicit, i.e., the relation of the robots' activities and properties was nonarbitrary.

Poor readers need concrete help before spontaneously generating elaborations that make material less arbitrary. Mere exposure to an explicit, nonarbitrary text is not a sufficient prompt to help the less successful students improve their ability to learn from a second arbitrary passage.

In a second study (Franks et al., 1982), concrete training on the effects of meaningful elaboration was provided. Academically less successful students were given an implicit version of a robot passage and tested for recall just as in the previous study. They performed poorly. After this experience they were shown how to make arbitrary sentences more meaningful by elaboration techniques. They learned that such activities were of great importance, dramatically improving their recall. Next they returned to the initial implicit passage and were helped to elaborate the implicit information contained within (e.g., why would a gardener robot need a basket?). Again, the students were shown how such techniques dramatically improved their retention of the robot's properties. Finally, the students were given a second implicit passage and told to study it. Performance on the second implicit passage was substantially better than on the first. Indeed, after training, the less successful students performed at about the same level as had the successful students in the first study.

These findings imply that one method of improving students' ability to learn is to modify the texts to make them more explicit. Whereas the development of such "considerate texts" (Anderson & Armbruster, 1984) may help students learn the content of those particular texts, it will not necessarily help poor readers learn to read better in general. If, however, explicit training is given in *why* certain texts are considerate, e.g., why elaboration of robot properties makes the memory task easier, then students may learn to make these elaborations on their own. As a result, they will have learned to work with texts to make them more considerate, i.e., to render difficult material more manageable. They will have learned something about reading all texts, not just those that are considerate.

Sensitivity to Textual Anomalies. One of the most active areas of current research is also one of the oldest; it addresses whether children are aware of inadequacies in text itself. Binet (1909) regarded insensitivity to the absurd a result of inadequate auto-criticism, for him one of the foundations of intelligence. He expressed the problem well:

> It is easy to test (the child's) lack of adequate self-criticism; it appears as a problem on tests in general, but we have an excellent exercise intended to demonstrate failures of auto criticism, i.e., sentences to critique. We tell the child that we are going to read a sentence in which something is wrong, and he will have to say what it is. These are some examples: 1) an unfortunate cyclist fractured his skull and died at once; he has been taken to the hospital and we are afraid that he won't be able to recover; 2) Yesterday there was a train crash, but nothing serious; only 48 people died; 3) I have three brothers, Pierre, Ernest, and me; 4) Yesterday we found a woman's body sliced in 18 pieces; we believe she killed herself. You would be surprised at how many of the "thoughtless young" are quite happy with this nonsense.

Binet included tests of logical absurdities in his original intelligence-testing battery and they still remain in current Stanford-Binet scales. Note that the problems in this test are presented aurally. Several recent studies have confirmed that grade school students experience considerable difficulty evaluating the adequacy of instructions or other aural communications (Flavell, Speer, Green, & August, 1981; Markman, 1977); of interest here is their proficiency in monitoring their comprehension of written materials.

There are several different standards or criteria that should be used to evaluate text comprehension (Baker, in press), and the novice reader may well be unaware of them. In a study by Markman (1979), children in third, fifth, and sixth grades listened to short essays containing sentences contradicting each other. For example, a passage about fish included the following two sentences: "They cannot even see colors. Some fish that live at the bottom of the ocean can see the color of their food." Despite the obviousness of inconsistencies such as this, children in all grades tested were equally unlikely to report the problem when later questioned. However, when warned in advance that problems would be present, the older children in particular were more likely to report the inconsistencies, indicating that comprehension can be monitored more effectively when criteria for evaluation are made explicit.

A series of experiments by Garner et al. (Garner, 1981; Garner & Kraus, 1981-1982; Garner & Taylor, 1982) has also shown that upper elementary and middle school children, especially those identified as poor readers, have difficulty evaluating written texts for internal consistency. The students were asked to rate brief passages for ease of understanding and to justify whatever low ratings they gave. Poor readers were less likely to rate inconsistent text as difficult to understand, although good readers were by no means proficient at this task either. Nevertheless, the poor readers were sensitive to one type of comprehension problem: difficult vocabulary words (Garner, 1981). This latter finding is in keeping with the word-decoding focus of less effective readers discussed earlier.

In the studies of both Markman (1979) and Garner (Garner & Kraus, 1981-1982), children were more likely to notice inconsistencies expressed within a single sentence or in adjacent sentences than those separated by intervening text. This suggests that one common shortcoming in children's comprehension monitoring is a failure to consider relations across noncontiguous sentences in text. Although capable of evaluating their understanding of single sentences, they still need to develop the skills to integrate and evaluate information across larger segments of text. Even college students have difficulty with this more demanding task (Baker, 1979; Baker & Anderson, 1982).

Baker (1983) has also shown that certain types of text distortions are easier to detect than others. She presented children, ages 5 to 11, with short narrative passages that contained three types of problems: nonsense words, internal inconsistencies, and prior knowledge violations. The older children were exceptionally good at detecting all types of problems, and even the 5-year-olds had detection rates superior to those reported in the literature for older children. A crucial difference in this study was that the children were explicitly told their task was to find the three different kinds of "mistakes." They were given extensive practice in doing so, along with immediate feedback, and were given second opportunities to find any nondetected problems. Nonsense words and prior knowledge violations were more readily detected than internal inconsistencies because of the greater difficulty of comparisons across nonadjacent textual segments. Moreover, there was a relatively slower rate of improvement with increasing age in the detection of inconsistencies, suggesting that expertise at evaluating text for internal consistency develops more slowly than expertise in evaluating text for word understanding or consistency with respect to what one already knows.

A general criticism of studies requiring children to report inadequacies in texts is that children's putative lack of sensitivity could reflect reluctance to criticize or difficulty in describing their own thoughts. The latter criticism does not hold up, however, because their insensitivity is also apparent when nonverbal responses provide the index of comprehension failure, such as relaying a recorded message (Flavell, Speer, Green, & August, 1981) or spending more time reading a particular sentence (Harris, Kruithof, Terwogt, & Visser, 1981). Nevertheless, when such "on-line" measures are used, children exhibit more sensitivity to textual anomalies than previously supposed. For example, in a listening comprehension study (Flavell et al., 1981), kindergarten children did look puzzled in response to poor messages, although they were not able to report their puzzlement to others.

An analogous finding was reported by Harris, Kruithof, Terwogt, and Visser (1981) in a reading task. Eight- and 11-year-olds were asked to read passages containing sentences that were or were not anomalous depending on the title. For example, the sentence "He sat in the chair and watched his hair get shorter" would be acceptable if the title were "A Visit to the Barber," but anomalous if the title were "A Visit to the Dentist." Children at both ages read the anomalous sentence more slowly, but the proportion of subjects reporting they had detected a text problem was much greater in the 11-year-old sample. Capelli and Markman (1980), Flavell et al. (1981), and Harris et al. (1981) all suggest that younger students have difficulty interpreting their own feelings of discomfort in the face of hitches in smooth comprehension.

Although we have ample evidence that young readers have problems monitoring their own understanding while reading, it is encouraging to note that their performance can be greatly improved by training. Even the simple technique of providing examples of the types of errors to look for substantially improves detection (Baker, 1983). Markman and Gorin (1981) gave 8- and 10-year-olds passages to read containing either false or internally inconsistent statements. Some of the students were given no indication of what type of error they might encounter; the remainder were told in advance and given practice looking for either inconsistencies or falsehoods. Advanced warning increased the detection rate in general, but students set to find falsehoods or inconsistencies excelled at identifying the particular error type they sought.

Poorer readers may require more extensive intervention. Garner and Taylor (1982) found differences in the amount of assistance required to notice inconsistencies. After reading a brief passage, fourth, sixth, and eighth graders were provided with increasingly more specific hints about the source of difficulty. Even after the experimenter underlined the two sentences that conflicted with one another and told the students they did not make sense, poor readers rarely were able to report the exact nature of the problem. However, the intervention did increase the likelihood of better readers noticing the inconsistency.

Task

Reading is not a unitary activity. Many differing tasks are subsumed, and if we add studying then the array of tasks and purposes multiplies. An important factor in learning from reading is knowing what will be required as a test of the acquired knowledge. If learners know about the type of test to be given, they can structure their learning activities appropriately.

An even more fundamental form of understanding is knowing that the primary goal of reading is to understand the content. The novice reader has problems with even this basic notion. Younger and poorer learners are not always aware that they must attempt to make sense of the text; to them, reading is a decoding process rather than an effort after meaning and means of learning

(Canney & Winograd, 1979; Denny & Weintraub, 1963, 1966; Johns & Ellis, 1976; Myers & Paris, 1978). If students are unaware that reading is supposed to lead to understanding, then it is difficult to see how they can monitor their own status in this regard.

Even if students do know that they must attend to the meaning of what they read, this is not enough to make them experts. They must also realize that different criteria are necessary for different kinds of reading tasks, and that they should adjust their behavior accordingly, slowing down when they encounter difficulties, speeding up if the material is trivial, and so on.

Skimming is one activity that reflects the student's understanding of adjusting reading rate for the purpose at hand. Young children have different ideas of what it means to skim. For example, Myers and Paris (1978) report that sixth graders understand that the purpose of skimming is to pick out the informative words, whereas second graders think they skim by reading the easy words. These different skimming strategies reflect conceptions of reading as meaning-getting and word-decoding, respectively.

Children's skimming behavior also has been examined experimentally. Kobasigawa, Ransom, and Holland (1980) directed fourth, sixth, and eighth graders to find specific types of information in short passages. In one passage, the information could be located most efficiently by skimming, using clues located in the first sentence of the paragraph; in another passage, the information could be found by skimming for a key word. Students were interviewed to determine their awareness of skimming techniques. Children at all three grade levels had knowledge of relevant text characteristics (i.e., the function of first sentences of paragraphs and how relevant information may be expressed in prose); children at all levels were also able to skim when explicitly instructed how to do so. However, spontaneous skimming as a strategy to meet task requirements developed only gradually with age. Thus, students may have relevant knowledge, including the implications of specific task demands, but still not be aware that they can use this knowledge to facilitate learning.

That children have difficulty modifying their reading strategies for purposes other than skimming has been demonstrated by Forrest and Waller (1979). Third and sixth graders were asked to read 500-word stories under each of four different instructions: (1) read for fun; (2) read to make up a title; (3) read as quickly as possible to find one specific piece of information (skim); and (4) read to study. After each story, the children took a multiple-choice comprehension test. The ability to adjust reading strategy in response to assigned purpose increased with age and reading ability. Only with sixth-grade good readers was retention significantly higher in the study conditions than in the skim condition.

The problem of adjusting reading activities to the task at hand is not just characteristic of the grade school student. Smith (1967) asked good and poor 12th-grade readers to read for two different purposes, to glean details or obtain general impressions. The good readers adjusted their reading behaviors appropriately, but poor readers used the same behaviors for both purposes. In addition, the poor readers were less able to report the procedures they used. Even at the college level there are students who still fail to set their own purposes; they read everything at the same rate, regardless of its difficulty or their reasons for reading (Bond & Tinker, 1973). Such students need help if they are to succeed in school. Unfortunately, explicit instruction in purpose setting may be quite rare, as suggested by Smith's (1967) report that neither good nor poor readers remembered being taught how to read for different purposes. It seems this is a skill good readers develop on their own.

Adjusting one's effort in response to task demands is, of course, the essential element of effective studying and it can demand very subtle forms of self- and text-monitoring. Sensitivity to the match between what is known now and what is still left to master is a particularly late developing metacognitive evaluation.

An excellent method for studying effort-allocation is the study-time apportionment task introduced by Masur, McIntyre, and Flavell (1973). Grade school children were given lists of pictures to learn over several trials. On each trial but the first, they were permitted to select half of the items for further study. Very young children chose randomly, but third graders selectively chose for extra study those items they had forgotten on previous tests, a successful study strategy.

This strategy is not so simple to apply to learning from texts. The learner must still select for extra study material she has failed to recall, but judging one's mastery of the gist of texts is more difficult than judging verbatim recall of a list of items. In attempting to learn a text to mastery, it is necessary to shift attention in tune with one's subjective impression that certain points are known well enough to risk a test while others need extra study. In addition, one must estimate which segments of the material are important enough to warrant attention and which are trivial and can, therefore, be ignored. The ideal strategy is to concentrate first on the most important elements of text and then, as these become well known, shift to lesser and lesser elements until a full representation of the text is built up.

Brown et al. have examined the changing effort and attention allocation that occurs during studying (Brown, Smiley, & Lawton, 1978). Students from fifth through twelfth grade, together with college students, were asked to study texts until they could recall all the details in their own words. They were given repeated tests of the current state of their knowledge. Passages were divided into constituent idea units rated in terms of four levels of importance to the theme. On each test students were allowed to select a subset of the idea units to keep with them while they attempted to recall the information (i.e., as cribs or prompts).

On the first test, the majority of students at all ages selected the most important units as recall aids. Children below high school age continued to do this, even though they became perfectly able to recall the most important information without aid, but persistently failed to recall additional details. College students, however, modified their selection as a function of their degree of learning: on the first test, they selected mainly important (Level 4) units for retrieval aids. On the second test they shifted to a preference for Level 3 units, and by the third test they preferred Level 2 units. As they learned more and more of the material, college students shifted their attention allocation to reflect their estimated state of knowledge. Older high school students performed like college students but took a little longer to shift their attention.

The ability to fine-tune one's allocation of attention to reflect mastery level is a late developing skill, perhaps because it requires the coordination of various forms of knowledge. To allocate attention according to one's present state of knowledge, the learner must have (1) information concerning current knowledge, i.e., what is known and not yet known; (2) knowledge of the task demands; (3) knowledge of the relative importance of various elements of texts, i.e., what is important to know and what can be disregarded; and (4) the strategic knowledge to adjust allocation of effort in response to the above information.

Strategies

The efficient learner employs appropriate strategies to help him learn better. There is a considerable literature on common study strategies used by experts. Some of the traditional ones are note taking, summary writing, underlining, self-questioning, and more elaborate systems such as mapping and networking (Anderson & Armbruster, 1984b; Armbruster & Anderson, 1980). The development of reading strategies in children has been examined recently in two types of studies, those aimed at "fix-up" strategies in response to comprehension failure and those examining the emergence of traditional study strategies such as outlining and summarizing (Armbruster, Echols, & Brown, 1982).

Fix-up Strategies.   When comprehension fails, the reader must make several important strategic decisions. First, the reader must decide whether to take *any* remedial action, a decision that depends largely on the purpose for reading (Alessi, Anderson, & Goetz, 1979). If the reader decides to take some action, he must choose from the following options: store the problem in memory as a pending question in the hope that clarification will be forthcoming; reread the text; look ahead in the text; or consult another source. These strategies have been called "fix-up" strategies (Alessi, Anderson, & Goetz, 1979), and are more prevalent in adults than in children.

Myers and Paris (1978) asked second and sixth graders questions tapping awareness of "fix-up" strategies for comprehension failures at the word and sentence level. Older children tended to say they would resolve a difficulty by using a dictionary or asking another person. Younger children had few strategies for deciphering the meaning of unknown words or sentences and were less sensitive to the need for resolving comprehension failures. Subsequently Paris and Myers (1981) obtained several measures of the comprehension monitoring and study strategies actually used by good and poor fourth-grade readers. Students were directed to read and remember a story containing some difficult vocabulary words. Provided with blank paper, a pencil, and a dictionary, they were told they could write or ask questions. Good readers asked questions, took notes, and used the dictionary more than poor readers. Furthermore, only good readers asked for the meanings of unknown words; poor readers were more interested in the pronunciation.

The "fix-up" strategy that has received the most attention is the "look-back" (Alessi, Anderson, & Goetz, 1979); that is, rereading relevant sections of previously read text to resolve comprehension failures. College students frequently look back at sentences that are inconsistent with subsequent information (Baker & Anderson, 1982). Alessi et al. (1979) operationalized comprehension failure as a failure to answer a text-based question correctly. They used questions interspersed in a text presented on a computer in order to help college students detect comprehension problems. When students answered a question incorrectly, the computer forced them to "look back" to the relevant section. This induced lookback procedure helped students resolve comprehension failures.

The Alessi et al. finding prompted Garner et al. to pursue research on the use of lookbacks in younger students. Garner and Reis (1981) had middle school students read narratives containing interspersed questions based on difficult-to-recall details presented on a previous page of the text. The students were observed for signs of comprehension monitoring (recognition of difficulty while answering the questions) and attempts to remedy question-answering failures by looking back. Poorer comprehenders at the sixth-, seventh-, and eighth-grade levels failed to either recognize the difficulty or correct it. Better comprehenders in grades 6 and 7 recognized the problem but did not spontaneously use lookbacks. Eighth-grade better comprehenders, on the other hand, did both.

Garner, Wagoner, and Smith (1982) observed the behavior of sixth-grade good and poor comprehenders as they tutored fourth graders. The task involved reading an expository passage and answering reader and text-based questions about the passage. Reader-based questions could be answered from the reader's existing knowledge; text-based questions could be answered from information presented in the passage. Results showed significant differences between good and poor sixth-grade comprehenders on several measures: the number of times they encouraged younger children to "look back" in the text, the number of times they encouraged lookbacks for text-based questions (where lookbacks are appropriate) versus reader-based questions (where lookbacks are inappropriate), and the ability to direct attention to the relevant text segment for answering the question. Good comprehenders encouraged their tutees to use lookbacks and informed them when and where to do so; poor comprehenders were less effective tutors. The fact that good readers attempt to teach the lookback strategy to younger children indicates that they are well aware of the usefulness of this strategy for learning.

Study Strategies.   Studying, or reading for remembering as well as understanding, involves all the activities of reading for meaning and more. It is obviously helpful, if not absolutely necessary, to understand the material you are studying. Failures to comprehend to-be-remembered materials result in reliance on difficult rote remembering techniques. Although students have been known to approach a studying task via rote learning methods, we restrict our attention here to studying that relies on an initial effort to understand, followed by additional efforts to retain critical information. In order to study, the learner must take purposive action to ensure that the material is not only comprehensible but memorable. In this section we consider selected evidence that highlights problems immature learners face when attempting to study.

In considering studying strategies, it is important to distinguish between a *technique* and a *strategy* (Armbruster, Echols, & Brown, 1982). Students can employ a technique "blindly," without using it strategically in processing text information. A technique becomes a strategy only if students have the knowledge of *when, where, and how* to use it (Brown, 1978). This distinction between techniques and strategies may explain the often ineffective outcome of inducing students to use study activities (see Anderson & Armbruster, 1984b).

Consider the common practices of note taking and underlining. Until recently, by far the majority of studies on underlining or note taking showed these activities to be no more effective than passive studying techniques such as rereading (Arnold, 1942; Hoon, 1974; Idstein & Jenkins, 1972; Kulhavy, Dyer, & Silver, 1975; Stordahl & Christensen, 1956; Todd & Kessler, 1971; Wilmore, 1966). However, as Brown and Smiley (1978) demonstrated, an important factor in these studies was that learners were randomly assigned to treatment groups. Thus, they were forced to adopt one or another strategy, whether or not they would have chosen that activity if left to their own devices. Brown and Smiley (1978) compared high school students who were spontaneous users of these strategies and those who were told to use them. Students who were spontaneous users underlined or took notes that favored the important information and subsequently remembered more. Students induced to use the strategies did not show a similar sensitivity to importance; they took notes or underlined more randomly, and failed to improve as a result of their activities. Taking notes or underlining is not in itself a useful strategy; a useful strategy also involves understanding how and when one should use these activities to focus attention appropriately.

In support of these findings, three studies that have shown positive results of underlining all report an advantage to active studiers. Richards and August (1975) found that college students who actively underlined passages recalled more than students who had appropriate sections underlined for them. Similarly, Schnell and Rocchio (1975) found that high school students who underlined their own text outperformed those who read a version underlined for them, who in turn recalled more than students reading an uncued text. Finally, Fowler and Barker (1974) found that college students who highlighted their texts recalled more of the material they marked than did students who received a premarked text.

Similar findings come from the note-taking and outlining literatures (Brown & Smiley, 1978). Again, more studies show that these activities are inefficient (Arnold, 1942; Stordahl & Christensen, 1956; Todd & Kessler, 1971; Wilmore, 1966) than report increased performance as a function of such pursuits (Barton, 1930; Brown & Smiley, 1978; Salisbury, 1935). As Anderson and Armbruster (1984b) point out, however, in none of the "failure" studies were students *taught how to outline*. But in the major successes, *fairly extensive training* in outlining was given. For example, Salisbury's (1935) training involved 30 lessons of instruction.

There is considerable evidence that high school and even college students need to be taught explicitly how to use an outlining strategy. Again we see that outlining itself is not a desired end product, and merely telling students it would be a good idea to outline, underline, take notes, and so forth, is not going to help them become more effective studiers (Brown & Smiley, 1978). Detailed, *informed* instruction in the purposes of outlining and methods of using the strategy intelligently are needed before sizable benefits accrue.

Learner Characteristics

A final major fact of metacognition is the learner's awareness of his/her own characteristics (such as background knowledge, interest, motivation, skills, and deficiencies), how these characteristics affect learning, and how reading and studying behaviors should be adjusted accordingly. Expert learners take into consideration their particular strengths and weaknesses when devising a plan for studying. Some report they "have a good rote memory," "tend to forget details," and so forth. Whatever the psychological reality behind such self-diagnoses, it is certainly true that everyone has a limited capacity for remembering large amounts of information. A reader can only keep a certain amount of information alive at any one time. Effective readers know this and do not overburden their memories by attempting to retain large segments of texts, too many pending questions, too many unresolved ambiguities, too many unknown words and abstract phrases, and the like. Similarly, as arbitrary material is difficult to comprehend and retain, experts try to make the text more meaningful by attempting to understand the significance of what they are reading, or by trying to fit the new material into their own personal experience (Bransford, Stein, Shelton, & Owings, 1981). In the Myers and Paris (1978) interview study, both second and sixth graders were aware that background knowledge and interest affect reading. However, there is a difference between knowing that these characteristics affect reading and knowing how to harness this information when learning from text.

One learner characteristic that has received attention in research on meta-cognition is the awareness and activation of relevant prior knowledge. Bransford et al. report several studies where academically unsuccessful fifth graders have difficulty using their existing knowledge to help them learn (Bransford, Stein, Arbitman-Smith, & Vye, 1985). For example, they asked fifth graders to read a passage about camels. Part of the passage emphasized problems such as surviving desert sandstorms; other parts discussed facts such as "Camels can close their nasal passages and have special eyelids to protect their eyes." Many of the academically less successful students failed to utilize information about the sandstorm to interpret the significance of facts about the camels' nasal passages and eyelids. However, successful students who did understand how various properties of camels help them survive desert sand-storms had a basis for understanding a new passage describing the clothing worn by desert people (e.g., these students could understand the significance of wearing veils or other forms of face protection). The less successful students had the background knowledge necessary to learn the information, but they consistently failed to use this knowledge. They failed to ask themselves how potentially available information could clarify the significance or relevance of new factual content. Fortunately, Bransford et al. (1985) report success in teaching students to ask themselves questions designed to activate relevant prior knowledge.

Individual differences in a learner's beliefs about studying can also affect monitoring activities. On the basis of interview and questionnaire data, Ryan (1982) classified college students as having either dualistic or relativistic beliefs about the nature of knowledge. Dualists apparently believe that knowl-edge consists of facts that are true or false, right or wrong, whereas relativists believe that knowledge is relativistic. Along with these beliefs come different standards for evaluating study activities. The dualist believes that the outcome of studying is the accumulation of facts and judges his comprehension by the number of propositions he can recall after reading a text. In contrast, the relativist views the outcome of studying as the discovery of a logical structure and correspondingly judges his comprehension by the degree to which clear and coherent relations can be established between text propositions. Dualists try to remember facts; relativists try to integrate what they read into a coherent interpretation (Svensson, 1977). Individual conceptions of understanding de-termine how learners evaluate their success while studying. The fact that the relativist approach leads to better grades suggests that some college students, i.e. dualists, need help in changing their conceptions of what learning is and would benefit from instruction in monitoring their understanding (Ryan, 1982).

In summary, a fundamental form of metacognition is the ability to monitor one's current state of learning. This ability depends on one's knowledge of four major factors: text, task, strategy, and learner characteristics. All of these influence the degree to which students will be able to coordinate their plans and engage in active monitoring, which in turn will lead to successful reading and studying outcomes.

METACOGNITION AND INSTRUCTION

Blind, Informed, and Self-Control Training

Inducing students to be more active studiers is an old pastime. Dewey (1910) had a set of prescriptions for inculcating more effective learning, as did Binet (1909), and how-to-study guides have been popular for a long time (Anderson, 1980). Encouraged by NIE's funding, there has been a resurgence of interest in study skills as a topic for scientific investigation, primarily because of the merging of educational psychology and cognitive science (Glaser, 1978). Hopes for a new discipline of cognitive engineering (Norman, 1980) are becoming realistic. A prime impetus for the new interest in cognitive skills training (Chipman, Segal, & Glaser, 1985) is the work on metacognition that stresses the learner's awareness and control of his own study activities.

We would like to contrast the current emphasis on training with awareness with the more traditional study skills training procedures (such as Robinson's SQ3R method, 1941) that Brown, Campione, and Day (1981) have termed blind training studies. Although there is nothing wrong in principle with the traditional methods, in practice, training in such cookbook methods often results in "blind rule following." Instructing a student to read a text, ask questions about the topic sentence (undefined), reread it twice (why not three times?) and so on, may be a reasonable recipe for learning certain texts for certain purposes— if the learner understands why these activities are appropriate. But if the learner does not understand the significance of these activities, does not know how to check that the strategies are resulting in the desired end result, does not know what the desired end result is, does not know how to adapt the recipe to slightly new situations, or invent a new recipe for various types of texts and tasks, then it is not surprising that instruction in the study recipe is less successful at producing expert studiers than one would like.

The typical procedure in blind training studies is to instruct students to perform particular activities, but without explaining the significance of such activities. They are told what to do, but not why, or that it is an activity appropriate to a particular class of situations, materials, or goals. Although these procedures are sufficient for some students because they can infer the significance of the strategy, this is not so for all.

Although blind training techniques can help people learn a *particular* set of materials, they do not necessarily help people change their general approach to the problem of learning new sets of materials (see the example of the robot passages in the second section). The outcome of such intervention is often that students neither perform the trained activities subsequently on their own volition nor transfer them to new but similar learning situations (Brown & Campione, 1981). Something other than "blind training" seems to be necessary to help many students learn on their own.

The main goal of cognitive training with awareness is to help students recognize the need to adapt their study activities to the demands of the task at hand, the nature of the material, and their personal preferences and abilities. The aim is to provide novice learners with the information, practice, and success necessary to design effective learning plans of their own. Such training would sensitize students to the active nature of critical reading and studying, and to the importance of employing problem-solving routines to enhance understanding. If less successful students can be made aware of basic *strategies* for reading and remembering, simple rules of *text* construction, differing demands of a variety of *tests* to which their knowledge may be put, and the importance of using any *background knowledge* they may have, they cannot help but become more effective learners. Such self-awareness is a prerequisite for self-regulation, the ability to monitor and check one's own cognitive activities while reading and studying (Baker & Brown, 1984a; Brown, Bransford, Ferrara, & Campione, 1983; Brown, Campione, & Day, 1981).

In the last few years, research aimed at assessing the effects of adding metacognitive supplements to strategy training has become popular (Brown, 1978). We consider two types of experiments, those involving *informed* training and those involving *self-control* training (Brown et al., 1983). Generally, subjects in informed training studies are given some additional information about the strategy they have been instructed to use; those in self-control studies are also given explicit instruction about overseeing, monitoring, or regulating the strategies.

Informed training involves instruction in the significance of the trained activity (Kennedy & Miller, 1976; Ringel & Springer, 1980). An example of this approach is a study by Paris, Newman, and McVey (1982). After 2 days of baseline performance on a task requiring children to learn lists of categorized pictures, Paris et al. divided their 7- and 8-year-old students into two training groups. In one, the nonelaboration (blind, in our terminology) group, students were told how to carry out some mnemonic activities; grouping, labeling, cumulative rehearsal, and recalling by groups. The second, or elaboration (informed) group, was given, in addition, a brief rationale for each of the different behaviors. They were also provided feedback about their performance after recall. The elaboration group outperformed the nonelaboration group in both training and subsequent sessions. Paris et al. argue that providing the rationale for each component strategy leads to an understanding of the significance of those activities, and this awareness contributes to continued unprompted use. To evaluate this possibility, they obtained metacognitive judgments throughout the course of the experiment. In fact, the students in the elaborated training condition showed increased awareness of the role of the trained strategies compared with those in the nonelaborated condition. Also, awareness scores were significantly correlated with both strategy use and remembering.

The second category of training studies involves self-control. The main feature of this set is the inclusion of explicit training of metacognitive skills, such as planning, checking, and monitoring. Although informed training includes provision of information about the study activity and its effects, self-control training also includes help with planning and overseeing one's action.

Although few self-control training studies have been conducted, the initial results are encouraging. For example, Day (1980) trained junior college students to use a variety of rules for summarizing texts. The students differed in ability and in the type of instruction they received. The "control" group was given traditional summary writing instructions: be economical with words, include all the main ideas, and so forth, but no further details were provided. The second condition involved information about suitable rules, demonstration, and practice; and the third condition included both the rules and explicit instructions regarding the management and overseeing of those rules (self-control training). The traditional (control) instruction was ineffective. Students with no diagnosed learning problems improved with the informed training. Students with diagnosed reading and writing problems, however, needed direct training in rule application and overseeing, i.e., self-control training, before any significant improvement was effected.

Criteria for a Successful Study

We believe that ideal cognitive skills training programs should include skills training, self-control training, and informed training. In addition, there are certain criteria of success necessary before the researchers can claim that the outcome has practical significance. The following major criteria of success have been suggested (Brown & Campione, 1978b, 1981):

1. There should be clear *improvement* on the target task. If students are being trained to summarize, it is essential to show improved summarization scores after training, and that improvement should be substantial if the instructional package is to have practical utility.

2. There should be independent evidence of *process change*, so that improvement on the target task can reasonably be attributed to the specific effects

of training, rather than to general effects due to motivational factors, such as increased attention.

3. The training effect must be reliable and *durable*. As instruction is time consuming, favorable outcomes should stand the test of time.

4. Several different kinds of *transfer* are desirable. For example, one would like to see transfer across settings (i.e., from the laboratory or other training site to the classroom); across tasks with the same underlying structure but different surface formats; and to improved scores on standardized reading tests, an important form of school evaluations.

5. The training should be *instructionally feasible*, so it can be implemented in regular classrooms by average classroom teachers.

Two NIE-funded programs meet the above criteria and provide good examples of successful training programs. The first, by Palincsar and Brown (1982), is typical of the type of training study that begins with laboratory practice and then moves by gradual extension to the classroom. The second, by Scott Paris and his associates, is typical of the curriculum development approach that begins in the classroom by introducing a specially designed curriculum. Both programs share the same aim—to improve general metacognitive skills of reading.

From the Laboratory to the Classroom

Palincsar and Brown (1982) sought to improve the comprehension-fostering and comprehension-monitoring skills of students in need of such help. Four training activities—self-directed summarizing (review), questioning, clarifying, and predicting—were combined in a package. Each activity was used in response to a concrete problem of text comprehension. Clarifying occurred only if there were confusions either in the text (unclear referent, etc.) or in the student's interpretation of the text. Summarizing was modeled as an activity of self-review; it was used to state to the group (or teacher) what had just happened in the text and as a test that the content had been understood. If an adequate synopsis could not be reached, this was regarded not as a failure to perform, but as an important source of information that comprehension was not proceeding as it should and remedial action (such as rereading or clarifying) was needed. Questioning, similarly, was not practiced as a teacher-directed isolated activity, but as a concerete task—what question could a teacher or test reasonably ask about that section of the text (Andre & Anderson, 1978-1979; Collins & Smith, 1982). Students reacted very positively to this concrete detective work, rather than the more typical isolated skills training approach.

In addition to these cognitive activities, every attempt was made to enhance the students' sense of competence and control. The teacher provided praise and feedback; the students graphed their record of success and the teachers paid considerable attention to the "metacognitive" setting. The students received explicit instruction, extensive modeling, and repeated practice in concrete versions of the trained activities; they were constantly reminded to engage in these activities while reading. They were instructed not to proceed until they could summarize, clarify, and answer questions on each segment of text. Finally, the students were constantly reminded that the target activities were to help them improve and monitor their comprehension, shown that their performance improved dramatically when they did so, and told that they should always engage in these activities while reading for academic purposes.

The students were from low socioeconomic backgrounds, had low "normal" IQ scores (mean IQ = 84) and were participants in remedial reading classes. Their decoding fluency was at grade level, but they were seriously delayed in their reading comprehension ability (2–3 year delays). In two replications of the procedure, instruction took place in small groups with one teacher (a researcher) and either one or two students. In the third study, instruction took place in larger, naturally constructed, reading groups, where the teacher was the regular classroom instructor.

Each day during reading, the teacher and students engaged in an interactive learning game (referred to as reciprocal teaching) that involved taking turns in leading a dialogue concerning each segment of text. If the passage was new, the teacher called the students' attention to the title, asked for predictions based upon the title, and discussed the relation of the passage to prior knowledge. If the passage was partially completed, the teacher asked the students to recall and state the topic of the text and several important points already covered in the passage.

Following this general orientation, the teacher assigned a segment of the passage to be read (usually a paragraph) and either indicated that it was her turn to be the teacher or assigned one of the students to teach that segment. The teacher and students then read the segment silently. After reading, the teacher (student or adult) for that segment summarized the content, discussed and clarified any difficulties, asked a question that a teacher or test might ask about the segment, and finally made a prediction about future content. All of these activities were conducted in as natural a dialogue as possible, with the teacher and students arguing and giving feedback to one another.

At first the students had difficulty taking part in the dialogue, particularly with summarizing and formulating questions. The teacher helped with a variety of prompting techniques such as "What questions did you think a teacher might ask?"; "Remember, a summary is a shortened version; it doesn't include detail." The teacher also provided praise and feedback specific to the student's participation: "You asked that question well; it was very clear what information you wanted"; "Excellent prediction; let's see if you're right." After this type of feedback, the teacher modeled any activity that continued to need improvement: "A question I would have asked would be . . . "; "I would summarize by saying . . ."

In this initial phase, the experimenter modeled effective comprehension-monitoring strategies but the student was a relatively passive observer. In the intermediate phase, the students became much more adept as dialogue leaders, and by the end of 10 sessions were providing paraphrases and questions of some sophistication. For example, in the initial sessions of the first study, 46% of student-produced questions were judged as non-questions or as needing clarification. By the end of the sessions only 2% of responses were judged as such. Unclear questions dropped out and were replaced over time with questions focusing on the main idea of each text segment. A similar improvement was found for summary statements: initially, only 11% of summary statements captured main ideas, whereas at the end 60% of the statements were so classified. A similar improvement in the quality of the dialogues over time was found in the two replication studies that took place in group settings (see Palincsar & Brown, 1982, for details).

In all three studies, with repeated interaction with an adult model performing appropriate questioning and paraphrasing activities, the students learned to perform these functions on their own. Over time, the students' questions became more like the tutor's, being classified as *inventions*, i.e., questions and summaries of gist in one's own words, rather than selections, repetitions of words actually occurring in text (Brown & Day, 1983). Given the steady improvement on daily comprehension tests (see below), it would appear that students internalize these activities as part of their repertoire of comprehension-fostering skills. This statement is supported by the data from peer tutoring sessions taken at the termination of the study. Trained tutees, faced with naive peers, did attempt to model main idea paraphrases and questions along with clarifying and predicting.

In addition to the qualitative changes in the students' dialogues, there was a steady improvement in the level of performance on daily comprehension tests. Each day, following the interactive learning sessions, the students read a novel passage and independently answered 10 comprehension questions. During pretesting prior to the introduction of the interactive sessions, students averaged 20% correct on such tests. After the reciprocal teaching sessions, students reached accuracy levels of 80%-90% correct. The improvement on the daily tests was large and reliable: of the 10 students taking part in the first two studies, 9 improved to the level set by good comprehenders. All 31 students in Study 3 taught in their reading group by volunteer teachers met this level. The effect was durable: maintenance probes showed no drop in the level of performance over 8 weeks. Although there was a decline after 6 months (levels dropping from 80% to 60%), only one session with the reciprocal teaching procedure was sufficient to raise performance back to the short-term maintenance level of 80%-90% correct.

The effect also generalized to the classroom. During the study, the students took comprehension tests as part of their regular science and social science instruction. They were not informed that these tests were related to the study, as all seventh graders took the tests. The students began the study with scores below the 20th percentile compared to all other seventh graders in their school (approx. 130), but after the study, 90% of the students showed a clear improvement, moving up to at least the average level for their age-mates. Given the difficulty reported in obtaining generalization of trained skills across settings (Brown & Campione, 1978, 1981; Meichenbaum, 1985), this is an impressive finding.

Training also resulted in reliable transfer to dissimilar laboratory tasks that demanded the same underlying processes. The tests of transfer were selected because they tapped the skills taught during the reciprocal teaching. Two of the four transfer tests were measures of the two most frequent activities during the reciprocal teaching sessions, summarizing (Brown & Day, 1983) and predicting questions that might be asked concerning each segment of text. In addition, two other tests were used as measures of general comprehension monitoring, detecting errors (Harris, Kruithof, Terwogt, & Visser, 1981; Markman, 1981) and rating importance of segments of narratives (Brown & Smiley, 1977).

The transfer tests were conducted in a pretest-posttest format. (For details of the transfer probes see Palincsar & Brown, 1982.) Briefly, three of the four tests showed a significant improvement: writing summaries, designing questions to be asked on a test, and detecting errors. The students did not improve on the Brown and Smiley (1977) task of rating narratives for variations in importance, although they did improve in their ability to select important elements in their summary writing.

Thus training resulted in reliable transfer to dissimilar tasks: summarizing, predicting questions, and detecting incongruities all improved. Again this is an impressive finding given prior difficulty with obtaining transfer of cognitive skills training (Brown & Campione, 1978, 1981). In addition, sizable improvements in standardized comprehension scores were recorded for the majority of students. And, of prime importance, the intervention was no less successful in natural group settings conducted by regular classroom teachers than it was in the laboratory when conducted by a researcher.

Some possible reasons for the success of the Palincsar and Brown studies include:

1. Training was extensive. Students received approximately 20 days of instruction.

2. The trained activities were well specified theoretically and well established empirically as particular problems for poor readers.

3. The training was tailored to the needs of these students (good decoders but passive comprehenders).

4. The skills could be expected to be trans-situational. Such ubiquitous activities as self-review and self-interrogation are pertinent in a wide variety of knowledge acquisition tasks.

5. A great deal of attention was paid to "metacognitive" variables: students were informed of the importance, generality and utility of these activities; they were trained in self-regulatory activities; and the skills themselves were general comprehension-monitoring activities applicable in a wide variety of reading/studying tasks.

6. The reciprocal teaching mode permitted extensive modeling in a reasonably natural setting, and forced the students to participate so teachers could evaluate current states and provide appropriate feedback and assistance.

7. Every attempt was made to increase the students' sense of personal efficacy: they plotted success, planned strategies, monitored progress, and were shown to be competent and in control.

A Metacognitive Curriculum for the Classroom

Paris et al. (1982) recently completed a longitudinal investigation of an instructional program designed to teach children metacognitive aspects of reading. The major question addressed by their experimental treatment was, "Can classroom instruction on metacognitive aspects of reading improve children's reading comprehension?" The initial data from this study suggest that the answer is yes.

Working with the directors of curriculum and research in the Ann Arbor Schools, Paris and his associates solicited the cooperation of four principals and ten teachers for the project. These four schools were roughly equivalent in demographic and achievement variables. One third-grade and one fifth-grade classroom in two different schools were designated as experimental classrooms. One third-grade and one fifth-grade classroom in each of the other two schools were designated as control classes. (In addition a third-grade and a fifth-grade classroom in one experimental school provided a within-school control condition.) Each class consisted of approximately 20 children.

A battery of reading tests was administered to the 200 participating children in the fall of 1980, spring of 1981, and December, 1981. The battery included more than a dozen different tasks, some given to the classes as groups and many presented individually. They included the Gates MacGinitie standardized reading test, cloze tasks, oral reading, recall of stories, and individual interviews with children to assess their knowledge about reading skills and reading activities. The multiple measures over time afford a rich and detailed picture of children's evolving reading abilities.

The instructional treatment was offered to approximately 100 children in the four experimental classrooms between November, 1980, and April, 1981. Weekly teaching modules included a brief description for the classroom teacher of the week's activities and the skill focus (e.g., making inferences, identifying main ideas). Two half-hour group lessons and a bulletin board on the skill were also prepared. Lessons were identical for both third and fifth grades except that the instructor adjusted her teaching style, rate, and difficulty of worksheets and materials for each grade. Children in control classes were provided with 4 months of nonreading activities including science lessons, movies, and individual tutoring. This was done to equate time spent with each group, as well as to ensure equal familiarity with the researchers and positive benefits for participating in the study for all children.

Each week's lessons involved the use of a bulletin board containing a metaphor for the strategy to be taught, a set of goals and plans for the lessons, and a set of focal questions for the children and classroom teachers. For example, the week devoted to *Understanding the Goals of Reading* had lessons entitled: "Reading is Like a Puzzle." The bulletin board was entitled "A Bag Full of Tricks for Reading" and provided illustrations of suitable activities such as "skimming-along" or fix-up strategies entitled "road repairs." Children were instructed to ask themselves certain questions before beginning their "reading trip." A "quiet zone" sign directed them to find a quiet place to prepare. A "stop sign" directed them to stop and think about what they were reading, and a "dead end" sign told them that they needed to retrace and reread because they had missed the meaning. Paris et al. claim that the concrete nature of these illustrations played a large part in the success of the program.

All the data have not yet been analyzed, but the results so far are very encouraging. The experimental and control classrooms were equivalent on standardized tests of reading comprehension before the project, but the experimental groups scored significantly higher afterwards. This pattern of improvement was evident in three different tests of reading comprehension (Gates-MacGinitie, Teaching of Reading Comprehension, cloze) and also in interviews of children's understanding about reading. The improvement was maintained for at least a 6-month period.

In summary, well-structured training programs aimed at both basic cognitive skills of reading *and* metacognitive factors of awareness and control can result in quite dramatic and durable improvements in children's reading proficiency. Current interventions have been more successful at generating significant improvement, maintenance, generalization, and transfer of learning than prior studies for several reasons. The training is based on a firmer understanding of the knowledge and strategies that poor readers lack. The training is intensive and focuses on concrete examples of what might otherwise seem like abstract skills. Students are fully informed about the reasons why the trained activities are important; they are given explicit information concerning the generality and utility of the activities; they are trained in self-regulatory activities including the checking and monitoring of their own comprehension; and finally the skills themselves are general comprehension-monitoring activities applicable in a wide variety of reading/studying tasks.

CRITICAL ISSUES FOR FUTURE RESEARCH

Given the great success of the current studies of metacognitive factors involved in reading, our primary suggestion for future research is "more of the same." We need to know a great deal more about the types of misunderstandings novice readers entertain about their roles as active learners and, in particular, the relation between a student's (mis)conception of learning and how she sets about the task of reading. Finally, although there have been a number of successful training studies that share a concentration on metacognitive factors (for example Bird, 1980; Brown, Campione, & Barclay, 1979; Dansereau, 1985; Day, 1980; Palincsar & Brown, 1982; Paris et al., 1982; Raphael, 1980; Wong & Jones, 1982), the number is still relatively small. Studies actually demonstrating instructional feasibility in the regular classroom are even scarcer. Given the importance of this line of research for improving educational practice, additional examples of successful metacognitive training are needed.

In addition to our call for more training studies to establish the generality of their success across student populations and across cognitive skills, research should address the issue of exactly what determines success. For example, in the Palincsar and Brown studies the successful intervention involved four activities, all trained with awareness. But would a single activity rather than all four (paraphrasing, questioning, prediction, and clarifying) have been successful? Similarly, the reciprocal teaching method is a complex mixture of activities. Would modeling alone, or just explicit instruction, be as successful as the reciprocal teaching game (see also Bird, 1980)? Just what features of the Paris et al. curriculum are essential for inducing change, and can the procedure be streamlined? Given that cognitive skills training studies are very time and labor consuming, we advocate first obtaining a sizable, durable, and generalized effect of training and then conducting the necessary experimentation to determine the subcomponents that are primarily responsible for the improvement.

To end on an optimistic note, the called-for research essentially requires replications and extensions to test the limits of the existing exciting findings and help streamline procedures. Given the state of the art, we can train instructionally relevant cognitive skills even in students who have a long history of academic failure. This training can be carried out under the pressures of normal classroom settings, and results in worthwhile and reliable improvements. In fact, poor students can be brought from the very bottom of the distribution for their age up to the average of their successful classmates (e.g., Palincsar & Brown, 1982). The success of such studies suggests that metacognitive training may have broad educational utility, but it may be particularly appropriate for children with diagnosed learning problems and a concomitant sense of helplessness in academic milieux.

5 Changing Linguistic Perspectives on Literacy

Roger W. Shuy
Georgetown University

THE HISTORICAL INTERACTION BETWEEN LINGUISTICS AND LITERACY

To a linguist, it seems odd to assert that language analysis has a role to play in literacy. To us, literacy *is* language, at least as the intermediary medium from the human mind to the printed page and back again. However obvious this may seem to linguists, it has not been so obvious from their work. Few have seemed very interested in literacy, except for those heroic missionaries who faced daily problems of reducing a new language to a writing system, translating the Bible into that language, then teaching people to read it. Unfortunately, the work of these missionary literacy specialists has gone relatively unnoticed. But even they were handicapped by the caveats of the then current view of linguistics and by physical isolation from other fields of knowledge that could have fed their analyses.

The caveats of historically held linguistic theory have done almost as much damage as good to the field of literacy. Early linguist pioneers to the field of reading, such as Charles Fries (1966), brought to reading that which was known and popular in linguistics. Since linguistic analysis in the forties and fifties was predominantly at the sound and word levels, it was only natural that such linguists would add their dimensions of language knowledge to what was known, or thought to be known, about letter-sound correspondence or word formation.

In the 1960s, however, within the field of reading a rebellion began. Researchers like Kenneth Goodman (1968) and Frank Smith (1971) began to assert that decoding skills play only a minor role in reading. The "linguistic approach" to reading (largely decoding) came under attack. The new school, referred to as "psycholinguistic," began to be associated with comprehension, and "linguistics" was relegated to phonology, morphology, and lexicon. This was unfortunate for the credibility of linguistics, and the field soon fell into disrepute among reading specialists.

In more recent years, it has become clear that the aspects of language structure which contribute to literacy include a great deal more than phonology (revealed through letter-sound correspondences), morphology (revealed through word formation), and lexicon or vocabulary. In the sixties and seventies, linguists focused their attention on sentence syntax, with the promise of applications to literacy, though little was done to connect this to reading. Efforts were made to associate what was then known about kernel sentences to developing writing ability (Roberts, 1970), but schools soon despaired of making little syntacticians out of their students. In any case, changes in linguistic theory soon made these materials out of date, so there was not much support from linguists either.

Two different paradigm shifts in linguistics were needed to move language analysis close enough to the issues of literacy to be helpful in any way. The first was the creation of sociolinguistics in the late sixties; the second was the focus on units of analysis larger than the sentence, or discourse analysis, in the seventies.

Sociolinguistics and Discourse Analysis

Definitions of sociolinguistics are numerous and confusing. Somewhat arbitrarily, sociolinguistics here refers to six concerns: (1) language in social context rather than in isolation; (2) variability in language in addition to universals; (3) the dynamics of language rather than its static representation; (4) empirical data in addition to intuitive analysis; (5) subjective reactions to language, not just objective language use; and (6) a concern for the functions of language, not just the forms.

In the sixties, sociolinguistic interest in the relation of literacy to language was focused mainly on units of language with which linguists were familiar, such as dialect interference from phonology and grammar. One question concerned the effect of nonstandard oral language on the ability to learn to read or write standard English. The research of Labov (1966, 1972), Wolfram (1969, 1971), Fasold (1972) and others had demonstrated clear patterns of variability among speakers of Vernacular Black English (VBE). Since there was little likelihood that existing literature would be rewritten in VBE, and since research on the attitudes of the Black community did not suggest any desire that written Black English be used in schools, researchers turned to the issue of dialect interference on learning to read or write (Shuy, 1979). Phonological interference or mismatch of oral language to reading was studied by Shuy (1968), Melmed (1971), Rystrom (1970), Rental and Kennedy (1972), and others who concluded that phonological differences had little effect on learning to read. For example, the habitual pronunciation of *des* for *desk* simply did not affect reading ability.

The major thrust of this work was on grammatical interference in beginning reading, but it was often flawed, as Simons (1973) and Venezky (1970) point out. There was extreme difficulty in obtaining adequate, naturalistic samples of reading, to provide consistent and realistic reading passages and to analyze the results in an appropriate manner (Shuy, 1979). It became clear that language research of any kind, including reading, required a great deal of contextual information because context affects both the productive and receptive aspects of language. Paradoxically, the more context the researcher notices and controls, the more complex the research becomes.

A variation on this search for the influence of vernacular language on literacy should also be noted. In 1969, attempts were made to develop beginning reading materials in Vernacular English, which would avoid the mismatch of spoken language to the printed page. The Chicago Board of Education's *Psycholinguistics Reading Series—A Bidialectal Approach* (Leaverton, Gladney, & Davis, 1969) started reading instruction in a written representation of VBE instead of in the usual Standard English form. The second program, developed by Baratz and Stewart (1969), produced materials that more closely approximate actual vernacular dialect. Although evaluations of the Chicago project claimed that children could be taught to read quicker using "everyday talk" rather than "school talk," the written representation of everyday talk in VBE ignored that variability of natural language, in which the nonstandard variant is *not* used every time it could potentially occur, causing deep concern for the premises of the theory. The Baratz and Stewart program ran afoul of negative public reaction to any language in print other than the standard code.

Efforts by linguists to apply the knowledge of their field to writing were considerably fewer. Whiteman (1981b) addressed the question of oral language influence in the writing of VBE speakers and found that some of the features of spoken language which are known to characterize VBE speakers show up even in the writing of working-class white children, although they do not occur in their casual speech. This suggested that there are general developmental influences in learning to write which are similar to VBE spoken features.

A second major rebellion in linguistics also took place in the seventies. This was the attack on sentence level linguistics. If any pattern in the recent history of linguistics is visible, it is the trend toward analyzing larger and larger chunks of data. If the forties and fifties can be characterized by the study of phonology and morphology and the sixties and early seventies by the study of syntax, the late seventies and early eighties can be seen as the time when interest in discourse, (units of language larger than a sentence) became prominent.

A consequence of these two rebellions is the changing definitions of terms. In the recent period, the definition of *context* took on a new dimension. Whereas in the forties and fifties, context meant the immediate phonological environment, and in the sixties and seventies it meant the relation between syntactic units, the work of sociolinguists in the sixties and seventies extended the meaning of *context* to the social environments in which language could be found. This included speaker/listener factors such as sex, race, socioeconomic status and age. Ethnographers of communication extended the meaning of *context* even further to include variability in language use due to differences in topic, participants, setting, genre, and so forth (Gumperz, 1964; Hymes, 1972; Sherzer, 1974). Thus *context* became a crucial dimension for analysis of any spoken or written data. All of these contextual variables influence the production and reception of literacy. Few have been researched in either the reading or the writing of children.

FUNCTIONAL LANGUAGE: DIFFERENT STRANDS AND DISCIPLINES COMING TOGETHER

In the seventies, linguists began to heed the work of language philosophers such as Searle (1969, 1975), Austin (1962) and Grice (1975), who were saying that the conveyed meaning of an utterance is not necessarily the same as its semantic meaning. This was the birth of pragmatics and speech act theory, which simply means "the way a person uses language to get things done." Linguists have become quite excited about this area and have made many contributions to our knowledge base (Saddock, 1974). Efforts to apply pragmatics to reading and writing have only begun, but show great promise.

Linguists interested in literacy are concerned that the convergence of these newer understandings of discourse not be considered simply another literacy gimmick. Whereas there may have been an overpromise of the potential of linguistics when the focus was on the *forms* of language, there is reason for great optimism about the relevance of the present focus on discourse and sociolinguistic factors. For one thing, this new movement is toward a *holistic* rather than a *reductionist* approach (Magoon, 1977), stressing a level of analysis which is at the very heart of education: function. In fact, the term used to represent the understandings of spoken and written language at the discourse level, *functional language*, may well address the fear that our newer views will be treated as gimmicks.

We need to learn how language is used in writing and speaking to get things done and how to process (in listening and reading) how others use language to get things done. To get at language functions, and the various strategies people use to reveal these functions (depending on topic, setting, participants, and group membership), language must be viewed from a different level than in the past. These generalizable functions (i.e., requesting information, denying, apologizing, reporting facts, evaluating, complaining, etc.) are both linguistic and cognitive. To study them as either alone is to miss much of the richness of their existence.

As obvious as it may seem to teach strategies that reveal language functions, we instead teach grammar, spelling, punctuation, and vocabulary—the *forms* of language. Instead of teaching ways of accomplishing the underlying construct (function) that relates to the speaker's intention to do something through language, school practice is to engage in straight task teaching (Fig. 5.1).

Straight task teaching is a weak replacement for generalizable function teaching (Fig. 5.2). For example, many strategies are available for getting oneself invited to dinner, including:

- Could I have dinner with you? (direct request).
- I'd like to get together with you for dinner sometime (report opinion).
- I'm getting hungry (reporting a fact).

A speaker's selection of one of these strategies depends on relevant contextual factors which obtain at the time. On certain occasions, directness is appropriate. On other occasions, indirectness is considered better. The maturing language learner gradually acquires a sense of when to use the most appropriate

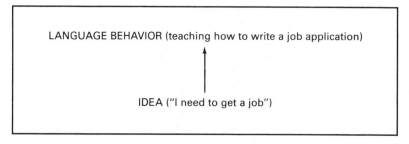

FIG. 5.1   Straight Task Teaching

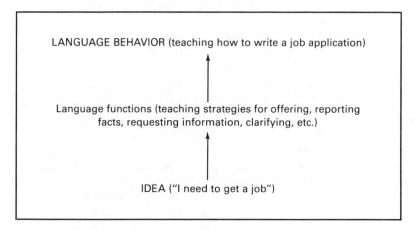

FIG. 5.2   Generalizable Function Teaching

strategy. The functional teaching task should be how to write, speak, read, or hear the appropriate language function strategies to get things done.

Teaching language function strategies differs from teaching language forms in two major ways. First, language forms are acceptable or unacceptable, with no alternatives. Functional strategies, in contrast, are alternative ways of saying the same thing. Appropriateness of the strategy will vary with the context, the role relationship of the participants, the topic, the formality of the interactive register, and other factors. Teaching such strategies involves providing alternatives from which to select, modeling, and otherwise leading the student toward communicative competence. Second, whereas form-organized teaching presents structures in what is presumed to be an increasing order of difficulty, functional strategy teaching starts with the student's communicative needs or intentions. In this sense, it is self-generated rather than teacher- or "other"-generated. Form-oriented instruction specifies practice or drills until mastery is attained. Teachers often encourage learners to use only those forms they have mastered. Such a practice is in direct opposition to communicative practice which is, by definition, self-initiated.

This is not to say that language forms are unimportant. There will certainly be no communication without such forms. But accuracy of forms should not be our sole purpose. The social acceptability of correct form must be weighed against the cognitive effectiveness of the intention as revealed through a functional strategy. Educators make great claims about the importance of comprehension in reading and the presentation of ideas in writing, but they tend to ignore the strategies used by writers to accomplish these intentions in favor of a stress on correct forms.

What We Need to Know About Discourse

One of the major problems facing literacy studies at the discourse level is that our theory and knowledge base are incomplete. Yet language use examined without a notion of discourse is not fruitful. This is an important problem, since the lack of a complete or adequate view of discourse means that the researcher cannot merely grind new data through an already successful and accepted model. If we knew all of the important language functions, we would simply collect new data and then find those functions in operation, noting the ages of the speakers as those functions are acquired and the contexts in which they are required. We would then infer notions of development and the degree of fit between what children can do and what school talk demands. However, not only do we not know what all the functions are, we do not know what strategies people use to carry them out.

Even more problematic is the question of whether a list of functions and a set of strategies associated with each (or which are alternate realizations of each) are in any way an adequate reflection of the nature of functional language. Such a model owes much to speech act theory and is somewhat reminiscent of some syntactic models, but whether it is safe to assume that it can capture all the important aspects of functional language is open to question. If our studies are totally dependent on such an approach, we might have not only the practical problems of locating all the alternative strategies, but also new theoretical problems.

Recent Trends in Research

Over a decade ago, the report of the NIE Summer Study Group in Linguistic Communication suggested a number of new directions for literacy research in this country (Miller, 1973). The report emphasized the need to stress the influence of the child's environment, "anthropological type observations" as well as experimental studies. It urged that we engage in cross-cultural studies, the influence of dialectal variation, and, above all, comprehension. The major focus was on reading, with little attention to writing. At that time, it could not have been suspected that there would be an increasing convergence of the work of anthropologists, philosophers, linguists, and psychologists in such areas as communicative competence and discourse analysis. Nor would it have been possible to imagine the increasing reassociation of reading and writing in literacy studies evident in current research.

Recent research projects funded by NIE show clear evidence of the trend toward analyzing *discourse* in reading and writing (Boggs, 1983; Green, 1978; Griffin, 1977; Hall & Guthrie, 1979; Herman, 1979; King, 1979; Reichman, 1978; Spiro & Taylor, 1980; Staton, 1980b; Tennenberg & Morine-Dershimer, 1978). Other recent research efforts display evidence of the concern for *pragmatics and speech act theory* in literacy (Brewer, 1977; Cohen, 1979; Freeman, 1981; Green, 1980; Morgan, 1977; Ortony, 1976). Other projects stress *communicative competence* (Brause & Bruno, 1980; Florio & Clark, 1979; Gearhart & Hall, 1979; Hall & Guthrie, 1979; Hymes, 1978; Staton, 1980b). Meanwhile, *sociolinguistic studies* of literacy also continue (Ainsworth, 1981; Chafe, 1982; Gearhart & Hall, 1979; Hall & Guthrie, 1979; Kroch & Hindle, 1978; Rubin, 1980b; Steffenson et al., 1978).

Recent research on the language of literacy is distinguished from earlier research by concern with four factors: (1) the natural directions of learning; (2) the context of learning; (3) holistic learning; and (4) the individual learner.

Natural Directions of Learning.   A major difference in perspective in recent years is the attempt to recapture the natural direction of language learning, both in spoken language and in literacy. This natural direction is from *deep* to *surface* rather than from surface to deep, as it is usually taught. Some psychologists refer to this as bottom-up rather than top-down (Fredericksen, 1981). The good language learner begins with a function, a need to do something requiring communication, and moves toward acquiring the language forms that reveal that function. Such learners worry more about getting things done with language than with its surface correctness. They have an underlying belief that there is a system in the world. They experiment freely, try things out unashamedly, and make many productive and useful mistakes. They adjust to contextual variables, even at an early stage of learning. This appears to be the way we all learned our native languages (Krashen, 1978; Schumann, 1978; Sajavaara, 1978).

Because it is easier to teach and test forms than functions and because of the reductionist philosophy long held by behavioral psychologists, we have developed a tradition of teaching reading and writing that goes in just the opposite direction—from surface to deep, from form to function. Certain accomplishments in research on the language of literacy in recent years have tried to set straight this imbalance of learning and teaching (Staton, Shuy, & Kreeft, 1982).

The Context for Language.   For years, linguistic work had focused on the universals and broad generalities that characterize language. Within the past decade, however, linguists have begun to examine the context of language in order to understand the variability of language. Linguists realized that this variability brings alternative ways of understanding and producing nuances that clearly reveal our humanity. This variability, in fact, allows for individual expression, apt phrasing, and even poetry. Without an understanding of the contextual constraints and opportunities for variability, our understanding of universals is subject to error since incomplete data can result in treating epiphenomena as phenomena.

Examining the system of language use demands a broader notion of context, going beyond the word, sentence, and discourse event, and into the institutional context, issues of speaker role, and nonlanguage aspects of the environment of an utterance. Although we have always known that context contributes heavily to children's development, only recently have we begun to identify the many dimensions of context to show how it actually works.

As Bloom has pointed out, we cannot decide between alternative interpretations of the same behavior without a systematic analysis of context (Bloom, 1974). Gumperz and Herasimchuck (1975), in their study of teacher-student interactions, show that children make use of a number of variables such as task expectancy, role differences, and previous utterances in the conversation to formulate interpretations for learning. It is not difficult to extend this list of variables to include factors related to classroom placement, size, competing or simultaneous activities, accoutrements, equipment, and so forth.

Further, the research of Scribner and Cole in Liberia demonstrates that literacy gains its power *from* context, not apart from it. Their predictable finding that restricted use of literacy produces restricted cognitive and behavioral effects is important for what it signifies about the interaction of literacy skills, language, and context (Scribner & Cole, 1978a, 1981).

Four different types of context have been recognized in the recent literature: physical, situational, social and linguistic. These categories are by no means mutually exclusive (R. Scollen, 1976). Context is not a fixed set of individual properties of the world which children take into account sequentially as they learn. Cook-Gumperz considers context a concurrent part of the communication and learning process, a set of fluctuating variables that are constantly being reevaluated by all participants in the learning process during the interaction (Cook-Gumperz & Corsaro, 1976).

Holistic Learning. We have also learned that the traditional approach to reading, the chaining together of the meaning of strings of decoded words, must be replaced by a view of the reader actively using complex mental processes to derive meaning from textual material. Building on the support of three relevant scientific disciplines—cognitive psychology, linguistics, and artificial intelligence, researchers at the Center for the Study of Reading, among others, have suggested that reading is a multilevel interactive process. The reader must process text as a whole, not just as sub-units. Even more crucial, the reader must bring considerable preexisting knowledge to the comprehension process. Researchers also believe that reading is a flexible, strategic process adapted to the purposes of the reader (Spiro, Bruce, & Brewer, 1980).

The Individual Learner. In addition to the naturalness, context, and holistic concerns of literacy, the past decade has seen a focus on the reader (or writer) himself, in contrast to the text or the curriculum. Much current research focuses on the individual engaged in real reading or writing efforts in school or work settings. In written composition, Graves and others have been observing the development of literacy skills in children which begins with the participatory stimulus of drawing, moves to writing about their drawing, and finally to writing without the stimulus of the drawing. Hayes and Flower have been carrying out promising research on the process of acquiring writing skills in adults using a method of simultaneous talk and writing, in which the writers talk their ideas out, note their blocks, and describe the generation of their ideas and language selection. In more functional contexts, Odell and Goswami, and Scribner and Jacob have been researching the literacy needs of employees in industrial and professional settings in an effort to develop the best curriculum to address such needs. Although such research may be generalizable, the work begins at the level of one person with an individual writing need.

DEVELOPMENT OF LITERACY SKILLS

With increased knowledge about the natural directions and context of learning, holistic learning, and the individual learner, we can move closer to

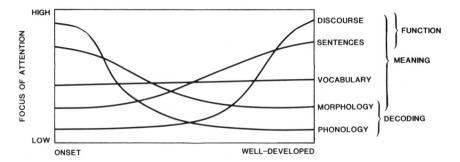

FIG. 5.3 Language Proficiency: Schematic representation of how a language learner calls on language accesses.

describing and analyzing the development of literacy. An acquisitional model of the language accesses to reading has been suggested in recent years (Shuy, 1968), as shown in Figure 5.3. The model suggests that different language accesses to reading are not discrete but operate simultaneously, in different relations to each other at various points in development. The reader varies the intensity of his focus on each component at various stages, but uses all of them at all times. The decoding focus is only a *starting* strategy which tends to decrease, whereas meaning and functional focuses increase. This supports the assertion that early skills are learned well enough to become unconscious to their users. This does not mean that form should be stressed over function or meaning. Rather, although function and meaning are the main thrust of reading, the earlier stages also require certain decoding skills, not as ends in themselves, but as means of assisting the more crucial functional levels. In terms of pedagogy, there appears to be a problem in teaching decoding skills too long, as well as not teaching the ability to process meaning and functional skills at all.

CONCLUSION

It is clear that we have learned a great deal about the language of literacy during the past decade. Most of this learning seems to have come about by the freeing of literacy study from the bind of education alone. It has clearly become the research topic of several disciplines, including psychology, linguistics, philosophy, and anthropology. But several future directions are indicated. We need more knowledge about the *contexts* of reading and writing and about the *goals* or purposes which such activities serve an individual reader or writer. According to Piaget, it is by intelligent interaction with the world, physical and linguistic, that knowledge is constructed (Piaget, 1972). Understanding the context of reading and writing goes hand in hand with understanding language functions as well as forms. The future of reading and writing research will need to be at the levels of meaning and function rather than at the level of decoding or encoding. In the area of writing we need to continue to conceptualize and carry out research toward a developmental basis for the acquisition of these skills and to free literacy from the rather negative and product-oriented pigeonhole in which it now resides in many educational settings. The concept of a personal literacy which is lifelong and tied to cognitive growth (even enabling such growth through its practice) is a radical but exciting suggestion for future development (Staton, 1979). Finally, our current state of knowledge about reading and writing suggests that the work on discourse cohesion, language use, text analysis, and the role of background knowledge and prior language experience be continued and extended. None of this work, of course, can exist outside of well-defined contextual understandings and all of it must be seen in a continuously emerging frame of developmental research. The context, the individual, and the text should continue to provide an even greater wealth of information about the language skills used in reading and writing than we have unveiled in the past decade.

6

Skilled Reading and Language Development: Some Key Issues

William S. Hall
University of Maryland

Thomas G. White
Kamahameha Research Institute

Larry Guthrie
Far West Laboratory

In the behavioral sciences, particular lines of research may progress in parallel fashion, seldom interacting, even though the phenomena they seek to understand are similar in many respects. This situation exists in reading and language development research.

Recent reading research has focused on comprehension and the ways skillful readers differ from less skillful readers (see Kleiman, 1982; Resnick & Weaver, 1979; Spiro, Bruce, and Brewer, 1980; Vellutino, 1979; Waller & MacKinnon, 1979). At the same time, developmental psychologists have attempted to identify the various structures and functions of language children acquire, to describe the stages children pass through, and to understand the process of acquisition, concentrating on grammatical and semantic development (see W. A. Collins, 1979; Fletcher & Garman, 1979; Kuczaj, 1982; K. E. Nelson, 1978, 1980; Whitehurst, 1982).

Overall, however, there have been few attempts to synthesize, coordinate, or draw connections between the two areas of research. Scholars in one area have generally not used the findings or profited from the perspectives of workers in the other area. We think this is unfortunate and would like to remedy the situation insofar as we can in this chapter. Our goal is to identify: (a) points of influence or contact between reading and language development, (b) questions reading scholars could ask developmental psychologists interested in language, or vice versa, and (c) questions neither child language scholars nor reading researchers seem to be asking, though perhaps they should. We hope a set of key issues lying at the interface will emerge and that our identification of them will stimulate future research and theoretical efforts.

We begin the task by characterizing current reading research and theories. Then we examine the nature of skilled reading and its relation to language development. The final part of the chapter highlights key issues.

READING: CURRENT RESEARCH AND THEORIES

Several assumptions underlie most current formulations of what constitutes skilled reading. First, it is immediately evident that reading is an extremely *complex task* that "depends on a multiplicity of perceptual, linguistic, and cognitive processes" (Adams, 1980a, p. 11). Similarly, according to Kleiman (1982), moving from printed text to comprehension involves: (a) knowledge of the world; (b) cognitive processes, including perceptual discrimination, short term memory, serial order encoding, attention allocation and direction, and inferential processing; and (c) language comprehension processes that include retrieval and integration of word meaning, syntactic parsing of sentences, determination of anaphoric references, and analysis of discourse structures.

Second, reading is an *interactive process* that does not proceed in strict sequence from basic perceptual units to overall interpretation of a text. Instead, the reader derives information from many levels simultaneously, integrating graphophonemic, morphemic, semantic, syntactic, pragmatic, schematic, and interpretive information at the same time (Adams, 1980a; Perfetti & Roth, 1981; Rumelhart, 1977a; Stanovich, West & Freeman, 1981).

Third, reading is constrained by the *limited capacity* of the human information processing system. Kleiman (1982, p.6) points to limits on "how much can be perceived in a single fixation, how quickly the eyes can move, how many chunks of information can be held in short term memory, and how quickly information can be retrieved from long term memory." Limited capacity may mean that in skilled reading, lower level processes such as encoding or decoding function so automatically that attention can be devoted to higher order comprehension processes (Adams, 1980a; Kleiman, 1982; Perfetti & Lesgold, 1979).

Fourth, reading is a *strategic process*. Skilled readers read for a purpose and continuously monitor their own comprehension (see Bower, 1982; Brown, 1980; Brown, Armbruster, & Baker, this volume). Alert to breakdowns in understanding, they selectively allocate attention to difficult passages and progressively refine their interpretation of the text.

Broadly speaking, we comprehend text when we "apprehend the intention of the writer and succeed in relating his message to the larger contexts of our system of knowledge" (Gibson & Levin, 1975, p. 400). This implies comprehending the meaning of individual words and relations among the words being read. In addition, the reader may go beyond the semantic and/or syntactic information directly given by the text to draw inferences. The reader may be said to build a "model" of what the text is about, based on preexisting knowledge (see Collins, Brown, & Larkin, 1980). There is evidence that skilled reading involves "building an interpretative structure for a text using the available text base together with one's prior and contextual knowledge" (J.R. Frederiksen, 1981, p. 316).

We have no doubt, then, that skilled reading involves building interpretive structures from the text and background knowledge. But we are left with the problem of selecting a level of analysis that allows us to relate research on reading to research on language development. We think it best to concentrate on whole words and sentences. Our analysis will be incomplete in many respects, but it should serve the synthetic purpose we have in mind.

SKILLED READING AND LANGUAGE DEVELOPMENT

Children come to the task of reading with substantial oral language skills, including basic syntactic competence, a sizeable vocabulary and the ability to produce and understand most of the sounds, or phonemes, of their language.

Yet we agree with Adams (1980a), Rubin (1980), and others (cf. Spiro, Bruce, & Brewer, 1980) who argue that reading comprehension is much more than decoding grafted onto oral language comprehension skills. Decoding aside, there are a number of significant differences between oral and written language that need to be taken into account to understand the contribution of children's oral language experience to skilled reading. Therefore, in subsequent discussion we ask, What are the special requirements of comprehension of written text as opposed to oral language? We also think it is important to see that "the relationship between language development and reading runs both ways" (Dale, 1976, p. 231). Our treatment is organized around the topics of word recognition, semantic processing, and syntactic processing.

Word Recognition

Perhaps the most salient difference between skilled readers and children just beginning to read is the ability to recognize single written words. Word recognition is actually a complicated skill comprising a number of distinct, interrelated subskills. In one scheme (J.R. Frederiksen, 1981), these subskills or subprocesses are (a) grapheme encoding; (b) identification and encoding of multiletter "chunks" that capture orthographic regularities occuring in English (e.g., *th*, *ing*); (c) decoding, translation of graphemic units into phonemic units; and (d) lexical access. In Frederiksen's (1981) interactive model of word recognition, the subprocesses of decoding and lexical access begin operating immediately with whatever information is available to them. Thus, in retrieving the meaning of a word from memory, the reader may use not only visual features, encoded multiletter units, or phonemic information, but also information from the sentence or larger discourse context in which the word occurs (see Fig. 6.1).

Interactive models provide a useful framework for interpreting developmental and individual differences in reading. To illustrate, children with low reading comprehension scores and younger children name printed words more slowly than their older or more skilled counterparts. These differences are augmented when the words are presented in degraded form, but attenuated when the words are frequent or preceded by a related (prime) word or congruous sentence context (Perfetti & Hogaboam, 1975; Simpson, Lorsbach & Whitehouse, 1983; Stanovich, West, & Freeman, 1981).

Another benefit of a model like Frederiksen's is that it points to alternative "routes to the lexicon," that is, different processes that may mediate lexical access (see Resnick & Weaver, 1979). The issue is whether there can be direct visual access to the lexicon without recording of print into some speech-like representation. But, the question should probably be; "What is the extent of phonological involvement in skilled reading?" (Perfetti & Lesgold, 1979, p. 69). It may be that some phonemic recoding is unavoidable for both children *and* adults (Shimron & Navon, 1981; see also Chomsky, 1970; Smith & Kleiman, 1979), especially when sentences are being read (Kleiman, 1975). In addition, there is evidence that good readers actually make better use of phonetic information in memory tasks than poor readers (e.g., Brady, Shankweiler, & Mann, 1983), although both may be equally capable of generating a phonological code when the task explicitly demands it (Briggs & Underwood, 1982).

Investigators in the area of reading are apt to be interested in developmental precursors of word recognition skill. Figure 6.1 suggests an obvious one, the ability to discriminate letters of the alphabet (e.g., by identifying, naming, or writing them). Mason (1983) reports that by the beginning of first grade, only a small percentage of children have any difficulty with letter naming. Those who do, however, know very little else about reading, and their prognosis for reading achievement at the end of the first grade is poor.

It may be especially critical for preschool children to learn names for consonants. Vowels are less important for word recognition than consonants, and account for the majority of the spelling-to-sound irregularities of English (Adams, 1980b). On the other hand, for 16 of the 21 consonants, the principal sound in the name of the letter is a phoneme that corresponds to the letter as it appears in print. Thus, preschool children may initially make use of their knowledge of consonant names to segment written words into graphemes—corresponding phonemes (Mason, 1983; see also Read, 1971; Snow, 1983).

A second conceivable forerunner of word recognition skill in young children may be termed "word consciousness" or "print/speech reference" (Mason, 1984). This is the child's realization that discrete units of print bound

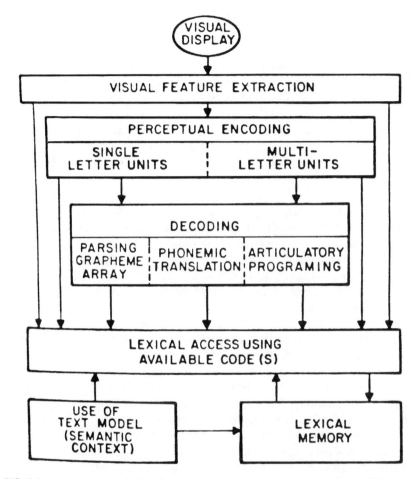

FIG. 6.1   A schematic rendering of a processing model representing component skills in word recognition. The diagram is meant to illustrate the notion of parallel inputs from lower level to higher level processes and from higher levels to lower levels of analysis, i.e., interactivity.

SOURCE: Frederiksen, 1981) Copyright 1981 by Lawrence Erlbaum Associates. Reprinted by permission.

by spaces (written words) correspond to both familiar objects and units of speech (spoken words). Since preschool children have difficulty segmenting speech into words (Holden & MacGinitie, 1972; Huttenlocher, 1964) but first graders have less difficulty (Ehri, 1975), it could be argued that this awareness is a product of being taught to read rather than a precursor or facilitator of early reading. Yet preschool children often begin reading, for example, names on cereal boxes, or on T-shirts (Mason, 1983; Snow, 1983). This may occur as the result of parental labeling or television segments displaying a printed word in conjunction with speech and a pictured referent.

When formal reading instruction begins, there is considerable emphasis on "sounding out" (decoding) visually unfamiliar words. This process can be described in the following steps: (a) parse the word into sets of one or more graphemes that correspond to phonemic units (see Adams, 1980b); (b) generate sounds corresponding to each graphemic set; (c) blend the sounds together (Adams, 1980b; see Fig. 6.1). Not much is known about how children learn to parse written words into graphemic sets. If parsing is graphophonemic, then the first well-known complication is identifying the phonemic units themselves, since they do not occur as discrete units in speech, and the child's preexisting linguistic skills are unlikely to be of much use. Research shows that preschool children are incapable of segmenting phonemes (Bruce, 1964; Liberman, Shankweiler, Fischer, & Carter, 1974). Nonetheless, the majority of first graders do succeed in phonetic segmentation (Liberman et al., 1974), so it appears that children develop this skill as a *result* of reading instruction (Mason, 1983). This aspect of language development is apparently facilitated by reading. But, interestingly, the reverse could be true if parsing of written words is primarily syllabic, since nearly half of the Liberman et al. (1974) sample of kindergarten children could segment spoken words by syllable (see Katz & Baldasare, 1983).

In learning to read, errors in decoding visually unfamiliar words most frequently occur due to misarticulation or incorrect parsing (e.g., no thing for nothing). Detection of such errors depends on previously acquired phonological and semantic knowledge. Vocabulary is obviously crucial. If a word has not been acquired through aural language experience, the child cannot check his or her "translation" for sense. Some decoding mistakes are probably caught and corrected because children hear themselves saying a "word" that contains a sound sequence that is either unlikely or impermissible in English. We do know that preschool children discriminate sound sequences that English disallows (Messer, 1967), but more research needs to be done on this topic.

Semantic Processing

To comprehend text, a reader must do more than recognize individual words; it is necessary to access and integrate the meanings of two, three, or many words. Plainly, the meaning of a word cannot be retrieved unless previously learned. Another more subtle comprehension problem could arise if a child has acquired only part of the meaning of a word. Assuming that multiple and complete word meanings are accessible, their retrieval and integration must be accomplished quickly and accurately, for working memory capacity is not infinite, and mistakes in interpretation are costly. In short, reading is a real-time processing task, suggesting three broad categories of factors that distinguish older or more skillful readers from younger or less skillful readers. The first is *word knowledge*, including both (a) quantitative differences in vocabulary, and (b) qualitative or semantic differences in the nature of meanings. The second is *speed of processing* semantic information, specifically the rate of lexical or semantic memory access. The third category is the *use of semantic information* in sentence comprehension, that is, the actual integration of word meanings into a unified whole or "interpretation of what the sentence means." Each of these is discussed in turn.

Word Knowledge

Vocabulary.   The number of words a child knows is deeply implicated in reading comprehension. Evidence comes from two sources. First, in an older research tradition of factor-analytic studies, vocabulary ("recalling word meanings") has consistently emerged as a unique factor accounting for most of the variance in comprehension scores (see Rosenshine, 1980, for a review of this work). Second, experimental studies manipulating word familiarity show that vocabulary difficulty does influence children's text comprehension directly (Freebody & Anderson, 1983; Wittrock, Marks, & Doctorow, 1975). Finally, as Beck, Perfetti, and McKeown (1982) have shown, it is possible to improve reading comprehension through vocabulary instruction.

Contemporary investigators of the reading process tend to underplay vocabulary. It is said that the vocabulary-reading comprehension correlation merely reflects the influence of a third variable, presence or absence of "underlying conceptual difficulties" or "general linguistic experience." This overlooks both experimental data cited above and the possibility of indirect effects on comprehension; e.g., vocabulary growth could contribute to development of grammatical skill (Hoff-Ginsberg & Shatz, 1982) or enhance motivation for reading.

Vocabulary is not presently an active area of investigation by developmental psychologists. In the early part of this century, studies of vocabulary growth were common (McCarthy, 1954), and there are some data on early vocabulary development, up to about 18 months (Benedict, 1979; Nelson, 1973; Rescorla, 1980). But to find a major comprehensive study covering the preschool years, one must go back to Smith (1926). Smith's data show a rapid increase in the number of words children know from 10 months of age through the fifth year.

What of vocabulary development during the elementary years, after the child commences reading? Unfortunately this is one of the murkiest areas of our knowledge. There is little agreement about either absolute size of vocabulary at particular ages or the rate of vocabulary development (Anderson & Freebody, 1981). Available estimates of vocabulary size differ by as much as a factor of ten. For example, for third-grade children, vocabulary size estimates range from 2,000 words (Dupuy, 1974, cited by Nagy & Anderson, 1982) to 7,425 words (Cuff, 1930) to 25,000 words (M. K. Smith, 1941). For seventh graders, the Dupuy (1974) and Smith (1926) estimates are 4,760 and 51,000 words, respectively.

On the question of rate of development, if the first grader starts with a vocabulary of 2,500 words (Smith, 1926) and has mastered 7,800 words by high school graduation (Dupuy), then just over one new wb03ord per day is learned across 12 years of schooling. However, Miller (1978) claims that young children learn new words at a rate of more than 20 per day. This is supported by Templin (1957) who calculates a vocabulary of 13,000 words for 6-year-olds and 28,300 for 8-year-olds; hence between 6 and 8 years the child learns 15,300 words or approximately 21 words per day.

If the rate of vocabulary growth is anywhere near as large as Miller and Templin suggest, then how are so many words learned so quickly? The question is obviously of more than purely theoretical interest. It seems that the process by which children acquire vocabulary is a topic very much in need of further investigation.

Semantics.   Reading scholars recognize that word meanings are subtle and complex, and in many cases considerable experience is necessary for the child to elaborate the meaning of a word. Developmental psychologists, on the other hand, have collected data specifying when particular word meanings are mastered, and it is natural to suppose that these data relate to text comprehension. However, much of this semantic development literature is of uncertain relevance to reading comprehension (see Blewitt, 1982; Greenberg & Kuczaj, 1982; Richards, 1979).

Children's early word meanings for normal or object words are neither overly general nor too specific. They overextend some words, applying them to a referent an adult would not (e.g., calling a sheep *doggie*); but they underextend other words, failing to apply them to referents appropriate by adult standards (e.g., saying a duck is not a bird). Many overextensions are based on perceptual similarity, but since some overextensions and underextensions are affected by functional properties of objects, a strong argument cannot be made for the primacy of either form or function. Finally, within hierarchically organized domains, development does not proceed from specific to more general terms, or vice versa; rather, many of the objects the child first learns to name are at some intermediate level of generality. For example, *dog* is apt to be learned before *collie* or *animal*, *flower* before *rose* or *plant*, and so on.

For dimensional adjectives, a consistent finding has been that general terms are acquired earlier than more specific ones. For example, *big* and *small* are produced and comprehended before the pairs *tall* and *short*, *high* and *low*, or *long* and *short*, and these latter pairs are understood before *wide* and *narrow*, *deep* and *shallow*, or *thick* and *thin*.

Perhaps the most important conclusion one can draw from the semantic development literature is that children understand words better in some contexts than others. There are numerous demonstrations of the effects of the semantic or syntactic form or complexity of test sentences, the syntactic or semantic role of the target word in test sentences, and the task or nonlinguistic context in which comprehension is assessed. This implies that it is not simple to isolate genuine semantic-developmental factors.

It is probably accurate to say that the literature on semantic development has been mainly concerned with: (1) young children under the age of 6 years; (2) concrete nouns, adjectives, and to a lesser extent, prepositions, but not verbs, conjunctions, pronouns, or articles; and (3) referential or extensional meaning as opposed to sense or intensional meaning (word-word relations, definitional or connotational meaning). In terms of motivating theoretical concerns, most studies are designed to test aspects of Eve Clark's (1973) semantic feature theory, or to establish the role of cognitive and perceptual factors in semantic acquisition.

Unfortunately, these foci are not the ones reading scholars and educational researchers might select to inform their work. Consider characteristic (1) first. Although information on early semantic development is helpful in understanding how the child has arrived at the point where he is when reading begins, it is later semantic development that impinges most directly upon skilled reading.

Regarding feature (2), a clear implication of our discussion of semantic strategies critical in sentence comprehension is that the development of verb meaning may be crucial. There is a real dearth of data on children's comprehension of verbs, however. To illustrate, Blewitt's (1982) review includes nine such studies, whereas Richard (1979) cites only two.

These points might be taken as suggesting that more research with older children and more studies of verb comprehension should be done. Such a shift in research focus might generally be useful. But it seems to us that, from the standpoint of improving understanding of text comprehension most rapidly, what is really needed is some additional basis for deciding *which* categories of verbs or conjunctions (or for that matter nouns, etc.) to investigate. One approach in this regard is to look at differences between oral and written language.

Turning lastly to the emphasis on referential meaning (point 3), there is some logic in the position that it ought to take precedence. For instance, the question of how a child comprehends and uses the word *bird* when dealing with the nonlinguistic world seems more basic than the question of how she recognizes the statement that "A robin is a bird" is true (thus demonstrating comprehension of the sense relation called hyponymy, or class inclusion). Nevertheless, what reading investigators are concerned with is the child's construction of meaning during the act of reading. They want to know how the child "makes sense" of whole sentences and larger units of discourse, or how the child "instantiates" the meaning of a word in context. This *is* a different problem from those that have captured the attention of developmental psychologists. To see this clearly, imagine a child who (1) underextends *bird,* failing to apply it to a duck; (2) overextends *doggie,* applying it to a sheep; and also

(3) correctly selects the "bigger" of two objects but fails to select the "taller" of two objects. Now suppose the child read—if he or she could do so—three sentences: (1) The bird flew right past Jimmy's nose. (2) The sheep went "baaa." (3) The truck was too tall for the tunnel. It seems likely that our child would instantiate a robin- or sparrow-like bird, a sheep, and a tall truck (or short tunnel), respectively—much as an adult would! Young children do include robins in the bird category (White, 1982); they may correctly comprehend words that are overextended in production (Fremgen & Fay, 1980); and they rely on their knowledge of the world in comprehending sentences they hear. Note, however, that these phenomena are typically not emphasized by semantic development researchers.

A developmental psychologist interested in semantic issues might ask how can I conduct research that contributes to a better understanding of reading? There is already growing sentiment for the view that semantic development cannot be effectively analyzed as based upon abstract, contextually independent semantic features, and this change in theoretical climate alone tends to encourage research on what might be called "the development of word meaning in context" or "semantic-developmental factors in sentence (as opposed to word) comprehension." Our aim is to highlight this critical topic and hopefully in that manner lay another plank bridging the areas of reading and language development research.

Both reading scholars and developmental psychologists have recently argued that efforts to pin down word meaning "as if it were a thing that had an independent existence" (Whitehurst, 1979, p. 116) are hopeless since most words show shifts in meaning from one context to another. Anderson and Shifrin (1980, p. 332) further suggest that when a word is considered in context, its meaning is "particularized" in a "process of inferential interpolation based on knowledge of the world." This particularization of meaning, termed *instantiation*, is a narrowing of the sense or reference of a term to a subset of the cases that would otherwise be denoted or connoted (if the word were considered without context).

A number of studies (see Anderson & Shifrin, 1980) have demonstrated that adult subjects do instantiate, but there has apparently been only one study of instantiation in children. In that study (Anderson, Stevens, Shifrin, & Osborn, 1978), first graders and fourth graders were read sentences like *Sally looked at the clock in her classroom*. For each sentence heard, the child pointed to one of four pictures that best fit the sentence (e.g., a typical alarm clock, a classroom-type wall clock, a grandfather clock, and a sponge). Results were that first graders chose the expected picture 92% of the time whereas fourth graders did so on nearly all (97%) of the trials. Although Anderson et al. (1978) found little evidence of a developmental trend in instantiation, future research may indeed show that older children are more likely to instantiate than younger children. If this turns out to be the case, then it will be interesting to discover whether the tendency to engage in instantiation of particular words follows the same or a different developmental course than other measures of comprehension of the same words (Gentner, 1975).

Speed of Processing

As already noted, skilled reading is a complex process involving both bottom-up skills, such as encoding or decoding, and top-down processes, such as lexical or semantic memory access (see Fig. 6.1). Rates of lexical and/or semantic memory access are closely tied to the development of reading skill. Semantic interpretations occur many times per minute in reading (Gitomer, Pellegrino, & Bisanz, 1983), at a rate two or three times greater than in listening, for adults. Hence, even small differences in the time required to access memory can have major impact. More efficient execution of these processes "may allow a reader to hold more material simultaneously in active memory . . . and may also permit more attentional capacity to be allocated to higher level processes" (Gitomer et al., 1983, p. 57).

Research on developmental changes in speed of semantic processing has just begun, due to the difficulty of measuring semantic processing independent of age-related changes in motoric or vocalization response times or encoding speed. These problems were addressed by Gitomer et al. (1983). In their first experiment, subjects searched through diagonal arrays of words for an instance of a prespecified category (e.g., fruit) and pressed a button as soon as this "target" was found. The slope of the function relating response time to target position in the array was steeper for 8- and 10-year-olds than for 19-year-olds. Therefore, apart from changes in motor response or vocalization speed (decoding speed), semantic processing speed increases with age. Different rates of development for decisions about category membership versus size attributes of words in arrays were found in the Gitomer et al. (1983) second experiment. This was interpreted as evidence that age differences in semantic decisions cannot be entirely due to differences in encoding words. A similar investigation by Chabot, Petros, and McCord (1983) demonstrated both developmental and reading ability differences in semantic processing speed.

How are these findings related to language development? Studies of children's definitions of concrete nouns show that although young children tend to mention use (e.g., for *orange,* "you eat them"), older children and adults define words in terms of a superordinate class and differentiate ("a citrus fruit") (see Anglin, 1977, 1984). These age and developmental changes in semantic category decisions presumably have common roots in the child's linguistic experience (see Olson, 1977; Whitehurst, 1979). Similarly, adult labeling of objects must be the basis both for word learning and increasing speed of lexical access with development. Consistent with this, Cirrin (1983) reports that lexical access speed as measured by children's picture-naming latency is significantly correlated with both word frequency and estimates of age of acquisition for names of stimuli.

Use of Semantic Information

We come now to what appears to be an important but poorly understood aspect of semantic processing in reading—use of semantic information. Such use entails integration of the meaning of encoded words into a coherent whole or "interpretation" of a sentence. Integration of word meanings is accomplished partly by semantic and partly by syntactic means. We treat the topic of syntactic integration in the next section. Here we consider whether there are developmental changes in integration apart from developmental changes in word meaning (or syntactic skills).

It has been known for some time that there is general improvement through middle childhood in the ability to integrate individual word meanings into sentence meaning. For example, in a classic study by Entwisle and Frasure (1974), children aged 6 to 9 years listened to "noisy" tapes containing meaningful, anomalous, and syntactically scrambled word strings (e.g., *Wild Indians spear heavy buffaloes; Little Indians eat nearby elevators;* and *Spear forms rocks fast old,* respectively). The dependent variable was the percentage of words repeated in the right order immediately after each sentence was heard. As shown in Fig. 6.2, from age seven on, performance was best on meaningful strings, next best on anomalous strings, and worst on scrambled strings; differences between these conditions increased with age. Because the syntax of the sentences used in the Entwisle and Frasure (1974) study was very simple, the improvement on anomalous strings seems to reflect a developing ability to integrate, and the difference between the anomalous and meaningful conditions does suggest a semantic integration ability (not vocabulary since the same words, differently arranged, occurred in all conditions). However, the alternative interpretation is that the older children had acquired more information about sense (word-word) relations or semantic selection restrictions.

Ackerman (1982) concludes that under some conditions there are developmental changes in semantic integration independent of the development of word meaning per se. Second-and fourth-grade children and college students were asked to recall target nouns (e.g., book) presented in three types of sentential context: congruous (e.g., *The boy placed the book on the table;* incongruous (*The boy placed the book on the dog*); and anomalous (*The boy placed the book on the bear*). There were two experimental conditions: a Read condition in which subjects read silently while the experimenter read aloud at a slow pace, and an integration condition in which the events described by the sentences were rated for likelihood prior to recall of the target word. The results showed a three-way interaction of Grade × Condition × Sentence

Congruity, in which there were significant developmental differences in the congruity effect in the Read condition but not in the Integration condition. Thus, the youngest children could make use of the semantic information and relations among words when the task required integration, but they did not spontaneously do so in "reading" the sentences.

Syntactic Processing

Although word recognition and semantic processing are important, as well as necessary, in skilled reading they are not sufficient alone. It is also important and necessary in skilled reading to know how words go together, i.e., how they relate to each other. This requirement of skilled reading, specifying the relations among words in sentences, is primarily the province of syntax. The special function of syntax in skilled reading is readily apparent when one

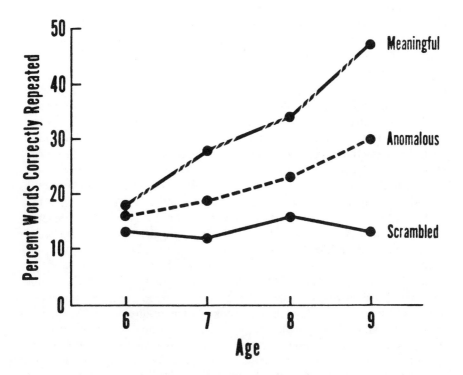

FIG. 6.2.   Percentage of words repeated at four age levels as a function of syntactic and semantic structure.

SOURCE: A contradiction resolved: Children's processing of syntactic cues. In D. R. Entwisle and N. E. Frasure, *Developmental Psychology*, 1974, 10, 852–857, Fig. 1. Copyright 1974 by the American Psychological Association.

considers the ways in which comprehension of a written text differs from that of an oral one.

When confronted with a written text, children do not have the cues present in an oral text to guide them (Adams, 1980a). Note first that real-world context and the speaker's pitch and stress patterns can be used as guides to understanding oral language. Second, at least fluent speakers tend to restrict pauses to syntactic boundaries; that is, they usually pause to take a breath between, not within, major constituents. Third, the duration of spoken elements such as vowels or phrases varies with the phrase structure of the speaker's utterance. In contrast, in written text comprehension, the task of segregating phrasal and clausal units is basically left to the reader. Although forms of punctuation do indicate some syntactic boundaries, they by no means indicate all. This implies both that reading "presumes a level of syntactic proficiency that is not required for listening (comprehension)," and that "processing differences between reading and listening do indeed extend beyond the level of word recognition" (Adams, 1980a, p. 20).

A second point Adams (1980a) makes in discussing the role of syntax in skilled reading is that skilled and unskilled or beginning readers differ in their ability to recognize and encode syntactic units. Skilled readers can somehow coordinate their eye movements and fixations with the phrase structure of the text. If the text is abruptly removed, their "reading" continues until a phrasal boundary has been reached. Similarly, when short sentences or phrases are tachistoscopically presented, skilled readers' recognition of them tends to be either complete or entirely absent. Beginning readers, on the other hand, engage in many fixations per line of print, and they do not "sample" the text in phrasal units (Adams, 1980a).

That skilled and unskilled readers are differentially sensitive to syntactic cues is also revealed in studies using cloze procedures (e.g., Willows & Ryan, 1981), eye-voice span (Gibson & Levin, 1975), or a semantic and syntactic violations paradigm (Isakson & Miller, 1976). These differences remain when IQ and decoding skill differences ae controlled (Willows & Ryan, 1981).

Syntactic segmentation ability may become increasingly important in reading as the child grows older. This follows from practical, theoretical, and empirical considerations. In the firstplace, syntactically complex sentences are much more common in the textbooks older children read; beginning readers are typically not challenged in this way, because the presumption is that they should be "learning to read" (decode) instead of reading for meaning. Now consider the limited-capacity assumption that is, as we have previously noted, a key element in most current models of reading. According to this view, less attention can be directed toward sentence comprehension (which entails both syntactic and semantic processing) when preliminary reading processes such as word recognition are slow, or not fully automatic. If decoding and encoding skills improve with age as, in fact, we have seen they do, then more attention will be available for comprehension, and comprehension factors should become the most important predictor of reading skill in the intermediate and upper elementary grades. This expectation is nicely confirmed in a study by Curtis (1980).

What have developmental psychologists learned about syntactic skills, given that such skills are crucial for reading at all levels and especially significant for skilled reading beyond the early grades? The beginning reader, entering grade school at age 5 or 6, comes to the task of reading with considerable knowledge of syntax. However, children continue to show important gains in their ability to produce and understand syntactic structures until adolescence (Adams, 1980a; Huggins & Adams, 1980; Palermo & Molfese, 1972). Bowerman's (1979) review of the literature on later syntactic development discusses several kinds of complex sentences that do not seem to be fully comprehended by age 5. All of these involve aspects of embedding and coordination. Specifically, children's understanding of object complementation seems to continue developing between the ages of 5 and 10, although the data on this topic are controversial (Chomsky, 1969; Maratsos, 1974; cf. Warder, 1981). Sentences containing adverbial clauses introduced by subordinating conjunctions (e.g., *before, after, when, until*, etc.) are not fully controlled until 6 or 7 years of age or older, and children's understanding of causal connectives (e.g., *because, so*) seems to develop late as well (around 7 or 8 years). Finally, coordination at the phrasal level does not seem to be fully developed by the time children enter school, and mature conjunction use involving logical connectives such as *or* and *if* develops throughout the elementary school years and beyond.

Clark and Clark (1977) maintain that the process of sentence comprehension involves (1) isolating and identifying the constituents of surface structure and (2) building corresponding propositions. Once this is done, the comprehender's goal is to discover the "underlying representation" of a sentence—its meaning. The critical question is *how* the listener or reader identifies constituents (or propositions) and their interrelations.

Clark and Clark (1977) identify two approaches—syntactic and semantic. Generally, the syntactic approach emphasizes "function words, suffixes, prefixes, and grammatical categories of content words as clues to the identity of constituents" (p. 85). The semantic approach focuses on *strategies* that "take advantage of the fact that sentences refer to real objects, states, and events, and fit the on-going discourse" (p. 85). Because these strategies "begin with propositions that make sense in context" (p. 85), it could be said that the semantic approach moves from propositions to constituents whereas the syntactic approach does the reverse. One of the most important semantic comprehension strategies is the "verb-centered strategy" (Clark & Clark,

1977). Listeners (or readers) center their attention on verbs and look for constituent noun phrases that fit the semantic or propositional requirements of each verb encountered.

What concerns us in the current context is how these data relate to text comprehension. Some studies have reported that reading skill differences are associated with comprehension of embedded sentences (Byrne, 1981; Goldman, 1976), but this is actually somewhat surprising. Since the measures of reading comprehension used in these studies presumably tap many different kinds of syntactic comprehension ability, it is not evident why there should be anything more than a very weak relationship. One would not expect to find a strong correlation between any *specific* facet of later syntactic development and reading comprehension broadly conceived.

Perhaps what we need to do here is break out of the usual mold of thinking about a one-way relationship between "language" and reading, namely, that oral language development contributes to the development of reading skill. It seems at least equally plausible that reading itself, or the onset of literacy, influences development of the aforementioned aspects of syntactic competence. As reading is a major activity in school aged children's lives it *ought* to have an impact on development, but research on this topic is limited.

SOME KEY ISSUES

So far we have discussed skilled reading at the word and sentence levels and what the developmental psychology research indicates about aspects of children's language that are relevant to reading. In this final part of the chapter, we bring into focus several issues that seem important in light of what has been said. Our choice of issues is selective, of course, but it is a reasonable sample of areas that scholars of language development and reading might explore with equal profit.

Issue #1: How Are So Many Words Learned?

Earlier we cited studies indicating that quite remarkable growth in vocabulary takes place not only in the preschool years, but also in later elementary and high school years. This "fact," if it is accepted as such, has clear implications for both educational policy and theories of language acquisition. Here are some statements to whet the appetites of developmental psychologists and reading educators alike: (1) "If some seventh graders have vocabularies of over 50,000 words, as is estimated by some researchers, a theory of language acquisition must include mechanisms that could account for this phenomenal accomplishment" (Nagy & Anderson, 1982, p. 2). (2) "If the year to year growth in vocabulary for the average child is as large as some figures suggest, then the best advice to school teachers would be to help children become independent word learners" (Anderson & Freebody, 1982, p. 5). (3) "Even the most ruthlessly systematic direct vocabulary instruction could neither account for a significant proportion of all the words children actually learn, nor cover more than a modest proportion of the words they will encounter in school reading materials" (Nagy & Anderson, 1982, p. 1).

Some of our readers may question the premises or "if" clauses in the above statements. This is well since there are some thorny problems that must be grappled with in reaching the conclusion that vocabulary growth is "phenomenal." To construct a vocabulary test, one must first identify a population of words from which to sample. An operational definition of a "word" is required, and what should be done with derivatives, compounds, proper names, homographs, and so on? Given an adequate sample of words, how should the child's knowledge of them be assessed? Is a multiple choice or some other format best? There is some recent work that we think represents substantial progress along these lines. We review it in some detail below, and refer the interested reader to the original papers (Anderson & Freebody, 1982; Nagy & Anderson, 1982).

Anderson and Freebody (1982) report development of a promising yes/no method of vocabulary assessment. Children simply indicate whether they know each item in a list of words and nonwords, and the child's proportion of words truly known is estimated from a formula that corrects for guessing ("false alarms"). Preliminary data suggest that relative to traditional standardized multiple-choice tests, the yes/no format is both more efficient, since three times as many words can be covered in the same time period, and more valid, since it reduces the effects of extraneous factors in testing. In this context it is worth noting that vocabulary research has consistently found a relationship between word knowledge and socioeconomic status (SES). Children of lower SES, and often minority children as well, tend to perform poorly vis-a-vis their higher SES counterparts on vocabulary tests and other standardized tests with important vocabulary subcomponents (e.g., intelligence tests). However, this could easily reflect, in addition to the child's vocabulary, his or her response to the testing situation, or test-taking strategies (Cazden, 1972; Steffensen & Guthrie, 1980). It may be that the yes/no method will avoid placing minority and low-SES children at a disadvantage in vocabulary testing, though some other obstacles remain (e.g., possible bias in the content of vocabulary tests—see Hall, Nagy, & Linn, 1984).

Nagy & Anderson (1982) address the problem of defining what a word is. Everyone recognizes that such regular inflectional forms as *walk* and *walked* or *dog* and *dogs* ought to be viewed as instances of the "same word"; even young children know most of the rules of regular pluralization and tense formation (Berko, 1958). Some linguists (Aronoff, 1976) reasonably argue that words derived by adding *ness* or *ly* should similarly not be regarded as separate lexical entries. There are, however, other types and degrees of relatedness among words that merit consideration in counting words and estimating vocabulary size, and previous researchers have taken quite different tacks in dealing with them. Some count inflectional variants as separate words, but others (e.g., Dupuy, 1974, cited by Nagy & Anderson, 1982) exclude from their count almost all suffixed, prefixed, and compound items, treating these as derived rather than "basic" words. Nagy and Anderson (1982) adopt an approach that will have considerable appeal for developmentalists and educators. They define five levels of semantic relatedness "in terms of the relative ease or difficulty with which a child could either learn the meaning of a target word, or infer its meaning in context while reading" (p. 9), assuming the child knows the target word's "immediate ancestor." Definitions and examples of the levels are presented in Table 6.1.

Nagy and Anderson (1982) drew a sample from the Carroll, Davies, and Richman (1971) *Word Frequency Book*. Projecting from it, they estimated that printed school English contains about 88,500 "distinct words" including (a) about 45,500 morphologically basic words that cannot be derived from any other word; and (b) another 43,000 "semantically opaque" derived words, defined as words coded at levels 3, 4, or 5 (see Table 6.1). Further, they suggested that high school students know somewhere between 25,000 and 50,000 words or more, based on comparison of their criteria for treating a word as distinct with those used in previous investigations of vocabulary size.

The figure of 50,000 words would imply learning of between 8 and 11 new words per day for a dozen years of school (depending on which estimate one uses for 6-year-olds beginning school). This is not exactly George Miller's (1978) 20 per day, but it is enough to raise the acquisition issue quite emphatically, as indeed Anderson and his colleagues have (see first paragraph of this section).

How *do* children acquire vocabulary? Experimental studies of word meaning acquisition in young children show that they are in general quite efficient word learners. K. E. Nelson (1982) reviews half a dozen published investigations demonstrating that under naturalistic conditions and with long delays between training and testing, 1- to 6-year-olds can learn to comprehend and produce novel labels for objects or actions on the basis of as few as one word-referent pairing, and they generalize the labels to similar referents not involved in original training. This kind of learning is especially rapid when an adult has labeled an object (e.g., an interesting toy) which is valuable to the child, or an object that is a typical instance of the concept being learned (Stewart & Hamilton, 1976; Whitehurst, Kedesdy, & White, 1982).

Yet it takes only a moment's reflection to convince oneself that school-age children do not have to be taken into the presence of a set of concrete referents

TABLE 6.1
Levels of Semantic Relatedness

Level	Definition	Examples	
		Target Word	Immediate Ancestors
0	Semantically transparent relationship between target word and immediate ancestor(s)	sensibly redness misinterpretation planktonburger	sensible red misinterpret plankton; burger
1	Target can be inferred from ancestor with minimal help from context	various entertainer misrepresent geneticist washcloth	vary entertain represent genetic wash; cloth
2	Target could be inferred from ancestor with reasonable help from context; one-exposure learning would be possible	mainly gunner knowledge therapeutic once additional theorist foglights	main gun know therapy one addition theory fog; lights
3	Target includes semantic features not inferrable from meaning of ancestor without substantial help from contact	collinear doctorate elevator visualize inlay mishap noblesse ominous percentile conclusive doctrinaire copperhead	linear doctor elevate visual lay happen noble omen percent conclusion doctrine copper; head
4	Target related to the meaning of ancestor, but only distantly	vicious motley inertia saucer go-getter	vice mottle inert sauce go; get
5	Lack of any discernible semantic connection (for "familiar" meanings of words)	clerical groovy dashboard shiftless	cleric groove dash; board shift; less

(Adapted from Nagy & Anderson, 1982)

for each new word they learn. In fact, many of the words they are learning *have* no concrete, easily pictured, referents (consider *doctrinaire, freedom,* or *democracy*). It is apparent, then, that as a child grows older and enters school, parental labeling—observational learning of word-referent relations (White-hurst, 1979) or the "original word game" (Brown, 1958)—is apt to diminish in importance while another, quite different semantic learning process comes to the fore. This is *intraverbal learning,* or learning the meaning of a word from the purely verbal context in which it occurs (Whitehurst & Vasta, 1977; Whitehurst, 1979). Intraverbal learning can take many forms, ranging from ordinary sentence contexts containing the unfamiliar word ("His excessively *doctrinaire* behavior had won him few friends and many enemies") to semi-formal, or relatively more precise and formal, definitions ("*Doctrinaire* is like dogmatic; *Doctrinaire* means imposing one's will or opinion on people, usually based on some abstract or impractical theory").

Very little is known about the process of intraverbal learning, in spite of its prevalence and educational significance. We are aware of two studies indicating that younger children are less able to derive word meanings from context than older children (Feldman & Klausmeier, 1974; Werner & Kaplan, 1952). It would be interesting to find out whether good and poor readers also differ in this respect. Much additional research is needed to find out whether certain contexts are more effective for some kinds of words, and so on.

The work we were discussing earlier by Anderson and associates (Anderson & Freebody, 1982; Nagy & Anderson, 1982) suggests a second, complementary line of investigation that is in our judgment most crucial for understanding how children—especially older children—acquire large vocabularies, principally through reading. They propose, in essence, that the child's knowledge of derivational morphology, or "word formation processes," is "one of the engines driving vocabulary growth" (Anderson & Freebody, 1982, p. 17). For example, if a second-grade child knows the meaning of *theory* and the function of the suffix *ist,* she can probably learn or infer the meaning of *theorist* when it occurs in context. This kind of thinking forms the basis for the classification system in Table 6.1. However, as Nagy and Anderson (1982) recognize, their coding categories must remain speculative until detailed studies of the relation between children's knowledge of morphology and word learning become available.

The likelihood that a child will know a word-formation process, and thus be able to learn a new word occurring in context, will be in part dependent on how many forms involving that word-formation process are already in the child's vocabulary. This in turn will depend on the frequency of those forms in the language, the overall size of the child's vocabulary, and the nature and amount of the child's exposure to language. The child's reading habits, for example, may determine breadth of exposure to root words and classes of suffixes or prefixes (Nagy & Anderson, 1982).

Issue #2: Does Reading or Literacy Facilitate Later Syntactic Development?

This question reflects our belief that the relation between skilled reading and language development is in many respects one of reciprocity. The nature and extent of this reciprocity are more assumed than known, however. We find all too few studies that attempt to locate school-aged children's developing knowledge of syntax in the activity of reading.

Let us examine, as an illustration of the kind of data we think are needed, a recent study by Richgels (1983). Children from the second, third, and fourth grades were tested, in both a written and an oral mode, for comprehension of both difficult, semantically anomalous sentences and less difficult, non-anomalous sentences. For example, the child was asked to point to a picture corresponding to the sentence "It was the woman wearing glasses who was scolded by the boy." Note that, in order to respond correctly to such a sentence, the child must pay close attention to its syntax. Richgels found that reading comprehension of difficult sentences improved at a faster rate than listening comprehension of the same sentences, and the advantage of print was specifically an advantage for difficult sentences read by older children. This suggests that as children grow older they are increasingly able to use their ability to read to help them understand difficult sentence structures.

To say that reading facilitates language development is to make a somewhat strong claim. But such a causal hypothesis seems definitely worth considering. Several observations from the developmental literature are germane here: (1) As we have previously mentioned, children do not fully control several kinds of complex sentences when they begin school, and they continue to demonstrate gains in syntactic skill until they are at least 12 years old (Bowerman, 1979; Palermo & Molfese, 1972). (2) Naturalistic and experimental studies suggest that syntax acquisition is influenced by the child's linguistic environment (Brown, 1979; Hoff-Ginsberg & Shatz, 1982; Whitehurst & Vasta, 1975). (3) Going to school, particularly learning to read and write, increases children's ability to use language in ways that are relatively abstract and removed from immediate context (Bowerman, 1981; Bruner, Olver, & Greenfield, 1966); such usage often entails complex syntax. Add to these points the obvious and undeniable fact that learning to read is easily the most dramatic and important language-related event of the elementary school years, and we have what appears to be a strong prima facie case for reading as a critical determinant of later syntactic development.

There is evidence, though not without its methodological flaws, that complex syntax is generously represented in written texts (Chafe, 1983). One goal of future research, then, might be to further document this finding through distributional analyses of texts children read in school, with concomitant investigation of the relation between this exposure and developing syntactic skill.

Issue #3: Differences between Oral and Written Language

One special theme has been present throughout this chapter, and it calls for further comment. This is the theme of how oral and written language differ. It is an issue that developmental psychologists and reading researchers have not made a central focus of their research, but both could benefit from its study.

What are the salient features of written language? We have found three papers especially useful in answering this question and refer the interested reader to them (Rubin, 1980b; Tannen, 1981; Chafe, 1983). These authors suggest that written language contains (1) more stative verbs; (2) more complement constructions and relative clauses; (3) more abstract nouns; (4) a preponderance of nominalized verbs; (5) chains of prepositions; (6) certain kinds of deixis; (7) more subordinate clauses; and (8) more compound verbs. Also, written fiction relies on "external evaluation," including explicit statements by authors about characters' plans, intentions, feelings, motives, and so on (Tannen, 1981).

As we stated or implied in our discussions of syntactic and semantic processing, several of the aspects of written language listed above have implications for research and advancement of our understanding of the relation between skilled reading and language development. Some possible instantiations occur to us, and we briefly present them here. The observation that fiction may include external evaluation by authors suggests that both internal state verbs and internal state words in general should be studied for their role in text comprehension (see Hall, Nagy, & Nottenberg, 1981). Although we have uncovered some research in the reading literature on pronominal reference and inference (Spiro, Bruce, & Brewer, 1980), a developmental focus is not the chief concern of this work. The finding that written language contains many nominalized verbs suggests that a profitable question for investigation might be how the child's knowledge of morphology enhances understanding of these verbs. We have already discussed possible research implications of the prevalence of complement constructions, relative clauses, and subordinate clauses in the previous section.

SUMMARY AND CONCLUSION

The purpose of this chapter was to characterize skilled reading and to relate it to language development in children. We have seen that skilled reading is a complex, interactive process in which the reader derives information from many levels simultaneously. We concentrated on two levels, whole words and sentences, i.e., on word recognition and comprehension of semantic and syntactic relations among the words in a sentence. This was done because these reading subskills make direct contact with (a) the child's linguistic experience (being affected by it), and (b) the child's linguistic abilities (in turn influencing them).

This two-way relationship between language and reading was apparent in each of the topics we covered. For instance, in word recognition and lexical access, decoding depends on vocabulary and phonological knowledge acquired through aural and oral language experience. However, phonetic segmentation, a linguistic skill, apparently develops as a result of reading instruction. Similarly, although vocabulary and semantic development constrain semantic processing in reading, the remarkable growth in vocabulary that occurs during the elementary years could well result from intraverbal learning of the meaning of unknown words encountered in written text.

Scholars of reading and of language development have large repertoires of theory, methods, and data, but they have often proceeded without due regard for each other's contributions. We hope our analysis here has shown that language development research has much to gain from consideration of the requirements of skilled reading, and that reading research can be advanced by studying aspects of language that develop after children begin formal reading instruction. Toward this end we offer three issues as signposts pointing to fertile zones for mutual exploration; (1) How are so many words learned? (2) Does reading or literacy facilitate later syntactic development? (3) What are the differences between oral and written language that modulate the language-reading relationship?

Instructional Implications

7 Instructional Research in Reading: A Retrospective

Isabel L. Beck
Margaret G. McKeown
University of Pittsburgh

INTRODUCTION

Recent changes in reading research are quite subtle in nature. They do not take us in novel directions so much as deepen our understanding of reading and allow us to pursue solutions to problems with greater precision. To paraphrase T.S. Eliot, they represent returning to the place where you began, and seeing it for the first time. This chapter reviews reading research of the last decade with attention to its instructional relevance. Instructional research is broader than training studies or investigations of instructional practices in classrooms. It includes attempts to expand knowledge of the reading process and to create new notions about practice. This chapter is organized around four topics that have been addressed in the psychological study of the reading process, learning, and reading instruction. These are (1) Decoding and Automaticity, (2) Background Knowledge, (3) Text Structure, (4) Metacognition.

DECODING AND AUTOMATICITY

Decoding Instruction

Decoding, the translation of print to speech, encompasses both "sounding out," using phonic principles, and instant recognition of word names. It is crucial to reading. Consequently, how to teach decoding has received abundant research attention.

During the 1960s the concern was whether procedures for word attack should be directly taught. A major paradigm for reading research of this period was the comparative study, a global approach that compared the outcomes of two or more reading curricula in their entirety. These comparative studies did little to advance knowledge of reading instruction. No general pattern of results was established that could direct the selection of reading methods. These studies were criticized for problems of design and methodology. Two of the most common criticisms (Diederich, 1973) were lack of control of variables and inadequate specification of methods or programs being compared.

The best known of the comparative studies was the Cooperative Research Program in First Grade Reading (Bond & Dykstra, 1967), which included 27 separate studies that compared an array of curriculum pairs. The key finding was that more variation in learning outcomes existed within programs than between programs. Another comparative study, done by Bliesmer and Yarborough (1965), stands out from the rest in its clarity of design and more careful experimental control (Diederich, 1973). The study compared five programs that taught decoding systematically and directly with five programs that taught phonics incidentally, following whole-word instruction. The results favored the direct teaching approach. The children under this condition averaged an additional half year of progress at the end of first grade.

Chall (1967), using a more qualitative approach, reanalyzed a massive amount of data on reading programs, analyzed program materials, and interviewed proponents of various approaches. In addition to looking at general outcomes, she investigated relations between the extent and kind of reading failures children experienced and the instructional methods used in beginning reading. Her conclusion was that systematic direct teaching of decoding should be part of initial reading instruction. Subsequent laboratory studies by Bishop (1964) and Jeffrey and Samuels (1967) confirmed Chall's conclusion that decoding is more effectively taught using a phonics approach than a whole-word approach.

Although research of this period supported direct teaching of the code as part of initial reading instruction, little evidence accumulated on the type and amount of instruction that would be most effective. The aim of phonics instruction of this period can be characterized as accuracy of response. It was deemed that a child had sufficient decoding ability if she or he learned, implicitly or explicitly, the rules for breaking the printed code and was able to give accurate pronunciations of words encountered.

Reading as an Interactive Process

From the mid-1970s to the present, the focus of research on decoding has changed notably. This change, due mainly to work in cognitive psychology, has greatly refined and enriched our knowledge about the reading process. This more precise understanding points to the need for certain subprocesses to be developed beyond the accurate level. That is, accurate decoding may not be sufficient for successful comprehension to occur; the efficiency of decoding may be a factor as well. For decoding to be efficient it must take place rapidly, without undue use of conscious attention.

The importance of the efficiency of subprocesses derives from a current view of reading as an interactive process. An interactive model assumes that information from print and the reader's knowledge act simultaneously and influence each other (Carpenter & Just, this volume; Frederiksen, 1981a; Perfetti & Roth, 1981; Rumelhart, 1977a; Stanovich, 1980). As visual information from a text page is perceived, it is acted upon by various sources of knowledge. These sources include awareness of letter-sound correspondences and spelling patterns, knowledge of word meaning, of syntactic possibilities and language patterns, and memory of the preceding context. The sources interact to compile information about the textual input, identify it, and integrate it with what has come before. Thus meaning of the textual message is constructed. For example, in reading the sentence "Jack made a sandwich by putting bologna between two slices of *bread,*" identification of the word *bread* might call three sources into play: memory for previous context, knowledge of the meaning of sandwich, and letter-sound correspondence knowledge. A decision about *bread* could not be made as efficiently if context memory or word meaning or letter-sound knowledge failed to supply information immediately. Slower identification of *bread* might result, and this would, in turn, act to slow down the whole reading process.

The importance of efficiency in the reading process is understood in the context that human information processing capacity is limited. That is, active attention cannot be directed to many tasks at once. This limited capacity requires that some subprocesses in a complex task such as reading be automated. The automation of lower level subprocesses (e.g., word access) is necessary to allow attention to be focused on higher level subprocesses (e.g., drawing inferences). If lower level processing does not proceed automatically, there will not be enough processing capacity for other components of the reading process to occur.

Perfetti and Hogaboam (1975) studied the relation between children's comprehension and speed of single-word decoding. Their results showed that although both good and poor comprehenders could accurately respond to the words presented, good comprehenders were reliably faster. Marr and Kamil (1981) replicated these results. Stanovich, Cunningham, and West (1981) investigated the development of automaticity in first graders, and found that automatic decoding developed as the year progressed, particularly for high-skilled readers.

Research on Instruction

Increased understanding of the reading process has important implications for instructional research. The role of efficient component processes in successful reading implies that a key to reading problems may be found in the reader's limited proficiency with components rather than whole missing skills. Two directions for instructional research have emerged from this view: (1) identifying vulnerable points within the reading process, and (2) alleviating reading problems through training aimed at increasing proficiency of vulnerable components.

A study of vulnerable points by Calfee and Piontkowski (1981) investigated acquisition of specific components of the reading process in first graders. The investigators broke down decoding into discrete subtasks. Over the school year, they analyzed student performance on each of these subtasks in relation to other components of reading (oral reading and comprehension) and classroom instruction. Their findings support earlier work indicating that children learn more from direct instruction, and that decoding skills lead to comprehension skills more often than the reverse. The investigators also concluded that poor student performance can be linked to specific classroom and program effects. More importantly, the fine-grained look at reading performance and instruction that characterizes this study represents a step toward unpacking the reading acquisition process so that we can begin to build an understanding of how students become good or poor readers.

Lesgold and Resnick (1983), in a 3-year longitudinal study, charted development of reading skills across ability levels in two different instructional approaches—direct-code instruction and whole-word instruction. The study traced the development of automaticity of word recognition in young readers. A major finding of their work was that the links between automaticity and comprehension were stronger than those between accuracy and comprehension. They also found that reading speed for children in the decoding program began slower, but became considerably faster than that for the other group.

Although the code program produced accelerating success in reading and greater accuracy in oral reading, neither program completely solved the problem of very low-skill children. These children achieved greater accuracy in the code program, but remained slow. This suggests that processing efficiency may be critical to expert reading ability. Lesgold and Resnick observed that early weakness in automaticity seems to be a better indicator of later comprehension difficulty than poor standardized achievement test scores.

Efforts to overcome some vulnerable point in processing have provided children with training focused on lower level processing. The relation between rapid access to word meaning and comprehension of text was investigated by Beck, Perfetti, and McKeown (1982). In this study, fourth graders received an intensive vocabulary program in which they learned the meanings of 104 words under two frequency conditions—either $10-16$ or $26-40$ instructional exposures. Children were given two response timed tasks: one in which they had to decide if a word "could be a person," and the other to decide if a sentence was true or false. Students were instructed to push a button to indicate their response to the word or sentence displayed on a small screen. In the single-word task, the words met more frequently in instruction were responded to faster and more accurately. In the sentence task there was no difference between the two instructional frequency conditions, although both were superior to a noninstructed control condition.

Fleisher, Jenkins, and Pany (1979) trained poor readers in single-word decoding until their speed equaled that of good readers. But in passage reading, the trained poor readers did not reach the level of the good readers either in reading speed or in comprehension. When compared with untrained poor readers, the trained readers' performance on comprehension measures did not differ. The authors surmised that short-term instruction on isolated words is not adequate to affect comprehension and speeded practice needs to focus on words in context instead. Another possibility is that automaticity or fast decoding does not transfer immediately to improved comprehension, but rather allows for the development of comprehension skill.

Further studies of processing efficiency have used words in context as the training material via a technique called repeated readings. In this technique, children work to improve their reading times and decrease errors by reading and rereading the same passage. The approach appears to be successful in improving reading speed, decreasing errors, and enhancing comprehension. Samuels (1979) and Chomsky (1978) have used variants of this technique with positive results. However, few of these studies have been rigorous enough to be considered conclusive.

The most rigorous test of the repeated readings technique was a study by Carver and Hoffman (1981). Their study involved students' interaction with a computer and programmed text. Both rate of reading and accuracy of responses improved substantially through training, and the improvements transferred to new training passages. However, only one of five standardized reading tests showed general improvement in comprehension.

Instructional Implications

The notion that automaticity of decoding is needed for efficient reading comprehension is powerful, although this relation is not fully understood. Lack of automaticity may limit comprehension because too much mental effort is devoted to decoding, leaving few resources to devote to comprehension. Research shows that poor comprehenders are often poor decoders.

The instructional implications of this relation are not clear. Given that the goal of reading is comprehending, the question is whether comprehension can be fostered by increasing decoding fluency. Research on this point is equivocal. Longitudinal studies show that children who are good decoders at an early stage in learning to read are good comprehenders at a later stage and not the reverse, suggesting that automaticity plays a causal role in comprehension development. On the other hand, training studies have not shown consistent improvement in comprehension as a result of efforts to impove decoding fluency.

The most reasonable interpretation of these findings is that automaticity is a necessary but not sufficient condition for comprehension. Children may never become good readers unless word processing skills are fluent, but even with fluency they may not be able to comprehend text. They need instruction in comprehension in addition to an increase in fluency.

The critical question is how to increase fluency. Practice is the most frequent recommendation, hardly a revolutionary idea. However, the conditions of practice and integration with comprehension instruction have yet to be worked out. Reading fluency has long been a concern of teachers. The difference is that we now understand not only that lack of fluency might prevent a reader from completing a reading task, but it might also interfere with comprehension of what *has* been read. The next step is to translate the directive to "practice" into particulars about which skills, practiced at which stages in reading acquisition and to what extent, will best promote reading ability.

BACKGROUND KNOWLEDGE

Schema Theory

There has been a veritable explosion of research on the background knowledge a reader brings to text and its effect on comprehension. The major view of how knowledge affects reading comprehension involves the theoretical notion of schemata—abstract knowledge structures that provide frameworks for related concepts. (For a fuller discussion of schemata, see Anderson, Spiro, & Anderson, 1978; Rumelhart, 1980; Rumelhart & Ortony, 1977; Stein & Trabasso, 1982; Thorndyke & Yekovitch, 1980; Wilson & Anderson, this volume).

A schema brought to bear on a reading task can be thought of as a framework containing slots to be filled by incoming text information. For example, if a reader is presented with a text about going on vacation, he or she would likely have a slot in the vacation schema for packing a suitcase. Text statements about folding clothes or carrying bags could then fill the slot. If a reader did not have a vacation schema with a "suitcase-packing slot," the information about clothes and bags might not be readily understood.

Historical Perspectives on Using Background Knowledge

On the most general level, the current research about background knowledge demonstrates that the knowledge one brings to a reading task helps to determine what one will get from reading. Of course, this relation was realized long before this period of current research. Several studies from the 1930s (Smith,

1963) demonstrated the relation between background knowledge and reading comprehension. Smith recommended that teachers enrich their students' store of knowledge through field trips, films, and class discussions. The acknowledgments of the relation between background experience and comprehension, accompanied by suggestions to provide enriching experiences, have been common in reading methods textbooks over many decades.

The basal reading lesson traditionally begins with a teacher-led discussion aimed at establishing a background for the story. Typically, the story setting might be discussed, new concepts to be encountered in the story introduced, and children asked to talk about any personal experiences relevant to the story topic. In a modification of the traditional basal-directed reading lesson, Stauffer's (1969a) Directed Reading Thinking Activity (DRTA), pupil-to-pupil interaction is encouraged, instead of the more common teacher-led discussion.

Another variation on activating background knowledge before reading is Ausubel's (1963) advance organizer. An advance organizer can be thought of as an organizing framework for a text topic, written on a higher level of abstraction or generality than the material to be read. Its purpose is to activate a reader's prior knowledge in a way that will help the reader organize and integrate the new text information.

The issue of background experience is handled in a different way by the Language Experience Approach (Lee & Allen, 1963; Stauffer, 1970). Rather than relate their own experiences to an upcoming story theme, children use their experiences to create stories that serve as their reading materials. In this way, background knowledge of reading topics is assured, since the topics are the child's own. However, the approach does not provide for growth of the child's knowledge base if no supplementary methods are used to introduce new concepts.

Although concern with the topic of background knowledge in reading is not new, investigation of its specific effects is a recent development. As a result, prior knowledge is seen to have much deeper implications for comprehension than previously assumed. Research is now under way to show how specific knowledge affects comprehension and to explore strategies to boost knowledge toward facilitating comprehension.

Knowledge and Comprehension

Voss and his associates (Chiesi, Spilich, & Voss, 1979; Spilich, Vesonder, Chiesi, & Voss, 1979) analyzed the comprehension of text by adults with high and low knowledge in a specific content area, baseball. Subjects were presented a passage about a baseball game and then asked to recall the text. Not only did the high-knowledge group recall more text information, but there were qualitative differences as well. High-knowledge subjects were more likely to recall information of greater significance to the game, whereas low-knowledge subjects were more likely to recall information about peripheral matters such as the weather. Although both groups recalled setting information, the initial event, and outcomes, only high-knowledge subjects were likely to recall the sequence of events that developed the theme. In addition to better recall of the event sequence, high-knowledge subjects were better able to integrate the events and construct a representation of the game described in the text.

Pearson, Hansen, and Gordon (1979) tested the comprehension of second-grade children with high and low knowledge on a passage about spiders. The children differed on spider knowledge but not on IQ and achievement test scores. Both explicit and implicit questions were asked to assess comprehension. The high-knowledge group performed significantly better overall, mainly due to their ability to answer the implicit questions. This suggests that comprehension requiring integration of text and world knowledge may be especially facilitated by strong knowledge of the content topic. An important point to be drawn from the Voss et al. and Pearson et al. work is that all subjects in the studies had some knowledge about the content subject being investigated. Clearly, it is the extent and quality of that knowledge that determines how well a text is comprehended.

Instructional Strategies

Let us turn to research that has the most direct implication for classroom practice—the exploration of prereading instructional strategies and their effect on comprehension. Two types of strategies have been developed in this research: helping students utilize knowledge they already possess, and imparting new concepts to students.

Studies of the first type assume comprehension may suffer when students have knowledge relevant to the content of the text but have difficulty linking what they know with concepts in the text. Langer (1981; Langer & Nicholich, 1980) developed a Pre-Reading Plan (PReP) to help students access relevant knowledge before reading. The activity also acts as a measure of prior knowledge, helping a teacher determine if student knowledge is adequate for the upcoming selection. PReP consists of three phases: (1) the teacher asks students to free associate about a concept that will be important in the upcoming text; (2) students explore why they came up with their associations; and (3) they discuss any new ideas about the topics as a result of the activity (Langer, 1981). Langer and Nicholich showed that judgments about students' levels of knowledge based on PReP were good predictors of the students' comprehension. In using PReP with high-, average-, and low-skilled sixth-grade readers, they found it influenced comprehension for the average group only. The authors reasoned that high-skilled readers could do for themselves what the PReP activity did for the average readers, whereas low-skilled readers needed direct concept instruction as opposed to refined concept awareness. These results suggest that PReP activity may be an effective tool for boosting comprehension for some readers and for alerting the teacher that some students need further preparation before reading.

Instruction aimed at increasing background knowledge prior to reading has been investigated by Graves and his colleagues (Graves & Cooke, 1980; Graves & Cooke, 1981; Graves & Palmer, 1981). Graves created short story previews designed to present relevant background knowledge and to introduce specific key story elements (characters, plot, point of view, and setting). The previews began with questions to elicit discussion on concepts related to the text. Then the teacher read a 400 − 600 word text. Four separate experiments involving upper elementary, junior high, and senior high school students yielded significant results for both high- and low-skilled readers as measured by explicit and implicit forced-choice questions, story recall, or short answer comprehension questions. Although these previews involved more than increasing general knowledge, their results suggest that increasing a student's knowledge may be an important step toward improved comprehension.

Beck, Omanson, and McKeown (1982) compared performance of third graders on traditional basal reading lessons with revised versions that introduced requisite prior knowledge and highlighted text concepts central to the story's meaning. Prior to reading, general concepts deemed important were introduced, and specific information was presented to help children identify and interrelate story events in terms of main concepts. Children who received the revised lessons recalled more of the story and correctly answered more questions, including those about implicit information, than did the control group. Here, as in the Graves et al. studies, background knowledge was not the only issue. However, the results again support the idea that greater background knowledge enhances text comprehension.

Although there appears to be a similarity between the traditional prereading component of basal reading lessons and current examples of prereading strategies, a deeper look suggests differences. The traditional establishment of background for reading was too often a rather perfunctory activity, as an analysis of basal reading lessons demonstrated (Beck, McKeown, McCaslin, & Burkes, 1979). These activities vary from more recent efforts in, at least, the level of analysis of what knowledge might be needed for comprehension and some recognition of the extent of knowledge that might be required to affect comprehension. Evidence that the traditional versions were not as effective as those currently being developed appears in one of the studies discussed earlier (Beck, Omanson, & McKeown, 1982). In both studies, the control groups, who showed poorer comprehension performance, received the background component as specified in a basal reader.

The picture that emerges from studies on the relation between background knowledge and comprehension is one of an active research area supported by a rich theoretical base. This stands in contrast to work on the topic of a decade or more ago, which was based largely on intuition with virtually no empirical evidence.

We note a conflict implicit in some of the issues discussed here and offer a resolution. We have discussed the importance of prior knowledge for concepts met in text. On the one hand, opportunities for students to expand their knowledge are provided by texts and unfamiliar concepts, but the concepts may place the text beyond the students' comprehension. On the other hand, texts without significant knowledge requirements are more comprehensible, but offer little opportunity for students to expand their knowledge. Few would take the position that the issue can be solved by simplifying all texts, thus eliminating knowledge problems. Studies have suggested that sufficient knowledge can be presented prior to reading to enhance comprehension of text containing unfamiliar concepts. Are we to suppose that the only solution is to provide detailed prereading strategies before each lesson? The problem may be handled more efficiently. One solution might be to organize basal readers around a few specific knowledge domains, such as marine life, colonial history, or whatever. Then concepts introduced about a specific topic could be built upon in a spiraling fashion by later, more difficult selections on the same general topic. Knowledge demands would not be so problematic, since topic familiarity would be programmed into the instruction.

Finally, a practical note is offered for teachers. Problems caused by inadequate prior knowledge may not be as readily spotted as one might think. That is, the effect may be much more complex than having a student explicitly indicate, "I don't know this stuff." The interaction of the student's knowledge gaps and the demands of the text may produce far more subtle difficulties. The underlying message is that teachers need to be on the lookout for lack of background knowledge as a potential contributor to reading difficulty.

TEXT STRUCTURE

Texts can differ from one another in many ways. They can be easy or hard, abstract or concrete, narrative or expository. In the instructional world, a key concern has been the description of text features to determine texts' comprehensibility. Traditionally this has been accomplished by readability formulas. Early attention to the readability of texts was guided by the difficulty of their vocabulary (Dolch, 1928; Thorndike, 1921). Later Gray and Leary (1935) added other factors such as sentence length, density of ideas, and personal preference. But Gray and Leary used only vocabulary difficulty and sentence length to calculate readability. These two aspects continue to characterize the readability formulas that are most frequently used today.

Readability Formulas

Readability formulas are widely used to set a difficulty level for reading and content area texts, as well as to create materials of specified difficulty. Beyond a broad sorting function, the wide use of readability formulas may be a disservice. The application of readability formulas is limited in that the variables used in them predict difficulty but do not control it. That is, attempts to simplify vocabulary and shorten sentences, while maintaining content, may or may not result in text that is easier to read.

Consider the following sentence: "Bill is a member of a Socialist organization." The words "Socialist" and "organization" would give this sentence a high level of difficulty, as calculated by readability formulas. If the sentence were altered to read, "Bill is a member of a left-wing group," the assigned readability would be eased, since it contains short, high-frequency words. However, the comprehensibility of the ideas has not been eased. The meaning of the two sentences is much more similar than readability analysis would reveal. These sentences represent an often criticized inadequacy of readability formulas—the lack of consideration for concept difficulty.

Now consider the effect of the other feature of text attended to by readability analysis, that of sentence length. Compare the following sentences:

1. Sam only spent a dollar on the gift because he didn't have much money.
2. Sam only spent a dollar on the gift. He didn't have much money.

Rather than being easier to understand, sentence set 2 requires an extra inference. The example represents what has been cited as the most serious limitation of readability formulas, the lack of attention to text organization (Anderson & Armbruster, this volume; Bruce, Rubin, & Starr, 1981; Kintsch & Vipond, 1979). Text organization or structure means relations between and among sentences or larger segments of a discourse.

Models of Text Structure

Although readability research examined discrete surface features of sentences in text, research on text structure aims at a formal description of a text as a whole. Recent models of text structure are concerned with what happens during reading. They incorporate notions of how readers process text or how they represent text in memory.

Efforts to create models of text structure have taken several directions. One is the development of story grammars which are schematic representations of narrative text that readers presumably use in comprehending and recalling stories (Mandler & Johnson, 1977; Rumelhart, 1975; Stein & Glenn, 1979;

Thorndyke, 1977). Another direction involves schemes for representing the relations among small units of text, including non-narratives, assumed to characterize the structure of a text that builds as the individual reads (Frederiksen, 1975; Kintsch, 1974; Meyer, 1975).

Story Grammars

A story grammar is actually a schema for stories that readers develop, based on acquisition of knowledge about human interactions and repeated exposure to stories. As a schema, a story grammar contains slots to be filled. These slots represent categories of story information readers come to expect from a story.

A story grammar consists of categories said to describe a well-formed narrative. The categories of Stein and Glenn's (1979) story grammar, for example, are (1) *setting,* which introduces the characters and surroundings; (2) *initiating event,* which marks a change in the story environment; (3) *internal response,* which includes the formation of a goal; (4) *attempt,* the effort to achieve the goal; (5) *consequence,* the attainment or nonattainment of the goal, and (6) *reaction,* a character's response to the consequence or broader outcomes of the immediate consequence.

One way in which the influence of story grammars has been demonstrated is to present readers with stories that lack a category. In such cases, the reader's recall of the story tended to conform to the grammar; i.e., the reader filled in the missing category (Stein & Glenn, 1978; Whaley, 1981). Older children do this more consistently than younger children (Whaley, 1981). Another finding is that these incomplete texts tended to depress the amount of story information that is recalled by all subjects (Stein & Glenn, 1978).

Another method of manipulating story structure for investigation purposes is to place the categories out of order within a story or intertwined with other information. In these cases subjects' recall tended to match the expected story structure rather than the disorganized one (Mandler, 1978; Stein & Glenn, 1978; Stein & Nezworski, 1978). But such disorganization took its toll, as it was associated with less recall of text information (Stein & Glenn, 1978) or more distortions and confusions within the recall, particularly for younger children (Mandler, 1978).

Given the findings just described, it appears that story grammar structure has a strong influence on comprehension and recall. Recall of text tends to conform to this structure even when the text itself deviates from it. The results of the studies also suggest that stories whose structure deviates from the expected disrupt comprehension. This seems to be especially pronounced for younger children. With these results in mind, it seems reasonable to recommend that texts for early reading instruction should present well-formed stories. This is most difficult at early levels because of young children's limited vocabulary. However, text publishers should make sure that any information missing from the text is clearly provided by pictures or by teacher dialogue. As Beck et al. (1979) have shown, such care is not always taken in basal readers.

Although story grammar seems to play an important role in comprehension, the results cited so far imply that the grammar of stories need not be taught directly because children acquire it readily. Indeed, Dreher and Singer (1980) report a study in which instruction in story grammar did not improve comprehension. On the other hand, Spiegal and Whaley (1980) have shown that direct instruction may enhance comprehension. They identified children who did not have a well-defined concept of story, and instructed them in story grammar. Their performance on four unfamiliar stories, in comparison to a control group, showed that the instruction had helped. The notion of enhancing comprehension by strengthening the child's concept of story is an intriguing possibility. It matches an intuitively powerful notion that making covert knowledge overt enables it to be used more effectively. The situation might be likened to one's ability to solve a mystery when it has been brought to one's attention that certain facts or events are clues to the solution.

Microstructure Models

The second research direction in text structure is based on a textual representation formed by dividing each sentence into smaller units (propositions) and establishing the interconnections between them. In this way, the representation is built using every concept in the text rather than general categories of text content as in story grammars. Another difference from story grammars is that these models based on small units, or microlevel representations, can apply to exposition. The models of text structure we consider are those created by Kintsch (1974), Frederiksen (1975), and Meyer (1975).

Although the models were developed mainly as research tools, several instructional implications have arisen from their study. Kintsch and Keenan (1973) compared texts with the same number of words but different numbers of propositional units. That is, one text was more dense in ideas. They found that the text with the greater number of propositions was more difficult for readers, as measured by reading time. Kintsch, Kozminsky, Streby, McKoon, and Keenan (1975) identified another text difficulty factor in the number of new concepts introduced in a text. That is, a text that said a little about many things seemed more difficult than one that said a lot about a few things. This was so even though the text containing fewer new concepts was quite complex. Another aspect of Kintsch's (1974) work is potentially useful for the assessment of comprehension. The model enables the prediction of which text propositions will be more readily recalled.

Research on Meyer's model has yielded instructional implications and even some direct suggestions for instructional practice. A characteristic of Meyer's model is its representation of a well-developed higher level organization for a text. This high-level organization is a framework or superstructure into which text concepts fit. The model has been likened to an outline (Pearson & Camperell, 1981; Reder, 1980). This description allows one to envision how a high-level organization might be established, based on levels of importance. Meyer (1975) found that the level of a text concept within the structure allowed accurate prediction of whether that concept would be recalled, a result similar to that from Kintsch's work, cited earlier. Meyer has identified five types of structure for expository text: problem/solution, comparison, antecedent/consequent, description, and collection, and found the problem/solution type to be most facilitative of learning text material (Meyer & Freedle, 1979). These top-level structures can be likened to story grammar for expository text. The two are not completely analogous, however, since Meyer's top-level structure is based on an analysis of relations between propositions in the text.

Meyer and her colleagues (Meyer, Brandt, & Bluth, 1980) also investigated the relation between text structure and ninth-grade students' organization of text in recall. They found that students who used the top-level organization of the text to organize their recall remembered more of the text and could better discriminate between text-consistent and text-inconsistent information. However, only 22% of the subjects used this recall organizing device.

These results beg the question of whether it would be useful to teach students to use a text's top-level organization in reading and studying text. In this regard, Meyer et al. cite two recent dissertations (Bartlett, 1978; McDonell, 1978) that investigated the effects of the teaching of top-level structure as a reading and study strategy. In both cases, recall of text content was facilitated.

Text Cohesion

The preceding section dealt with how text relations contribute to global text structure. Now we turn our attention to the actual expression of relations between concepts in text, or cohesion. Cohesion refers to the devices by which meaning relations are established, thereby giving the text unity as a whole (Halliday & Hasan, 1976). These devices include nominal coreference and pronouns, where interpretation of one text element depends on the meaning of another (usually prior) element. For example,

> Mary and Donna planned to go shopping. *Their* mother said she didn't want to go with *them*. Since it was a nice day, *the girls* decided to walk rather than take the bus.

In this example, *their, them,* and *the girls* all refer to Mary and Donna and could not be understood in the absence of the first sentence.

Halliday and Hasan's work has laid the foundation for the study of cohesion in texts and its role in comprehension, although they did not address the latter issue. Their work has been an exploration of the properties of text and identification of features that differentiate text from disconnected sequences.

A useful notion for extending the discussion of cohesion to the interaction between reader and text consists of the constructs of *given* and *new* information (Clark, 1977; Clark & Haviland, 1977). As a reader proceeds through sentences in a text, he or she meets two kinds of information—given, which refers to information in previous sentences, and new, which is added information that carries the text forward. If comprehension is to occur, a reader must be able to identify which concepts represent given information and the previous information to which it refers, and then fit the new information into the representation of text that is forming. A cohesive text is worded to help a reader with these processes, whereas lack of cohesion may hinder him or her.

Regarding the identification of given information with its referent, Lesgold, Roth, and Curtis (1979) discuss three situations that can occur. In the first, the given information refers to information still actively in mind, and can be matched immediately with its referent. In the second, the information referred to is no longer actively in mind, and must be reinstated before comprehension can occur. In the third, the given information has no direct referent, and an inference must be made. Although such reinstatements and inferences seem rather easy for a skilled reader to make, they do take longer than if the information is immediately available. Thus the reading process becomes less efficient, and comprehension may at some point be affected negatively.

Virtually all texts require some reinstatements and inferences, and we are not implying that this is always a bad situation. But, early basal readers often require a disproportionate amount because words for story concepts are not in the child's reading vocabulary. In these instances, the concept is usually supplied in a picture and referred to by a pronoun in text. Imagine the following exchange, which resembles one found in a basal:

"Why is the baby crying?" asked Andy. "What does he want?"

"Don't you see, Andy? This is what he wants," said Sally.

Clearly this text excerpt is not complete in itself. "This" has myriad possible meanings. Getting meaning depends on how clearly a referent is depicted in the picture. Often pictures accompanying the stories either do not offer a strong candidate or offer more than one possibility (Beck et al., 1979). Even if the picture establishes the target concept clearly, the child may need to go through a reinstatement process if the pictured concept is not actively in mind when the sentence referring to it is read. These situations can be especially troublesome for beginning readers, since they are just getting accustomed to the reading process. Merely getting through the words requires a lot of attention. Potential reading problems caused by the use of referring expressions such as pronouns have also been discussed by Barnitz (1980), Frederiksen (1981b), Schallert, Kleiman, and Rubin (1977), and Webber (1980).

Now we turn from cohesion between given information and its referent to cohesion between given and new information. Inferences may be required when a reader must relate new information to given information without the benefit of logical relations explicitly stated in the text. That is, if causal, temporal, or conditional relationships are not stated, the reader must supply the links through inference. These logical relations are often signaled by connectives such as *because, if-then, unless*. Studies support the view that the use of such connectives facilitates comprehension. For example, Marshall and Glock (1978 – 79) found that less fluent readers benefited by the use of explicit connectives. Pearson (1974 – 75) found that longer sentences with explicit connectives often facilitated children's comprehension, even when the material involved easy, familiar concepts in which it might seem children would have little trouble realizing the connections. For example: (1) Ann loved the clown. The clown was funny. versus (2) Ann loved the clown because he was funny.

Logical relations frequently remain unstated in children's materials for two reasons. One is that traditional readability formulas are based on sentence length, so sentences are often shortened by removing connectives and forming two sentences from one, as in the above example. Second, in very early reading the connectives may not be in the children's reading vocabulary and are avoided. The result can produce quite abstract text as shown by the following adaptation of a basal excerpt:

Sandy wants a train for Christmas.

Christmas will be no fun for her.

Here the child must infer that the second sentence is conditional upon events described in the first sentence not happening.

Creating Comprehensible Texts

Now let us examine work aimed at solving problems in text cohesion. This work is based on an understanding of the variables that influence comprehension, and is driven by the goal of effective communication (Pearson, 1974 – 75). Some researchers have attempted to describe the problems and derive guidelines for writing and editing texts that are maximally comprehensible.

Davison (1981) stresses that any procedures for creating or changing texts toward readability must be based on knowledge of how humans process language. Without such knowledge the causes of difficulty cannot be identified, and only broad, predictive measures will result. Davison states that the best present substitute for readability formulas is simply the informed judgment of a writer or editor. By "informed" she means that one should possess knowledge of language, and literary style, and how best to communicate the specific content and its relationships.

Anderson and Armbruster (1984a) have studied content subject texts to identify their problematic aspects and to suggest how to overcome these problems. They have created the concept of "considerateness" as a goal for text. A considerate text is designed to maximize the possibility for the reader to gain information from text and to establish relations among concepts. Adapted from Grice's (1975) notion of a "cooperative principle" that governs conversation, the authors define four maxims of cooperation that characterize considerate text: (1) a text's structure should be chosen to convey its purpose; (2) the relations among concepts should be coherently drawn; (3) there should be a unity of purpose; (4) the content should be appropriate for the target audiences. Anderson and Armbruster have designed a procedure, based on these characteristics, to evaluate the considerateness of a text. The work of Anderson and Armbruster and of Davison represents a valuable initial step toward developing usable alternatives to readability formulas.

Although recent work on the influence of text variables on comprehension has not enabled the creation of some sure-fire new readability formula, notions have become refined enough to be useful in describing and evaluating texts. Some preliminary notions about instructional strategies to help students employ text structures to enhance their comprehension have also been gained.

METACOGNITION

Metacognition is the least understood phenomenon discussed in this chapter, and is also the least developed research area. Only in the last 5 or 6 years has it been an area of serious consideration by researchers, and only recently have efforts been made to apply knowledge about metacognition to reading problems (Brown, 1980; Brown, Armbruster, & Baker, this volume). There are two common elements of metacognition. First, there is a recognition of a problem: the reading process has broken down. Second, there are strategies used to deal with the problem (Flavell & Wellman, 1977).

As Baker and Brown (1984) point out, the activities associated with metacognition, such as planning, checking, and evaluating one's reading process, have long been included in descriptions of successful reading (e.g., Dewey, 1910; Huey, 1908/1968; Thorndike, 1917). But now such activities, under the label metacognition, are receiving attention as a specific area of study. The current research in metacognition involves describing its function, providing evidence that metacognition develops as reading ability matures, exploring whether it is a factor in differentiating good and poor readers, and investigating whether training in metacognitive skills enhances reading comprehension.

Baker (1979) has reported two studies addressing the function of metacognition in reading. In one study, Baker asked college students to read paragraphs that contained inconsistencies and to report about their comprehension. The retrospective reports indicated that students used a variety of strategies to deal with the inconsistencies. Some students reread previous text to check if certain concepts had been missed, whereas others decided that the problem was trivial and needed no strategic attention. Many students made inferences to supplement the text, often filling in perceived gaps with prior knowledge. Interestingly, over half of the students did not report noticing inconsistencies in their initial reading of the text. Baker concluded that this occurred because students had resolved the inconsistency in the course of reading, rather than that they had failed to monitor their comprehension.

In the second study, Baker attempted to observe reading behavior more directly by having students read text presented sentence-by-sentence on a computer terminal. The computer recorded reading times and movement through the text, such as rereading previous sections. Baker found that students took more time and looked back at previous text more often when passages contained inconsistencies.

Several studies have explored developmental and ability differences in metacognitive skill. Markman (1977) studied developmental changes in how first, second, and third graders monitor their own comprehension. Children were presented with inadequate instructions to play a game and perform a magic trick. In interviews designed to determine if children perceived the problems, first graders needed significantly more probing before realizing they had not understood the instructions. Often the younger children did not discover the inadequacies until asked to carry out the instructions.

In an effort to analyze children's metacognitive knowledge about reading, Myers and Paris (1978) interviewed second and sixth graders about various aspects of reading. Children were asked what they do when they do not understand a whole sentence and if they ever have to go back to the beginning of a paragraph or a story to figure out what a sentence means. In general, the younger children revealed fewer resources for working out the meanings of unknown words or unclear sentences. They seemed insensitive to the need for resolving comprehension failures.

Although the work just discussed dealt with metacognitive skills in reading for meaning, metacognitive skill also is involved in reading for remembering, i.e., studying. Brown and Smiley (1978) investigated how students of various ages took advantage of extra study time. They observed the behavior of children in grades 5 through 8, 11, and 12, and college students, all of whom were given extra study time and then asked to recall text material. The researchers found that fifth through eighth graders were much less efficient in their use of extra study time. Older students were able to improve their recall of essential text information, but younger students' recall still lacked many important elements.

Brown and Smiley also investigated the use of study strategies such as underlining and note taking. They found clear developmental differences in that most older students used these techniques spontaneously, but some younger children also used these strategies. The recall of these children showed a more sophisticated pattern, like that of the older readers. Thus, it seems that skill level, as well as age, is a factor influencing whether a reader uses metacognitive skills.

More evidence that metacognition differentiates good from poor readers comes from studies by Clay (1972) and Olshavsky (1976–77). Clay (1972) investigated children's awareness of problems during reading by studying first-graders' oral reading. They found that more of the better readers spontaneously corrected their errors and did so more often than poorer readers.

Olshavsky (1976-77) identified 10 strategies used by tenth graders to help understand a story they had been asked to read. The strategies included identification of problems, such as failure to understand a word or sentence, and solution strategies such as making inferences. Olshavsky found that good and poor readers employed the same kind of strategies, but that good readers did so more often.

A fourth aspect of metacognition being studied is most pertinent to reading instruction. This aspect comprises efforts to train metacognitive skills to improve comprehension. The training activities are similar to the kind of activities traditionally labeled study skills in the reading field. These activities, such as summarizing, note taking, underlining, and reciting of important text concepts, are described in numerous reading methods textbooks (for example, Fry, 1977; Harris & Sipay, 1975; Spache & Spache, 1977).

In general, traditional study skill activities are presented to students so they will adopt certain behaviors that represent aspects of efficient reading and studying. For example, a teacher will ask students to underline as they read to help them recognize the main points of a text and to remember them. The use of such activities to foster development of metacognitive skills is somewhat different. Metacognitive instruction not only aims to induce explicit behaviors in students; it focuses attention on the processes of reading and the reader's control over them. Brown, Campione, and Day (1981) discuss three types of instruction that further define the differences between metacognitive instruction and traditional instructional strategies. They are:

- *Blind training.* With this instruction, students are merely told or induced to employ a certain strategy. Nothing is communicated about how or why the strategy is helpful. An example of this type of instruction would be a teacher telling students to underline important parts of the text.

● *Informed training*. In addition to being induced to perform the strategy, the student is given information about how the strategy may be helpful and feedback about his or her performance. In this case, the teacher would tell the students to underline, tell them that it will help them remember the important points in a text, and check to see that they have underlined the important points.

● *Self-control training*. The child is taught how to apply the strategy and how to monitor and evaluate the strategy's use. The difference between self-control and informed training is that in the latter, students are instructed in how to select text ideas to be underlined and how to evaluate their own performance.

Brown et al. have shown the success of this third type of training and its long-term effects both with retarded and normal students. Brown, Campione, and Barclay (1979) taught mentally retarded children strategies to help them perform, monitor, and test themselves on a memory task. The children significantly outperformed a control group and the gains held on a similar task for the more advanced children a year later. Brown, Campione, and Day (1981) taught the skill of summarizing text passages to junior college students. Instructional conditions included blind, informed, and self-control training. Better students improved similarly in all conditions, whereas the poorer students benefited most from self-control training.

Andre and Anderson (1978 – 79) also studied different types of training, using self-questioning as the study strategy. High school students were (1) instructed to reread as a study aid; (2) told to formulate questions and answer them as they read; or (3) instructed in how to formulate questions and use them to monitor their learning. The result was that both question groups did better than the reread group, but the question-plus-training group's gain was larger. Andre and Anderson also found that lower ability students received the most benefit from the training. The above studies suggest that metacognitive skill may be lacking in poorer readers and may be improved with appropriate instruction.

The work reported here shows metacognition as a promising avenue toward improved instruction in reading. A large part of its appeal is that metacognition merges ideas from detailed psychological work on the reading process with traditional notions about activities of efficient learners (Brown, 1980).

Although the investigation of metacognition in reading is still quite new, we believe that some practical conclusions can be drawn for immediate use. Experience and observations suggest that many teachers employ the kinds of reading and study strategies discussed here as part of their instructional repertoire. But what may be missing are the components that separate blind training from self-control training. For example, children are often not told why they are being asked to perform certain activities, or why certain instructional procedures are carried out. It seems that such information could help children to control their own learning processes, which, as data reported here suggest, yields benefits in improved comprehension.

SUMMARY AND CONCLUSIONS

At the outset, we suggested that changes have occurred in reading research over the last decade, and that these changes are subtle in nature. Let us now review the major aspects of this chapter to show why we have likened the changes to "returning to the place where one began and seeing it for the first time."

In the section on decoding and automaticity, we discussed the notion that accuracy of decoding is not sufficient for successful comprehension, and that automaticity and speed of decoding also must be considered. Automaticity of decoding was likened to reading fluency, which has always been a goal of reading instruction. What has changed is that the concept of automaticity allows us to define precisely the traditional notion of fluency and to be more aware of its role in promoting successful reading.

In the section on background knowledge, we discussed the longstanding recognition that one's prior knowledge influences one's reading comprehension. We pointed out that traditional activities done in consideration of this influence were at a general, often superficial level. Recent research has shown that background knowledge may be a major factor in reading failure. It is also becoming evident that the extent and quality of one's knowledge about a subject affect comprehension of text about that subject. It may indeed be the case that a little knowledge is not enough. An implied change for practice is that teachers need to be on alert for knowledge problems masquerading as reading problems.

In the third section, we discussed the weakness of readability formulas and indicated that new work on text structure may dismantle the readability myth. A major point here was the importance of recognizing aspects of texts that can influence a reader's comprehension. Through the understanding of these influences, it may be possible to develop some principles for constructing texts that communicate best for specific purposes. However, it is not likely that one set of principles will work for all domains of text used for vastly different audiences.

In the final section on metacognition, we noted that many of the strategies used to teach metacognitive skills are those long used as study skill techniques. The change is that under the rubric of metacognition, the rationale for the activities and methods needed to implement them effectively are made explicit for the students. The belief is that this explicitness will help to bring these activities under the control of the learner, and thus make them useful as part of his or her general repertoire.

Common to all the topics presented in this paper are advances in knowledge that have brought insight into traditional approaches. This insight makes us more able to discriminate among the older notions, recognize those of most value, and describe in more precise ways why those notions are valid. This greater discrimination and precision provide a more solid base from which to conduct research related to instruction and allow the refinement of instructional practice. Our seeing, as if for the first time, is a sight of greater clarity and deeper understanding.

Recent Theory and Research into the Reading Process: Implications for Reading Assessment

8

Roger Farr
Robert Carey
Bruce Tone
Indiana University

The assessment of reading performance is a pragmatic, immutable phenomenon in the world of education. Often criticized, reading tests continue nevertheless to be developed, administered, and—theoretical issues notwithstanding—believed in. These tests and their progeny—norms, test scores, placement of students, criticisms of teachers and schools, funding—are, above all, a *political* reality. They are a constant with which all students, teachers, and administrators know they will have to contend. And because of this constancy, persistent questions about the assessments of reading performance should be of keen interest to all of us concerned with reading education.

The importance of reading assessment has not been reflected in the general explosion of research on the reading process. Despite the many advances in knowledge about reading during the last decade, the issue of assessment has not been accorded a position that reflects its quotidian significance.

From one point of view, this neglect makes considerable sense. How can we hope to improve the diagnosis and measurement of the process until we have a more adequate understanding of the essential nature of reading? The logic in this question may explain why most of the recent research has focused on the basic aspects of reading, especially the elements and processes of comprehension. During this time, however, testing has continued unabated, largely unaffected by the basic process research, even when that research has been relevant to assessment issues. There is a need to synthesize that relevant research, to address the issues and problems raised by the recent wealth of information on reading, and to provide a context for direct application of solutions to the assessment of reading performance. This chapter takes a step in that direction by discussing the implications for assessment of recent advances in reading theory (Part I) and text analysis research (Part II). Part III includes recommendations for research and practice.

IMPLICATIONS FOR ASSESSMENT EMERGING FROM READING THEORY

Recent theories and studies in reading have come from different scholarly perspectives, all addressing the difficult question: *What happens when we read and understand?* Although we do not have a unified theory of reading, certain theoretical formulations have received abundant empirical support. Many of these have resulted from cross-fertilization among disciplines, including linguistics, psychology, education, and computer science.

The Emerging Comprehension Model

The emerging model of comprehension asserts that comprehension is an active process in which the reader constructs meaning from text cues, calling upon knowledge of language, text structure and conventions, content concepts, and communication. This process is essentially inferential, with readers using their existing knowledge to link discrete pieces of information in the text, to ascribe appropriate meanings to words, and to fill in implied information. In addition, readers monitor their state of understanding and engage various strategies according to different reading purposes and genre, or to encountered difficulties. (See Brown, Armbruster, & Baker; Carpenter & Just; Shuy; Wilson & Anderson; in this volume).

Current theorists believe their new analyses should enable us to assess the subprocesses they describe. The consensus is that most existing tests have failed to do so for three major reasons: First, test designers have arbitrarily selected the subskills to be measured without reference to any theory, and in so doing have failed to define those subskills adequately. Second, extant reading assessments have not developed technologies to guarantee the validity of the data produced. Third, those data are produced by a limited number of items supposedly measuring each subskill.

The critical question now is whether reading can be separated into sub-operations that can be diagnosed through assessment. There is every reason to expect assessment instruments to provide diagnostic information about specific aspects of reading relevant to instruction (Anderson, Wardrop, et al., 1978). Current editions of some standardized tests perform that service to a higher degree than many realize. Although the terminology may seem archaic, some of the tested skills clearly relate to aspects of comprehension in current psychological models. The more dependable available instruments indicate whether a child's instructional level is lower than his or her grade level (Farr, 1978). Some relate this discrepancy to more specific skills. The teacher can use such test results as one piece of information recommending further inquiry.

Haertel's careful study (1980) of standardized tests published prior to 1970 tends to support the criticisms of existing assessment instruments. He analyzed test items and large samples of responses in terms of nine comprehension subskills. He found that none of the subskills could be distinguished, but that reading comprehension appeared to be a "single dichotomous skill" (i.e., a reader can or cannot comprehend). However, Haertel's nine subskills were not the specific skills the tests professed to measure. Rather, they were research-based subprocesses identified after the tests were published. Consequently, there is some question of whether comprehension is a unitary skill, whether Haertel's analysis of subskills was inappropriate, or whether the subskills would have been distinguished had he analyzed the data according to those the tests purported to measure. He concluded that the tests could only tell us if an examinee could comprehend.

All of these points, of course, ignore the contention of some theorists (especially Goodman and Smith) that subskills, per se, are not the issue. These theorists contend that the reading process is a natural, organic process rather than a mechanistic one and to decontextualize certain aspects of the process is to study something other than reading. This school of thought, called the "whole language" school, is, to say the least, controversial. The whole language point of view may have important implications for reading assessment; but since it tends to exclude all other theories and almost all existing reading assessment, it is difficult to accommodate in an inclusive discussion of research relevant to issues of assessment.

Analyses of Inferencing Suggest Some Immediate Implications

Although the emerging theory of comprehension has served as a springboard for changing reading instruction, it does not provide direct or easy guidance for assessment. To illustrate, let us deal with an example based on one aspect of comprehension—inferencing. By inferencing we mean "going beyond the information given" (Bruner, 1957), using one's existing knowledge to generate the meaning of the text. It has been selected because it is central to comprehension, relevant to instruction (and thus for assessment), and illustrates the need for extensive clarification.

In assessing the inferences a reader draws, the first problem will be to develop the technology to distinguish among different types of inferences. This seems both promising and challenging.

A second problem will be to decide which taxonomy to use and whether any is both suitable and adequately structured. Although recent analyses of inferences do not appear to be exhaustive, they are complete enough to merit experimentation. The three classification schemes developed by Warren, Nicholas, and Trabasso (1979) and Trabasso (1980) appear to be adequately enough related to the construction of instructional materials to serve as experimental assessment taxonomies as well. It would be difficult, however, to use more than one on any one assessment because the relations among the three are not clear.

Trabasso (1980) describes a reader's operations in coping with text features: solve lexical ambiguity, resolve anaphora, establish context, and establish a larger framework for context. The Warren et al. (1979) taxonomy yields information more valuable for instruction: informational, spatial or temporal, script-related or knowledge-based concepts. Trabasso's (1980) other analysis classifies inferences by "protagonist actions."

It is possible that much can be learned from experimenting with item types for each of the sets separately. Continued research efforts to operationalize such schemes in assessment could well revise each of the above category sets and expand, clarify, or merge them into a single set.

A third problem may be in clearly defining and expanding the notion of inference drawing to include an analysis of reasoning. Johnston (1981) says the direction of research is to make reasoning strategies explicit. Although he does not suggest that reasoning and inferencing are synonymous, he acknowledges that both are inherent parts of comprehension:

> While there is still some willingness to separate inferencing and problem solving, they are no longer generally considered to be removable from the comprehension process, but rather are considered an integral part of it, like the apple in apple pie. (p.12)

It seems possible that in any taxonomy of reasoning, all classifications will involve inferencing; the type involved may help distinguish the classifications. It seems arguable that all inferencing is some type of reasoning as well. If so, it might be possible to match inference and reasoning types.

Reader Background Is a Unifying Theme

One aspect of the reading process of concern to most contemporary reading theorists is reader background knowledge. Such disparate theorists as Searle (1975), Kintsch (1974), and Schank (1975) all employ some version of reader background as a central feature of their work. They envision it as, respectively, awareness of the functions of speech acts, deep-structure word concepts, and "scripts" for behavior and knowledge. In these theories background knowledge is the basis for drawing inferences during comprehension and for relating to the content of the text. Authors assume certain kinds of knowledge on the part of their readers, and leave much unstated for the reader to fill in.

The emerging descriptions of the role of background knowledge pose a dilemma for the assessment designer. If background knowledge is integral to reading comprehension, an assessment instrument must account for it. Factoring background knowledge out of reading assessment is next to impossible; yet background knowledge must be controlled so that it will not account for an indeterminate amount of assessment results. The problem becomes obvious to the test designer concerned about the passage dependency of test items. A general charge against reading tests is that they do not adequately account for the role of such factors as background knowledge and reasoning ability, and therefore measure intelligence and experience as well as reading ability. Consequently, their usefulness in diagnosing certain aspects of reading is called into question.

Johnston (1981) contends that the question of whether such factors as background knowledge, long-term memory, and reasoning ability can or should be factored out of reading assessment is now moot. Research unequivocally shows that comprehension includes those factors. Some theorists and researchers who helped describe the essential role of background knowledge have also been concerned with how it could be factored out of reading assessment (e.g., Koslin, Koslin, & Zeno, 1979; Royer & Cunningham, 1978; Tuinman, 1973-74). Yet to factor reader background out of assessment, as Royer and Cunningham suggest, is to assess something other than reading comprehension.

Items based on single sentences or larger units of discourse depend on the reader's knowledge of syntax, semantics, and real-world knowledge. Obviously, these will be reflected in test performance. The higher up the process ladder assessment aims, the more involved meaning—and potentially background knowledge—becomes. As Haertel (1980) points out, if one attempts to assess inferencing by using in a test item a synonym for a word in the text, one is also testing whether the subject recognizes that those words mean the same thing.

To control for background knowledge, Royer and Cunningham (1978) suggest that texts be written to fall within the knowledge base of the target populations. A dependable analysis of concepts people know at various stages of life, verified by observation of curricula or life tasks, could help test designers select topics with equal relevance to subjects across geographic regions, socio-economic differences, and among an urban/rural continuum of environments. Commonsense editorial judgment is presently used.

The same objective has led to the construction of passages on relatively esoteric topics that designers hope are not part of the target readers' backgrounds. Yet the test designers want such passages to be of high interest to potential readers. Therefore, in selecting such passages, it is assumed that the examinee has general background that will make the esoteric material meaningful and interesting.

Most attempts to evade or anticipate the need for background knowledge fail because they demand a commonality of experience among readers. Even if it were possible to assure common curricula, it is not likely that individuals would assimilate "generic concepts" in the same way and acquire the same knowledge structures. The effects of out-of-school differences in experience and language remain pervasive.

To distinguish the contribution of background knowledge from other processing skills, Johnston (1981) suggests the development of background measures. If matched to the content of a particular assessment instrument and administered at a time close to the reading assessment, the results might be deductible from the reading test score, yielding a more valid measure of reading skills.

Background Knowledge is the Key Factor in the Issue of Test Bias

One prevalent issue related to the effect of reader background on test results is whether standardized instruments are fair to groups whose cultural experience and background knowledge are distinctly different from that assumed by the test. Broad administration of standardized tests has yielded lower scores for urban and black populations and for readers for whom English is a second language.

Instruments must be selected on the basis of valid information needs that are clearly defined and related to assessable instructional goals for the particular population. The widespread use of standardized tests with non-mainstream students may be justified only when educators need to assess individual students' ability in a curriculum that adequately matches the test or for selecting materials at appropriate difficulty levels. However, the scores tell so little about the student's actual reading abilities and the test's demands might be so frustrating to students that instructional guidance might be more efficiently sought from other sources.

Tailoring is being recommended for special populations (Royer & Cunningham, 1978). Tests tailored for specific populations are analogous to the instruments with the assured background relevance mentioned earlier (Johnston, 1981). These would also have the same potential measurement problems. However, an issue unique to tailored tests is that they may not always match real-life tasks (Johnston, 1981). Assuming that the child will want to compete in American society at large, should instruction be geared more to the communication demands of the broader arena? If so, assessment should reflect that goal.

The development of tests tailored to special populations would need to be subsidized due to the expense of careful test development. Because tailored tests have a limited audience, the development of informal assessment techniques is an attractive alternative. Since the purpose of these tests is to gather information relevant to instruction, teacher-made assessments have greater potential for answering the need.

The Role of Reader Purpose in Literacy Assessment

A reader's purpose determines whether and how a reader interacts with a particular text. The importance of purpose obligates the test designer to frame reading assessment passages with clear purposes. Comprehension is greatly affected by a reader's ability to grasp how the text at hand answers his or her immediate needs. This awareness should have more real-life relevance than "I better do my best on this test," a point that relates to concerns about the impact of test environments (Spiro, 1980; Steffensen & Guthrie, 1980).

Assessment designers ought to consider:

- How test passages can be selected and presented so they engage the subject in valid purposes for reading.
- How test items can be presented so the reader does not treat them as a very atypical kind of text, thus setting an artificial purpose for reading.
- How generic processes can be assessed without disrupting any natural purposes for reading that have been established.

Consideration of different literacies raises other issues: What types of literacies should be represented on a test for school children? What kind of assessment will best reveal what educators need to know in order to develop their students' ability to comprehend different kinds of text? How literacy-specific should a particular instrument be?

The answer to the last of these questions is highly contingent on another purpose—the assessor's purpose for seeking the information. The more task-specific the need for information is, the more literacy-specific the assessment ought to be. This would include matching assessments to particular curricula and philosophies of reading, as well as determining if the test actually produces the needed data.

TEXT ANALYSIS: IMPLICATIONS FOR ASSESSMENT

Until relatively recently text analysis was exceedingly limited as a domain of inquiry. Generally, the available analyses were of two kinds: text difficulty and syntactic complexity. They were used primarily to match texts to readers of presumed reading ability levels. The most common form of text difficulty analysis is the readability formula. Although pervasive, there are serious questions about the efficacy of these analyses (Anderson & Armbruster, this volume; Davison, 1984). The syntactic complexity measures are the products of the Chomskyan revolution in linguistics, reflecting advances in knowledge about linguistic structure engendered by transformational-generative grammars.

Both types of analysis are essentially structural; that is, form is considered dominant to function. In general, these ways of characterizing texts tend to dismiss meaning as either inconsequential or too complex to be amenable to analysis. Both approaches use the sentence as the unit of analysis.

Text Analysis and Text Linguistics

More recent developments have tended to be more theoretically based and operationally sound. Indeed, the movement toward consistent text analyses has been so swift and popular that a new subdiscipline has evolved: text linguistics. Its hallmark is the analysis of text units larger than single sentences. It is worth noting that this field is interdisciplinary in nature. It draws on precepts and specific analytic techniques not only from linguistics, but also from cognitive psychology, artificial intelligence, sociology, literary theory, and pedagogy. These fields have provided new tools, new theoretical insights and, perhaps most importantly, a context of awareness for examining texts at a variety of levels and in a variety of modes.

The burgeoning field of text linguistics has provided numerous analytic techniques. (See especially de Beaugrande & Dressler, 1982, for a thorough introduction.) Those techniques most often used for reading research have tended to be variations of one of three specific modes: propositional analysis, cohesion analysis, and story grammars. Propositional analysis and its variants (e.g., Davison, 1980) reduce texts to a series of semantic structures called propositions, which represent the potential meaning of the text below the surface level. Cohesion analysis (Halliday & Hasan, 1976) examines those aspects of text that cause it to "hang together" as a text, especially those aspects of the linguistic system that operate across sentence boundaries in narrative or exposition. Story grammars characterize the overall structure of traditional stories and have served as a basis for analyzing the implicit match between the way in which stories are put together and the way a reader expects them to be put together (for both cultural and cognitive reasons).

Each of these modes of analysis has implications for reading assessment. They should help test developers to design reading passages at relatively specific levels of comprehensibility and provide a basis for determining what makes a text easy or difficult. Ideally, these analyses will serve as the basis for developing tests that unambiguously assess various reading skills. This would give greater control and specificity to the tests, reducing error variance. At present, it is not possible to synthesize text analysis procedures to the point where we can avail ourselves of all the information in a given text; some techniques simply preclude others. A recent study by Feathers (1983) suggests the staggering complexity of data yielded by the simultaneous application of these procedures.

Fillmore and Kay's (1983) analysis of several existing reading tests based on recent linguistic and cognitive approaches to text analysis provides guidelines for improving reading test items. With regard to test questions, he suggests:

1. Don't test for skills not related to reading, e.g., mathematics.
2. Don't use harder vocabulary in questions than in the text.
3. Don't test for incidental, insignificant information.
4. All questions should have one and only one correct answer.
5. Write questions so that if a child understands the text, he or she can answer the question; if the child does not understand the text, she or he cannot answer the question.
6. Don't require inferences based on background knowledge children are unlikely to have.
7. Don't allow rejection of alternatives on grammatical grounds.
8. Avoid questions that require stylistic or other ambiguous judgments, e.g., "What is the best title for this passage?"
9. Questions shouldn't require as correct answers false or questionable statements.

From this analysis Langer (1983) has identified several major characteristics of text that increase difficulty of the passage or test items, and hence reduce item validity:

1. Extreme density of ideas, especially if list-like or lacking explicit connectives.
2. Overreliance on the reader's background knowledge to make sense of a passage, yielding implicit rather than explicit text.
3. "Imitation genre" in which a genre is implied (e.g., joke, riddle, or exposition) but where the test question may not be appropriate to the genre.
4. Deceptive simplicity in which a passage appears simple (based on a readability formula), but the concepts are in fact difficult or unknown to the reader.

We currently have neither the technology nor the theoretical expertise to take full advantage of all text analytic approaches for either assessment or instruction. The point may be moot, however, since test developers have shown little interest in going beyond readability analyses in designing their instruments. They may be uneasy about applying the results of a new field such as text linguistics, or it may simply be more economically feasible to stick with more conventional, albeit unproductive, linguistic approaches such as readability formulae.

Establishing Valid Functional Literacies

An entirely different kind of text analysis is of equal or greater relevance to assessment. This kind of text research has focused on literacy requirements and demands of various contexts. For educational purposes, we need to know whether there is a minimum level of literacy needed by all citizens for coping with everyday literacy demands, as well as varying levels or types of literacy skills for specific tasks. This requirement has generated analyses of written materials essential to particular occupations and life tasks in an effort to determine the proficiencies required.

The Adult Proficiency Levels (APL) study (Northcutt, 1975) has been perhaps the most influential study—at least among the general public. When its findings have been used to describe national literacy, however, questions have been raised about the literacy levels set in the study, and those questions have gone unanswered (Fisher, 1978). That proficiency levels of individuals who were succeeding at some jobs were lower than requisite levels described for the jobs indicates that although the study may provide literacy descriptions for those occupations, the functional literacy levels are not appropriate.

Other researchers whose work includes text analysis that relates to specific occupations and tasks include Sticht et al. (1973), Sticht and Caylor (1972), and Sticht and McFann (1975), all of whom have done extensive analyses of materials essential to the armed forces. Mikulecky and Diehl (1979, 1980) and Mikulecky (1980) have analyzed materials used in several occupations, and Holland and Redish (1981) have analyzed strategies required to read and understand forms and other public documents.

The work in this area is quite fragmented, but that is appropriate. Each researcher identifies and isolates specific occupations or tasks and collects relevant written material for analysis. In addition, the studies are diverse in terms of the analytic techniques used.

The potential implications of text analysis for reading assessment are obvious. Reading assessments ought to reflect the schema domains, syntax, vocabulary, style, and structure of materials that individuals taking the tests will need to read.

"Learner Literacy"

The oft-heard question, "What is real-life reading for a school child?" implies that much of the reading children do in the classroom is different from what they do outside. On the surface, the question suggests that by requiring, teaching, and testing a literacy alien to non-school activities, reading instruction in school is a relatively esoteric experience unrelated to real life.

Such a line of reasoning ignores two obvious facts. First, classroom experience is an important part of a child's life, comprising a significant part of a child's total activities. Thus, it is a major real-life experience for the child. Society has determined that childhood should be devoted to learning, not productivity, necessitating the second qualification to be considered: Instructional materials in content areas are apt to deal with more complex concepts and be more heavily laden with facts than materials the child encounters outside the classroom. In order to handle this load, the materials may also be more syntactically complex. The facts and concepts also may be presented in more tightly and logically structured frameworks than those encountered outside the classroom. This suggests that a student needs to develop a kind of "learner literacy" to handle highly informative, usually expository, texts.

If we accept the existence of a generic "learner literacy" requirement, we will need a fuller characterization of it and assessment measures to guide instruction in it. An essential component of learner literacy is acquiring the skills to learn independently. Research indicates that this includes learning about texts: the characteristics of genres, such as poems, narrative stories, jokes, instructions, and exposition, including their structure and purpose, conventions used to signify important information and what the author intends the reader to do with the information (Anderson & Armbruster, 1984a, and this volume). It also involves developing metacognitive skills, such as monitoring whether or not you have understood what you are reading, and whether you have satisfied your purpose. They include as well the flexible application of strategies according to the genre and purpose for reading and also to cope with comprehension difficulties when encountered (Brown, Armbruster, & Baker, this volume).

The argument for "learner literacy" offered above is not presented as a rationale for ignoring the obligation to wed instructional texts and reading instruction to the real-world interests of children—by developing convincing purposes for learning specific things, by engaging in satisfactory play, and by otherwise living and growing outside the classroom.

Definitive tests to reveal a subject's ability will depend on extensive acceleration of analyses of many kinds of written materials and on careful syntheses of the findings of such studies. Steps are being taken by school districts that need more sensitive measures of students' progress than currently available. For example, Schuder (this volume) reports that CRTs designed to measure comprehension skills for narration and exposition are more sensitive to instruction in these forms than are standardized tests. Likewise, Mikulecky (this volume) reports substantial gains by workers on job-related literacy tasks following a job-literacy program, but little progress on standardized tests. Clearly, further research is needed to determine whether and what reading skills are generalizable, and hence what kinds of tests are needed to assess them.

IMPLEMENTING AND EXTENDING THE RESEARCH: QUESTIONS AND RECOMMENDATIONS

The preceding discussions are representative of the questions and issues that assessment-relevant research has addressed in recent years. Following are recommendations for future efforts.

Analyze existing instruments

Close analyses of assessment instruments are rare and should be encouraged in an effort to answer pertinent questions provoked by recent research. There is a great deal that might be learned from analyses of assessment instruments, especially when such analyses are crossed, as Haertel (1980) did, with extant score data. Specific areas for improving the quality, validity, and integration of assessment instruments with theory and instructional design should be studied. These include:

- the identification, definition, and relation of item designations to emerging taxonomies,
- the development of items that require higher order skills (e.g., inferencing, synthesis, and critical evaluation),
- a determination of relevance to daily life, student ability, and the naturally occurring reading act, and
- a comparison of test item technologies in terms of reading assessment validity.

Analyze Written Materials

Increased analysis of various types of written materials promises to contribute significantly to the construction of reading assessments, especially to develop levels of difficulty based on sound linguistic principles. Text analysis will make it possible for assessment to reflect the kinds of materials particular groups of readers need to read. In addition, text analysis may illuminate specific reader purposes and reading tasks, information that could be used to establish reader purpose during assessment. We also need to know how the reader's perception of the writer's purpose, and the mood and tone of the text, affect comprehension, so perhaps they can be controlled or measured during assessment.

Survey Test Uses and Misuses

A thorough study of test uses and misuses is needed. Such a study could help stop the misuse of tests resulting from political motivation (Levine, 1976) and ignorance. To do this, the effort must clearly explain what tests can do and recommend how they should be used. Such a study might also identify assessment needs that are not being met by existing instruments.

This effort should specifically target tests yielding grade equivalents. As Miller (1973) noted, "We believe that grade level criteria may often be more misleading than informative." The use of grade equivalents is so entrenched that explaining how they lead to misunderstanding is like attacking apple pie and motherhood.

Develop Assessment Strategies That Reflect Emerging Models of Reading

Perhaps the most exciting aspect of the research of recent years is the promise that we may soon be able to identify specific aspects of reading comprehension with some certainty. Meanwhile we need to devise methods of measuring them, using the definitions we now have. As Johnston (1981) put it:

> We are approaching the stage of being able to classify items and item clusters with respect to the information they could yield. Thus we approach a position from which to select items which have a clear relationship to the structure of the text, the reader's prior knowledge, and the nature of the requisite cognitive processes. Knowing the characteristics of these item clusters, we should be able to generate tests which provide more, and more meaningful, information. (p. 69)

The response to this charge will be varied. Those who argue strongly that the cloze procedure is the technology that assures we are measuring the reading act should be experimenting with deletions controlled to reveal various types of inferences, reasoning, and linguistic, psychological, and psycholinguistic features of text and the reading process. Obviously any single deletion is going to cross types and features, and the cloze assessor is going to have to analyze the requirements for filling each deletion carefully, crossing the multifacets of groups of deletions to yield some kind of gross distinctions.

As domain referencing guides assessment experimentation (Anderson et al., 1978; Anderson, Wardrop, et al., 1978), various aspects of the reading act may be better isolated and categorized for diagnosis. Then different domain controls can be implemented in single assessments to test whether they yield distinctions among subprocesses.

Those who would rely on the statistically clean reporting potential of latent-trait theory will probably engage computer technology and its branching potential to channel subjects to assessments of increasingly specific sub-processes. This potential is discussed by Frederiksen (1979). Haertel (1980) notes the relevance of such use to the latent trait theory of assessment.

Text designers who construct multiple-choice items face a challenge that has yet to be addressed by research on the potential of distractor control. It is possible to pinpoint the reason for an error by noting, for example, that an examinee frequently selects a distractor representing the same faulty line of reasoning or that the wrong pronoun antecedent has been identified.

Sentence verification techniques (Royer et al., 1979) will be tested to see how they can distinguish between levels of memory, which in turn may help distinguish subprocesses. We can only speculate on the development of new assessment techniques. Someday technology may allow us to analyze open-ended responses in a manner that yields data that can clearly direct instruction. If so, schema theory and comprehension models described in terms of net-works may be the theoretical bases of such measurement.

It is hoped that future technology will allow us some way to assess reading comprehension in terms of what the reader does with what is read, which is, after all, the ultimate gauge of how well it was understood. Such assessment might dissolve the distinction between product and process measurement.

Explore the Potential and Limitations of Criterion-Referenced Measures

Criterion-referenced testing (CRT) can be highly effective in the classroom setting. Teacher-made assessments based on objectives set and defined by the teacher are, in the purest sense, criterion-referenced measures. The use of this general technique for broader measurement to assess grade-, school-, city-, or state-wide populations is becoming widespread practice as an accountability system. Minimum competence exams, which have swept the country, are criterion-referenced measures. A possible benefit of this movement is that it requires educators to define their goals, objectives, and philosophies.

The reliability of such measures, however, is usually undetermined, and their validity is no more assured than the validity of standardized measures. Results of a nation-wide study of criterion-referenced tests could be far-reaching, since we know relatively little about how CRTs are affecting instruction.

Explore the Full Potential of Informal Assessment

In the light of the current high regard for individualized instruction, the general distrust of standardized measures, and what is being learned about the role background knowledge plays in comprehension, it is surprising that so little has been done to analyze the potential of informal assessment. Observation, the most informal and perhaps valuable of all assessments of reading, needs to be studied too. The most important aspect of an extensive study of informal reading assessment would be its synthesis and reporting.

Experiment with Tailored Assessments

Schema theory should be used as the basis for constructing reading assessments tailored for special groups. The results of recent studies of test bias, linguistic capabilities of special groups, and the role of both reader purpose and background should be analyzed and incorporated in the development of such measures.

Researchers Should Accept a Share of the Responsibility for the Implementation of Findings

If basic and applied research findings are to have an impact on practice, it will be necessary for someone to synthesize the findings and present the information in a form that is meaningful and useful to teachers, teacher trainers, and the public. Given the increasing involvement of the public in curriculum decisions, it behooves researchers to make their findings accessible, to eliminate jargon, and to relate their findings to concepts familiar to the lay person. Likewise, teacher educators, methods text authors, and designers of instructional material must understand the emerging concepts if they are to assure that training programs, curricula and materials reflect that new knowledge.

9 Readable Textbooks, or, Selecting a Textbook Is Not Like Buying a Pair of Shoes

Thomas H. Anderson
Bonnie B. Armbruster
University of Illinois at Urbana-Champaign

Determining how easy a text is to read and understand (readability) has been a fascinating topic of investigation for psychologists and educators. Kintsch and Vipond (1979) point out that the flurry of excitement for psychologists may have ended 20 years ago, but research on the topic is still flourishing among educators. This continued interest highlights the need for a metric that is useful, in addition to being scientifically interesting.

This chapter addresses the usefulness of readability measures, and concludes that currently they are not very useful and perhaps never will be. As evidence, we present a brief history of research in readability, describing how well it works in a decision-making model, and discuss new work on text variables that may help students understand text.

THE QUEST FOR PREDICTION

There is a 60-year history of active research on what characteristics of text make it easy or difficult to read. E.L. Thorndike's work in the 1920s helped shape this critical look at the influence of text on learning. Today, Klare (1984) and Kintsch and Vipond (1979) estimate that more than 50 readability indices have been developed. This relatively small number is impressive, considering the potentially large number of text variables. For example, Bormuth (1966) presents data from more than 48 text variables in one of his studies. Only a few of the readability indices have received wide recognition and usage.

Six of the more widely used ones, as reported by Selden (1981), are by Dale and Chall (1948), Dolch (1948), Fry (1968), Gunning (1952), Spache (1953), and Sticht (1972, 1975). All are based on a combination of three basic measures: vocabulary frequency, word length, and sentence length. These six indices account for most of the current usage patterns.

The intended uses of readability indices fall into two broad categories: *prediction* and *production* (Klare, 1984). In *prediction*, readability indices are correlated with comprehension measures. In *production*, these indices serve as a guideline for writing text. In this chapter we make little reference to the production aspect (but see Davison, 1984; Klare, 1984).

The intended use of a readability formula as a *prediction* index can be illustrated by the following analogy. Consider the process of buying a pair of shoes. Because of the close relationship between foot and shoe size, anyone who knows his or her foot size can reliably select a pair of shoes that will fit. Likewise, in selecting an appropriate book, the teacher first determines the student's "reading size" by referring to a few indices: standardized reading scores and the latest scores on quizzes from the student's reading workbook. Then the teacher determines the appropriate "book size" by referring to a "reading size" to "book size" conversion chart, and sends the student to the bookshelf to search for a book that has a certain "book size."

In this system, can the teacher and student be confident that the student will get an appropriate book? Our conclusion is that readability formulas are probably not very useful in predicting text difficulty. This conclusion is based on the following argument. The correlation between ability (a measure of how well students can read) and readability (a measure of text difficulty) is not very high due to the complex nature of the constructs. Motivation, interest, prior knowledge, and strategy training remain unaccounted for in the current reading ability construct, and text style and coherence remain unaccounted for in the current readability measures. Because the correlation between reading ability and readability is not particularly strong, the reading ability of a student cannot be a very accurate predictor of the appropriate readability level of a text that a student can read with understanding.

How Precise a Prediction Can Be Made?

Theoretically, we can estimate how much error would be made in selecting text for children to read based on their reading ability. Table 9.1 shows some estimations of text reading levels for a student with a reading ability of 6.0 given three different possible correlations between text readability and student reading ability.

When the correlation between reading ability and readability is approximately 0.5, a reasonable estimate based on research reviewed by Selden (1981) and Klare (1984), Table 9.1 shows that a teacher can be reasonably confident (68%) that the needed book for the student with a 6.0 grade reading ability ranges somewhere in difficulty from the 4.1 to the 7.9 grade level. Table 9.1 also shows that the teacher can be 90% confident that the required text lies between the 2.9 and the 9.1 grade level. This range is larger, but is more likely to capture the needs of the student than the 68% one.

Theoretically, then, it appears that students whose reading ability is at the 6.0 grade level can read and comprehend text with a wide range of difficulty. Results provided by Kern (1980) provide some support for this conjecture. Kern (1980) scaled 18 passages using two types of indices—level of comprehension difficulty and readability. He determined level of comprehension difficulty by administering a standardized reading test to the readers to identify their reading grade level. Then, the readers were given experimental passages in the form of cloze tests. Comprehension difficulty indices were determined by identifying the lowest reading grade level in which 50% of the students achieved a cloze score at or above the 35% correct criterion level. At least five standard readability formulas also provided indices of text difficulty. Kern found that students with 7th- and 8th- grade-level reading skills could read and understand materials ranging in readability from 7th to 11th grade and 9th- and 10th-grade-level readers had a reading and understanding range from the 6th- to the 12th-grade level. These ranges are similar to those shown in Table 9.1 when $r = .8$.

TABLE 9.1
Theoretical Grade Levels of Suitable Text for a Student
Who has a Measured Reading Ability at the 6.0 Grade

Correlation Between Text Readability and Student Reading Ability	Standard Error of Estimate[a]	Text Grade Levels for 68% Confidence Level	Text Grade Levels for 90% Confidence Level
$r = .2$	2.1	3.9–8.1	2.6–9.4
$r = .5$	1.9	4.1–7.9	2.9–9.1
$r = .8$	1.3	4.7–7.3	3.9–8.1

[a]Based on a standard deviation of reading ability and of readability in grade 6.0 equaling 2.2 grade levels. (SRA, 1972)

Our point is made. Theory and practice suggest that current prediction technology tells the teacher nothing to help reduce the uncertainty in selecting a text. Knowing that the text a sixth-grade student needs is equally likely to be *any* level between 2.9 and 9.1 is of no value. Functionally, this means virtually any book on the teacher's shelf is likely to be *the* one for any student reading at the sixth-grade level. Surely, teachers are able to select texts more accurately based on intuition than on current "science."

RESEARCH ON TEXT VARIABLES

Reading a textbook is similar to driving through a city. For the most part, the flow of ideas from the page into and through the reader's mind is a smooth one. When barriers are encountered, the reader must know how to work around them. Likewise, writers must know what to do to help increase the likelihood that this smooth flow of ideas is maintained. Thus, we see research on text variables as a way to forewarn authors about potential rough spots for readers and a way to help teachers prepare readers to overcome these trouble spots.

Some of these trouble spots are caused by writers who fail to use, or misuse, appropriate writing conventions. Examples of these include poorly structured discourse; choice of either too technical or too general words; abrupt changes in idea flow without signaling the reader; misleading titles and headings; causal sequences that have no effects; and pronouns with unclear referents.

We believe the most important text characteristic in comprehension and learning is *textual coherence*. The more coherent the text, the more likely it is the reader will construct a coherent cognitive model of text meaning. Textual coherence is not a unitary concept (Armbruster & Anderson, 1981; Cirilo, 1981). Texts cohere both globally and locally. *Global coherence* is achieved by text characteristics that facilitate the integration of high-level, important ideas across the entire discourse. *Local coherence* is achieved by several kinds of simple links that connect ideas together within and between sentences.

Global Coherence

Global coherence is mediated primarily by the overall structure or organization of the text. Generally, structure refers to the arrangement of ideas and the relations connecting the ideas in text. A few basic text structures appear to capture fundamental patterns of human thought. The most common structures are (1) *simple listing*—where the order of presentation of ideas is not significant; (2) *comparison/contrast*—a description of similarities and differences between two or more things; (3) *temporal sequence*—sequential relations between ideas or events described in terms of the passage of time; (4) *cause/effect*—an interaction between at least two ideas or events, one considered a cause or reason and the other an effect or result; (5) *problem/solution*—similar to the cause/effect pattern in that two factors interact, one citing a problem and the other a solution to that problem.

Another way to define text structures has been to identify somewhat more specialized organizational patterns appropriate to specific genres. For example, a generic structure for *narratives* has been defined by so-called story grammars, which specify the relations among categories of content (e.g., goals, actions, and outcomes). Another generic organizational scheme is used to describe *systems*. A description of a system (such as the circulatory system of the human body) typically includes information on the function of the system in the larger entity, the components of the system and their individual functions, and the operation of the system. Specialized structures for content-area text are just beginning to be identified (Dansereau, 1985; Lunzer, Davies, & Greene, 1980).

Perhaps the most compelling evidence that structure makes a difference in learning from text comes from research using story grammars. The consistent result of this research is that memory for stories is superior when the content is organized according to the stereotypical story grammar (e.g., Kintsch, Mandel, & Kozminsky, 1977; Mandler, 1978; Mandler & Johnson, 1977; Stein, 1976; Thorndyke, 1977). Altering the structure by displacing or deleting elements results in poorer memory for the stories and lower ratings of story comprehensibility (Thorndyke, 1977).

Other evidence for the importance of structure comes from the research of Meyer et al. using informative, "textbook-like" prose. Meyer and Freedle (1984) showed that manipulating structure while leaving everything else constant affected memory for text. Meyer, Brandt, and Bluth (1980) found that ninth graders who identified the structure of well-organized text and used this structure as the basis of their own recall could remember more from a passage than those who did not. Furthermore, ninth graders taught to identify and use the author's structure dramatically improved their memory for text (Bartlett, 1978).

Other research has shown that learning can be affected by how clearly structure is indicated in text. Information about structure is provided in two ways. One way is through "signaling." Meyer (1979) has defined signaling as information in the text that emphasizes certain ideas in the content or points out aspects of the structure. Types of signaling include (1) explicit statements of the structure, (2) previews or introductory statements, including titles, (3) summary statements, (4) pointer words and phrases such as "an important point is . . . ," and (5) textual cues such as underlining, italics, and boldface. Some evidence suggests that average students, in particular, remember more from text that contains signaling (see Meyer, 1979).

Another means of providing information about structure is through repeated, consistent use of a particular structure. Presumably, the reader learns the structure in early presentations of text and comes to expect that ideas in later presentations will be organized in the same way. Research by Thorndyke (1977) lends support to the facilitative effect of repeated structure.

Another important contributor to global coherence is *content*. One area of research indicates that learning and memory are improved when people are given information clarifying the significance of facts that might otherwise seem arbitrary (Bransford & Johnson, 1973; Bransford, Stein, Shelton, & Owings, 1980; Dooling & Mullet, 1973). Consider the following simple example from Bransford et al. (1980). College students who read sentences such as "The tall man bought the crackers, The bald man read the newspaper, The old man purchased the paint" tend to perform poorly on questions such as "Which man bought the crackers?" The students rate such sentences as comprehensible but have difficulty remembering the sentences because the relation between each type of man and the actions performed seems arbitrary. Recall improves dramatically for sentences such as "The tall man bought the crackers that were on the top shelf; The bald man read the newspaper to look for a hat sale; The funny man bought the ring that squirted water." The elaborations clarify the significance of the relation between each type of man and the action he performs.

Drawing once again on the research with story grammars, we know that information about the character's goal and events leading up to the goal has a significant effect on comprehension and memory for narratives (Kintsch & van Dijk, 1978; Rumelhart, 1977b; Thorndyke, 1977). Presumably, knowledge of the goal and the events leading up to the goal helps readers understand the significance of the character's actions and the consequences of those actions, and thus aids the reader's effort to build a coherent model of the text. Bransford (1984) has suggested that the reciprocal relationship between structure and function provides another type of significance-imparting information. For example, knowing the different functions of veins and arteries helps in understanding the significance of differences in their structure. In sum, the content an author chooses to include can influence the global coherence of the text. In particular, global coherence is greater when the author establishes a meaningful context for facts in the text.

Evaluating Structure in Textbooks.   A way to evaluate structure in textbooks, short of reading the entire text, is to look at signaling devices. In particular, titles and subtitles, introductions, and topic sentences can be particularly revealing about the relative degree of structure in the text. For example, compare these chapter outlines from two different American history textbooks.

Textbook 1   (1)
    What Were the Problems of the New Government?
      A. The Basic Problem
      B. Economic Troubles
        1. An Empty Treasury
        2. Economic Depression
        3. The Money Problem
      C. Conflicts Among the States
      D. Unfriendly Foreign Countries
      E. Calling the Constitutional Convention

Textbook 2   (2)

   Growing Cities, Growing Industries
     Early Cities
     More Cities Grow
     Industrial Growth and Immigration
       Americans All
       Labor Unions
       Jane Addams
       Americans Prosper
     Cities Today
     Industrial and Technical Progress
       Progress Through Inventions
       Technology

The chapter outline from Textbook 1 suggests a better, clearer structure than the chapter outline from Textbook 2. The Textbook 1 chapter outline has an overall structure of "simple listing"; it is easy to predict that each subtopic will probably be cast in a "cause/effect" or "problem/solution" structure. On the other hand, it is difficult to determine any logical structure for the topics from Textbook 2, other than a general "early to late" progression.

Some introductions give the reader a good overview of the content and structure of the ideas to follow:

> Do you remember that, in Unit 2, we said that part of our nation's heritage was change? A terribly important change began in 1776, with the Declaration of Independence. Before that, the people of America were colonists under the rule of England. But after that, they were citizens of an independent country. This unit will tell you about the causes of the Revolution, the war itself, and the early years of the United States.   (3)

Here's the beginning of another good introduction:

> In this chapter, we are going to look at how people in the 13 English colonies lived in the middle of the 1700's. Ways of life differed from colony to colony in 1750. Black slaves in Maryland lived differently from white merchants in Massachusetts. German-speaking farmers in Pennsylvania lived very differently from large land owners living in Virginia.
>
> Yet there were ways many people in the colonies were alike. . . .   (4)

The reader is nicely set up for a compare/contrast structure.

Now read the following chapter introduction:

> People worked hard to rebuild and unify America after the Civil War. It was time to move ahead. In 1790 the first census (sen' səs) of the United States was taken. A

census is an official count of people. Every 10 years a census is taken in the United States. In 1790 there were 4 million Americans. Most of them were living in small settlements or on farms. Today the United States has more than 220 million people. Most of these people live and work in or near cities.   (5)

The introduction itself is terribly confusing. The first two sentences lead the reader to believe that the chapter will discuss the post-Civil War years, the Reconstruction perhaps. The third sentence changes the topic *and* the time frame. The reader is left wondering what the chapter will be about, not to mention what its structure will be.

Topic sentences also alert the reader to the organization of upcoming text. The following is a good example of such a topic sentence as well as the use of markers to reinforce the indicated structure.

There were five main areas of change related to nationalism. Four of these were *domestic* changes. One involved foreign policy.

1. There was a decline in political party struggles. . . .
2. The national government gained more power through legislation. . . .
3. The national government was also strengthened by the decisions of the Supreme Court. . . .
4. The population of the United States began to move west. . . .
5. In foreign policy, the United States began to assert itself as a power in the Western Hemisphere. . . .   (6)

The global coherence of textbooks may also be evaluated by looking at the content itself: Does the author include information that clarifies the significance of facts? For example, in history textbooks, check to see whether events are explained by referring to the motivations and goals behind those events. Below is a textbook excerpt on the building of the first transcontinental railroad.

Many Americans wanted a railroad that would connect the East to the West. In 1862, Congress passed a law to build the first transcontinental rail line. The Central Pacific and Union Pacific railroad companies were formed to do the work. Find these railroads on the map on page 251.

The Central Pacific's line headed east from Sacramento, California. Workers laid track through the Sierra Nevada, which are high mountains. The workers built trestles and hauled dirt to make a level roadbed. They hunted for passes through the mountains. They blasted tunnels through solid rock. Once across the mountains, they worked in the heat of the deserts.

The Union Pacific's line headed west from Omaha, Nebraska. Its workers faced attacks by Indians who knew that the railroads would bring millions of white people to their lands. The builders also had trouble with herds of buffalo tearing up tracks. The Union Pacific hired hunters to kill the buffalo. Armed guards fought the Indians.

On both lines, the rail companies began running trains as soon as a section of track was laid. Now settlers could go west by train.

On May 10, 1869, the two lines met at Promontory, Utah. A golden spike was hammered to hold the last rail in place. A worker described what happened:

When they came to drive the last spike, Governor Stanford, president of the Central Pacific, took the hammer. The first time he struck he missed the spike and hit the rail.

What a howl went up! Irish, Chinese, Mexican, and everybody yelled with delight. "He missed it. Yee." The engineers blew the whistles and rang their bells. Then Stanford tried it again and tapped the spike. The tap was reported by telegraph in all the offices east and west. It set bells to ringing in hundreds of towns and cities. (7)

This text presents a colorful, interesting, detailed description of the event; however, the text includes nothing about the *significance* of the event: Why was the railroad built in the first place? What important changes did it precipitate?

The following excerpt does a better job of establishing the significance of building railroads by answering the question "Why were railroads needed?"

To make a profit from their land, farmers had to send their crops to market. To work their land, they needed tools from city factories. As factories grew to supply the nation's wants, the factories consumed more and more raw materials—iron, wood, and cotton. To keep the whole process going, the vast nation, spread across a continent, needed transportation. The nation was already served by its broad rivers, its many canals, and roadways. But there had to be easier, speedier ways. (8)

In summary, globally coherent text is organized so that the sequencing of ideas within the text is predictable according to some convention or standard.

Local Coherence

Local coherence functions like a linguistic mortar to connect ideas in text (Tierney & Mosenthal, 1982). It is achieved by means of cohesive ties— linguistic forms that carry meaning across phrase, clause, and sentence boundaries. Examples of common cohesive ties are *pronoun reference,* use of a pronoun to refer to a previously mentioned noun ("The doctor will be back shortly; *he's* with a patient now"); *substitution,* replacement of a word or words for a previously mentioned phrase or clause ("My pen is out of ink; I need a new *one*"); and conjunctions or connectives ("I'd give you a hand, *but* I'm busy").

A large body of research has established the importance of cohesive ties in understanding and remembering text. Repeated references that carry meaning across sentence boundaries can decrease reading time and increase recall of text as an integrated unit (de Villiers, 1974; Haviland & Clark, 1974; Kintsch, Kozminsky, Streby, McKoon, & Keenan, 1975; Manelis & Yekovich, 1976;

Miller & Kintsch, 1980). For example, Manelis and Yekovich (1976) found people can read faster and remember better sentences such as "Arnold lunged at Norman; Norman called the doctor; The doctor arrived," than the sentences "Arnold lunged; Norman called; The doctor arrived." Even though the first sentence set is longer, cohesive referential ties render it easier to learn and remember than the second sentence set.

Children prefer to read, read faster, and have better memory for sentences connected by explicit conjunctions, particularly causal connectives, than sentences in which the conjunction is left to be inferred (Katz & Brent, 1968; Marshall & Glock, 1978-1979; Pearson, 1974-1975). For example, in the study by Pearson (1974-1975), third and fourth graders were asked which of several sentences they would prefer to use in answering a "Why" question. They selected sentences like "Because John was lazy, he slept all day," over sentences such as "John was lazy; he slept all day." The children also recalled sentences with an explicit conjunction better than sentences in which the connective was left implicit. Thus, sentences with explicit conjunctions produced better comprehension and recall even though the added conjunction increased the grammatical complexity of the sentence.

More cohesive text is read faster and remembered better because it helps readers construct a coherent model or interpretation of the text. When an incohesive text makes this difficult, readers spend extra time and cognitive energy to remediate the problem. They reread for the link, search through their memories to retrieve the connection, or make an inference about a possible relationship. With this extra effort, mature readers *may* be able to form a coherent interpretation of the text. Children, however, have less chance for success. They are less likely to know that rereading text and searching memory are appropriate "fix-up" strategies (Armbruster, Echols, & Brown, 1982). Children are also less likely to be able to infer connections simply because they have less world knowledge to draw upon. Thus, local coherence in the form of strong, explicit cohesive ties is particularly important in textbooks for children.

Evaluating Local Coherence in Textbooks.   The evaluator should first check to see that relations among ideas, particularly causal relations, are stated explicitly in the text. The following paragraph is an excerpt from a sixth-grade textbook. Many of the connectives are missing and left to be inferred.

> In the evening, the light fades. Photosynthesis slows down. The amount of carbon dioxide in the air space builds up again. This buildup of carbon dioxide makes the guard cells relax. The openings are closed.   (9)

The paragraph below is a more coherent version of the same content because the relations are more explicit.

What happens to these processes in the evening? The fading light of evening causes photosynthesis to slow down. Respiration, however, does not depend on light and thus continues to produce carbon dioxide. The carbon dioxide in the air spaces builds up again, which makes the guard cells relax. The relaxing of the guard cells closes the leaf openings. Consequently, the leaf openings close in the evening as photosynthesis slows down.   (10)

The evaluator should also check for order of presentation of events in a temporal or causal sequence. Young readers can become confused if the order of events in the text does not match the order of actual occurrence. For older readers, the direction may not be so critical. However, for most purposes, it would seem that the text should remain consistent and not skip around in time.

The following is an example of a text that changes time frame. The sentences are numbered so that the commentary is easier to follow.

[1]Adult female alligators make large cone-shaped nests from mud and compost. [2]The female lays from 15 to 100 eggs with leathery shells in the nest and then covers it. [3]The heat from both the sun and the decaying compost keeps the eggs warm. [4]The eggs hatch in about nine weeks. [5]Unlike other reptiles that hatch from eggs, baby alligators make sounds while they are still in the shell. [6]The mother then bites off the nest so the baby alligators can get out. [7]When first hatched, baby alligators are about 15 to 25 cm long.   (11)

Note the many shifts in the temporal sequence. The first four sentences are fine; they present the order of events from earliest to latest. The fifth sentence reverts back to when the baby alligators were still in the shell. The time frame for the sixth sentence is when the baby alligators are sufficiently mature to leave the nest. The final sentence returns to when the baby alligators were first hatched.

Finally, the evaluator should check for clarity of references. The following excerpt illustrates a confusing use of pronoun reference—the pronoun "they." Does "they" refer to "the people from the North" or "the Bronze Age people"?

The people from the North learned from the Bronze Age people. They were skilled workers and traders. They made fine tools and jewelry from metals. They traded their beautiful cloth and pottery to peoples around the Mediterranean. They kept records of their trade on clay tablets.   (12)

In sum, the preceding section has reviewed research establishing the importance of textual coherence—structure and cohesion—in learning from text. The more coherent the text itself, the more coherent the cognitive model the reader is likely to construct. Textual coherence is particularly important for children, who may not have sufficient background knowledge to infer the content and relations absent in incoherent text. Some guidelines for assessing the coherence of textbooks were suggested.

Conclusion

Many characteristics of text have an important influence on *how much* and *what* students will learn from reading a textbook. Students understand and learn more from text that is *coherent,* that is, text that has a clear overall structure that establishes the significance of the facts presented, and tight cohesive ties binding the ideas together.

In this chapter we included many "real" textbook examples of text *not* conducive to learning in general or to the learning of important information. We cannot really estimate how widespread the situation is, because we have not systematically sampled a scientifically acceptable number of textbooks. However, our perusal of textbooks over the past 3 years has led us to conclude that during elementary school years, at least, children read many pages of poorly written text.

In hopes of getting better textbooks into the hands of teachers and students, we urge textbook adoption committees to give serious consideration to factors of *coherence* and *importance* in evaluating and selecting textbooks. These factors are not captured by readability formulas or other currently proposed objective, quantitative indices. But with a little extra effort they *can* be identified by using some of the guidelines outlined in this chapter.

TEXT EXCERPT CITATIONS

1. Schwartz, S., & O'Connor, J. R. *Exploring our nation's history (Vol. 1): The developing years.* N.Y.: Globe Book Co., 1971.
2. King, A. Y., Dennis, I., & Potter, F. *The United States and the other Americas.* New York: Macmillan, 1982.
3. Gross, H. H., Follett, D. W., Gabler, R. E., Burton, W. L., & Ahlschwede, B. F. *Exploring our world: The Americas.* Chicago: Follett, 1980, p. 173.
4. Klein, S. *Our country's history.* New York: Scholastic Book Services, 1981, p. 117.
5. King, A. Y., Dennis, I., & Potter, F. *The United States and the other Americas.* New York: Macmillan, 1982, p. 126.
6. Abramowitz, J. *American History* (5th ed.). Chicago: Follett, 1979, p. 231.
7. Berg, R. M. Scott, Foresman Social Studies (Grade 5). Glenview, IL: Scott, Foresman, 1979.
8. Boorstin, D. J., & Kelley, B. M. *A History of the United States.* Lexington, Mass.: Ginn, 1981, p. 344.
9. Bendick, J., & Gallant, R. *Elementary Science 6.* Lexington, Mass.: Ginn, 1980, p. 71.
10. Senesh, L. *The American way of life.* Chicago: Science Research Associates, 1973, p. 149.
11. Berger, C. F., Berkheimer, G. D., Lewis, L. E., Jr., & Neuberger, H. J. *Houghton Mifflin Science (6).* Boston: Houghton Mifflin, 1979, p. 55.
12. Dawson, G. S. *Our world.* Lexington, Mass.: Ginn, 1979, p. 29.

10

Reading and Writing: How Are the First Two "R's" Related?

Andee Rubin
Bolt Beranek and Newman Inc.

Jane Hansen
University of New Hampshire

People use language to make connections. As in other spheres, connections established through language are complex; sometimes superficial, sometimes profound. Just as guests bring their wine, their jokes, their good will, their intentions, and even their disguises to a party, language users bring their knowledge, their biases, their gifts, their disguises, and their goals to communication. It cannot occur without people and it depends on all the participants' contributions. Even in written text, where author and reader may never meet, communication depends on an interpersonal connection (Bruce, 1981c).

Susan is a first grader. Her behavior reflects her growing appreciation of reading and writing as ways people communicate. From the very beginning of the school year, she expected text to communicate because she wrote her own pieces (Hansen, 1983a). However, she learned that to make other authors' stories communicate, she often needed to add her own commentary. For example, Susan once read a trade book to her class. After each page, she held up the book to show the pictures. At one point a boy called out, "I like the part about chocolate frosting." Susan responded, "So do I," and then asked the class, "How many of you like chocolate frosting?"

Susan's decisions about the text and the way she read it illustrate several critical aspects of her appreciation of language. First, she chose a text that could communicate with her audience. She knew her own stories had messages, because she had written them. She knew many stories from basal readers contained so little information that the message was difficult to understand. So she chose a text with more potential and encouraged the story to grow into a true communicative event by making her own contribution to the meaning and eliciting contributions from the rest of the class.

Susan is not typical. Many children view reading and writing as piecemeal and problematic because their instruction has often created or widened distinctions between reading and writing. This chapter attempts to close this gulf by presenting recent research on relations between reading and writing.

Until recently, the dominant view of reading and writing emphasized their differences. Reading was defined as a receptive process, whereas writing was considered expressive (Hennings, 1982; Petty & Jensen, 1980). Reading was seen as a non-creative process, with meaning existing in the text itself, to be ferreted out using the author's clues. Writing, on the other hand, was seen as creative. As Shanklin (1981) puts it, this paradigm held that "reading involves a one-way transmission of meaning from graphics to readers' minds. In contrast, writing involves a one-way transmission from writers' minds to the working out of graphic displays" (p. 164). At the same time that this view prevailed, superficial similarities between reading and writing guided language arts education. In both cases, students were required to master mechanical details, e.g., decoding, punctuation, spelling, and grammar.

Recent research has uncovered more basic similarities between reading and writing, and has focused attention on the author's and reader's contributions to communication. In reading, schema theorists (e.g., Anderson, 1977; Bransford, 1979) found that the messages readers construct are heavily influenced by their own knowledge. At the same time, studies of writers have shifted the emphasis from the product of composition to the process (e.g., Emig, 1971; Flower & Hayes, 1981a; Graves, 1982; Stotsky, 1983).

The interaction of these two insights has produced a view that emphasizes the essential connectedness of reading and writing. Research advancing this perspective has suggested that reading, like writing, is composition (Petrosky, 1982); that both processes involve "transactions" between reader and text (Rosenblatt, 1978); that an awareness of the author-reader relationship is central to both reading and writing (Tierney & LaZansky, 1980); and that the writing process includes reading (Graves & Hansen, 1983). This view recognizes the central fact of reading and writing—both are communicative acts.

New technology makes possible language activities that further blur the distinctions. Microcomputer activities such as Story Maker (Rubin, 1983) and the Interactive Text Interpreter (Levin, Boruta, & Vasconcellos, 1983) allow one "composer" to construct a structured set of choices from which a partner "composer" constructs a final text. Who is the author of the finished product? The reading performed by the second "composer" is as integral to the process as the writing performed by the first.

Research also suggests that the knowledge readers and writers use when they compose fits into several categories:

- Information knowledge
- Structural knowledge
- Transactional knowledge

- Aesthetic knowledge
- Process knowledge

Because all five are critical to expertise in both reading and writing, it is possible that knowledge gained through one can facilitate the other. The following discussions include hypotheses about how instruction in reading or writing might transfer to the other.

The children cited in the following discussions are in the same first-grade classroom as Susan. They write every day and confer with their teacher and peers about their writing. As they learn to read, they have similar conferences and routinely connect writing and reading in class discussions. They explore connections between reading and writing that until recently have been largely ignored.

Information Knowledge

This category includes vocabulary, world knowledge, concepts, and general "book learning." When readers compose messages, they need both the text and information from their own memories. When writers compose messages, they begin with information and use text to convey it. Information is the key to successful reading and writing.

Writers recognize the centrality of rich information to good writing. When asked what makes a good writer, one first grader answered, "Someone who does lots of things. I don't mean in school. We all do the same things in school. I mean on the weekends" (Hansen, 1983). Another child in the class commented on his own revision process. The first draft of his story read, "Some days are pouring. Some days are REALLY pouring." He elaborated this brief description into a story of several sentences, then commented on his first draft, "That didn't have much information in it, did it?"

One connection between informational knowledge in reading and writing is that information gained in reading is one possible source of content for writing; research papers make explicit use of this connection. The possibility of using information gained in writing to facilitate reading is being investigated. Gould, Haas, and Marino (1982) demonstrated that when students wrote about a topic before reading a related text, they recalled the text better than students who wrote on topics unrelated to the text. They concluded that the writing supplied the reader with a "set for understanding."

Structural Knowledge

This category comprises knowledge of discourse structure and writing formulas such as paragraph structure, compare and contrast paragraphs, problem-solution frames (Armbruster & Anderson, 1981), story grammars (Mandler & Johnson, 1977; Meyer, 1975; Stein & Glenn, 1979), and cohesion and coherence devices (Halliday & Hasan, 1976). Writers produce texts with structure; readers use structure to construct meaning. Writers and readers learn that various genres have associated conventions. Sophisticated readers and writers understand how purposely breaking structural conventions also communicates a message.

Studies of the interaction between structural knowledge in reading and writing are relatively rare. Gordon and Braun (1983) demonstrated the transfer of structural knowledge gained through reading to writing. They taught fifth graders to discover the story grammar structure in appropriate texts. The stories these students later wrote fit story grammars more closely than those of the control group. Conversely, Taylor (1982) found that students who practiced writing in particular expository formats showed improvement in reading texts written in those structures.

Part of the reason it is difficult to assess the effects of structural knowledge is that we do not fully understand the role such knowledge plays in either reading or writing as separate processes. Several experiments have shown that structural knowledge can improve reading comprehension. Such studies have been carried out using both narrative (Gordon, 1980) and expository texts (Meyer, Brandt & Bluth, 1980; Meyer & Freedle, 1979). Case study evidence in writing indicates that knowledge of structure can initiate a qualitative change in children's compositions. For example, when Marie first wrote a piece about Christmas, it included information on attending a play, a hockey game, gifts, sledding, and a visit to her grandmother. This confused her readers until she organized her piece into several chapters. This in turn started a wave of "chapter" books in her classroom, because the other children recognized the value of chapters as a mechanism for comunicating complex subject matter.

Transactional Knowledge

This category relates primarily to the conceptualization of texts as a medium of communication between author and reader (Booth, 1961; Holland, 1975; Bruce, 1981). An appreciation of author/reader relationships leads to discussions of purpose in reading and writing. What was the author trying to achieve? Does the reader's comprehension of the text include an understanding of the author's reason for producing it?

Transactional knowledge develops early. In a literate environment, young children learn that print can fulfill different purposes, many of which are social. Harste, Burke, and Woodward (1982) found that preschool children know what type of information everyday labels and signs contain. Slightly older writers use more complex knowledge of social interactions and human emotions when they write and read. In a sixth-grade class where students use a computer to write, one girl included in her own review of a school event the following comments on her friend's review: "When the Glee-Club was singing so nice, Melinda got very jealous and asked Mrs. Elbert to be in the Glee-Club. But when Mrs. Elbert said no she wrote bad things about the Glee-Club on the computer up-stairs."

Consideration of audience also influences topic choice and revision. Children's choice of topic is governed by their conception of audience reaction ("They'll think it's funny"). They decide what to add when they revise based on their understanding of the purpose of their piece. Randy, for example, decided to add information on scurvy to his piece on Good Food because, "The kids don't know about scurvy." His comment displayed an understanding of one purpose of expository text—to impart information—as well as knowledge about his specific audience's background knowledge.

In reading, transactional knowledge leads to investigating and questioning the author's purpose and style. Green and Laff (1980) showed that kindergartners can identify authors by conventions such as rhyme and attributes of the main characters. A group of first graders in Susan's classroom demonstrated their perspective on reading and writing with their explanation of the differences between original texts and simplified versions in basal readers (Graves & Hansen, 1983). Faced with the basal's watered-down version, they hypothesized that the author had produced it first, received feedback on its lack of detail, then improved it for the final (original) version!

Graves and Hansen also have identified several phases in children's developing sense of the concept of authorship—a concept that affects both their reading and writing competence. Among their hypotheses:

• Children realize authors have options, because children do the following when they write: exercise topic choice, revise by choice, compose in different genres, and receive feedback from many people.

• Children who learn to exercise options become more assertive when they read. At first an author is distant; then an author is self; finally, the self-author questions all authors and assertive readers emerge.

Evidence from the classroom in which Graves and Hansen worked points to the tremendous effect early writing can have on children's developing sense of transaction in reading and writing. They argue that when children write, they become aware of author/reader relationships and use that knowledge in the reading arena.

Aesthetic Knowledge

Knowledge of aesthetic devices constitutes another strong link between reading and writing. A certain alliterative style, the way a single interjection focuses an entire paragraph, or the relative length and stress patterns of consecutive words all echo in readers' and writers' ears and affect their choices.

Danny had just read the trade book "More Spaghetti, I Say" in which the following segment is frequently repeated:

I love it,
I love it,
I love it,
I do!

He had also heard Langston Hughes' "April Rain Song," which ends, "I love the rain." And he had heard Eve Merriam's poem "Weather," which includes:

. . . flick a flack fleck
Freckling the window pane . . .
A puddle a jump puddle splosh
A juddle a pump a luddle a dump a
puddmuddle jump in and slide!

This fun language prompted Danny to write the following piece in April of first grade:

When rain comes down it dances in the puddles and splashes
in the air. pssss
It splashes on the window. Goes pat, pat, pat, and I catch
it in my mouth.
When I walk in the puddles I try to splash it.
When I come home I change my clothessss
I love it.
I love it.
I love it.
I love the rain.

Aesthetic knowledge also has to do with the affective side of communication. Brewer and Lichtenstein (1981) studied adult readers' concept of story by presenting different versions of the same narrative in which suspense and surprise were manipulated. They discovered a high correlation between readers' sense that the narrative was a story and the amount of suspense it contained. In this case, a reaction that might be considered outside the cognitive domain influenced readers' perceptions of text.

The affective domain also includes revelations about self. Children who choose their own topics become emotionally involved, often writing personal narratives about their families; for example, "My nana has a hump on her back. That's why I love her." Children who have experienced this involvement assume other authors have important messages to share. When they find a text that doesn't "grab" them, either they quit reading, elaborate it so that it DOES involve them, or start to question the author's purpose and technique.

Process Knowledge

The four previous knowledge categories—informational, structural, transactional, and aesthetic—are all necessary components of reading and writing, but are not sufficient by themselves. Also needed is knowledge about the process by which they are combined. The writing process—choosing a topic, brainstorming, drafting, organizing ideas, revising, editing and publishing— gives us a metaphor for describing and examining reading. Seeing the parallels between the two may emphasize the constructive nature of reading comprehension.

For example, awareness of the importance of revision in writing may facilitate reading. Writers who are aware of their writing processes can make conscious decisions about revising. Similarly, readers who are aware of their reading processes can make conscious decisions about strategies to use in rereading an unsatisfactory message. If more children were aware at an earlier age of their reading and writing processes, we probably would hear fewer graduate students echo, "It wasn't until college that I realized there was something to do other than 'read harder' when I didn't understand a text."

INSTRUCTIONAL IMPLICATIONS

If writing and reading facilitate one another, as the accumulating evidence suggests, then educational contexts that take advantage of the communicative nature of both can be created. We describe two such environments in which reading and writing are taught as related processes.

QUILL (Rubin & Bruce, 1983), a set of microcomputer-based writing activities for upper elementary children, includes a child-oriented text editor, a data base management system, an electronic mail system, and a program to help students plan and organize their thoughts. Although officially designed to teach writing, QUILL stimulates a large amount of reading by creating an environment in which children's writing is naturally read by their peers. The electronic mail system encourages students to write messages to other students in the class and to students in distant schools.

The classroom activities QUILL facilitates—such as a class newspaper— foster conections between reading and writing by inducing students to communicate for valid purposes. When provided with an electronic mail system, one group of fourth graders wrote each other riddles, invited each other to parties and even commented on each other's writing. Without being told, these students created a situation not present in many classrooms—the full cycle of author/reader feedback critical to communication. In one sixth-grade class the presence of the computer changed the amount of each other's writing students read. Students tended to "mill around" the computer, reading partially finished pieces over the author's shoulder, and sometimes included comments on friends' work in their own texts.

A second rich educational context is the first-grade classroom described throughout this chapter. From observing this class, the researchers Blackburn, Graves, and Hansen have generated four implications for instruction:

1. Children must compose messages frequently. The children began in September by inventing stories in both reading and writing. They could write and read early because when they wrote they used invented spelling and when they read they invented stories loosely based on the books in front of them.

2. Children must choose their topics and books because they then feel committed to the effort. In writing they will pursue a piece until it is clear. In reading they will stay with a piece because they want the satisfaction of knowing they can read it themselves. It is when they stay with a piece that breakthroughs occur.

3. Children's composition attempts in both reading and writing must be accepted by their peers and teacher. If we expect children to write, we must provide an environment that supports risk-taking. Children's earliest attempts at reading must be supported so they will persist.

4. Children must share books and their own writing with peers and teacher. Whenever students realize their friends do not understand their message, the decision about rereading or revision must be their own.

If we want students to continue writing and reading then control of these processes must remain in their hands. They must have options and they must make their own decisions about these options. If the message is worth communicating, they will choose to remain with it until it is clear. One sixth-grader using QUILL learned only recently that he had control over his own writing. The researcher noticed Ken consistently copying into his piece words from planning questions the computer offered. The researcher commented, "You don't have to use those words." Ken responded, "Do you mean I can use my own words?" "Yes." "Do you mean words like 'tuff'?" "Yes."

ACKNOWLEDGMENT

We would like to thank Chip Bruce, Allan Collins, Donald Graves, Vicki Jacobs, Sarah Michaels, Trika Smith-Burke, and Rob Tierney for their substantial contributions to the content and style of this paper. Special thanks to Tom Hansen for saving the manuscript from a tired computer. We also thank Cindy Hunt and Cheryl Przekwas for their help in preparing the manuscript.

11 Teaching Reading and Writing with Personal Computers

Allan Collins
Bolt Beranek and Newman Inc.

The invention of the printing press created a revolution in education: the literacy revolution. Before the printing of books, almost no one learned to read and write. Today, in literate societies practically everyone learns to read and write. The invention of the computer will have equally profound effects on education, though the extent of its impact cannot yet be gauged.

Computers already are at work in the nation's schools. They have begun to change the teaching of math and science (Abelson & diSessa, 1981; Bork, 1981; Dugdale & Kibbee, 1975; Papert, 1980), and will soon change the teaching of reading and writing.

To glimpse what the future will look like, let us describe three visions of personal computers in teaching reading and writing.

Vision 1. A preschool child has a hand-held computer about the size of Speak and Spell with a keyboard and a graphics screen—what I will call "Speakie" and what Alan Kay (1977) has called Dynabook. Children can play many different letter and word games with Speakie, learning which letters go with what sounds. Speakie can even read Dr. Seuss books aloud, highlighting each word it says and illustrating the book with color animation. Every child can thus have a grownup to read to him or her at command. The technology to build Speakie is essentially here.

Vision 2. In a third-grade classroom, the children do their language assignments on personal computers. There is a publication system that allows them to print books, newspapers, and letters. There is a message system that allows them to send messages and stories to third graders in Alaska. There is an information storage and retrieval system, accessible to all third graders in

171

the country, that allows them to create a library of knowledge about the things that children are interested in. There are reading and writing games that children find both challenging and fun. And there are kits (Goldberg & Robson, 1980) that allow them to modify existing games or create new ones for other kids to play. This vision is being designed now (Collins, Bruce, & Rubin, 1982; Levin, Boruta, & Vasconcellos, 1983; Rubin, 1983).

Vision 3.   For high school students, the personal computer is a resource in their school, library, or home to help them prepare papers for their classes. The computer has text-handling programs designed to help inexperienced writers, a coach that makes suggestions about revisions, and a text editor that makes it possible to change things easily. Source materials are available directly on the computer from anywhere in the country. There is a graphics editor for preparing tables and figures to go with the text. Parts of this vision are happening now (Goldberg & Robson, 1980; MacDonald, Frase, Gingrich, & Keenan, 1982).

Computers offer three new capabilities with significance for teaching reading and writing. They allow us to create *communication environments* where children read and write because they wish to communicate with other children in different places and times. As such, reading and writing function for children in the same way they do for adults. Second, we can create *activity environments* where children play games or solve problems that require reading and writing, providing highly motivating practice opportunities. Third, computers provide *tools* to make the reading and writing tasks students perform easier and more rewarding. We examine some developments in educational technology in terms of these new capabilities.

TEACHING READING

The programs being developed to teach reading may be grouped in three categories: (1) those directed toward decoding, (2) those directed toward reading comprehension, and (3) texts that interact with readers to provide various kinds of help.

Decoding

Frederiksen, Warren, Gillotte, and Weaver (1982) have been investigating skills that differentiate good from poor readers. They have found three critical skills:

- Speed in identifying letter groups, such as PLE, CL, GEN
- Speed in pronouncing pseudo-words, such as BRENCH, DRAP, SLENG
- Ability to predict words from context, as in "The stream flowed through the _____."

Because of the need for automaticity in these skills (see Beck, this volume; Weaver et al., 1982), they have designed arcade-like games to provide practice. The games resemble Space Invaders, because the player feels that if he had just been a little bit faster or had done something different, he would have had a better score.

One of their games, *Speed,* focuses on identifying letter groups. The player must decide whether a target-letter cluster (e.g., PLE) occurs within stimulus words appearing on the screen one at a time in rapid succession (e.g., APPLE, PLATE). Students begin at a base speed (e.g., 80 words per minute). With each correct response, the speed accelerates slightly, and registers on a speedometer at the bottom of the screen. For each run there is a target speed (e.g., 126 words per minute). An incorrect response activates a light, and the speed is reduced. But, with each correct response, the student turns off one light. If five lights appear, the student crashes and the run ends.

Another game, *Racer,* teaches automaticity in decoding whole words. The game requires pronouncing words as quickly and accurately as possible. Twenty words are presented in each race. The speed of response controls how fast the student moves in a race shown on the screen, with the computer as opponent. Because the computer cannot judge whether the student has pronounced the words correctly, there is a second phase called *Soundtrap.* In this game, the student hears eight pairs of similar words (e.g., moose–mouse) and decides which word in the pair actually was presented during the race. The student's final score is based on a combination of speed during the race and accuracy in *Soundtrap.*

The third game, *Ski Jump,* requires word predictions based on context. Students read a sentence with a word missing. A target word is then flashed on the screen, and students must decide whether it fits. The goal of the game is to recognize and judge the word at the shortest exposure possible.

Beck has taken another approach to teaching decoding skills. Her game, Build-a-Word, emphasizes skills in blending word parts. The touch-sensitive screen has two columns of word parts. In the left-hand column there might be C, CL, and CH. In the right-hand column there might be OCK, ED, IP, AP, OG. Children point to the combinations they think might make a word (e.g., CLOCK, CHAP). The child tries to match as many pairs as possible in a given amount of time.

The speech capabilities in "Speak and Read" and "Speak and Spell" by Texas Instruments suggest other reading games. Speeded games where children choose between similar words displayed on a screen, when one is spoken, would teach sound-to-letter correspondences. Simple word games such as Boggle, Hangman, or Jotto could be built around small sets of letters like *A, B, D, L,* and *M,* to emphasize blending skills. In a reading detective game, children would watch a text while a computerized voice reads the text aloud, their task being to catch reading errors made by the computer, by pointing to the misspoken or omitted word. In short, there are many potential games to teach children to read, and preschoolers exposed to them will probably arrive at school reading on their own.

Reading Comprehension

Rubin (1980b, 1983; Zacchei, 1982) has developed two reading activities, *Story Maker* and *Textman*, to teach young children about higher level aspects of texts, including the structure of genres and the use of themes and rhetorical devices.

In *Story Maker,* the child constructs a story by selecting a sequence of episodes. The child reads the initial episode, then chooses the next episode from several options. The choices affect the immediate story and its subsequent options. To construct a story in which the main character succeeds at a particular task, the child must select the proper episodes along the way—or the protagonist may end up totally botching the job. *Story Maker* helps motivate children to evaluate their choice of episodes by providing high-level constraints:

- "Try to construct a story in which the main character gets his enemies to like him."
- "Try to construct a story that uses suspense."
- "Try to construct a story that illustrates the theme that it is important to take risks in order to succeed."

Rubin (1980b) sees a natural sequence in using *Story Maker*. Children begin by tracing different story paths freely, move to more goal-oriented tasks, and then construct their own stories for others to read. Thus, *Story Maker* turns from a reading activity into a writing activity.

In *Textman,* a variation on Hangman, players select sentences that come from a particular kind of text (e.g., a conversation between Alice-in-Wonderland and the Cheshire cat or a thank-you letter from a girl to her grandmother). The author, intended audience, and purpose of the selection may be specified, as well as some context. The player chooses the sentences that comprise the text from a list and puts them in proper order. The activity is designed to teach children the constraints of different genres and intersentential connections in paragraphs.

Schnitz has developed a system, IRIS, to teach reading comprehension in grades 3 to 8. IRIS is a set of activities that stress different aspects of reading comprehension:

- *Making inferences.* Children read a short passage and then choose which of several inferences can be made. Having made their choice, they must point to the words in the text that best justify their answer. After students make their choices, the system lists both the students' words and the computer-preferred words, and gives the reason for its answer to the inference question.

• *Recognizing inappropriate sentences.* IRIS has students edit a fictional newspaper such as the *Chicago Fun Times* or the *Gettysburg Address*. They read articles to determine which sentences are inappropriate. Sentences might be inappropriate because they are irrelevant or in a different style. When the student decides to delete a particular line, IRIS explains why the line should be deleted or retained. If the student misses any lines that should be deleted, IRIS points them out.

• *Analyzing arguments.* IRIS also teaches students the structure of arguments. It displays the first paragraph of an argument and asks students to identify what position the writer is arguing (again using a multiple-choice format). IRIS then displays the next paragraph and asks if the author makes the points needed to support the argument. This pattern of inquiry continues for all the paragraphs in the argument.

• *Understanding graphs and charts.* The texts in IRIS include graphs and charts. The text first explains the type of information given in the chart. The student then must choose from among four choices what the chart will show. IRIS gives the student feedback and displays the chart. At this point various inferential questions are posed that require reading the chart to find the answer.

IRIS incorporates much of the recent research on reading comprehension described in this volume, such as how skilled readers make inferences based on their prior knowledge (Wilson & Anderson, this volume) and how the structure of different genres guides understanding(Anderson & Armbruster, this volume; Armbruster & Anderson, 1980). The computer makes it possible to continuously monitor how well the student is understanding and to redirect him to easier reading levels when necessary.

Interactive Texts

Weyer (1982) has developed the first dynamic social studies textbook. Its central element is a browser for finding information about particular topics or questions. The browser provides a table of contents and a subject index, parts of which appear on the screen simultaneous with the text. When the reader selects a topic, the text automatically moves to that section, and the headings for the table of contents reset themselves around the piece of text shown. Weyer sees dynamic books being used to locate information without reading the entire text.

Another kind of interactive text developed by McConkie allows readers who cannot recognize a word in the text to touch the word on the screen and the system says the word and underlines it. So far, it has been used with semi-literate adults to improve their sight vocabulary by reading texts of interest to them. The same technique should work with young children who have a small sight vocabulary.

Interactive books may change the nature of reading to be more like conversation (Rubin, 1980a). For example, an interactive book can ask questions to check readers' understanding (Anderson & Biddle, 1975). If readers do not understand, the book might explain things in simpler terms. In fact, any text could be written at several levels of difficulty or detail. Based on the reader's ability to answer different questions, the computer could present the text best geared to the readers' prior knowledge. This gauging of the student's sophistication is what teachers do in conversation (Collins, Warnock, & Passafiume, 1975).

TEACHING WRITING

The introduction of personal computers into the school may have even more profound effects upon the teaching of writing. Text editors are already becoming widespread in schools, and they appear to ease the problems some children have in writing. Text editors for children can incorporate a variety of aids and coaches. Programs are being developed that allow students to explore how sentence syntax can be manipulated. Moreover, computers will foster a new form of writing: writing to create games and activities for other children to play.

Text Editors

Levin has provided third- and fourth-grade students with a text editor called the Writer's Assistant (Levin et al., 1983). Students see the text on a display screen as they type it, which makes it easy for them to make changes. By simply pressing a few keys the text editor automatically moves text, making room for additions and removing extra space caused by deletions. In response to the question: "How is writing with the computer different from writing with pencil and paper?" fourth graders have responded, "Because it's funner and easier then writing with pencil and paper. Also it does not hurt your hand," and "You can write faster and better. You also don't need to erase" (Levin et al., 1983).

Daiute (1982) has studied the use of text editors across the country. She has identified several reasons why writing on computers benefits children:

● *Less concern about making mistakes.*   When they write by hand, many children crumple up the paper every time they make a mistake. On the computer mistakes can be fixed easily, so the consequences are less devastating.

- *Texts look better.*   Children hate messy pages. The computer print increases pride in their work. As one 10-year-old honestly noted, "The computer makes my writing look better than it is." This increases motivation to write.
- *Fewer motor-control problems.*   Some kids have great difficulty with handwriting. The motor control needed to hit keys is much simpler to master, although learning the letter-finger correspondences may take some time.
- *Students produce longer papers.*   Teachers find that students produce longer texts on the computer. Research shows that the more children write, the better they learn to write.
- *Students revise more.*   Because text editors make revision easier, students tend to rewrite and experiment more. This helps them discover their awkward sentences and disorganized prose. Daiute even argues that it fosters a greater range of choice and comparison, helping students focus more on what they want to say.

Fales (personal communication, 1981) found that children working with a text editor paid more attention to low-level editing skills such as punctuation, capitalization, and spelling, and made greater use of the dictionary. This was especially striking among children with spelling difficulties. She also found improved ability to notice errors. The text editor makes errors more apparent, so children pay more attention to them. Additionally, students who benefit most were those who had problems with neatness and spelling, or who "block" when they write on paper. Unlike most educational innovations, it is not the most gifted children who benefit most; rather it is the ones who have the most difficulty in learning to write.

Writing Aids and Coaches

MacDonald et al. (1982) have developed the Writer's Workbench, a system that advises writers on how to edit their prose. Features include proof-reading advice; a spelling checker that lists all the words it does not recognize; a checker for some, but not all, errors; a detector for split infinitives and words that are repeated by mistake; and a Diction program that looks for wordy phrases. It also can perform stylistic analyses. It can compute readability levels by several indexes, the average length of words and sentences, and the proportions of simple and complex sentences. Additionally, it can count the frequency of passive sentences, the noun forms of verbs, and the use of phrases such as "there are" or "it is." Writer's Workbench will even compare the text to well-written texts, and give general advice on how to improve the text.

Writer's Workbench is one of the first computerized coaches that can check writing and make useful suggestions. It will not find every error, and it will sometimes make bad suggestions. Therefore, writers cannot follow its advice blindly. Instead, they must decide whether to use suggestions it makes. In short, it forces the individual to think about writing style and editing.

Coaches can prompt writers when they are getting started. Levin et al. (1983) provided a variety of prompts and models for children to use in composing. For example, in one case they provided a basic story structure, requiring only that children fill in the blanks in "mad-lib" style:

ONCE A ##### WAS ##### IN A #####.

HE TRIED TO GET ##### THROUGH THE #####.

HE ##### WITH ##### AND #####, BUT HE #####.

One child filled in these blanks to produce the following little "story":

ONCE A FROG WAS IN A POND. HE WANTED TO SEE THE WORLD. HE TRIED TO GET THROUGH THE CAGE. HE TRIED WITH ALL HIS MIGHT, BUT HE CHOULDN'T.

This writing environment, unlike paper and pencil worksheets, allows children easily to go beyond the support provided.

Levin (1982a) is experimenting with still other kinds of prompts in a system he calls Interactive Text Interpreter. He may provide the beginning of a story and allow the students to provide their own conclusions. For poetry Levin provides the set of constraints the child must meet, together with suggestions on how to fill them and a model of how to do it. For example, he developed prompts for some of the poetry formats (such as the "With a friend") that Kenneth Koch (1970) describes in his book, *Wishes, Lies and Dreams.*

Another level of prompts, called the Planner, has been developed for the QUILL project by Bruce and Rubin (see section on Reading and Writing Environments). The Planner prompts students in planning the structure of the piece they are writing. For example, in a movie review, it might prompt the writer to name the movie and some of its actors and actresses, describe what type of movie it is (comedy, western, mystery, etc.), and then indicate whether they liked the movie or not, and the reasons for that opinion.

Scardamalia and Bereiter (1981, 1983) have studied extensively the writing difficulties children experience and devised methods to improve their writing. *Procedural facilitation* has been effective in helping children develop ideas in writing opinion essays. This technique prompts students with such leads as, "A good point on the other side of the argument is . . . ," or "I need some facts to support my argument so. . . ." Based on their experimental success, a version has been adapted for a microcomputer and is being tried with sixth-grade students. These same kinds of prompts could be useful in helping students revise essays, since they force students to reflect on their arguments.

The kinds of writing coaches described here provide help in planning before writing, give advice as writing progresses, and suggest how to evaluate and revise a completed draft. Novice writers are particularly weak in planning and revising (Flower & Hayes, 1980; Scardamalia & Bereiter, 1983), and writing coaches have the potential to improve significantly their writing skills.

Syntactic Manipulation Activities

Bates, Beinashowitz, Ingria, and Wilson (1981) have developed *Iliad,* a program that can generate and transform sentences according to syntactic rules of transformational grammar (Chomsky, 1957). For example, ''Bill ate the cake'' can be transformed into variations such as:

Did Bill eat the cake?
It was eaten by Bill.
Bill should eat the cake.
Who ate the cake?

With this capability, activities can be designed to develop children's ability to express their ideas in a variety of forms and to revise texts by transforming sentences appropriately. This ability is crucial to good writing. *Iliad* provides basic practice in these skills.

Sharples (1980) developed two syntactic manipulation programs, along with a set of activities used to teach writing to fifth-grade children. *Gram* generates text on the basis of a context-free grammar. Children use the program to explore sentence structure. They begin by typing sentence patterns such as ''The noun verb with a adjective noun'' and the program generates a sentence by replacing each part of speech by an appropriate word chosen at random from its vocabulary (for example, ''The mouse danced with a huge bicycle''). The children then add further examples of each part of speech or create their own rewrite rules to generate a phrase, a sentence, or a poem.

Gram becomes a poetry generator by specifying that a poem can be rewritten as a title and a body. The title can be any noun phrase. The body can be any number of lines. There are many different possible definitions for a line (e.g., noun phrase + intransitive verb phrase + preposition + noun phrase). A noun phrase in turn can be, among other things, a plural noun, and a plural noun might be ''lilies'' or ''frogs.'' The poetry generator makes each of these choices randomly, producing a poem that is essentially meaningless, but within the constraints of the grammar. By manipulating the grammar, students see how different constraints produce different kinds of poems.

Sharples also developed *Walter,* a text processor that allows students to create stories and then modify them by writing transformations, like those in *Iliad.* These are written as pattern-action rules: If a piece of text matches the pattern on the left side of the rule, that part of the text is replaced by the right-hand side of the rule. For example, the rule "noun1 1 noun2→ noun2 1 noun1" swaps the first two nouns in a sentence (the 1 between noun1 and noun2 allows for any number of words to go in between). *Walter* was used in an activity to encourage children to produce unusual descriptions by using as many adjectives as they could that the computer did not know. The computer replaced all the adjectives it knew by a star. The appeal of this kind of activity for children is the opportunity to outwit the computer.

Programs like *Iliad, Gram,* and *Walter* allow students to explore how syntactic manipulations affect text. This enables them to think about language in a new light, as a thing in itself that can be transformed in different ways to achieve different stylistic effects.

Activity Kits

One of the most intriguing ideas for teaching writing is to provide children with kits (Collins, Bruce, & Rubin, 1982; Goldberg & Robson, 1980) to create games and activities for other children. The fact that the product is a game or text for other children provides strong motivation for producing these texts.

One example of a kit is Rubin's *Story Maker Maker* (Rubin, 1980b), based on *Story Maker* described earlier. To create a *Story Maker* using *Story Maker Maker,* students write each episode. They specify the starting episode, the set of ending episodes, and the links from each episode to its possible successors. They can also specify goals for the kids playing their *Story Maker* (e.g., Construct a story where the good guys outwit the bad guy). Constructing a *Story Maker* forces children to think about the different ways stories can unfold.

Sharples (1980) provided fifth-grade children with a kit to create fantasy games. The game involves a protagonist who wanders through a large series of caves, reading descriptions of each cave and any characters in it, and taking actions to overcome problems that arise (e.g., killing the dragon that attacks him). The general goal is to find hidden treasures and to escape with them. These games can be endlessly fascinating to people who like to solve puzzles.

In creating a fantasy game, students must write a description for each room and character. The student specifies the possible actions and their effects. Starting and ending places also must be specified. Constructing fantasy games provides practice in descriptive writing.

The kit provides facilities for creating such games, so the child does not have to program the game. He or she only has to specify the texts and the connections from cave to cave or episode to episode. Creating such activities is challenging because it forces children to write under unusual constraints. They are highly motivated to do so, because they are creating a real product that is interesting to other children.

READING AND WRITING ENVIRONMENTS

Computers can create environments where children communicate with each other through written language. Such communication occurs naturally in the adult world via newspapers, letters, and books. But in the classroom, written communication is directed from adults to children (e.g., textbooks, the *Weekly Reader*) or from children to adults (stories or papers written for the teacher to read). Some teachers overcome this by introducing class newspapers or books, but it is hard work for them to do so. The wonderful thing about the computer is that it creates child-to-child communication environments natural to the children and easy on the teachers.

Computer-generated environments foster the teaching of reading and writing as parts of the same whole (see Rubin & Hansen, this volume). Children write to communicate ideas they care about. If other children cannot make sense out of the message, they either complain or ignore the writer. In either case, the writer gets the message: It is important to be interesting, clear, persuasive, and succinct. The computer promises to bring reading and writing education back together again.

We examine some of these environments under the headings: publication systems, message systems, information retrieval systems, and automated dictionaries.

Publication Systems

A publication system (Collins et al., 1982) enables students to create texts in different formats and with different page layouts. Students simply select the format, and queries from the system prompt the input of the various items. For newspapers, it sets up columns, headlines and bylines, a masthead for the editorial board, an index to sections, and the front page layout. For letters, the system sets up the date, salutation, body, and closing. For books, the system can set up chapters and headings, table of contents, title page and dedication, a forward, index, acknowledgments, and a description of the author.

Third/fourth graders in Oceanside used a publication system in Levin's Writer's Assistant to produce several class newspapers (Levin et al., 1983). The students were encouraged to produce different kinds of articles, including class news items, book reviews, poems, stories, sports reports, and notices. Each article had a headline and byline, and was written by groups or individuals. Models of each kind of text were available for reference.

Students also can use the publishing system to produce different kinds of letters. The system provides models of different "genres" of letters, e.g., the invitation, the request letter, the thank-you letter. Students can be encouraged to write and mail at least one letter in each genre.

Within a publication system books also can be produced by an individual or group of students. Where a graphics program or tablet is available, illustrations are possible. When the book is completed, multiple copies can be made for family and friends.

Teachers have known for years that newspapers, letters, and books are effective ways to motivate students to write in a variety of genres. But the computer adds another dimension: Children see their names and texts nicely laid out in print. They can produce as many copies as they like for parents and friends. In time, children's newspapers even may become a real communication medium for elementary schools.

Message Systems

Message systems provide a variety of capabilities for reading and sending messages. Messages can be sent in multiple copies by defining a group of people (e.g., Book Lovers) who are to receive a message, or by listing all the people who are to receive the message. When messages are received, students are notified the next time they use the computer. Then they can list the topics and sources for all their messages to see which ones they want to read. Once they have read the message, they can keep it, throw it away, or send it on to someone else.

An interschool message system makes possible a variety of activities where writing for different purposes and in different genres occurs naturally (Collins et al., 1982; Levin, 1982b). Levin set up a message system to enable school children in California to communicate with children in a rural school district in Alaska. He also plans to develop interschool clubs. Children interested in dinosaurs might form a Dinosaur Club to tell each other about different dinosaurs and their characteristics. Children who like to read might join a book club to share information and opinions. Clubs foster explanatory and descriptive writing. Because their audience is remote, club members must make themselves understood in writing.

Another activity made possible by the message system is Confidential Chat (Collins et al., 1982), a computerized variation of the personal problem-solving section that appears in some newspapers. Students can present problems, (e.g., "Our classroom is too noisy to be able to study" or "My mother won't let me go out after dinner") and anyone can offer solutions. All messages are sent under code names. The value of Confidential Chat is its ability to encourage children to write problem descriptions and provide possible solutions in writing.

Collins, Bruce, and Rubin have developed Ice Cream Price Wars, a reading and writing game. Designed around the message system developed for the QUILL project (Collins et al., 1982), the game is an extension of the Lemonade Stand game developed by the Minnesota Educational Computer Consortium. In the simulation, groups of students run ice cream stands. Each week the groups must decide how much to produce, what price to charge, and how much and what kind of advertising to have. Sales depend on the price relative to the other stands. A random element is added by changes in the weather: When it is hot and sunny, many more cones are sold than when it is cold and rainy. The discussion within groups and between groups is by typed messages. The goal is to argue persuasively for the best strategy. Ice Cream Price Wars is designed to teach persuasive writing, both within your group and in negotiating with other groups.

Message systems are becoming widespread in our society, carrying electronic mail between and within businesses and universities. In learning to use a message system, children will be preparing for a society where they will be commonplace. More important, when message systems connect different schools, they create an environment where written language is the only means to communicate. They provide a natural way to make reading and writing as functional for children as they are for adults.

Information Retrieval Systems

As part of the QUILL project, Bruce and Rubin (Bruce & Rubin, 1984; Collins et al., 1982; Rubin, 1983; Rubin & Bruce, in press) have developed the *Library,* an information storage and retrieval system for elementary school children. The *Library* is a general purpose system that lets students store and retrieve information under different descriptors. For example, fourth graders in Brookline, Massachusetts, used the *Library* to create a file of game reviews.

Bruce and Rubin plan to have elementary school children create the first Kids' Computerized Library using this system. Working in groups of two or three, students would produce entries on different topics of particular interest to them (such as how to make chocolate chip cookies), develop different descriptors for their material, and fit them into a general indexing scheme provided in the program. Ideally, the computerized Library produced by students would be available to their peers all over the country via a message system.

Since information retrieval systems of this kind will become common in our society as computers enter homes and libraries, these activities give children experience in finding and using information stored in such systems. But the *Library* can also perform other functions: (1) It provides easy access to information useful in writing for different classes; (2) it is a communication environment, where meaningful reading and writing occur among peers; and (3) it is a record keeper that maintains a portfolio of students' work.

An Automated Dictionary and Thesaurus

Miller (1979) has been exploring the possibilities of an automated dictionary and thesaurus for children. As an online aid in reading and writing, it would be easier to use and would offer new capabilities not possible with a printed dictionary or thesaurus. For example, if readers do not understand a word, an online dictionary allows them to point to the word to find the definition.

In writing, when unsure of the spelling of a particular word, you can type in the parts you are sure of (e.g., th-gh) as in Writer's Workbench, or your best guess (e.g., thogh) as in Writer's Assistant. In either case the system suggests different possibilities to choose from. If you are not sure of the meaning or use, you could then ask for the word's definition. If you are not sure of pronunciation, the system can say the word for you. With an automated thesaurus, you would then ask for words that are similar in meaning to see if you like any of them better. Their definitions also would be available. Such a system would help find the best word in a given context.

Lawler and Papert (1982) have developed the automated dictionary idea to meet the needs of pre-readers. They plan to tie the computer to a video disc with a picture dictionary for preschoolers to explore word-picture correspondences. Action terms might be represented by motion sequences. They envision these uses:

- *Browsing.*   The children could type in letters (e.g., DUK), and the entry with the closest match in letters would be shown (e.g., a duck). They could move back or forth alphabetically by pushing an arrow. Keying a single letter would start at the set of entries under that letter (e.g., *R* might put them at the entry for rabbit).
- *Look up.*   The children would be able to scan quickly through entries to find what they want and stop there. Entries might be grouped by conceptual categories as well as letters, so that children could look more slowly through animals or human actions for an entry.
- *Labeling.*   Children could make up their own labels for entries, so they can later retrieve them by the names they make up. Children would begin to learn how to create labels they could remember later, and how to use modifiers to differentiate similar entries.

Automated dictionaries of the kind described would be powerful tools in both reading and writing. But they will have to be tailored to people of all different ages. In the long run, they will be integrated and used with many different kinds of systems in ways never anticipated for printed dictionaries.

CRITICAL ISSUES FOR FUTURE RESEARCH

We cannot count on publishers or computer manufacturers to develop educationally effective software. Development of good programs will have to occur at universities and research centers. This will require research funding from the federal government, directed to three critical areas.

Development of Educational Programs and Activities

The most critical need is simply for development of software. What I have described is promising, but covers only a small proportion of the curriculum in schools. In the reading area there is need to include vocabulary and texts that cover the whole span of instruction. In writing, coaches and activities are needed that address every age level from first grade to college. Research has made a good start on providing programs and environments where reading and writing can take place. What is now needed are supporting activities and materials on the scale of those now produced for teaching reading and writing in the textbook publishing industry.

Evaluating the Educational Effectiveness of Activities

A critical issue regarding programs that have been developed is their educational effectiveness. Sometimes programs that appear educationally sound can be counterproductive. This problem pervades the development of educational materials, and is exacerbated by the many arbitrary decisions that go into designing a program, any one of which might lead to unintended side effects.

Such a side effect occurred in one version of Darts (Dugdale & Kibbee, 1975) developed by John Seely Brown (personal communication). In Darts, students aim at balloons arranged on a number line by typing fractions that specify points on the number line. The line is unmarked except for the numbers at the end points and any points where darts are thrown. In the version Brown developed, children learned they could control the darts by increasing the numerator to aim the dart higher on the number line and increasing the denominator to aim the dart lower. This treats a fraction as two separate variables rather than as a single unit—entirely the wrong concept. Because of this, students' understanding of fractions failed to improve, despite many hours of playing Darts.

Unintended side effects may occur with any of the activities and environments described above. For example, suppose we design a game to teach automaticity in reading words. It might turn out that students who are most successful at the game pay no attention to the meaning of the word—doing so slows them down. The educational question then is whether the benefit of the automaticity in recognizing words is offset by some sort of loss in reading comprehension. As another example, it may be that if we provide spelling correctors for students in writing, they will come to expect them to correct their spelling errors. We don't know whether these are real problems, but they illustrate the general issue. It is important to measure the effects of any activities that are developed in terms of the skills we are trying to teach.

Integrated Teaching and Testing Environments

With the introduction of computers in the classroom, a new kind of interaction between teaching and testing becomes possible (Tyler & White, 1979). Instead of tests that interrupt learning, tests could become measures of students' progress in daily reading and writing activities. The computer can unobtrusively monitor students' performance, collecting measures of each student's progress. It can also guide the selection of tasks as problems are detected (Brown & Burton, 1979). A student's successes, which can be automatically preserved in a computer "library" (Dugdale & Kibbee, 1975), become the student's portfolio. Consider the kinds of automatic observations that are possible for some of the reading and writing activities described above:

- *Interactive texts.* If students read stories and texts in an interactive mode, the computer can keep track of words or sentences the students need help with, or questions the students cannot answer. As students progress, the computer measures the vocabulary level of the words or the reading level of the sentences not understood. It can track the difficulty of inferences in questions put to students, and evaluate students' progress in terms of their answers. Reading texts can be selected automatically for students to challenge but not to overtax them. Records of students' progress and accomplishments can be printed automatically for teachers, administrators, and parents.
- *Text Editors and Writing Aids.* As students produce texts throughout their school years, it is possible to track their progress in several ways. The computer can track length of sentences, sophistication of the vocabulary used, and use of empty phrases and passive sentences. With the text editor, it is also possible to see if students progress from making minor edits, such as spelling and punctuation changes, to more major edits, like revising whole sentences and paragraphs or moving parts of the text around (Levin et al., 1983).

What we can track in reading and writing are only indicators of the progress the student is making. It is impossible to evaluate with a computer the students' depth of reading comprehension or the interest, ideas, and expressiveness in their writing. But the indicators can be helpful, as long as teachers, administrators and parents do not treat them as the end goals of learning to read and write.

CONCLUSION

The computer heralds a new kind of learning in our society. It can create environments where reading and writing are instrumental to the goals of children. The computer can challenge children through games and activities that require reading and writing skills for success. Computers can provide reading and writing aids that remove frustrations and compensate for the deficiencies that block learning for many students with motor, visual, planning, or attention difficulties. In such a setting reading and writing are not just for teachers. All the reasons for written communication and for different genres arise naturally in such communication environments.

12 Computer Technology and Reading Instruction: Perspectives and Directions

Judith A. Langer
Stanford University

The computer revolution is well under way. One need not look far to see the great impact it has had on our daily lives. Computer games, text editors, and microcomputers are widely advertised and can be seen in computer shops everywhere.

In addition to having captured the public's imagination with innovative and highly absorbing games, the microcomputer industry has developed an extensive home computer offering, with options for family budgeting, personal investment, business management, and record keeping. Many computer games include instructional components, and parents are encouraged to buy them as educational toys. More directly, instructional and quasi-instructional programs are rapidly being developed for home use.

In spite of these studies, the existing instructional software for school use is inadequate. Although new programs are being developed by a rapidly growing number of software-for-education companies, educators and educational researchers are rarely consulted to help set the goals, functions, or implementation of the new instructional programs. A revolutionary mode of learning has been developed, but the instructional aspects are being permitted to *happen to* rather than be *shaped by* professional educators who know about children, schools, and learning.

OBSERVATIONS ON THE USE OF TECHNOLOGY IN SCHOOLS

A walk through many school storage rooms discloses dusty stacks of one-time "high tech" equipment. Overhead projectors, individual filmstrip viewers, opaque projectors, microfiche readers, and single-concept film loop viewers were purchased in large scale during the late 1960s and early 1970s, when federal funds for educational innovation were relatively easy to come by and alternative methods for individualizing instruction were being sought. At that time, audiovisual courses were offered as regular in-service training, and aides were hired to assist in the changing modes of instruction. Yet, this technology failed to take substantial hold in education. These instructional aids were used relatively little except by the smitten few, teachers who became excited by the motivational and educational potential of the new technology. As for computer-assisted instruction (CAI) in particular, early CAI programs (of the 1960s) were often designed as independent curriculum packages, focusing on drill and practice of identifiable and testable subskills and responsive to the individual student's ability and progress. Sophisticated diagnostic and record-keeping systems designed to save teacher time were often an integral part of these programs. Yet, schools often found that after a few years teachers and students became disenchanted and returned to more conventional materials.

Before we can hope to see widespread acceptance of computers in classrooms, we must ask what went wrong with these earlier efforts. Why were teachers unwilling to use the available educational technology? Why did they become disenchanted after trying it?

In the mid-1970s this researcher, then a K-12 director of reading, and a teacher trainer, studied the reactions of teachers in the New York area to computers and other technology in the schools. They said:

1. The software either did not relate to the curriculum or was designed to be the entire curriculum—and differed from the teachers' or schools' goals.
2. The equipment was often kept in a separate "instructional resource room," taking students away from other important in-class activities.
3. Despite periodic mastery tests, teachers were not sure their students were learning. They described a sense of loss of control.
4. Teachers often found it difficult to recognize and understand the components of the instructional programs.
5. Teachers and administrators suspected the technology was a "fad." Some professed that students needed "real live human beings" and that they were personally uncomfortable with the "machinery."

When asked to comment about CAI in particular, teachers often voiced frustration, claiming it fostered learning in isolation and focused on skills practiced out of context. Many felt it fostered the teaching-by-objective approach with which many felt uncomfortable. Elementary teachers in particular reported feeling "guilty" and "old fashioned" for not using the technology, but uncomfortable and less effective as teachers if they did.

In a more recent study, Sheingold et al. (1981) found many of these concerns still prevalent. She investigated how three school systems across the country were using microcomputers. Although the districts varied considerably in instructional philosophies, curriculum and instructional organization, and willingness to innovate and experiment, they experienced similar problems and pressures associated with the introduction of microcomputers. Some of these are:

1. Lack of integration of microcomputers into elementary classrooms and curricula. Since the computers tended to be kept physically separate from the classroom, there was little integration with regular class work. In addition, no real teacher-stated goals were evident.

2. Inadequate quality and quantity of software. This was particularly apparent in non-math areas.

3. Inadequate preparation of teachers for using microcomputers. The teachers judged the in-service courses, university courses, and resource personnel to be inadequate.

4. Emergence of new specialized roles in response to microcomputer introduction. Aides were hired to work with computers in separate resource rooms, which often discouraged regular classroom teachers from acquiring computer skills. Teachers who spent personal time with computers, and student experts who took on instructional roles in school, placed new demands on the system.

5. Lack of knowledge of effects of the instructional use of microcomputers. Although the technology was not intended to change or replace the existing curriculum in any of the sites, the teachers noted changes in social interaction, status, and self-esteem after computers were introduced.

Clearly, teachers are unwilling to embrace technology that does not fit their teaching goals and whose educational advantages are not apparent. If use of that technology means taking children away from other activities teachers feel are more valuable, or if the computers are not accessible so they can be easily incorporated into everyday classroom activities, they are not likely to be used. Finally, if teachers are not comfortable with the technology, they will not be good instructional models for the students or express enthusiasm for this mode of learning. This opens the way for unequal access to computers: math and science teachers (or other teachers who have computers at home) may be more comfortable with the machines and likely to use them. This may foster the idea that computers are only for math-science use and limit access in other classrooms.

Sheingold concludes that microcomputers, as they were used in the three school systems she observed, "will not promote particular outcomes. Their impact will depend, not only on the hardware and software, but on how they are used and on the educational context in which they are embedded."

Based on the observations and reports cited, it is clear that before computer technology can make a positive impact on instructional programs, the technology must (1) reflect the best professional judgments regarding what is known about students and learning, and (2) reflect knowledgeable views of schools and teaching.

SCHOOLS AND TECHNOLOGY—WHY?

From this bleak description of technology in schools, it should come as no surprise that computer and software manufacturers are designing instructional products primarily for the home rather than the school market, and that school administrators have been less than enthusiastic in their support for computer technology in schools. Nonetheless, there are sound reasons for schools to embrace the use of computers and to become involved in the development of educational software. These fall into three categories: instructional, policy, and administrative.

Instructional

Interactive computers available today can provide strong support of basic instructional programs across grades and curriculum. For reading, the most promising of these applications stems from a view that emphasizes *problem solving* and *strategy development* as essential parts of the reading process. Such process-oriented instruction is time consuming and frequently individualized, and requires the teacher to make quick decisions about specific task demands and the student's momentary interaction with the text. Computer technology, which can provide instant process-oriented feedback, is ideally suited to such instruction.

Computers are also well adapted to diagnose individual differences in performance, to trace the variations in process that underlie these differences, and to provide activities that permit students to try alternative strategies and make decisions about their effectiveness.

Students frequently find computer activities fun, engaging, and highly motivating. They often become particularly attentive when receiving immediate response and guidance from the computer. Also, there is an element of "kid-power" in the acquisition of strategy control and increased understanding. Because of the increased motivation and involvement, student time-on-task also increases.

Policy Issues

The major policy issue related to computers is educational equity. Given the ubiquity of computers in our world and the likelihood that today's school children will need to use computers when they grow up, it is important for our educational system to assure that all children have an opportunity to become computer literate. Given the costs involved, public schools will need to provide computer learning experiences for all students before the "new literacy" becomes a prerogative of only the more affluent.

A second equality issue has to do with providing quality instruction to all children, regardless of cultural or economic background. Studies investigating student-teacher interaction have indicated that poorer readers receive qualitatively and quantitatively different reading instruction than their higher achieving classmates. Lower achieving students tend to spend less time with their teachers on reading instruction activities and to have fewer opportunities to read silently than their peers (Allington, 1980; McDermott, 1978). Similarly, Gumperz, Simons, and Cook-Gumperz (1981) report that poor readers' errors tend to be treated out of context and that teachers' corrections focus primarily on phonics and letter recognition drill. Collins (1980) suggests the prosodic strategies (oral rhythm and parsing) of poor readers and speakers of certain dialects also provoke word-level corrections by teachers. On the other hand, when better performers and standard-dialect speakers make errors, teachers tend to respond with thought-provoking questions focused on meaning within the context of the whole work. These studies suggest that the teacher's instructional focus may unwittingly be determined by who the children are rather than by instructional needs. Although this is a major problem that needs to be dealt with directly by all educators, instructional technology can help ameliorate the problem by providing reading experiences in a more interactively neutral environment.

Innovative instructional software can also allow the use of computers across the curriculum to reduce sex and achievement biases found today in use of computers. Sheingold (1981) reports that in many secondary schools higher achievers learn to control the technology through courses in computer logic, computer languages, and system analysis, while their classmates in business and vocational programs learn clerical and caretaking tasks such as keypunching, data input, and the repair and maintenance of the computer hardware. If familiarity with computers is to become another mark of the "literate" person, it is important that schools provide equitable computer opportunities for all youngsters.

Administrative Reasons

The third reason for using computers in schools is administrative, both at the classroom and school levels.

Teacher Benefits. The realities of the usual classroom instructional program preclude personalized process-oriented instruction without some assistance for teachers. Often teachers know the kind of instructional interactions youngsters need but do not have time for them. At times teachers know that a strategy-based activity is in order, but do not always know how to provide the necessary guidance. In either case, computer-based programs would be useful because specific activities could be chosen based on the teacher's perception of what is instructionally appropriate for each child. Computer technology would also permit teachers to organize better the time spent with individuals or groups, to make decisions about how best to develop the reading skills of their students, and to integrate this into the subject area curriculum.

A teacher-as-programmer option might also be provided. Although only a few teachers may presently avail themselves of it, computer technology is becoming so common in our society that it is likely that programming skills will soon be sought by many school systems and teachers. Because teacher-as-programmer would permit the teacher to maintain ultimate control over instructional activities, this would be a pedagogically sound component of any program. Teachers then would benefit from computer-based programs in two ways: (1) they would maintain autonomy in selecting learning goals while providing interactive activities with feedback to their students, and (2) they would be able to reallocate instructional time among whole class, large-group, and small-group activities, relying on the technology for specific blocks of instructional time.

Administrator Benefits.   Instructional programs must, of course, be developed with a thorough understanding of administrative as well as classroom needs. Administrators presently have a number of concerns that cannot be addressed adequately by traditional programs and methodologies, but may be addressed successfully by computer technology. Because administrators are well aware of the varying instructional approaches and offerings from class to class, they often seek to adopt curriculum materials that provide instructional continuity over and above what might be offered in any individual classroom. Therefore, a process-oriented system that augments, but does not supplant, the basic instructional program may help minimize differences in approaches to teaching while providing useful personalized instruction. With the national stress on literacy skills, activities that develop reading and writing across the curriculum would be considered an instructional asset by many administrators. Because process-oriented computer programs can potentially benefit the entire age and achievement range of students, this aspect of innovative technology becomes a desirable instructional component from an administrative standpoint.

DIRECTIONS FOR COMPUTER-BASED READING INSTRUCTION

If computers are to fulfill their promise as significant instructional tools, the design of software must reflect recent advances in knowledge about the reading process and the organization and presentation of instruction. The critical question is, How can computers enhance the instructional process, increasing the effectiveness of the teacher? In the following sections I discuss possibilities that capitalize on the computer's special capacities and on new understandings about reading.

Reading research over the past decade has focused on two major topics: (1) the psychological processes involved in comprehending written text, and (2) learning how to learn from text. This research suggests that three important points must be taken into consideration in developing new instructional approaches:

1. Reading is an interactive process between reader and author, involving a construction of meaning based on the reader's background knowledge and information given in text.
2. If we can help readers know what text-based clues to use in a particular situation, and if we can help them to know when and how to use these clues, then their reading comprehension will also improve.
3. Reading instruction should be learner based and heuristic, encouraging invididuals to develop metacognitive control over their own skills and strategies.

If computer-based instruction is to offer the most meaningful learning experiences for the student, then it must focus on the development of highly motivating programs to help youngsters gain facility in each of these areas. This requires the development of programs that go beyond the drill and practice exercises characteristic of so many of the CAI programs of the 1960s.

Reading as an Interactive Process

Reading is considered an interactive process because it involves coordination of a number of knowledge sources, including reader's background knowledge and the actual text (Rumelhart, 1977a). When the reader is more expert and/or more familiar with the language or content of the text, reliance on text cues diminishes and the construction of meaning tends to become more concept driven (Bobrow & Norman, 1975). When idea processing breaks down and the language or content is difficult, more attention is given to text details, and analysis tends to focus on smaller units of language (Spiro, 1980). Purpose for reading also affects the extent to which a reader relies on the printed page (Tierney & Spiro, 1979). Both top-down (concept-driven) and bottom-up (text-driven) processes can and should occur.

Presently there are many instructional programs that provide practice in bottom-up tasks. Often these stress decoding at the word level, sentence parsing or sentence combining at the sentence and intersentential level, and surface level questions at the text level. New instructional programs need to provide activities designed to help students develop efficient meaning-based strategies which recognize the relation between world knowledge and each reading situation (Adams, 1980a).

Instruction in concept-driven strategies is often extremely difficult because it requires a great deal of dialogue with each individual student. The teacher must assess what meaning chunks the student is anticipating, what text cues are being used, and whether these are being used appropriately. Teachers must also provide activities designed to stretch or alter their student's meaning construction procedures, and provide strategy-based and concept-based feedback. Computer-based top-down strategy instruction would therefore be a valuable asset.

Instructional Needs: A Process View

When writing a text, authors use their sense of audience to select specific content and language to convey ideas. Any gap between reader and author must be bridged for efficient reading comprehension to occur. Instruction in reading comprehension involves assisting students to develop flexible decision-making strategies that help them interpret the author's message.

Factors that Influence Reading: The Reader, the Text and the Context

Current reading research suggests a number of variables affecting the reader during every moment of the reading experience. These include factors inherent in the *reader* such as personal experience, language, and content knowledge (Langer, 1982b, 1984), and factors inherent in the *text* such as concepts, vocabulary, and organizational structure (Tierney & Mosenthal, 1982), the linguistic nature of the text itself such as sentence structure and cohesive ties (Halliday & Hasan, 1976), and genre, point of view, and style.

In addition to the reader and the text, we must also consider the context for reading—the context in its largest sense, from the classroom environment and the student-teacher and student-student relationships, to the environment for learning in the school, to the context for literacy in the home and within the community at large.

Multiple Constraints on the Reading Process

At the center of each specific reading experience is the reader and text interaction, which is always affected by the purpose for reading (Fig. 12.1). This purpose for reading directly affects the extent to which a reader relies on the printed page or goes beyond it to relevant background knowledge and experiences. Although a reader may have efficient text-driven as well as concept-driven strategies, the reading strategies actually used will be influ-

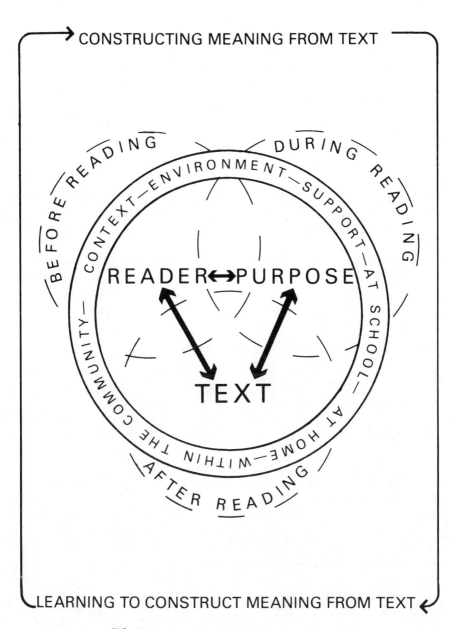

FIG. 12.1   Multiple constraints on the reading process

enced by the individual's purpose for reading in that specific instance. When reading becomes difficult or things go wrong, the most appropriate fix-up strategies will also differ. Different purposes for reading will permit smaller or larger gaps to exist between reader and author. At other times it is necessary for the reader to be aware of specific personal biases—and to keep them aside—so that the view of the author can be interpreted as openly as possible. Students must learn to become aware of the strategies they use when reading for different purposes, and teachers must be aware that what the reader gets out of the text is a function of the *purpose* as well as of the text itself.

Developers of computer-based instructional programs must be aware of the many variables that influence the manner in which text is processed. Because it is difficult for teachers to provide personalized instruction in all of the strategies appropriate for various reading tasks, this sort of decision-making activity might be developed using on-line processing of a variety of texts read for a variety of purposes. Decisions might also be made about the interactive and hypothesis-testing strategies that could be used if the reader had more or less prior knowledge about the topic. Because text-based learning is an important aspect of reading, activities that require students to decide which text-based clues are helpful in which situations would also become an excellent project for computer technology.

Metacomprehension and Reading Instruction

Metacomprehension refers to the strategic monitoring system, which involves self-reflection and awareness of what an individual knows, what he or she needs to know in a particular situation, and what needs to be done if things go wrong (Brown, Armbrusher, & Baker, this volume). Metacomprehension can be thought of as having two separate components: awareness and action.

- Awareness-reflecting one's own cognitive processes:
  1. Awareness of task goal.
  2. Awareness of what is known.
  3. Awareness of what needs to be known.
  4. Awareness of appropriate strategies.
- Action-using self-regulatory mechanisms:
  1. Relating the problem to similar problems.
  2. Checking problem solving attempts.
  3. Revising strategies.
  4. Anticipating what to do next.

Metacomprehension activities serve as a "third eye" which permits the reader to check his/her own state of understanding, and whether ideas in the text make sense and are consistent with one another (Baker & Brown, 1984b). Because there are varying levels of "how much you need to understand," readers must make this judgment based on the purpose for reading. Poor readers are less aware of the strategies they use during reading and when things go wrong. Similarly, young readers do not seem to notice inconsistencies even when capable of doing so (Markman, 1979). Therefore young and poor readers are less likely to seek clarification.

Instructional activities can be developed that help students learn to learn (Brown, Campione, & Day, 1981). In classrooms it is often the teacher rather than the student who makes decisions about what the students need to know. Learning to choose which strategies to use is often excluded from classroom practice because it is extremely time consuming and requires individual conferences. Computer-based activities designed to develop awareness of the demands of the reading task, to make judgments about what needs to be known, and to use the self-regulatory mechanisms to gain that information would be an important contribution to learning technology.

Stages of Reading

Although reading is in many ways a recursive activity in which the mind races ahead to anticipate what will come next and skips backward to review and revise interpretations that have already been made, it is helpful for purposes of analysis to focus on three stages of reading; before the text is read; while the text is being read; and after the eyes have left the page (Robinson, 1978a). This provides a framework for considering comprehension-fostering possibilities at each of these points. Instructional decisions before reading might focus on the vocabulary and conceptual background appropriate to a specific text, using pre-questions (Anderson, 1978) or analogies (Hayes & Tierney, 1982; Rumelhart & Ortony, 1977). During-reading activities might focus on helping the reader develop self-questions or respond to inserted questions (Andre & Anderson, 1978). Anticipation of large structural, organizational, or rhetorical elements might be developed. Sensitivity to the cohesive aspects of text might also be fostered. Interventions after reading might focus on post-questions (Anderson & Biddle, 1975), feedback (Gagne, 1978), and text-and-script-based recall (Pearson & Johnson, 1978). It must be remembered, however, the comprehension is multidimensional and that the multiple constraints described above must be considered simultaneously in a multifaceted approach (see Fig. 12.1).

Following are some suggestions software developers might consider when planning instructional activities.

Some Computer-Based Activities for Teaching Comprehension

1. Increase student awareness of text features (a) to meet text-based needs, and (b) to override text-based problems.

2. Model a metacognitive strategy in the presentation of a particular reading activity. Gradually turn the decision making, and later the question generation, over to the student.
3. Provide concept and language awareness activities prior to reading to help students think about what they already know about a specific topic. Have them anticipate what they will read in the text.
4. Provide activities requiring decisions about ideas in the text that may or may not make sense or are not necessarily consistent with one another.
5. Help students decide how thoroughly they must learn the text material based on the purpose for reading.
6. Develop activities involving adjunct questions to teach self-questioning before, during, and after reading.
7. Vary audience, author, or voice to help students become aware of these shifts.
8. Vary text clues at word, sentence, and text level and have students develop sensitivity to varying levels of usefulness.
9. Have students judge what they think will be easy/difficult for their classmates to understand and why.
10. Present writing-in-progress and have students determine if the author is exercising strategies that they know.

GAINING ACCEPTANCE IN SCHOOLS

Computer technology has progressed to the point where significant contributions to instructional effectiveness and student learning can be made at comparatively low cost. Computers are well adapted to focus on individual strategies to trace variations in process, and to provide personalized, strategy-based instruction. However, gaining acceptance for computer technology remains a major problem.

If computer technology is to be widely used in schools, at least four conditions must be met:

1. Terminals and software must be easily accessible to teachers and students.
2. Program activities must be adaptable to the teacher's instructional goals.
3. Program components and instructional goals must be easily identified.
4. Teachers and administrators must become comfortable with computers.

Although each is important, the last point may prove to be the major stumbling block. If teachers and administrators fail to become comfortable with computers, the technology may be used poorly at first, and ultimately allowed to gather dust next to the microfiche readers and other technical aids. The students will be the losers.

Decisions about large expenditures such as for computers are best made when both teachers and administrators are involved in the planning and development. Often, a pilot program is begun with enthusiastic teachers, principals, and curriculum coordinators who end up "selling" the program to others. In this same way it is possible for a school librarian and a few classroom teachers to begin together to use computer-based technology both in classrooms and in library media centers as part of the ongoing instructional program. It is likely that other students and teachers would become curious and even totally involved. It cannot be suggested too strongly, however, that administrators and teachers should be exposed to the "literacy" program over an extended period of time until they are comfortable with the technology. Neither in-service courses nor one- or two-week summer courses seem to work. An ongoing support network supplied "on call" seems to make a greater difference in learning, attitudes, and acceptance.

Many computer companies have become actively involved in the support of innovative microcomputer use, generally through grants for equipment and software development. Boards of advisors review grants and encourage the development of new applications of the technology. Large public-access educational computer centers for children have also been supported. Users' groups are being formed in local areas across the country. They are made up of educators and members of the computer industry, and have rich potential to plan and implement "literacy" projects in local communities and provide a forum for articulating ideas about the future use of computers for teaching literacy skills. New approaches to multilevel cooperation with computer companies might effect changes in attitudes about computer-based instruction, and influence the development of software and systems that will make an instructional difference.

SUMMARY

There is no doubt that the computer revolution is with us, that it is affecting schools, and that this trend will continue with or without the involvement of the educational community. Today's students need to be prepared for a technological society requiring some computer literacy even for entry-level jobs. Instructional use of computer technology is presently limited in scope, haphazardly organized and administered, and accompanied by software that does not reflect current knowledge of the reading process. The majority of teachers and administrators are uncomfortable with computer technology, and are uncertain about its ability to benefit school programs.

Based on what is known about computers, reading strategies, and cognitive theory, there is no doubt that computer technology has the potential to make a difference in schools. However, program development and school site implementation need careful guidance from educators and researchers who are knowledgeable about process research, aware of school needs, and sensitive to school conditions. If the issues of implementation and acceptance are not jointly addressed by educators and the computer industry, innovative learning experiences and computer literacy may only be accessible to select groups— increasing rather than helping eliminate equity problems in both school and society.

13 Literacy in the Secondary School

Gladys P. Knott
Kent State University

Complex and dynamic changes in our society have stimulated concern about trends, purposes, and goals of education. One of the prevalent trends is the adoption of minimum competency standards for high school graduation. Currently, different competency policies have been instituted in approximately 38 states, with others considering this alternative. This chapter argues that educators and others concerned with secondary students' education need to reconsider not only minimum competencies, but also the nature of reading and writing instruction itself.

There is ample research to support the contention that students' reading development continues beyond the elementary level if instruction is provided (Berkey, 1967; Crisucuolo & Rossman, 1977; Cushenberry, 1977; Knott, 1979; Seifert, 1978; Stevens, 1980). In addition, appropriate instruction in the functions of writing results in effective written expression (Bailey, 1979; Benson, 1979; Collins, 1979; Howie, 1979; Odell, 1980).

This chapter comprises three sections. The first section, Triggers for Concern about Literacy, highlights certain events that led to current research on reading and writing at the secondary level. The second section, Recent Literacy Research and Present Classroom Practice, indicates advances in understanding secondary students' literacy learning and forecasts classroom practices that corroborate current research. The final section, Extensions and Future Directions, suggests research needs to better understand broad areas of secondary education.

TRIGGERS FOR CONCERN ABOUT SECONDARY
STUDENTS' LITERACY ACHIEVEMENT

During the past decade, various events in society and education affected secondary students. At a societal level, taxpayers, educators, parents, and state and federal legislators began to question the effectiveness of increased annual spending for education in American schools. The U. S. Department of Education funded and continues to monitor the National Assessment of Educational Progress (NAEP).

Nationwide surveys conducted by NAEP in 1970–71, 1974–75, and 1979–80 document changes in secondary students' literacy learning during the 1970s. Reading scores for 13-year-olds did not change significantly between 1970 and 1974. However, the 1980 assessment revealed significant improvement in basic reading skills, but no improvement in higher level skills. The writing abilities of 13-year-olds did not change across the three assessments.

Data from the 17-year-olds indicated no significant overall changes in reading ability between 1970 and 1974. However, there was a decline in inferential comprehension between 1970 and 1974 and again in 1980. This suggests a need for improvement of secondary students' comprehension beyond the literal level.

Across the three assessments, there were no significant changes in 17-year-olds' writing abilities. Dearman and Plisko (1981) suggested that this lack of improvement was not surprising, since not much attention was given to writing instruction in schools during that time. Seventeen-year-olds, they noted, "were not required to do much writing. ... few appeared to have access to a writing program that included pre-writing instruction, oral and written feedback on writing assignments, or opportunities to redraft papers" (p. 17).

With the initial NAEP reports interpreted for public information and discussion, the educational accountability and back-to-basics movement gained momentum. Higher education and public school personnel examined the quality of what was taught and how well it was taught in public schools. Standards of educational achievement, known as minimal competency tests, were developed to measure how well schools were providing students with a basic education. Public school systems in 38 states had instituted minimal competency tests by the end of 1979. Thus, the NAEP reports can be cited as having had a pivotal influence on secondary education.

Although the NAEP reports provided global accounts of secondary students' literacy achievement during the past decade, a few researchers made specific observations about the essence of literacy instruction, particularly reading. Their reports corroborate the NAEP results for secondary students.

Early (1973) surveyed secondary reading instruction and arrived at four major findings: (1) Developmental reading translated into skills-oriented reading programs, suggesting that reading instruction consisted of decoding letters into words, words into phrases and finally, phrases into sentences to derive meaning. (2) The secondary student body had a wide range of reading achievement, which can be attributed to the country's campaign to keep students in school. Therefore, more students who previously would have dropped out remained in secondary school, contributing to the variability. (3) Preservice and in-service secondary teachers needed preparation in the teaching of reading. Previously, teachers of content subjects, such as mathematics and biology, had rejected the responsibility for teaching reading and referred problem readers to the reading teachers. These teachers, in turn, taught the skills they hoped would transfer to content subjects. However, this transfer was not happening. (4) The structure and organization of secondary schools varied with the student population. These included modular scheduling and an elective course system, as well as an array of less demanding courses, such as Recreation, Bachelor Living, and Food for Thought, which required little substantive reading and writing. Consequently, many secondary students were unable to perform basic literacy tasks when they graduated.

Harker (1975) characterized the philosophy underlying many educational approaches as motivational. In order to motivate students to read, materials that appealed to secondary students' personal interests and aspirations were used. However, it has been argued that motivational appeal is insufficient, by itself, to encourage students to overcome their reading and writing difficulties.

Shafer (1978) suggested a possible explanation for the proliferation of skills-oriented reading programs: the accountability and back-to-basics movements of the past decade reinforced the skills model. He claimed that not only was the skills model the basis for in-service education of teachers, but "courses on the development of skills in word recognition, literal comprehension, and the so-called higher levels of comprehension multiplied" (p. 308) in colleges and universities. Shafer concluded that programs developed on the skills model failed to accomplish their intended goal—the improvement of reading achievement, namely comprehension, of secondary students.

Sager (1980) characterized the state of the art of secondary reading instruction in the United States in a report on secondary reading practices in six New England states. On the basis of a comprehensive survey of practices, which included types of reading programs, instructional approaches, selection of students for reading instruction, evaluation of student achievement, and other related concerns, she concluded that few programs at the secondary level could be considered adequate. Sager attributed this to the following: Student achievement in reading is not monitored from elementary to secondary school; classroom and clinic or resource room reading procedures are not coordinated; content area teachers have experienced little preservice instruction and demonstrate little concern with teaching reading; and few schools have implemented a comprehensive or schoolwide approach to secondary reading.

New Beginnings: Alternatives to Literacy Achievement

As problems pertaining to secondary students' literacy achievement were identified, some researchers offered alternative approaches to secondary school literacy. A representative sample of new orientations to reading is presented.

Cooper and Petrosky (1976) expressed dismay at the skills-oriented reading program prescription for secondary students and the failure of the Right to Read slogan "every teacher is a teacher of reading" to have an impact on the secondary school. Instead of the usual secondary reading instruction, Cooper and Petrosky offered a reading strategies program. Described as "a planned, monitored, intensive reading program" (p. 201), it consisted of sustained silent reading in which time to read books and student opportunity to make free-choice reading selections within and across content areas were important elements. These researchers termed the model "psycholinguistic-information processing" and suggested that all students in the first semester of grades 7 and 9 complete the one-semester program.

Goodman (1976a) and Smith (1975) argued that fluent mature reading has its origin in cognitive processing of verbal or linguistic information. For example, Goodman described reading as a "psycholinguistic guessing game" in which readers use past experiences and knowledge of language to test hypotheses and make predictions about what they expect to discover from reading text.

Harker (1979) proposed that learning tasks could be clarified by assisting students to outline text; teachers could consider the amount of information they present students to process to avoid information overload; students could be encouraged to take risks while reading and predict what will come next in the text; and students could develop self-feedback as a way of validating hypotheses. Finally, as the decade ended, Artley (1980) recommended that reading in the content area include creating a need for students to read and to solve problems. Comprehension could be promoted, he suggested, by having students read texts, engage in problem solving, and compare their solutions and decisions with those of other students in the classroom.

Although a few researchers offered alternatives to the prevailing skills model of reading of the 1970s, a search of the literature indicates that the call for change in reading methodology in secondary schools has not been realized. The status of reading instruction during the past decade, as evidenced by several analyses, indicates that extensive research is still needed to uncover and correct diverse literacy learning problems in the secondary schools.

RECENT LITERACY RESEARCH AND PRESENT CLASSROOM PRACTICE

Much research attention during the 1970s was focused either on reading acquisition in elementary students or on models of skilled reading comprehension. As a result, our knowledge of secondary students' literacy development is minimal and does not reflect organized, systematic or sequential patterns of inquiry. Rather, research topics of interest to individual researchers and topics that previously had been explored with younger children were selected for study with secondary students. For example, the influence of background knowledge on reading comprehension (discussed in this volume by Wilson and Anderson), which has been explored extensively with younger children, has recently become important in learning more about secondary students' comprehension of text (Langer & Nicolich, 1981; Santa, this volume; Stevens, 1980).

The intent of this section is to examine how recent theoretical constructs apply to secondary students. Research on reading comprehension and writing is presented first, followed by a section on classroom practice.

Reading Comprehension

In this discussion, reading is viewed as comprising several perceptual, cognitive, linguistic and social processes and is defined as the process of comprehending the meaning of connected discourse. Kinds of knowlege that contribute to comprehension include concept formation and application, background knowledge, and text structure.

Concept Formation.   Both cognitive and linguistic processes are inherent in comprehension. On the surface, comprehension involves syntactic and semantic processing of information. The reader may experience difficulty with either process, and comprehension may be impeded as a result. However, concept formation and utilization represent a major difficulty (Adams, 1980a). This difficulty may include an inability to access, structure, and organize new concepts in relation to background knowledge, text, or personal experience. On the basis of a series of standardized tests of intellectual ability, reading, and verbal concept formation, significant differences between achieving and underachieving ninth graders were found in concept formation. Vogel (1981) noted that the students differed in their abilities to advance in levels of conceptualization, in their expressions of solutions to problems, and in their basic concept formation abilities. This study points to important differences that must be considered in efforts to facilitate literacy achievement of some secondary students. For example, some students may encounter difficulty when tasks require integration of cognitive and linguistic abilities. Difficulty in verbalizing a concept may well affect comprehension as well as production of text. Problems in concept formation suggest that some secondary students experience difficulty in categorizing information, in attaching labels to experiences and, generally, in solving conceptual problems.

Background Knowledge.   Prior knowledge and its effects on comprehension have received much attention from researchers (Adams & Collins, 1979;

Bransford, Nitsch, & Franks, 1977; Brown & Campione, 1978a; Wilson & Anderson, this volume).

Two recent studies examined the effect of background knowledge on reading comprehension of secondary students. Stevens (1980) studied ninth graders of varying ability levels. She assigned high- and low-familiarity paragraphs and administered multiple-choice questions about the paragraphs. Scores indicated that background knowledge was a significant factor in all ability groups. Possessing high prior knowledge about a topic greatly aided understanding of that topic.

Langer and Nicolich (1981) hypothesized that "text specific concept and vocabulary knowledge affect the processing and recall of text and that a measure of this knowledge might assist teachers in determining whether a reader possesses adequate background to successfully comprehend and recall a particular text" (p. 374). In their study, high school seniors enrolled in an advanced placement course in English literature were asked to free associate to specific content words taken from passages they were later asked to read. After reading the passage, students were asked to write what they remembered from it. Level of prior knowledge was greatly related to ability to recall a passage and prior knowledge predicted recall independent of intellectual ability of normal and above-average students.

At present, the relation between background knowledge and reading comprehension is still not fully understood. Topics currently under investigation include the nature of retrieval of appropriate prior knowledge, how background knowledge should be developed in classroom settings, and whether classroom-developed background knowledge actually increases a student's repertoire of information for use in novel reading situations. Solutions to these problems should lead to improved instruction in reading comprehension.

Text Structure.   Variations in text structure and the effects of text structure on comprehension and retrieval of information have been subjected to research during recent years. Goetz and Armbruster (1980) reported several psychological correlates of text structure: (1) Connected discourse facilitates greater learning than groups of unrelated sentences or lists of isolated words; (2) texts that correspond with the reader's knowledge and expectations are better understood; (3) within texts, readers identify particular elements that are important to remember; and (4) the internal representation of text is constructed through interaction of the reader, the context in which text occurs, and the text itself.

Implications from the researchers' findings are important and practical. For example, lists of information such as modes of transportation, biological species, and chemical elements are better retrieved when learned in a meaningful narrative context. Texts should be related to students' existing knowledge. Students should not be expected to remember insignificant details from text; main points are easier to remember.

Kreider (1981) examined the effect of the presence, absence and placement of topic sentences in paragraphs on reading comprehension. Three types of readers were subjects in the study: superior, average, and difference readers (students whose reading comprehension was average but whose vocabulary knowledge was above average). Results indicated that topic sentences in any position improve reading comprehension, particularly of main ideas, for all three groups of readers.

Researchers have shown, with a limited sample of secondary students, that expectations, knowledge of different text structures, and purposes students bring to reading interact and affect comprehension. Recent research efforts have focused on text structure of prose material, mainly narratives. Future research involving more complicated text will have special significance for secondary students, especially those experiencing difficulty with technical and scientifically oriented text.

Summarizing this section, research on secondary students' comprehension is minimal in view of the volume and variety of recent theory on reading comprehension. Nevertheless, the studies reported in this discussion illustrate that much research is needed to understand better the nature of reading comprehension of secondary students. The theoretical orientations, research-based theories and constructs that are grounded in scientific methodology and interpretation have been useful and informative in initiating research. However, the studies reported in the discussion are not comprehensive enough to suggest thorough practical programs. What has been illustrated is the need for continued research to provide a scientific foundation for reading instruction to be developed and applied in secondary schools.

Writing

Recent volumes on writing (DeFord, 1980; Frederiksen & Dominic, 1981; Whiteman, 1981a) attest to researchers' recognition of needs to address a "writing crisis" in American schools (Dearman & Plisko, 1981; Scribner & Cole, 1978b; Whiteman, 1980). Research advances have been made. However, the focus has been the acquisition and development of young children's writing. Definitive approaches to improve secondary students' written expression are needed.

Efforts toward improvement of writing instruction are being made. For example, one group of researchers (Bruce, Collins, Rubin, & Gentner, 1978) explored writing from a cognitive science framework. Presented as a mechanism for generating ideas rather than a unified theory, these researchers discussed writing from several perspectives. First, it is a communicative process built on four principles of communication: comprehensibility makes text easy to read; enticing devices hold the reader's attention; persuasion techniques convince the reader that ideas are true; and memorability assists the reader in retaining essential information. Second, writing is considered in the context of a taxonomy of communicative acts. These researchers explore differences between writing and conversing, writing a story and a skit, and writing and lecturing. When elaborated, these differences will have theoretical as well as instructional implications. Third, writing is seen as a "decomposable" process.

Odell (1980) offered suggestions for helping students develop effective writing. He examined samples of official business writing to illustrate problems. Suggestions for classroom teachers included preparation for writing in the form of class discussion and role playing, assisting students in identifying audiences and purposes for writing, and using methods that result in students receiving responses to their writing.

Whiteman (1980) described several National Institute of Education funded writing projects whose objectives and goals pertained to secondary students' writing. At Boston University, researchers are studying secondary students' ability to "detect ambiguity and to produce paraphrase." The research focus at the University of Iowa is syntactic and rhetorical fluency in the writing of 17-year-olds. At the National Council of Teachers of English, researchers are examining the types of writings students produce in school, the context in which writing occurs, and teacher variation in writing instruction. Descriptions of the projects suggest that researchers are pursuing knowledge of secondary students' ability to engage in writing as an ideation process. The focus represents an advance beyond the early mechanistic, craftsmanship view of writing, which emphasized capitalization, punctuation, appearance, and the like.

Researchers have responded to the "writing crisis" in American schools. The primary objective of their research is to formulate definitive theories of writing. A second is to translate theory into effective classroom practices. In several efforts at development of theory and practice, indicators are that secondary students are being nurtured.

Present Classroom Practice

Two succinct evaluative statements by prominent researchers in the field of reading provide a general picture of reading instruction at the secondary level. One decade ago, Early (1973) wrote: "In the past thirty years, the status of reading instruction in the secondary school has changed very little. In 1972 as in 1942, we are still debating the merits of special reading services and urging the whole school faculty to teach reading in the content fields" (p. 364).

Presenting a general description of current reading programs in secondary schools, Nelson and Herber (1982) stated: "In spite of the growing concern for the improvement of reading instruction, the organization and management of secondary reading programs has changed relatively little over the past two decades. The predominant mode of organization is the creation of special reading classes for limited groups of students" (p. 143).

According to Nelson and Herber, in any given secondary school, local resources and perceived needs dictate the number of classes and the balance among three types of reading classes: (1) small remedial classes serving students who are severely deficient in reading achievement; (2) corrective reading classes serving larger groups of students who demonstrate reading achievement a year or two below their potential; and (3) developmental reading classes for average to above average achieving students to refine their present reading skills and to assist them in developing more advanced study skills. In Nelson and Herber's view, this organization of secondary school reading programs should be altered. The primary structure would be reading instruction in the content areas; however, remedial and corrective reading classes would supplement content area reading instruction on a student need basis.

Similar evaluative statements on the status of secondary students' writing have been reported. Scribner and Cole (1978) stated: "the kind of writing that goes on in school has a very special status. It generates products that meet teacher demands and academic requirements but may not fulfill any other immediate instrumental needs" (p. 35).

Applebee (1981) conducted a comprehensive study of writing tasks secondary students perform, teachers' instructional strategies, purposes, and techniques in making assignments, and characteristics of students' writing across grade and subject areas. Describing current instructional practice, he wrote: "The most obvious finding to emerge from looking at the instructional techniques adopted to help students with this writing is that very few such techniques are used at all . . . so much of the writing students do is assigned in a test situation, rather than an instructional one . . . it comes from a conceptualization of writing as a simple skill which a given student has or does not have" (p. 102).

Applebee outlined several principles and elements of an effective secondary school writing program. Steps he suggested to improve secondary students' writing include (1) providing students opportunities in which "writing can serve as a tool for learning rather than as a means to display acquired knowledge" (p. 101), (2) translating research for classroom teachers to provide them with a framework for understanding teacher-student interaction in the writing process, and (3) creating contexts in which writing lessons serve a natural purpose, that is, where writing is motivated by a need to communicate.

The dismal picture of present practice in secondary school literacy instruction is brightened by a few model demonstration literary programs (Santa, this volume; Shallert & Tierney, 1982; Stallings, 1980) which point the way to more effective classroom practice.

Overall, current literacy instruction practices in secondary schools warrant more attention. One of the major problems is that literacy instruction practices in secondary schools largely duplicate elementary school instruction practices. Improvements in literacy instruction at the secondary level will result from increased understanding of reading and writing processes, and from effective translation of research contributions in preservice and in-service education, including those for school administrators. In other words, school administrators and teachers, and the quality of information they possess, are the keys to change in literacy instruction and thus, student achievement.

EXTENSIONS AND FUTURE DIRECTIONS

Throughout this chapter, it has been necessary to call for scientific research that addresses various aspects of secondary students' reading and writing. Additionally, if we are sensitive to the numerous educational, social, political, and economic consequences of widespread ineffective literacy instruction, there are related problems and issues that require consideration. Generally, these include students' transition from elementary to secondary school, the prevailing use of skills-building models of reading, and the structure and organization of secondary school literacy programs.

In the 1960s and 1970s, "financial support was not given to programs that emphasized reading instruction for all students in content areas" (Nelson & Herber, 1982, p. 145). Rather, financial support was appropriated for special groups of students who demonstrated moderate to severe problems in reading. During the same period, teaching of reading in higher education stressed preparation of reading specialists and remedial reading teachers. These personnel were prepared to assist secondary students through a skills-building model of reading (Harker, 1979; Nelson & Herber, 1982). Only recently have colleges begun to offer courses on teaching reading in various secondary content areas. However, our present scientific knowledge of the reading process and especially reading comprehension raises questions about the content of these courses. But progress has been slow in translating our best theoretical knowledge into classroom practices. A final issue concerns who bears the burden of providing secondary teachers access to opportunities to learn and implement more effective reading instruction. These problems must be resolved in order to establish clearly defined directions in providing effective literacy instruction at the secondary level.

Beyond the issue of teacher training is the question of the instructional impact of minimum competency tests. Although the intent is to assure that all students graduate with at least minimum literacy skills, the fear is that only the minimum will be taught. If this minimum does not include higher level comprehension skills, we run the risk of further handicapping these students.

Another concern is the management of literacy instruction for secondary students enrolled in various educational programs that place different emphases on literacy achievement. Some secondary schools present an academic type of education; others are primarily vocational; and still others present a combination of the two. Questions suggested by these different educational programs in view of current reading research include the following: Are different literacy-related perceptual, cognitive, and linguistic processes involved in the different content areas? How should a teacher structure a student's interaction with a science text *versus* a wood shop text? What criteria can be applied to discern if students enrolled in the different programs need different literacy instruction? There are few answers from current literacy research to these questions. However, conventional wisdom, intuition, and trial and error teaching are costly, and in many cases result in teacher and student frustration and failure. Clearly, further research is needed to explore students' needs in different contexts.

Although there are many more problems and issues that could be addressed in this section, one final issue is raised: Who should teach reading at the secondary level—reading specialists or content-area teachers? For many reasons, the slogan "every teacher a teacher of reading" has not been implemented. Although both pedagogical and political factors are bound to influence the outcome of this controversy, certain questions must be addressed. These are raised in the context of students' differing instructional needs and the absence of a coherent, research-based theory of reading comprehension or instruction. First, is it reasonable for schools to expect that every content teacher will also teach reading? Can we assume that a teacher who possesses extensive knowledge of a content area can also acquire adequate knowledge of a process as complex as reading? Second, are we assuming that most students have achieved their maximum developmental reading potential by the time they enter secondary school and that providing specific skill instruction to meet specific content demands is sufficient to meet ever-increasing requirements for efficient reading performance? The problems surrounding content area reading are not new to secondary educators or educational researchers. Perhaps, as in the case of our improved knowledge of the reading process, researchers representing other disciplines can offer suggestions that will improve present conditions.

In summary, several questions have been raised regarding not only the present status of secondary school literacy instruction, but also current research and the need to extend present knowledge. Questions pertinent to different students' needs in different teaching/learning contexts have been asked. Issues related to promoting and developing students' maximum literacy potential and issues related to the continuation of reading instruction by content area teachers have been highlighted. The questions, problems, and issues demand research to improve the existing status of secondary students' literacy instruction, achievement, and application in home, school, community, and work environments.

IV From Research to Practice: Case Studies

14 STAR: Teaching Reading and Writing

M. Trika Smith-Burke
Lenore H. Ringler
New York University

BACKGROUND

New York City Community School District 4, located in East Harlem, or El Barrio, has boundaries extending from 96th Street to 125th Street and from the East River to 5th Avenue. Attending twenty schools, 16 elementary and 4 junior high, the district's 16,000 students are approximately 61% Hispanic, 35% Black, .5% Asian and 3.5% other.

The following portrayal from an ESEA Title VII (1976) proposal describes the district:

> Every problem of slum life plagues East Harlem. There are endless blocks of overcrowded and crumbling tenements, glass-strewn sidewalks, stripped and abandoned cars, and boarded-up stores spread across the district, interrupted here and there by tall, impersonal towers of public housing projects. The cumulative effect of poverty, unemployment, under-education, and illness aggravagated by consumer frauds and rackets has had a devastating impact on the people. Many Black and Puerto Rican families earn less than $3,000 per year and unemployment rates are higher than the citywide averages. East Harlem has the eighth highest rate of welfare recipients of the 26 poverty areas in New York City. (pp. 1–2)

In 1973 only 15% of the students were reading at or above grade level, and no district-wide reading curriculum existed. This chapter described how the district resolved this problem through the development of an innovative program called STAR, Structured Teaching in the Areas of Reading and Writing.

215

Context for Change

A new Community School District Superintendent was appointed in 1973. In one of his first policy decisions, he mandated in consultation with the Director of Communication Arts that each school (1) select and consistently use one basal reading program through all grades, and (2) establish a High Intensity Reading Laboratory (Cohen, 1974). As a result of the second decision, a management approach for teaching hundreds of skills was implemented. Emphasis in the program was on diagnosing reading problems. Students, who attended 4 to 5 periods a week, were then assigned exercises to remediate deficient skills. These exercises were chosen primarily from basal and supplemental workbooks and skill kits.

By 1976, due to these changes, approximately 26% of the district's students were reading at or above grade level—an 11% increase over the 1973 average. Between 1976 and 1978, however, reading scores did not continue to improve as expected. District 4 teachers reported that students were bored with the High Intensity Program because of (1) repeated exposure to the same drill materials, (2) the individualized approach, limiting interaction among students, and (3) the unrealistic number of isolated skills to be mastered, which slowed movement through the program. Recent teacher questionnaires confirmed this dissatisfaction and revealed additional problems. There was little application of skills to real reading materials, the teachers functioned as managers, not teachers, and there was a lack of direct instruction.

As a result, a teacher committee to work with district staff was formed to develop a new Title 1 reading program. Lenore Ringler of New York University and her colleagues served as consultants. Two key goals guided the evolution of STAR:

1. to change the role of the teacher from classroom manager to teacher, and
2. to stress comprehension of "real materials for real purposes," and the interrelatedness of the language arts.

A DESCRIPTION OF STAR

The STAR Program for Grades 3–9 is grounded in current research on oral and written language. Its basic philosophy assumes respect and acceptance of the language and experiences students bring to school. Only with self-respect and a sense of their own language abilities can students respect, understand, and use the language of others.

Through the integrated use of communication arts, students learn to read for meaning and to express ideas by talking and writing. Real materials—trade books, stories, poems, encyclopedias, newspapers, magazine articles, textbooks, and students' writings—are used for instruction so that students begin to see reading as a purposeful, meaningful activity.

The teachers help students bridge the gap between their experiences and the author's ideas through prereading activities and the use of carefully constructed questions. These activities necessitate thorough lesson planning by teachers who must (1) select appropriate materials based on student strengths, (2) analyze the text for content, structure, and style, (3) prepare questions to elicit critical inferences, and (4) create lesson activities.

The teaching techniques of eliciting information, modeling reading and writing strategies, and facilitating discussion form the instructional core of the STAR Program. The content of the STAR Program is divided into six teaching strands: narrative reading, expository reading, strategy lessons, writing, skills reinforcement, and readership.

Narrative Reading

Narrative reading uses literature, poetry, and drama to develop basic concepts such as the role of language in communication, the nature of the reading act (including the roles of an author and reader), the types of genre, and the primary characteristics of stories (theme, plot, character, mood, and setting). These foundation lessons create a shared set of concepts and terms allowing students and teachers to communicate.

Eliciting and building background knowledge and setting a purpose for reading are prereading activities. Post-reading activities include retelling, writing, and discussion. Prepared structured questions are used only if needed to extend comprehension. Emphasis is placed on examining diverse interpretations and how these responses were derived.

Expository Reading

Expository reading focuses on comprehension of content area materials, particularly social studies and science. Teachers analyze expository text in order to understand the relation between the text and the curriculum and to teach the comprehension and study strategies most effective in promoting learning in these areas.

Strategy Lessons

Strategy lessons are based on specific text characteristics that may present comprehension difficulties (i.e., flashback, metaphor, analogy, first person narrative, complex logical argument, bias, or character motivation). These lessons utilize short passages containing a particular text characteristic. Structured questioning addresses the major goals of (1) understanding the particular rhetorical structure or stylistic convention, (2) increasing vocabulary in that content area, and (3) learning to comprehend unknown words in context.

Lessons on rhetorical or stylistic cues to meaning help students understand the primary characteristics of narrative and expository texts. The goal of these sessions is *not* to produce formal scholars of rhetoric, but instead to enhance students' understanding of the text. Part of this process is helping students make the critical inferences that are a generic part of comprehension.

Lessons on sentence or word level cues stress the role of certain types of words or phrases and punctuation in signaling syntactic relationships and stylistic conventions such as dialogue or listing of examples. Other lessons teach students to monitor for meaning and include strategies for trying to maintain meaning even when difficult words are encountered. Reasoning, based on students' prior knowledge and information from the text, is a significant part of all lessons. Each strategy lesson is followed by applying the strategy to a complete text.

Skills Reinforcement

Skills reinforcement, which is more direct and specific than strategy teaching, is used selectively for small groups of students identified on the basis of results of criterion-referenced tests, analysis of standardized test items, and informal teacher diagnosis. The central staff has prepared a manual correlating the comprehension and vocabulary skills from these diagnostic instruments with appropriate practice materials. These activities tend to be isolated drills usually at the sentence or short paragraph level.

Writing

The philosophy of the writing strand closely reflects the influence of recent research on teaching writing. Initially developed as an extension of the reading activities, the writing strand, now in its third year, is finally being developed and given emphasis in its own right.

Modeled on the work of Graves (New Hampshire Writing Project), Sterling and Perl (Lehman College, CUNY), and the Weehawken Writing Project, composing emphasizes student generation of topics, using techniques such as memory chains, brainstorming, and non-stop writing. Revision includes peer rethinking, rewriting, and editing. Strategies for self-evaluation and peer conferences are taught through teacher modeling, with primary emphasis on content. The importance of clearly conveying ideas is initially stressed over more mechanical editing activities. Holistic and primary trait assessment techniques are also used.

Varied writing acitivites are encouraged. Some stress writing for personal expression such as diary or journal writing; others are related to STAR reading assignments such as personal response to story, paraphrasing plot, developing a particular aspect of a story, or developing a story based on a specific situation. Report writing and writing for learning become more salient as more emphasis is placed on expository reading.

Readership

Readership was designed to build the "reading habit" and prepare students for more difficult materials. Teachers read aloud to pupils every day, stopping to explain difficult words, asking children to predict, elaborating unclear sections, summarizing, and discussing the author's ideas. Students are encouraged to engage in oral reading activities such as radio or echo reading to develop fluency and dramatic intonation. Sustained Silent Reading (SSR) is also scheduled (see Tierney, Readence, & Dishner, 1980, for a description of the above techniques).

Parents are encouraged to read to their children, to discuss what they have read, and to talk about school day events. These activities emphasize developing language, concepts, and the reading habit. In addition, parents receive information from the school about the location of their public library and how to obtain library cards for their children.

FROM THEORY TO PRACTICE

STAR rests on a theoretical base created primarily by the following researchers. Kenneth Goodman's work (1969, 1976a, 1976b) was seminal in moving reading research and practice toward comprehension. According to Goodman, the reader anticipates and reconstructs the author's message from selected cues represented in print. Goodman also stresses the importance of the reader's resources during comprehension. Consistent with Goodman's view, later research from the Center for the Study of Reading (Anderson, Spiro, & Montague, 1977) and others (Rumelhart, 1977a; Wittrock, Marks, & Doctorow, 1975) emphasized the underlying cognitive processes which influence comprehension and learning from text. Word recognition, the primary focus of earlier research and instruction, is now seen as a tool for comprehension.

Three approaches for generating curriculum evolved: (1) highlighting appropriate techniques already in use, (2) designing new activities consistent with research findings, and (3) redesigning techniques created by researchers that were too complex for classroom use. Appendix A presents a summary of the research base and the activities presented and developed during STAR in-service sessions. Findings in the following five areas of comprehension research led to the development of the curriculum:

1. the reader/learner as active participant
2. the role of background knowledge
3. rhetorical and stylistic conventions in text
4. questioning and inferences
5. reading to learn.

The Reader/Learner as Active Participant

Researchers no longer view readers or learners as passive recipients of information. Rather, using their knowledge, readers infuse print with meaning and actively construct an interpretation of the text, making inferences whenever necessary. Learners must actively organize and relate new information to what they already know to retain it (Goodman, 1976a; Rumelhart, 1977a; Wittrock et al., 1975). STAR teachers, functioning as facilitators, (1) involve students in small or large group discussions; and (2) help them actively engage in and assume responsibility for reading and learning.

The Role of Background Knowledge

Research has shown that prior knowledge significantly influences how readers comprehend text (Anderson, 1983; Anderson, Reynolds, Schallert, & Goetz, 1977; Anderson, Spiro, & Anderson, 1975). In the narrative and expository strands of STAR, activities are designed to stimulate and build background knowledge. The goal of these activities is to elicit background knowledge or to develop key concepts to facilitate comprehension. To conduct effective prereading sessions, teachers analyze the text for prerequisite information necessary to understanding the text.

Prereading activities include discussing an important topic, relating the topic to the student's personal experiences, reading orally and discussing another story or filmstrip to provide needed information, developing language experience stories on a given topic, using Langer's Prereading Plan (1982a), eliciting a semantic word map (Pearson & Johnson, 1978), or using free association to a key concept and categorizing the responses (Herber, 1978). When unexpected comments occur, students are asked to elaborate and explain how they arrived at their conclusions. These explanations provide valuable diagnostic information about students' knowledge and thinking. Teachers are encouraged to spend as much time as needed to develop the prereading component of every lesson.

Rhetorical and Stylistic Conventions in Text

Because research has shown the importance of text structure in facilitating comprehension and recall (Meyer, 1975; Stein & Glenn, 1979), STAR teachers are taught to analyze text for rhetorical and stylistic conventions that may create comprehension problems. In narrative this includes understanding the role of elements such as plot, theme, mood, setting, style, genre, and voice. Plot includes critical event(s), character beliefs, attitudes, goals, and attempts to solve the problem(s) and the final resolution (or lack of it) in stories (Mandler & Johnson, 1977; Stein & Glenn, 1979). In expository text this includes identifying major points and supporting evidence, and explicit and implicit relations among concepts (Armbruster & Anderson, 1980, 1982a; Meyer, 1975, 1979).

Based on this analysis, teachers construct questions to stimulate discussion of text elements, concepts, relations between ideas, and important inferences. Teachers may anticipate problems and use prereading activities to develop necessary background related to either content or form.

Questioning and Inferences

Questioning to elicit important inferences is seen as an integral part of comprehension and an aid to retention. Through the use of the Pearson and Johnson (1978) questioning taxonomy, teachers are encouraged to think about the relations among the text, questions, and student responses. This framework allows teachers to monitor whether students are just restating information, making inferences by relating ideas in the text, or integrating their knowledge with the author's message. Teachers may also use the Warren, Nicholas, and Trabasso taxonomy (1979; Trabasso, 1981) to construct questions that will elicit critical inferences needed to create a coherent interpretation of text. Questions are used to stress aspects of text the teacher considers important that have not surfaced during retelling or discussion. Explanations of how students derived their responses (i.e., from the text, other students, or prior knowledge) are elicited.

Reading to Learn

Research findings on reading to learn relate specifically to the expository reading strand. Brown's model of learning (Baker & Brown, 1984) was modified by Smith-Burke (1982) to include the concepts of strategies and critical tasks. Research has shown that the strategies used for reading and learning should vary as a function of the criterial task, what the teacher requires of the students—tests, projects, or written assignments (Baker & Brown, 1984a;

Brown, 1980; Brown, Armbruster & Baker, this volume). For example, if retention of information is the objective, study strategies that allow the students to organize the material and elaborate what they already know by relating new information to it are appropriate. These strategies include activating prior knowledge, creating structured overviews, underlining, note taking, and summarizing.

PLANNING, DEVELOPMENT, AND IMPLEMENTATION

A description of the formal and informal administrative processes used during the planning, development, and implementation phases of STAR are summarized in Fig. 14.1.

On paper this framework may not look different from other programs. However, certain characteristics of each phase give STAR its dynamic, vital quality and are critical to its success.

Phase I: Planning

The planning phase was conceived as an on-going process including both initial planning and revision based on feedback from central staff and other participants. An unusual characteristic of this phase was the involvement of university-based consultants and a representative group of teachers.

To start, long-range goals and a budget for the overall program were set by the Director of Communication Arts and the Community School District Superintendent. Due to the superintendent's decentralized style of leadership, the Director was then free to continue the planning, development, and implementation with periodic progress reports to him.

In the second stage of planning the Director met with university-based consultants to plan development and implementation activities that balanced current theory and research with a practical sense of the classroom. Then, the Director of Communication Arts, the consultants, central staff, and a representative group of teachers determined the materials and teaching techniques to be employed. This interactive process led to a natural problem-solving atmosphere fostering a sense of involvement by personnel at all levels.

Phase II: Development

The development phase of the program included the instruction of central staff trainers, reading teachers and, later, classroom teachers. In-service workshops led by university consultants followed by meetings in the schools conducted by the central staff provided the training for the central staff and the Title I reading teachers. After using the program and working out the inevitable problems, the

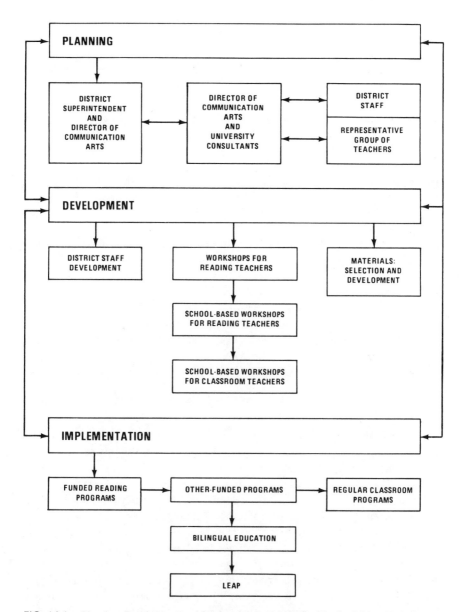

FIG. 14.1.   Planning, Development and Implementation Model for District 4, New York City

223

reading teachers became trainers for classroom and supplemental program teachers in their schools.

Materials were selected, developed, and purchased or reproduced. Whenever the reading teachers needed additional materials, the central staff helped to find and/or reproduce them. As the program evolved, a teacher's manual was written and revised several times as new elements and techniques were incorporated in sample lessons.

Three important characteristics of this phase were (1) stress on professional growth, (2) utilization of insights from theory and research, and (3) continuous support of teachers. The Director of Communication Arts emphasized and modeled professional growth by energetically attending Leadership Training Workshops sponsored by New York State and by inviting university-based personnel to share the latest theories and research with her staff. She gave her staff coordinators release time to attend conferences and encouraged them to watch Sunrise Semester (Smith-Burke, 1979).

The second characteristic, grounding classroom activities in a theoretical and research-based framework, was stressed throughout. Each in-service workshop started with a model of comprehension and/or learning from which the principles for the teaching techniques were derived. All levels of personnel were assumed to be interested and able to comprehend theoretical as well as practical information.

The third unusual characteristic of this phase was the support the classroom and reading teachers received. This was provided through on-site workshops by central staff who elaborated information and techniques developed in the university consultants' workshops and through provision of needed materials.

Phase III: Implementation

STAR was first implemented as part of the Title I Program. Eventually bilingual classes and the program for holdovers, Learning Experiences and Achievement Program (LEAP), began to utilize STAR techniques. The final step was to help classroom teachers incorporate those components that best fit their regular language and reading programs. This ability to adapt STAR to new situations is a characteristic worthy of note.

A final characteristic of this phase, feedback loops, allowed for flexibility and change (illustrated in Fig. 14.1). Some feedback was built into the system as problem-solving periods during in-service workshops. However, most of the feedback took place through an informal system that allowed information to flow "up" the hierarchy. This feature, which gave teachers a sense of ownership and importance, was imperative for program success.

The recursive nature of the three phases is evident in the planning, development, and implementation of the modified Reading Miscue Inventory (Ringler & Weber, 1984). Because the modified RMI reflected the theoretical framework of the STAR Program, its use was the first in-service topic. Throughout this series of workshops teachers were encouraged to use the modified RMI and to bring protocols and problems to the sessions for discussion. The central staff promoted its use by providing necessary materials and developing a manual for administration, coding, and interpretation.

After using the modified RMI for several months, teachers reported that it was too cumbersome and time consuming. However, they felt it was a valuable technique and should be part of in-service training because it forced them to get to know their students in a new way. It had helped them internalize the new model of the reading process and they suggested that the modified RMI could be used with children who are difficult to diagnose. This type of teacher feedback guided development of the STAR Program.

DESIGNING AND IMPLEMENTING IN-SERVICE TRAINING

The major problem for district staff and university consultants was how to help teachers adopt a new orientation to reading based on comprehension as an active contructive process in search of meaning in place of the skills orientation of their previous program.

Planning In-Service Training: Teaching Narrative Reading

The Director of Communication Arts and Ringler made seven important decisions in planning in-service training. First, teaching an adapted version of the Reading Miscue Inventory (Ringler & Weber, 1984) would help teachers understand the new model of reading as well as students' strengths and weaknesses.

Second, "real" materials encountered at home, in school or in the community would be used for instruction. The rationale was that by using actual books, magazines, stories, and newspapers, as opposed to skill exercises, students would begin to understand the relevance and communicative function of reading.

Third, narrative text would be the first area for instruction because both teachers and students were familiar with the genre and a wide variety of story material was available in basal readers, literature kits, and the library.

Fourth, during in-service workshops, consultants would model elicitation teaching, modeling and facilitating discussion. Activities were designed to provide an experiential foundation for teachers as well as motivation so that they would shift their instruction to include interaction in small groups and open discussion with the whole class, quite different from the individualized, isolated learning activities used before.

Fifth, because teachers needed to learn to ask higher level questions to elicit inferences, two taxonomies were selected from the research literature; those by Pearson and Johnson (1978) and by Warren, Nicholas, and Trabasso (1979; Trabasso, 1981).

Sixth, use of the language experience approach (LEA; Hall, 1976; Stauffer, 1970; Veatch, Sawicki, Elliot, Barnette, & Blakey, 1973) was expanded to supplement the curriculum, since this would help to develop children's ideas through their own language, moving from oral to written form. LEA often could be used to bridge from the students' experiences to the text.

Seventh, a three-level diagnostic writing technique was designed to evaluate the success of reading narrative text (Ringler & Weber, 1984). Teachers had an intuitive sense of their students' progress but wanted a more objective evaluation. Steps in this procedure ranged from writing a complete "retelling" to checking events from a story and writing about one of them.

Planning In-Service: Teaching Expository Reading

In planning the in-service training for the expository strand, the Director of Communication Arts and the university consultants decided to expand the reading/learning model and demonstrate how some of the techniques used for narrative could be adapted to expository prose. These included prereading activities, the Pearson and Johnson (1978) questioning taxonomy, and the use of the language experience approach. Two new techniques, the PreReading Plan (PReP; Langer, 1982a) and reasoning guides (Herber, 1978), were also introduced.

To teach a system of expository text analysis, a modified version of Meyer's (1975, 1979) system was tried, but dropped since teachers thought it was too cumbersome to use. Instead, text "mapping" (Armbruster & Anderson, 1980, 1982) was presented. Again teachers felt this system was far too complex and time consuming to use on a regular basis but that it should be included as part of in-service training to demonstrate the complex, nonlinear relations among ideas in expository prose.

Finally, study techniques such as structured overview, note taking, summarizing, and other strategies for retaining information (T. H. Anderson, 1980; Brown, Campione & Day, 1981; Brown & Day, 1983; Earle, 1969) were included during the spring, 1982, sessions. Due to teachers' lack of familiarity with this area, even more in-service training for teaching expository prose was needed than for teaching narrative.

The development of expository reading evolved more slowly than the narrative strand. Strategies for teaching expository writing, materials for reading teachers that coordinate with classroom content instruction and the expository section of the STAR Manual, still need to be developed (as of fall,

1982). Several factors may have contributed to the lag in the development of this strand, the primary one being that research on expository prose has lagged behind the research on narrative. Much of the work by Anderson and Armbruster (T. H. Anderson, 1980; Anderson & Armbruster, 1984b; Anderson, Armbruster, & Kantor, 1980; Armbruster & Anderson, 1980, 1982) such as the concepts of "mapping" or "considerate text" did not become readily available until 1980 and thereafter.

Another factor may have been teacher overload. Teachers had been concentrating on the teaching of narrative for almost 2 years. Consequently, they may not have been ready for training in how to teach expository prose.

A final reason may have involved the selection of teaching materials. Despite a clear state mandate that children learn to comprehend science and social studies texts, the staff and reading teachers were reluctant to use required textbooks, for fear of infringing on the classroom teachers' domain. This resulted in little coordination with content instruction in classrooms and no use of "real" expository materials for transfer to real-life situations.

PROGRAM EVALUATION

It is impossible to assess definitively STAR's effectiveness because standardized tests are the only available measures. Unfortunately, different tests were used in 1974, when the High Intensity Program was in practice, and after 1978, when STAR was established, making comparisons impossible. In addition, district-wide tests reflect the effects of other funded programs as well as the STAR Program

Results of District-wide Testing[1]

Teachers had just begun to try some of the STAR ideas in 1978–79. Therefore, spring testing in both 1978 and 1979 can be considered baseline for the program. In those years, 25.5% and 25.7%, respectively, of District 4 students were reading at or above grade level compared with 43% city-wide. As STAR was implemented the percentage increased. In 1980 35.6% and in 1981 44.3% of the students were reading at or above grade level. In 1982 the percentage had increased to 48.5%, only 2.5% lower than the city-wide average, a gain of 22.6% since the first year of the program. Preliminary April, 1983, data indicate that the percentage of District 4 students reading at or above grade level (52.3%) is above the national average and close to the city-wide average (55.5%).

---

[1]Test data are from the annual reports on Pupil Reading Achievement, N.Y.C. Board of Education, 1979–1982.

TABLE 14.1
Percentage of Students Reading at and above Grade Level
A Comparison of N.Y.C. and District 4[a]
1978 - 1982

Grade	1978 4	1978 NYC	1979 4	1979 NYC	1980 4	1980 NYC	1981 4	1981 NYC	1982[b] 4	1982[b] NYC
2	35.3	42.9	32.4	40.5	42.5	49.6	48.2	48.5	54.2	51.0
3	26.7	40.4	26.3	34.7	42.3	42.3	45.7	50.4	50.7	45.6
4	26.5	44.2	25.7	40.2	41.7	47.2	41.6	48.6	48.0	50.3
5	29.8	47.7	27.8	42.0	37.5	49.2	47.5	54.7	45.6	54.7
6	23.5	41.0	27.8	40.1	37.6	47.8	52.1	51.1	49.4	52.3
7	23.5	38.5	21.5	38.9	28.1	42.5	42.8	50.3	52.5	45.9
8	23.8	43.9	24.5	42.5	29.8	46.3	37.4	50.0	46.7	56.4
9	18.4	48.4	19.3	47.8	29.7	50.7	40.8	50.5	37.3	52.3
TOTAL	25.4	43.0	25.7	40.3	35.6	46.7	44.3	50.7	48.5	51.0

[a]The following forms of the California Achievement Test were used: 1982 CAT - Form C; 1981 CAT - Form D; 1980 CAT - Form C; 1979 CAT - Form C; 1978 CAT - Form D. The percentages were determined by including the students (in the total number of students) who were excluded from testing due to limited English proficiency. Had these language-excused students not been included in the calculations, the percentage of students at or above grade level would have been higher (Division of Curriculum and Instruction, 1981).

[b]Preliminary April, 1983, data indicate that the percentage of District 4 students reading at or above grade level (52.3) is above national average and close to the city-wide average (55.5).

Another way to view trends in the data is to compare a given cohort of students as they progress through the grades. For example, in 1978–79 25.7% of the fourth graders were reading at or above grade levels. As STAR was used systematically in 1979–80, when these students were fifth graders, 37.5% of them scored above the criterion. In sixth grade the percentage rose to 52.1%, the same as the city-wide average for that level. By seventh grade 52.5% of this cohort scored at or above grade level, 6.5% higher than the city-wide average.

Before STAR was implemented there was a decrease in achievement between second and third grades (e.g., 1978 to 1979, from 35.3% to 26.3%). Over the next 3 years this pattern changed (i.e., 1979 to 1980 from 32.4% to 42.3%; 1980 to 1981 from 42.5% to 45.7%; 1981 to 1982 from 48.2% to 50.7%). It appears that students are no longer experiencing a loss from second to third grade.

A comparison of District 4 with four other New York City districts with high percentages of bilingual students indicates that reading achievement has increased in all of these districts. However, the improvement in District 4 has been much greater. The percentage of children reading at or above grade level in 1982 in the other districts ranged from 32.8% to 37.4% compared with 48.5% in District 4.

TABLE 14.2
Percentage of Students Reading at or above Grade Level
A Comparison of Bilingual Districts and N.Y.C.[a]

District	1979	1980	1981	1982
A	24.7	29.2	32.2	32.8
B	22.0	28.9	32.7	34.2
C	22.3	27.8	30.8	34.0
D	25.2	30.0	36.1	37.4
4	25.7	35.6	44.3	48.5
City-wide	40.3	46.7	50.8	51.0

[a]The following forms of the California Achievement Test were used: 1982 CAT - Form C; 1981 CAT - Form D; 1980 CAT - Form C; 1979 CAT - Form C; 1978 CAT - Form D. The percentages were determined by including the students (in the total number of students) who were excluded from testing due to limited English proficiency. Had these language-excused students not been included in the calculations, the percentage of students at or above grade level would have been higher (Division of Curriculum and Instruction, 1981).

STAFFING CHANGES

Although the theoretical orientation of the program has remained constant, a number of changes in staff were necessitated by the selection of STAR in 1981 as one of four exemplary reading programs to be used in the Promotional Gates Program, a holdover program in fourth and seventh grades throughout New York City.

This designation provided the impetus to hire a full-time curriculum writer from among Title I reading teachers in spring, 1981. A new edition of the STAR Manual was written for use that fall by classroom teachers in the Gates Program who had had minimal training.

The roles of district staff and reading teachers also changed significantly in response to demands from other New York city districts and from within District 4. The Director of Communication Arts and the district reading and writing staff coordinators served as resource people to other districts using STAR in their Promotional Gates classes. They provided workshops and ran a special "hot-line" for teachers and supervisors throughout the city.

Within District 4, supervisors and classroom teachers were the focus of training. Staff coordinators trained building supervisors, particularly in the teaching of writing. One of the STAR staff members who was appointed Assistant Director of LEAP (the special program within District 4 for holdover students) began training LEAP teachers in the use of STAR.

The reading teachers functioned as resource people and conducted STAR workshops at faculty and grade level meetings, and held individual conferences with teachers in their schools. Time was specifically allocated in their weekly program for this in-service training. They also served as liaisons between the schools and the district office. This aspect of their work has been recognized as crucial to the inclusion of STAR techniques in the district-wide language arts curriculum.

An important change occurred in September, 1982, when the Director of Communication Arts accepted an appointment as Community School District Superintendent in another district. Three key staff coordinators who had worked closely with STAR transferred to this same new district. As a result of these changes, the District 4 central staff was restructured for 1982–83. A language arts committee, representing six programs (including STAR), was established to make curriculum decisions. In addition, the number of central staff directly involved with STAR was reduced from four and one half to one and one-half people.

At this same time a building principal, deeply committed to the STAR Program, was appointed Community School District Superintendent in another borough of the city. He selected one of the experienced STAR reading teachers to serve as a teacher trainer in his new district.

The final staff change occurred as this article went to press. The Assistant Director of the LEAP Program has been appointed Director of Communication Arts in District 4 effective September, 1983. This administrative change shifts decision making from a team approach, back to centralized control by the Director. Under this new leadership and structure, we predict that STAR will continue to utilize current research to improve instruction.

Even though the STAR Program is now being used well beyond the confines of District 4, the crucial question that can only be answered with time is what effect will the recent personnel changes and the return to a former administrative structure have on the continuity and success of STAR within District 4?

CONCLUSIONS

Three factors have been crucial to the success of the program: long-term commitment, a new research base, and strong administrative leadership.

Most important has been the commitment of people to a long-term project. From the beginning, district administrators, staff, teachers, and university consultants realized that program change would take time. As Samuels (1981) stated in his article on exemplary reading programs, the minimal commitment to a new program before progress can be reliably documented is usually 3 to 5 years. STAR is no exception. Now in its fifth year, it is still developing.

Second, STAR could not have been developed without a new model of reading/learning that stressed the active participation of the reader/learner, and new research on comprehension, writing, and study skills. Clear and consistent long-term goals were developed from this base. Relevant research influenced in-service training and the selection and development of teaching techniques and materials.

Third, without the strong administrative leadership of the Superintendent of District 4 and the Director of Communication Arts, STAR would never have been designed nor implemented. Their decentralized style of leadership and their expectations that other professionals share their concern for children and the professionalism of teachers created the atmosphere that enabled STAR to evolve.

Collaboration between university and school personnel ensured that there would be continuity and a consistent view of the reading process reflected in the training sessions and materials. The involvement of university consultants in all aspects of planning as well as teacher training was unusual, particularly in an urban district of this size. Teachers, respected for their knowledge and experience, also contributed many suggestions that were used to modify the program. Consequently, they felt free to share ideas and discuss the problems that arose in implementing new techniques. As new ideas were incorporated, support from the staff was always available.

We are concerned with how STAR will be implemented in other districts. We fear that the availability of the STAR Manual will lead to program implementation without what we believe are the critical factors of STAR's success: time, commitment, training leadership, administrative support, and an atmosphere of professionalism at ALL levels.

Mandating a curriculum is not the same as providing a context in which staff, teachers, and university-based teacher educators reflect on a particular situation, consider the new research, and come to an understanding of what is needed. Reading a manual of sample lessons is not the same as being involved in an on-going program of teacher training in which explanations of research and implications for practice are discussed and consistent techniques are presented. Also, the importance of on-going administrative support for teachers cannot be overemphasized.

Summary

This may be a statement of the obvious, but worth emphasis: It takes time to change curriculum and behavior. The cycle of research, planning, development, and implementation with all the necessary feedback to guarantee a usable program and a sense of teacher ownership takes time. We are convinced that this process must take place within the context of schools—with university and school-based personnel working in collaboration as peers. It is the cooperation and sharing of expertise that lead to the development of a successful program for translating theory and research into realistic practice.

APPENDIX A

Narrative Text

Year	Research Base	In-Service Topics
1978–79	Rumelhart, 1977a Wittrock et al., 1975	Reading as a constructive process
	K. Goodman, 1969, 1976a, 1976b Y. Goodman & Burke, 1972 Ringler & Weber, 1984	Adapted Reading Miscue Inventory
	Applebee, 1978 Bruce & Newman, 1978 Bruce, 1977, 1978, 1981a, 1981b Thorndyke, 1977 Stein & Glenn, 1979 Mandler & Johnson, 1977	Using stories for teaching reading Analysis of stories for elements (theme, plot, character, setting, mood, language) and genre
	Ringler & Weber, 1984 Rumelhart, 1977b	Developing general questions from this analysis
1979–80	Anderson, 1983 Anderson, Reynolds, Schallert, & Goetz, 1977	Prereading activities to elicit/develop background knowledge
	Anderson, Spiro, & Anderson, 1978 Anderson, Spiro, & Montague, 1977 Y. Goodman & Burke, 1972 Pearson & Johnson, 1978	Retelling and probe questions; Structured comprehension questions to follow retelling and probe
	Warren, Nicholas, & Trabasso, 1979 Trabasso, 1981	Inferencing
	Stauffer, 1970 Veatch et al., 1973 Hall, 1976	Language Experience Approach
1980–81	Ringler & Weber, 1984	Assessment of narrative reading through writing
1981–82	Ringler & Weber, 1984	Narrative lesson planning

Expository Text

Year	Research Base	In-Service Topics
1978–79 (Spring Semester Only)	Robinson, H.A., 1978b Hittleman, 1978	Patterns of writing Enumeration, classification, generalization, comparison/contrast, problem/solution, sequence; vocabulary development
1979–80	Robinson, F.P., 1961 Brown, 1980 Smith-Burke, 1979, 1982	SQ3R Model of comprehension and learning Importance of background knowledge, structure of the text, purpose for reading, reading strategies in relation to criterion task
	Davis, 1972 Smith-Burke, 1979	Analysis of content by finding key concepts and vocabulary words representing them
	Meyer, 1975, 1979 Smith-Burke, 1979	Analysis of text structure
	Anderson et al., 1977 Langer, 1982a	Prereading activities Eliciting/developing prior knowledge Pre Reading Plan (PReP)
	Herber, 1978 Pearson & Johnson, 1978	Post-reading activities Reasoning guides, questioning
	Baker & Brown, 1984a Brown, 1980	Process of learning Metacognition
1980–81	Pearson & Johnson, 1978 Ringler & Weber 1984	Pre-reading activities-eliciting/developing prior knowledge through semantic word maps

Expository Text

Year	Research Base	In-Service Topics
	Anderson & Armbruster, 1982 Armbruster & Anderson, 1980, 1982 Ringler & Weber, 1984	Mapping Text Structure
	Stauffer, 1970 Veatch et al., 1973 Hall, 1976	Language experience based on content area textbooks to elaborate concepts for learning
1981–82	Ringler & Weber, 1984 Ringler, 1982	Applying mapping more generally; identifying key concepts and relationships Relating textbook concepts to city-wide curriculum Using additional materials to develop concepts Prereading; eliciting/ developing prior knowledge
	Anderson, T. H., 1980 Brown & Day, 1983 Brown, Campione, & Day, 1981	Study strategies Underlining, notetaking, summarizing, outlining

15 Development and Implementation of the KEEP Reading Program

Kathryn Hu-pei Au, Doris C. Crowell, Cathie Jordan,
Kim C. M. Sloat, Gisela E. Speidel, Thomas W. Klein, and
Roland G. Tharp
Kamehameha Educational Research Institute

The Kamehameha Early Education Program (KEEP) was launched in 1971 to combat reading problems of disadvantaged Hawaiian youth in elementary school. Its target children are descendants of the original Polynesian inhabitants of the Hawaiian Islands. Native Hawaiians comprise 17% of the state's population; their school-age children number 30,000. Social and economic characteristics indicate that problems faced by this group are similar to those encountered by disadvantaged minorities on the mainland. Many live at or below the poverty level, with unemployment rates higher than the state-wide average. Their incarceration rate is high, and their lack of school success is indicative of a broader pattern of social and economic conditions.

Based on Stanford Achievment Test scores, native Hawaiian students are poor readers. In 1978 at fourth grade, 45% performed below average compared to 23% nationally; 51% were average compared to 54% nationally; and 4% scored above average compared to 23% nationally. By eighth grade, 68% were performing below average, 31% were average, and none were above average (Thompson & Hannahs, 1979).

A major factor in developing and implementing KEEP in the public schools was the unique nature of the Kamehameha Schools/Bishop Estate. A landed trust, Bishop Estate is the single largest private landowner in Hawaii owning 10% of the state's land area, the remaining crown lands from the Hawaiian monarchy. The schools, sole beneficiaries of the trust, provide educational services to children of Hawaiian ancestry. Entirely funded by the estate, KEEP's funding has been stable, allowing staff to work steadily to improve the reading program. This undoubtedly has played a role in KEEP's success.

KEEP's initial focus was to develop a reading program enabling primary grade disadvantaged Hawaiian students to achieve average reading levels. Following 6 years of laboratory school work, KEEP staff developed an effective prototype. That model has undergone extensive field testing, and has been implemented in five public schools. Adjustments are now underway to resolve problems encountered in the field and to incorporate the results of new research. Training and implementation procedures are being refined, and the scope of the program expanded. Originally designed for kindergarten through third grade, it is now being extended through the sixth grade, and is moving from a narrow reading focus to a total language arts approach.

The Ginn 360 was the original reading curriculum in the KEEP laboratory school. It is a conventional phonics-oriented basal reading program, widely used in Hawaii and on the U. S. mainland in the early seventies. This curriculum was faithfully and thoroughly implemented. Additionally, KEEP staff developed criterion-referenced tests for all program objectives and initiated systematic testing and charting of students' progress. They also made efforts to increase students' attentiveness and motivation to maximize the likelihood of success. Results obtained using this conventional phonics-oriented program were entirely negative: KEEP students did no better than control students in the public schools (Tharp, 1982).

This poor outcome prompted major changes in the program. Based on several lines of research, staff members reached consensus about the needed changes. All agreed the new program should emphasize comprehension of text meaning, not phonics. Instruction should be carried out in small reading groups. Classrooms should be reorganized around well-planned learning centers, emphasizing small-group formats. A switch to a program with these characteristics was made in the fall of 1976.

PROGRAM DESCRIPTION AND CURRICULUM RESEARCH

One of the hallmarks of the KEEP reading program is its emphasis on comprehension. This emphasis is reinforced in the program's prescriptions for small-group lessons, in assignments given to the children, and in the skills students are to learn. These skills and the basic content and organization of the curriculum are set out in the Kamehameha Reading Objectives System or KROS (Crowell, 1981).

KROS

KROS, the framework for the developmental reading program (K-3), is designed to help students develop into mature readers who can adjust their skills to meet the demands of both informational and recreational reading. KROS' major component is a comprehension strand composed of substrands in listening and reading comprehension, information retrieval, vocabulary development, use of context, and analogous thinking. The system also includes a decoding strand divided into sight vocabulary, structural analysis, and phonics substrands.

KROS is based on objectives, and includes criterion-referenced tests to determine when the student has met the objectives. The KROS comprehension objectives are derived from a series of studies exploring thinking skills or cognitive processes required to answer comprehension questions correctly (e.g., Crowell & Au, 1981). A scale of questions operationally defining thinking skills serves to guide teachers' questioning during small-group reading lessons and provides the structure for criterion-referenced tests. The scale of questions contains five levels: association, categorization, seriation, integration, and extension. Association questions are designed to elicit any details the child can recall. Categorization questions require the student to classify story characters (e.g., as good or bad) and to justify the response with information from the story. Seriation questions deal with relations among details, including cause and effect or sequence of events. Integration questions require story elements to be combined into a coherent structure not necessarily provided by the story (e.g., summarizing the story or giving the main idea). Finally, extension questions require the child to apply her understanding of the story (e.g., relate the story to other stories or suggest a plausible alternate ending).

ETR Lessons

In addition to asking questions at the five levels, KEEP teachers structure lessons by using the experience-text-relationship (ETR) method (Au, 1979). This method enables students to comprehend text in ways increasingly independent of direct teacher assistance. In ETR lessons, the teacher models and guides the children through the process of using background knowledge to understand and interpret text. At the beginning of each lesson (the E phase), the teacher focuses questions on the children's personal experiences or background knowledge relevant to the topic of the text to be read (usually, a basal reader story). Next, during the T phase, the children silently read a section of the text, usually a page or two, and the teacher specifies pieces of information the children are to find (e.g., the characters and the setting). After reading, the details of the story are discussed. In the R or relationship phase, the teacher uses questions to help the children draw relations between their background knowledge and text information, encouraging the children to speculate about what will happen later in the story. Relationship phases generally alternate with text phases: the children read and discuss the text at a literal level, then interpret it in terms of their existing knowledge structures.

Essential Features of the KEEP Reading Program

The small-group reading comprehension lessons, although central to the program, are just one part of it. Other "essential features" (Au, 1981) characterize the program for students in the primary grades; some of the features vary at the kindergarten and upper elementary levels. The following characteristics are considered standard in the program for grades 1 through 3 with enrollments of 25 to 30 students per class.

Schedule. Two hours and 15 minutes is allocated daily for the reading/language arts period. Most classes have reading groups of about five children; the meeting time for each group is 20 to 25 minutes. Reading/language arts time is usually divided into five periods. Each group spends one period receiving direct teacher instruction, and the remaining four working independently.

Monitoring Student Progress. The teacher or KEEP trainer requests KROS criterion-referenced tests at least every 2 weeks. Over a month, at least one test is requested for every child; the mean number of tests is between two and three. The average pass rate is 70% or better for all tests. Students get feedback on test results from an aide, the teacher, or the trainer.

Small-Group Instruction. Children are assigned to homogeneous reading groups based on their KROS test results. The teacher provides instruction for each group at the level and on the objectives indicated by test results. Two thirds of the time is spent on comprehension instruction, and one third on word identification skills. Children in the reading group are attentive nearly all the time. The teacher tries to involve them all in discussions, resulting in a high level of student participation.

There is an identifiable organizing strategy for comprehension instruction, supported by the use of effective teaching techniques, both appropriate to the children's reading level and the purposes of the lesson. The organizing strategy used most often is the Experience-Text-Relationship method described earlier; another is the Directed Reading-Thinking Activity (Stauffer, 1975). A supporting technique is the use of visual structures displaying text information.

Word identification skills are taught in the service of reading comprehension, and instruction in word identification follows the sequence of KROS objectives. Instruction aimed at enabling students to apply the KROS word-identification strategies occurs on a regular and frequent basis. The assumptions are (1) the most efficient means of word identification is sight recognition, (2) the next resort is use of context to identify the word, and (3) phonic and structural analysis are exercised if the word is still not known. Phonics is taught by analytic, as opposed to synthetic, methods.

Learning Centers: Successful Practice.   The classroom is organized into work areas, each with appropriate materials and supplies. There are usually 10 to 12 such learning centers in a classroom, and three to four children are generally present at each. At least half of the assignments at centers are directly related to the KROS objectives, and individual student work is consistent with KROS test results (i.e., covers objectives following those they have just mastered). One half of the time is spent on comprehension activities, one fourth on word identification skills and one fourth on other language arts skills. Assignments are designed so the children can complete them independently with at least 80% accuracy, and children generally spend at least 75% of the time at centers working on their assignments.

Cultural Compatibility.   Considerations of cultural relevance have contributed to program decisions on a number of "essential features." The following are highlighted as additional "marker" features of full implementation of the culturally compatible program:

1. Children are responsible for the setup and cleanup of the centers and are allowed to operate without direct teacher supervision.
2. The teacher allows peer interaction in centers. Teaching/learning interactions occur fairly frequently among children at centers and are allowed and encouraged by the teacher.
3. Talk-story-like participation structures as defined below are present in small-group lessons.

CULTURAL RESEARCH AND EDUCATIONAL PROGRAM

One of KEEP's basic premises has been that an educational program will be effective only if it is compatible with the culture of the children it serves. KEEP's anthropologists have studied modern Hawaiian culture as manifested in the home and as it interacts with the school setting, and have used that knowledge to contribute to program decisions regarding appropriate educational practices for Hawaiian children. One cultural facet which has been especially important in educational decisions consists of the contexts and interactions in which teaching and learning customarily take place.

Home and community ethnographic research (Gallimore, Boggs, & Jordan, 1974) has found that children are highly valued in Hawaiian families, which tend to be large. The socialization system is not organized to train children for leaving the family but to teach them to become increasingly responsible and competent *within* the family system. Basic family values are interdependence rather than independence, responsibility, sharing of work and resources, cooperation, and obedience and respect toward parents. Young people's responsibilities begin early and involve critical family functions to which children typically contribute as members of a work force of siblings, operating without close adult supervision. Childcare is shared by parents and older children. After infancy, children are expected to function as part of the sibling group and to turn to siblings for routine kinds of help and information. In many matters, adults tend to relate to the sibling group as a whole or to a teenage "top sergeant" of the group, rather than one-to-one with each child. Children learn to make requests of their elders indirectly, to accept decisions without protest, and not to confront or negotiate with adults.

Community ethnographic data (Jordan, 1981) reveal that Hawaiian children acquire knowledge and learn skills by observing adult and older child models and by participating in family tasks and activities with, and initially under the supervision of, older children. They are socialized to attend to and to learn from a variety of people, and to use other children as major sources of help, skill, and information. They also learn to switch roles, from that of learner to that of teacher, depending on their competence relative to others in the setting.

Hawaiian children learn in a whole-task or whole-skill context. Although they may be doing only some small part of a task, they participate within the context of the whole task, be it cooking a meal or dancing a hula. Finally, they are allowed to judge for themselves when they have learned enough to perform a more demanding part of a skill or task. Performance of new skills is voluntary, not forced.

A controlled-setting, comparative study of teaching interactions between mothers and their 5-year-old children (Jordan, 1976) found that although Hawaiian mothers and a comparison group of Midwestern middle-class mothers showed similar rates of teaching interaction overall, the forms of teaching used were quite different. The mainland mothers more often relied exclusively on verbal control and direction. The Hawaiian mothers' teaching involved nonverbal modeling/demonstration or co-participation in the task with their children, sometimes combined with task-oriented talk.

Naturalistic study of the behavior of Hawaiian children in school settings (Jordan, 1978a, 1978b) has found that as siblings and older children are important at home, so peers are important in school, as companions, as socializers, and as teachers. In school, Hawaiian children show a high peer orientation and do not automatically attend to adults. They spend a high proportion of classroom time in peer interaction, and turn to peers when in need of help. In turn, they offer help to other children, and are sensitive to cues that classmates are in difficulty. The major teaching strategies employed by peers in classrooms are reminiscent of those used by siblings and mothers: modeling and co-participation or intervention (that is, partially or wholly "taking over" a task).

The KEEP reading program is designed to be totally compatible with the children's culture. The following examples relate to major structural features of the program.

First, the small-group nature of the learning centers is in line with the importance of peers and siblings to Hawaiian children, since it allows them the company of other children in adult-approved circumstances. It is compatible with familiar home contexts for *working,* because the working group has a degree of autonomy and independence from the adult teacher, and other children are available as resources. Further, the potential for *cooperative* work is present, since there is likely to be at least one child present who is doing or has already done the same work. Because the center organization encourages peer interaction and cooperative work, peer teaching/learning interactions occur at a considerable rate, and the children can and do mobilize accustomed *strategies* for teaching and learning such as demonstration, co-participation, prompting, and error-cued teaching (Jordan, 1981).

In addition, the small working group provides a more culturally appropriate context for interacting with an adult than performing individually for the teacher. Also, pupil performance in the lesson is largely voluntary. Both these factors contribute to the children's willing participation in verbal interchanges (Jordan, 1981).

Secondly, the reading lesson shares task features with nonschool learning situations that help to elicit appropriate cognitive responses. There is co-participation by the more knowledgeable individual (the teacher) and the less knowledgeable individuals in the task. As at home, learning takes place in the context of performance of the whole task as the teacher guides the children in learning to read by engaging them in the whole process. The children learn by reading, comprehending, and incorporating the written text into their thought processes, not by learning rules for reading or by doing some decontextualized subpart of the task.

Finally, the reading lesson resembles the Hawaiian speech event of "talk story" (Watson-Gegeo & Boggs, 1977). "Talk-story" is a complex and rich narrative event, which is marked by joint performances and co-narration by two or more speakers. The KEEP reading lesson is orchestrated by the teacher to allow and encourage talk-story-like participation by the children, and thus to encourage rich verbal interaction and idea manipulation (Au & Jordan, 1981; Au & Mason, 1981).

As should be clear from these examples, cultural compatibility does not mean cultural isomorphism. We are neither attempting nor recommending the reproduction of Hawaiian culture or any other natal culture in the classroom. The KEEP classroom, although it is culturally compatible for Hawaiian children, is still a classroom. It is more like all other classrooms than it is like a Hawaiian home. Cultural compatibility relates not only to the home culture, but also to the culture of teachers. School settings need to be designed so teachers and students can work together to accomplish their prescribed purposes.

Cultural compatibility also does not imply complete cultural specificity. Other programs might be designed to work just as well for Hawaiian children as

KEEP does. Conversely, it is not necessarily true that KEEP will work only for Hawaiian children and not for any other group of children. We are in the early stages of research designed to investigate this issue. Our experience leads us to believe that the KEEP program, taken as a whole, works especially well for Hawaiian and other Polynesian children, but does not at all detract from the achievement of the other ethnic groups found in Hawaii's schools (see later section on evaluation data).

LANGUAGE RESEARCH

Since KEEP's target students are native speakers of a creole called Hawaiian English, the language-reading issue has received close attention (Speidel, 1982). Language factors seem to be implicated in the following way. Speaking a dialect does not in itself hamper learning to read; the problem lies in asking the children to learn to read standard English, a language code somewhat unfamiliar to them. Evidence for this unfamiliarity is of several kinds. For example, they understand connected discourse better in Hawaiian English than in standard English (Speidel, Tharp, & Kobayashi, 1982), and they are less likely to apply certain standard English grammatical rules than standard-speaking peers (Speidel, 1981). For Hawaiian children, familiarity with standard English is highly predictive of reading achievement (Speidel, 1981). Therefore, school curricula must be responsive to their language differences.

Rather than conducting separate language development sessions to promote the children's school language and standard English skills, KEEP has integrated language development with reading instruction in a unique and effective manner. Research knowledge on language development, observations of how language is acquired and used at home (Dore, 1979; Grimm, 1982; Moerk, 1983) and analyses of steps in reading acquisition (Speidel, 1979, 1981; Vellutino & Scanlon, 1982) have been important in the design of this program. We have evidence that an integrated approach to reading and language development is effective both for the acquisition of reading skills and for the comprehension and production of the less familiar standard code (Speidel, 1982). The following is an interpretation of reading program features from the language perspective.

During the small-group reading lesson, the teacher employs strategies similar to those used by mothers of middle- and upper-middle-class mainland children (Cross, 1977; Moerk, 1983) to promote language development (Dowhower-Vuyk & Speidel, 1982; Speidel & Dowhower-Vuyk, 1982). The teacher elicits language in context by asking various questions, elaborates on the children's utterances, introduces new vocabulary, and provides ample opportunity for the children to express their ideas. She creates a warm and accepting emotional climate in which the children feel their contributions are valued.

Textbooks written in the less familiar standard code are introduced gradually. Stories dictated by children and recorded in their own language patterns are the major material for early reading instruction. Use of these language experience stories eases the transition to standard basal texts.

Instructional strategies aimed at the development of reading comprehension also promote language learning. Discussions structured according to the ETR method allow for the learning of new vocabulary and language patterns on the basis of familiar ones. Discussion stimulated by comprehension questions at the five levels provides children with the opportunity to use language in ever more complicated ways.

RELATIONS BETWEEN RESEARCH AND PROGRAM IMPLEMENTATION EFFORTS

Various relations exist between the work of KEEP's training and dissemination unit and its research departments. Training and dissemination staff are usually the first to identify difficulties with the program, often when new features are being tested in the field. Their ideas may point to topics which are then studied by one of the research departments. Therefore, not only are research and program implementation closely tied to one another, they are often one and the same. Although tensions resulting from the different perspectives of researchers and teacher trainers are inevitable, such tensions are important to KEEP's work.

At present, the teacher training and program implementation process is itself the subject of major research efforts, like those that resulted in the design of KEEP's comprehension-oriented reading program. The following illustrates the teacher training and implementation process.

TRAINING AND IMPLEMENTATION

The Schools/Estate and the Public School System

KEEP's affiliation with the Kamehameha Schools/Bishop Estate has influenced its efforts to disseminate the reading program to the public schools in a number of ways. The Schools/Estate is a powerful, important force in Hawaii, influencing the lives of thousands. Association with the Schools is very important to those within the Hawaiian community. Parents want their children to attend the Schools, and many graduates want to work at the Schools. Thus, association with any Kamehameha program is desired by many Hawaiian parents, and this includes wanting their children to participate in KEEP-affected public school classrooms.

KEEP's adoption by public schools was a major change in direction for the Schools. Throughout most of their life, the Kamehameha Schools operated a private day and boarding school for Hawaiian students (affecting, perhaps, 5% of the school-age Hawaiian population) and had minimal interaction with the public school system. But 15 years ago the Schools began a number of cooperative ventures with the public schools. In most of these ventures, the Schools have borne all or most of the cost, and the relationships between the two organizations have been informal. Implementation of the KEEP reading program in public school classrooms could take place only after more formal working arrangements were established. The gradual development of these arrangements has involved a great deal of time and effort.

The characteristics of the public school system in Hawaii are in some ways unique, and the nature of the system has had important effects on KEEP's dissemination efforts. The system is funded at the state level, and there is a single board of education. When KEEP was started, the board approved in very general terms a cooperative working relationship. Over the years, the details of that relationship have been worked out at lower levels with those directly affected. From time to time presentations have been made to the board, which has continued to endorse the general nature of the relationship.

Some areas, such as personnel practices, are standardized and uniform throughout the public school system. In others, including curriculum, there is a fair amount of autonomy and discretion at the district and even at the school and building level. The seven districts in the public school system vary in the amount of control they exert over curriculum decisions at the building level.

The result is considerable variation in curriculum both across and within districts. In 1981-1982, KEEP was operating in five schools with 40 teachers. Previously, two of these schools used a single program, the locally developed Hawaii English Program (HEP), across all grades and classes. The others used HEP in one classroom per grade and a basal reader program in the other classrooms.

HEP is substantially different in concept and practice from KEEP in that it is based on self-instruction and peer tutoring. The teacher functions as an administrator of the system and has few, if any, instructional interchanges with students. Some public school teachers who decided to try the KEEP reading program had used HEP for 6 years; some younger teachers had never used anything else.

Establishing Relationships with Individual Schools

KEEP's relations with two of the five public schools began under unique circumstances. Its relations with the other three were established according to a common pattern. Relations with the first school were initiated 10 years ago, shortly after KEEP came into existence. The school's decision to implement the reading program came when a fire destroyed most of the language arts material used by the primary grade classes, and the teachers elected to discontinue use of HEP and adopt the KEEP reading program. The relationship with the second school began when KEEP was prepared to field test the reading program. As it happened, one of KEEP's periodic meetings with the state board occurred at this time, and the special requirements for a controlled field test were discussed. In effect, the district and this second school were directed to cooperate with KEEP.

The other school sites were established 3 to 4 years later. District superintendents and principals were contacted to discuss potential KEEP participation. The typical strategy for approaching the teachers involved an after-school presentation by KEEP staff, accompanied by invitations for teachers to visit a site where the reading program could be observed. The teachers spent a full day observing the program in action and discussing its details with KEEP teachers and trainers. In a subsequent meeting implications of adopting the program were discussed in detail. Teachers still interested then signed a voluntary, non-binding letter of agreement. The goal of these efforts was to establish a foothold in the school with the expectation that program results would persuade additional teachers to participate. The number of teachers volunteering initially ranged from two to four from faculties of 15 to 50 members.

Teacher Training

At all five sites, 3 to 4 months usually elapsed between the first contact with the principal, usually in late winter, and the signing of agreements by the teachers, usually in late spring. Concentrated efforts in teacher training start with about a week of workshops just before school resumes in the fall. For new teachers, up to 5 full days of training may be involved. The focus is on an overview of the curriculum and the specific things they should do in the first months of school. For teachers experienced in the program, the emphasis is on advanced teaching techniques, changes in the scope or sequence of the curriculum, and variations in the basic program.

The process of training teachers to implement the KEEP reading program is influenced by the teachers' previous experience and the features of the program. At the beginning of the school year, training efforts focus on helping the teacher organize and manage her classroom according to the learning center system. This may involve everything from helping the teacher learn to make decisions about which kinds of assignments should be placed in centers for different children to rearranging the furniture in the classroom. Part of the teacher's ability to implement the system properly depends on her spending considerable time training her students to function effectively in it. This takes from 2 to 4 weeks, depending on the students and on the teacher's previous experience. The center system certainly has value for student learning in and of itself. From a teacher training point of view, however, much of its value is that it frees the teacher to concentrate on providing lessons to small, homogeneous reading groups. The teacher begins these lessons soon after the center system has been implemented.

Proper implementation of many features of the KEEP reading program depends on the availability of KROS criterion-referenced test results, since direct teacher instruction and center assignments are both tied to these results. Testing all students thoroughly usually takes the first 4 weeks of school. While students are adjusting to the center system, their instructional needs are being diagnosed.

Trainers spend a considerable amount of time at this early point in helping teachers learn to make use of KROS test results. New KEEP teachers are unaccustomed to using data systematically for instructional purposes. Training in this set of skills occurs simultaneously with training in the running of the center system.

Because of all the learning and behavioral change required, this early period in the teacher training process is very stressful. Running 10 to 12 learning centers, with appropriate assignments for five different groups, is a complex and even overwhelming task for many new teachers. Most are concerned with survival, being prepared for the next day or week, and trying to understand what it is they are doing. Gradually, this part of the program becomes easier and absorbs less energy. As this occurs, there is a shift in emphasis in training.

With the centers running adequately, attention can be directed to the small-group, teacher-led lessons. The trainer's goal is to have the teacher master the instructional strategies and techniques described earlier. For weeks, a trainer may spend most of his/her time working on strategy or technique with a given teacher. As these are mastered, attention shifts to how they are related to one another, and when each should be used.

In most cases a minimum of a year is required for teachers to achieve general competence. More consistent and polished performance, including mastery of most of the techniques demanded by the program, is usually evident after 2 years.

Trainers are assigned full time to participating schools. As a rule, each trainer works with four to six teachers—observing each teacher's classroom two to four times a week. There is usually one long meeting a week (30 to 45 minutes) with each teacher and a number of shorter ones.

The observations and meetings serve several purposes. For newer teachers, the emphasis is on mastery of the basic teaching and management skills and the concepts underlying the KEEP program. General consultation affords the teacher an opportunity to use the trainer as a resource. Most teachers need encouragement, assistance, and a sympathetic ear from time to time, and trainers think that such encouragement is one of their most important functions. Since the trainer is an implicit part of the accountability system associated with the KEEP reading program, these meetings may also serve to improve the teacher's level of performance by reminding him/her of the program's standards. The presence of curriculum goals, along with the feedback provided by the trainer and the KROS test results, no doubt contributes to the teachers' high levels of performance.

The biggest obstacle trainers face is not having enough time to spend with teachers. Very limited meeting time is available, usually after the school day ends. KEEP provides funds to the public school system to hire substitutes so that teachers may leave their classrooms for training. But it has proved difficult to make arrangements for any teacher to be away for more than 4 days a year. If teachers could be removed from classroom responsibilities altogether, very thorough training could be done in less than a semester. Alternate training strategies are certainly possible.

In summary, the KEEP reading program is disseminated to the public schools through interactions between personnel from two separate institutions. Implementation is complicated by the complex nature of the reading program, the high level of teacher expertise required, and accountability pressures. The job of KEEP's teacher trainers is very demanding for all these reasons. The joint efforts of KEEP's trainers and cooperating public school teachers, however, have led to substantial improvements in student achievement, as indicated by evaluation data.

EVALUATION DATA

When the KEEP reading program was being developed, cohort analysis and true experiments were used to assess program effectiveness through standardized tests of reading achievement. Results obtained through the first 7 years have been reported (Gallimore, Tharp, Klein, & Sloat, 1982; Klein, 1981; Tharp, 1982). The true experiment was the evaluation design executed during the first 2 years of field testing the KEEP reading program. At each of two public school sites there were two KEEP classrooms and two control classes. At the end of the test, KEEP classrooms were performing at approximately the 50th percentile, control classrooms at the 30th, as measured by the Metropolitan Achievement Test (MAT).

This was the first opportunity to assess any differential effects of the curriculum for students of Hawaiian and non-Hawaiian ancestry. Reading achievement as measured by the MAT and the first-grade data were pooled over the 2 years of the field test. Results of this analysis are presented in Fig. 15.1 (mean scores are presented as normal curve equivalents (NCE), a linear scale with a mean of 50 and a standard deviation of 20.6). At each grade level, students in KEEP classes performed at a higher level than their controls in both ethnic classifications. The greater effect of the KEEP program on Hawaiians may be attributed in part to the lower performance of control children in that

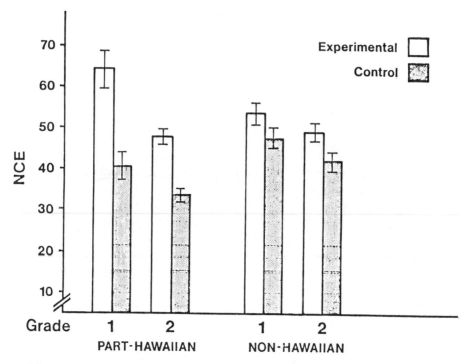

FIG. 15.1   Mean (± 1 standard error) total reading on the Metropolitan Achievement Test as a function of grade and ethnicity.

ethnic group, a difference that is significant at first- and second-grade levels. The higher performance of Hawaiians compared to non-Hawaiians in the KEEP classes is significant only at first grade.

With this initial demonstration of the effectiveness of the KEEP program in public school classrooms, broader dissemination of the program was undertaken and the focus changed from evaluation of the program itself to evaluation of the effectiveness of program implementation.

Results in the first year of dissemination were similar to those observed during field testing in the first and second grades. However, the third-grade results were lower. At this grade level, there were no previous control group data for comparison. The number of years a child had received the KEEP program was expected to be a critical variable, but was inextricably confounded with grade level. The effects of this factor could not be assessed in third grade in the absence of a control group. Effects of a second factor, the teacher's years of experience in the KEEP program, *could* be analyzed, although this factor was at least partially confounded with grade level and tenure of students. Results for the first 2 years of dissemination are shown in Fig. 15.2, presented as a function of grade level and years of teacher experience.

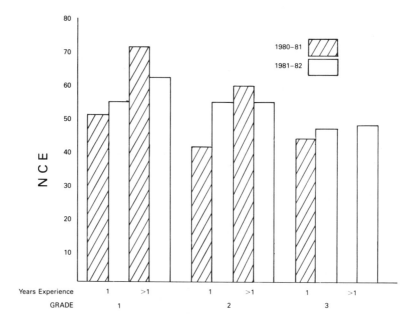

FIG. 15.2   Mean (± 1 standard error) total reading on the Metropolitan Achievement Test as a function of grade and teachers' experience for academic years 1980–1981 and 1981–1982.

Results of the first year of dissemination, 1980–1981, show a marked difference between first-year teachers and those with 2 or more years of experience in the KEEP program. All third-grade teachers were in their first year with KEEP, so no comparison was possible at this grade level. The data for 1981–1982 point to improvement in the effectiveness of program implementation efforts in two ways. Classes of first-year teachers showed an average greater than those of first-year teachers at all grade levels during the previous year. In addition, average achievement in classes of teachers in their second year with KEEP suggests improvement by those teachers who had been new to the program in 1980–1981 (assuming that continuing veterans' achievement scores remained constant across the 2 years).

In summary, KEEP's experience in public school field sites suggests the following conclusions:

● The field test demonstrated the probable success of the KEEP program in public school classrooms.

● Program success can, in part, be attributed to the increased achievement of Hawaiian students, who typically fare poorly in public school settings.

● Teacher experience with the KEEP program is an important variable to be considered in assessing the degree of program implementation and effectiveness. Two years of teaching experience may be required to achieve complete implementation and realize program benefits.

- Changes in strategies for teacher training may reduce the time required for effective implementation.

KEEP'S RESEARCH PROCESS

The KEEP reading program, lines of research, teacher training and implementation procedures, and evaluation data are all the products of a particular inquiry process. They are unfinished products since they continue to be revised by this process. Each separate inquiry occurs in the context of the process, and findings are evaluated within the accumulating body of knowledge. This process has been described in detail (Tharp, 1981; Tharp & Gallimore, 1979, 1982). It is composed of three assumptions, four methods or ways of knowing, and seven steps.

Assumptions

- *The phenomena are highly complex.* Understanding of the learning child, for the purposes of developing educational programs, requires the broadest and most intense analysis possible. This means that research must rely on multiple theories, disciplines, and methods.
- *Programs have multiple components.* Any educational program is both a single thing and an assemblage of elements. Elements may be studied one at a time, but that requires research strategies different from those used to study the whole.
- *The goal is viability.* The external validity of research requires that inquiry be conducted in the environments where it must ultimately survive, and developed programs must be viable in actual classrooms. Therefore, research and development must be conducted not only in laboratories but in real classrooms. Indeed, the basic laboratory must be the classroom itself.

Methods

Many research methods are employed at KEEP: psychometrics, discourse analysis, direct behavioral observation, microethnography, participant observation, task analysis, interview, analogue experimentation, and so forth. The following classification is intended to make clear the inquiry process appropriate for different purposes.

- *Experimentation.* The experiment is only one of four methods of research. As the term is used at KEEP, experimentation is that method which studies elements one-at-a-time, while attempting control over other elements.

• *Program evaluation.* At the other extreme, program evaluation refers to research which takes the program elements all at a time, and compares the outcome to some variety of non-program.

• *Data guidance.* Experimentation and program evaluation both are plagued with the complex interactions of multiple program components, and their findings are limited to the status quo of these interactions. Data guidance is a method that involves tinkering, fine-tuning, and balancing of a multicomponent, interactive system. It involves frequently or continuously taken "stream data" on the performance of the system, in the light of which one or more features are altered, and other features balanced to compensate. At KEEP, this process is continuous, as research findings call for program modifications. The stream data, on both child and teacher performance, provide the basis for judgments.

• *Personal knowing.* The first three methods are quantitative. Personal knowing refers to the qualitative aspect of inquiry: personal memories, opinions, and judgments; it includes disciplined participant observation, ethnography, and textual analysis. Personal knowing relies on the individuality of the observer, and accepts the unique unmanipulated event as datum.

Each of these methods has strengths and weaknesses; all are necessary to meet the three assumptions. The methods have been arranged in a typical sequence which is recursive, as shown in Fig. 15.3.

Step	Description	Method
One	Creation of a prototype assembly of elements	Personal Knowing
Two	Estimation of effects of elements one at a time	Experimentation
Three	Addition and Subtraction of elements	Personal Knowing
Four	Refinement of elements and balancing of the system	Data Guidance
Five	Formal inclusion, and definition of elements	Personal Knowing
Six	Measurement of the effects of the assemblage	Program Evaluation
Seven	Decision to continue, loop back, or abort	Personal Knowing

FIG. 15.3 The Model Sequence of Methods.

All methods are simultaneously employed, with answers for a variety of questions being sought through the sequence of steps. As shown in previous sections of this chapter, the KEEP reading program is complex, with many different features. There are several different lines of research all contributing to its development. Teacher training and implementation procedures may also influence changes in the program, and are themselves the subject of study. Evaluation designs change as time goes on, and different types of data are sought. Thus, the inquiry process outlined above is useful in ordering and channeling the cataract of data to produce educational improvement. It would be impossible to understand the complex but necessary interactions among KEEP's different arenas of activity without such a well-defined inquiry process.

CONCLUSION

Although KEEP is like many university-based research groups in having well-developed lines of inquiry continued over a period of years, it is unlike most of these groups in having ongoing, day-to-day responsibilities for the performance of large numbers of teachers and children. KEEP is like many school system-based projects in its concern for the practical realities of reading program development and implementation, but it is unlike most of these projects in having been in existence long enough to acquire a high level of process, as well as product, sophistication.

KEEP's work involves many theories, disciplines, and methods. The shape of the reading program was influenced by psycholinguistic, sociolinguistic, and schema theoretic views of the reading process. Education, psychology, anthropology, and linguistics are prominent among the disciplines represented at KEEP, and a wide variety of methods associated with these disciplines is used. At times, work with a particular theory, in a particular discipline, employing a particular method, yields especially rich results. But although the influence of particular theories or scientific perspectives can be seen in individual studies, none can be said to be more influential than another in shaping this reading program as a whole. It is the inquiry process itself that has proved to be paramount and of continuing value in permitting systematic evaluation of the usefulness of many different ideas.

The Step Up Language Arts Program: A Study of Effective Change

16

Gloria M. McDonell
Fairfax County Public Schools, Virginia

An educational community must be committed to examining the effectiveness of its practices and develop workable strategies for change or it is in danger of failing to fulfill its primary function—to create literate thinking citizens. This chapter describes and analyzes change designed to improve a reading program for low-achieving children. It is an example of current research put into practice.

It is not the intent of the paper to make sweeping generalizations about program impact. Clear causal relations are difficult to establish in a natural school setting where evaluation designs, test measures, and instructional practices have all been modified over the 16 years of program operation. This case study simply presents an empirical view of data gathered through intensive interview and personal observation, as well as test scores. An integrated picture of past experience, environmental forces, and present status should provide insight into factors that contribute to successful change.

BACKGROUND AND HISTORY

Step Up Language Arts (SULA), a Title I program for low-achieving children in grades 1 through 3, functions in the large, affluent suburban school district of Fairfax County. Though the county's test scores are well above the national norm, many of its schools are populated with educationally disadvantaged students who need additional help in reading and language arts. The children served by this program are much like other low achievers in primary grades. Their achievement level is below the 40th percentile. They lack experience with books and print. Their view of the reading process is distorted, because they do not always get a message from print. They may or may not have letter-sound identification skills, but they usually have difficulty in applying these skills to an unknown word. They have few strategies to help them deal with difficult text, and unfortunately, some are so used to not understanding that they do not perceive this as a problem. These children are highly dependent on the teacher, and by second grade have an additional problem—lack of self-esteem.

When SULA was first conceived in the late sixties, it was largely an enrichment program. Its purpose was to provide children with varied experiences and to build vocabulary. Activities such as field trips, art, and popcorn making helped children think of school as a warm inviting place to learn. As the focus in all federal programs shifted to a more academic approach, readiness became the new goal. Students were expected to demonstrate ability in the following skill areas:

- Body Motor—Body control and parts recognition, left-right differentiation.
- Visual Motor—Likenesses-differences in symbols and color-shape recognition.
- Auditory Perception—Source of likenesses-differences in sounds, rhythm patterns, memory for digits, syllables, oral direction, and rhyming words.
- Reading—Letter naming and matching, letter reproduction, color words, initial sounds, and vowels.

Utilizing commercially prepared materials, teachers attempted to develop reading readiness. Decoding skills were taught. Through a synthetic phonics approach, students received intensive drill on isolated sounds and blending. Worksheets provided further practice. An additional program attempted to increase language competence in a stimulus-response fashion. Teachers were warm and loving and tried to pace instruction so students felt success and developed an improved self-concept. Unfortunately, that fragile self-concept often disappeared in the regular classroom, and the carryover of skills was minimal.

The Impetus for Change

Seven years ago classroom teachers began to express dissatisfaction with the existing program. Like many remedial programs, SULA was governed by a commercial product with a totally different teaching method than the basal approach used in regular classrooms. Children were often confused by conflicting instruction. Teachers and principals were concerned by the lack of skill carryover, particularly the failure of newly developed decoding skills to improve comprehension.

An internal review of the program was conducted by the Director of Curriculum Services. Three perspectives were considered: classroom teachers, building administrators, and parents. The major finding was that lack of coordination between the Title I resource teachers and the classroom teacher had negated the long-range goal of the program: to increase student success in the classroom. Although students succeeded in the resource room, their classroom performance did not improve. Indeed, there were many indications that the instruction caused students to develop a great dependence on the resource instructor, and they were not able to function in an independent mode when necessary. With the aid of a newly appointed Title I coordinator, a decision was made to change the program.

Goals of the New Program

Relying on current research developments, the new coordinator designed a theoretical framework for the instructional program, and a cooperative venture between teachers and specialists was launched. The goals for the new program, set by a committee of principals, teachers, and specialists, were as follows:

- Provide instructional carryover into the classroom.
- Increase student independence.
- Enlist parental support through parent education.

The goals were not complex, but long-range planning and time were needed before these goals could be met. The initial step was to eliminate the old materials. Since the major reason for change was to provide students with a coordinated plan of learning, teachers were advised that the commercially produced program was to be phased out and new materials (primarily books for reading) would be purchased. Teacher reaction to removal of materials, used for a number of years, was initially negative. Although many had been supplementing and enriching the commercial products with good activities, the thought of providing daily instruction without a manual seemed a difficult, if not impossible, task.

There were several reasons for adopting a variety of books rather than a product with its own manual. Few commercial programs are exactly alike, and since the classroom objectives were to govern the general content of SULA, it was important not to introduce a manual that might not correlate with these objectives. Additionally, many students possessed some isolated skills, so it seemed reasonable to help them understand the relation of those skills to longer discourse. As time progressed, it became apparent that the most important task of the SULA teacher was to help students "put it all together."

THE NEW SULA

In the past decade, reading research has moved away from determining what the disabled reader lacks to identifying factors that affect reading achievement and pinpointing strategies that successful readers employ while reading. This new focus has been particularly helpful for practitioners, because it allows a positive approach to remediation and lends itself to the development of instructional techniques to help disabled readers acquire strategies used by efficient readers.

Since the early seventies, research from many disciplines has shown that reading should be viewed as only one part of the communication process, the child must be an active participant in this process, and reading should be taught within a total language framework. SULA has been greatly influenced by research supporting this view.

Teachers' views of how to teach reading have been affected by research findings indicating that reading is an interactive process (Anderson, Reynolds, Schallert, & Goetz, 1977; Frederiksen, 1977b; Rumelhart, 1977a); activation and organization of prior knowledge is critical to comprehension (Adams & Collins, 1979; Anderson, 1977; Spiro, 1977); the structure of text can impede or assist comprehension (Meyer, 1975; Stein, 1978); the ability to make an inference is based on prior knowledge and an understanding of textual relations (Pearson, Hansen, & Gordon, 1979; Trabasso, 1980); the writing process can be used to reinforce skills (Graves, 1975, 1982) and finally, metacognition is an important factor in successful learning (Baker, 1979; Brown & Campione, 1981). How these research findings have been used in revising SULA is described below.

Prior Knowledge

Poor readers do not always use prior knowledge to assist them in understanding what they read (Anderson, 1977); in fact, they sometimes activate an incorrect schema which causes additional problems in comprehension (McDonell, 1978). Teachers initially try to use reading topics with which students are familiar. Existing knowledge is expanded gradually through real or vicarious experience. Teachers are aware that just building vocabulary is not enough. Instead, prelistening, prereading, and prewriting activities help students make the link between what they know and what they are about to hear, read, or write. Built into each lesson is a survey of what is already known about the topic. Through brainstorming, categorizing, and simple graphic organizers, children expand concepts, integrate some new ones, and are able to activate appropriate schemata to aid comprehension. To avoid misconceptions, teachers provide time for sharing and use discussion for clarifying and explaining relationships.

Text Organization

Many low-achieving students come to school having had no exposure to a written form of story. Even the television they watch is frequently confined to cartoons, many of which can hardly be said to have a plot. There are many first-grade students who, when asked to tell a story, are unable to narrate a tale, real or imagined, which contains the components for a simple episode (Mandler & Johnson, 1977; Stein, 1978). Other students have a concept of story structure but are unable to use it as an aid to comprehension. Instruction in story structure has provided noticeable improvement in recall of important information (McDonell, 1978; Whaley, 1981). Through teacher modeling and direct teaching of story parts, students are able to use a story schema as an internal outline for retelling and for understanding. When a basal has been completed, students become literary critics by rereading the stories to pick out those that conform to an ideal structure (Stein & Glenn, 1979). They label stories "good" or "bad" depending on the presence or absence of a setting, conflict, and so on.

Although young students do not have frequent opportunities to read expository text, reports about such topics as animals and food are often part of their writing activities in the SULA classroom. Using these reports and any other non-narrative text, students practice deleting information until only the most important statements remain, thereby gaining practice in summarizing (Brown, 1980).

Writing is used as an important tool for learning about text structure. Through pupil-teacher or pupil-pupil conferences children learn that writing is easier to understand when it is explicit, stories can be rewritten or new ones generated with the help of a story structure chart, and simple reports can be written by using reminders such as "What is my most important idea?" "What is my proof?"

Inferences

Poor readers have difficulty in understanding textual relations, in being able to predict, and in drawing from their own bank of experience when confronted with a question not explicitly answered in the text. Using the revision process in writing helps children understand the difference between implicit and explicit text. This understanding is frequently the initial step in learning to make text-based inferences. Teachers also help students use their background of experience to make "gap-filling" inferences, a very useful strategy in the justification procedure. Students are required to justify answers whether they are right or wrong. One important factor in the low-achiever's outlook toward learning is that learning is frequently seen as a guessing game (Byers & Byers,

1972; McDermott, 1974). Justification removes this notion and helps students learn to rely on their knowledge. Requiring students to make inferences when reading about familiar, everyday situations and to justify their answers helps them recognize that answers are not always written into the text, and that their own experience can help them draw conclusions, predict outcomes, and recognize relationships.

Writing

Writing is consistently used to improve students' ability to communicate. The four-step writing process—prewriting, composing, revising, and sharing—is frequently the basis for teaching many skills and concepts about reading. Teachers use it for instruction in oral expression, for organizing language into units of thought, for illustrating the relations between oral and written language and the conventions of print, for developing sound-symbol relationships, and for stressing that the purpose of reading is to receive a message. Each of these skills or concepts appears to be especially critical for the low-achieving student (Cazden, 1972; Clay, 1972; Clay & Imlach, 1971; Loban, 1976).

Writing is used to ensure a coordinated program between classroom objectives and lessons conducted by the resource teacher. The basal is extended and basal vocabulary reinforced through written retellings of the basal story or through a thematic unit dealing with basal story topics. Teachers of low-achieving students frequently complain that students "learn" a word today and act as if they had never seen it tomorrow, especially when it is presented in another context. Instead of drilling basal words on flash cards, teachers and students create little stories and make "big books" (Clay, 1972) and "little books" so children can review words in the context of a story. Cloze procedures using basal stories provide instructional focus for beginning sounds, phonograms, and so forth.

Metacognition: Fostering Self-Monitoring

Low achieving students are frequently confused about the world of school. This confusion starts in kindergarten and continues to grow. They many not understand what is expected of them or that the purpose of reading is to get a message from print. They many not even recognize when they do not comprehend, because this lack of understanding has become a part of their school day. The SULA program attempts to correct this critical failure in the instructional process.

Many first-grade children do not know the difference between a letter and a word. This lack of metalinguistic awareness frequently causes confusion until interaction with print through writing and language manipulation promotes understanding.

The emphasis on reading for meaning has helped teachers develop a standard set of questions which students eventually learn to use themselves. The major question "Does that make sense?" helps them learn self-correction strategies. Although teachers may say, "Skip the word and go on," they also insist, when it doesn't interrupt meaning, that students go back, or use forward and backward context cues as well as sound-symbol relationships for identifying an unknown word. Teachers constantly attempt to expand the development of self-monitoring strategies for each student.

Teacher modeling of reading and writing processes helps students understand that even the teacher does not always comprehend and sometimes makes mistakes, but that there are strategies for solving these problems. Through direct teaching, students gradually learn to ask themselves questions such as "Do I have a problem?" "Does what I read make sense to me?" "What do I know now that I didn't know before?" In an atmosphere where mistakes are considered an integral part of learning, students learn the importance of self-correction, of developing search behaviors that allow them to use one cue to check another. Group conferencing during the revision process helps children recognize that learning takes place through errors. By third grade, many are able to revise their own writing, because they realize their classmates may have difficulty understanding what they wrote.

Teaching Materials

Commercial materials used to support these activities have been primarily limited to books, basal stories, magazines, and newspapers. Understanding reading as an interactive process has helped teachers focus on comprehension and meaning. Intuitive knowledge of language, sound-symbol relationships and meaning are brought together for the student so he or she learns to use all cues simultaneously, rather than to rely on only one. A typical lesson now reflects the teacher's belief that it is possible to teach most skills within the context of a story or through writing. Workbooks and worksheets are seldom used and rote drill has been replaced by thoughtful learning and by helping students make sense of the world of reading.

THE PROCESS OF CHANGE

The research-based changes just described did not emerge full blown overnight. They evolved through the joint efforts of the Title I coordinator, central office staff, Title I teachers and principals, and university-based researchers who served as consultants to the district. Translating research findings and theoretical notions about the reading process into instructional practices was brought about through a series of staff development efforts over 7 years. These included workshops and a university course for Title I teachers, an in-service training seminar series involving researchers, and summer staff development institutes. The vehicle for change in Title I classes throughout the district was a checklist used by teachers to monitor children's progress and identify areas needing work. The checklist served as an instructional guide.

Staff Development

An organization cannot grow or change unless the individuals in that organization have an opportunity for self-renewal and professional development. The potential for successful change is greatly augmented when teachers are given time to recognize a genuine need, when they have opportunities to share information and exchange ideas, and when they are involved in the plan for change. With this in mind, a needs assessment was conducted 7 years ago. Title I teachers were interviewed to determine what they knew about three aspects of instruction that were significant according to the emerging research: language development in young children, current research findings in reading as a language and meaning-oriented process, and writing as a functional way to teach reading skills. Although teachers were knowledgeable about language experience as a means to teach reading, they did not necessarily know how to structure a lesson plan to support the classroom program. Teachers also indicated their lack of knowledge about recent research in language development or in reading as a language process. Initial staff development focused on these areas.

A set of teacher workshops was conducted by Title I program assistants. Through tape recordings and examples, they demonstrated the progress of normal language development to show how teachers could assist in this process and to provide a forum for sharing. At the same time, a specially-designed university course was offered after contract hours. This class partially fulfilled a new district requirement that all teachers, to maintain certification, take two graduate courses in reading. The course was intended to help the teachers understand the language competence of the child, to acquaint them with various diagnostic procedures in reading, and to provide them with a background of research findings on which instructional techniques might be built. Over half the teachers in the program completed this course.

At the end of one year, it became clear that the skills checklists the teachers had been using to evaluate student progress were in conflict with the new research-based concepts of reading. Reading for meaning was not included in the checklist nor was it measured in any other way. Even the standardized instrument used to evaluate progress assessed reading through word recognition.

The checklist had been viewed by teachers as an instructional guide. They enjoyed seeing their students progress and master each new skill because, in a way, it was a measure of their own success. Since what was measured was what was taught, it became obvious that the checklist had to be changed if the objective was to measure progress in reading comprehension.

The Language Arts Skills Inventory

A summer staff development institute, with university credit for teachers, provided the impetus for generating a new checklist—one that reflected the research and could be used as a diagnostic tool for teaching. This checklist was developed on the premise that reading is a language process, that children come to school with some language competence, and that reading instruction should build on that competence.

The Language Arts Skills Inventory (LASI), still in use, was designed to assess four skill areas: speaking, listening, reading, and writing (see Fig. 16.1). The LASI assessed skills in the context of a sentence or longer discourse. Since efficient readers use knowledge of language, sound-symbol relationships and meaning in constant interaction, the checklist should measure this interaction of skills rather than isolate any one skill for the purpose of testing. If students could be taught to use a number of textual cues simultaneously, then transfer of skills would be more likely to occur. With this understanding, teachers were provided an outline and, with the coordinator and program assistants, worked in groups to develop items or procedures for testing a learning area, e.g., writing. Research information and pertinent studies, such as the Grosse Pointe Study (McCaig, 1972) were available for teachers to use as references.

Each year for 4 years during curriculum workshops, the checklist was modified to reflect new research findings and teacher feedback. Certain sections were more helpful than others and changes were made based on teachers' interactions with students. For example, because transfer of skills was a program goal, only reading comprehension was measured. When the checklist was first developed it was impossible for teachers to construct a totally new instrument to measure all four language areas, so the Scott Foresman Reading Survey was used as a measure of comprehension. The Reading Survey did not prove useful for diagnosis and was subsequently abandoned in favor of a modified informal reading inventory that used quality as well as number of errors for determining student strengths and weaknesses (Goodman and Burke, 1972). Later, teachers felt it would be helpful to measure student knowledge of beginning sounds. A group of sentences, using the cloze procedure, was developed to measure a student's ability to use more than one cue simultaneously: sounds, symbols, and context.

Finally, Marie Clay's research findings were used to develop the third reading subtest—the Beginning Reading Assessment Section. The original beginning reading section measured progress on 11 skills. Two provided very little useful information and were dropped.

TITLE I—#9 SULA
Skills Checklist (LASI)   (9/81)

Program_____
School   _____
Teacher _____
School Year ___1981-82___
Program No. ☐
School No. ☐☐☐☐
Group Time _____

Indicate when mastered:
1 — Pretest
2 — 1st Quarter
3 — 2nd Quarter
4 — 3rd Quarter
5 — Posttest
9 — Passed in
    previous year

DISTRIBUTION
Goldenrod—Pre
Pink—1st Qtr
Canary—2nd Qtr
Green—3rd Qtr
Blue—Teacher's Copy
White—Post

STUDENT NAME	Student ID	GR	Colors	Shapes	Composition	Function	Addit. Characteristics	Oral Prediction	Identifies character	Events—Beg. Md. End	Main idea/plot	Draws conclusions/theme

ORAL LANGUAGE

OBJECT DESCRIPTION

ORAL CLOZE

RETELLING

FIG. 16.1   SULA Skills Checklist.

READING / WRITING

READING

BEGINNING READING ASSESSMENT
- Left/Right—Top/Bot. Pro.
- Picture cues
- Concept of word
- Concept of letter
- Rec. words in context
- Inv. story from pict.
- Uses book talk
- Uses memory/pict. cues
- Voice-print match

BEGINNING SOUNDS
- Beg. Consonant Sounds

INFORMAL READING INVENTORY
- Self-corrects
- Sensible substitutions
- Pretest level
- 1st Quarter level
- 2nd Quarter level
- 3rd Quarter level
- Posttest level

WRITING

BEGINNING WRITING LEVEL
- Garble/letters
- Garble/words
- 1 M-unit with garble
- 1 M-unit — no garble
- 2 or more M-units

TRANSITION
- Description
- Movement of thought

COMPOSITION LEVEL
- Retelling: Prt. BME
- Retelling: Comp. BME
- Gen. St.: Prt. BME
- Gen. St.: Comp. BME
- Expository
- Cap. Punt. — Partial
- Cap. Punt. — Consistent
- Good Spelling — Partial
- Good Spelling—Consistent
- Uses conjunctions
- Uses descriptive words
- Uses quotations
- Expresses feelings
- Involves reader

Additional modifications were made in the listening section of the LASI. This section was composed of stories to be listened to and retold. When research indicated the importance of story schema (Stein & Glenn, 1978), the retelling format was modified to include critical story elements.

The evolution of this new checklist took 4 years, but it was a key factor in providing structure for the SULA program and in continuing the process of change. The teachers' role in developing it ensured their acceptance of the new ideas. The checklist became their instrument, one they were proud of and they felt provided useful information for teaching. A handbook of activities, based on the reading and writing sections of the checklist, was eventually developed by groups of teachers proud to share their newly gained expertise.

The LASI is the understructure of the instructional plan for each student. Teachers combine the results of the LASI and information on classroom progress to use in a diagnose-plan-teach-evaluate cycle. Unlike other skills checklists, there are no established hierarchies in the LASI. Of course, students usually master the beginning reading skills before they are able to read longer discourse, but within this set no one skill must be mastered before another is taught.

Activities geared to help students master the skills within a learning area are created or taken from the SULA Activity Guide. Some basic teaching-learning strategies such as assisted reading, controlled language experience, cloze procedures, story structure, and teacher modeling can be adapted to any grade level or to any instructional focus. Other activities are geared to specific skills on the checklist and district-wide objectives. Whenever possible, activities center around the basal stories assigned in the classroom.

Consultant Support.   Another year-round staff development program was designed to inform as well as motivate teachers to try new ideas and to understand reading and writing as processes that must actively involve the learner. The general plan was to bring in consultants, usually two a year, who would present the research in day-long in-service training sessions. This meeting would be followed by regularly scheduled monthly in-service conducted in smaller groups by program assistants to clarify and expand on the information. On-site support also was provided. Program assistants, assigned to 12 to 14 schools, observed teachers, supplied assistance, feedback, and encouragement, and perceived new needs as they arose. These needs became the topics for future group in-service sessions.

During the first year, consultants focused on helping teachers understand the language development of the primary-aged child. Several linguists provided the disequilibrium necessary to initiate change. Reading was presented as a natural facet of language; assisted reading, a teaching strategy, was presented as "immersion in the total language process" (Hoskisson & Krohm, 1974). Teachers liked it and started using it.

After the first year, consultants were brought in to share research in many disciplines: cultural anthropology, to show how teachers could communicate success or failure to their students; psychology, to demonstrate the behaviors exhibited by children as they acquire the ability to read; writing, to illustrate the writing process and the importance of using it to reinforce reading skills; and reading comprehension, to discuss the factors that affect understanding.

As a result of this staff development design, teachers broadened their horizons to view reading from a research-based conceptual framework. They expanded their repertoire of teaching strategies through the creative use of research and through opportunities to share new ideas with one another. They were able to build a program for each group of students, primarily through the use of books, writing material, and their own understanding of the reading and writing processes.

In previous years, there had been a large annual migration of Title I teachers back to the regular classroom. Now the teachers leave only if they move out of the school district. Requests from classroom teachers to be assigned to the program became the norm. One of the most frequently cited reasons for these requests was the opportunity for professional growth.

Parent Education

Parents were willing partners in attempts to improve instruction. They attended three or four meetings a year and learned to use daily experiences as opportunities for learning. Although the primary focus was to help parents understand and communicate with their children and the school, some specific activities increased parental involvement in their child's learning. For example, assisted reading was taught to every parent who attended the meetings. Hoskisson and Krohm (1974) describe assisted reading as a natural extension of what many parents do: read aloud to their children. Using this technique, a parent reads aloud to his or her child, pointing to the words as they are read, and the child repeats the words or phrases. The parent also guides the child in pointing to the words as they are repeated. After the story or book is read, both parent and child discuss the main events. As the child learns more words, the parent is gradually required to supply only those words that are unknown.

When parents first learned this technique, they were somewhat skeptical that anything so simple would work. But many parents wanted to help their children, and they soon found this to be a pleasant way of doing so. Fifteen minutes of assisted reading each day created a warm close feeling between parent and child. Since the parent did not have to assume the role of teacher, assisted reading became a rewarding experience.

An extremely successful parent-child venture was the annual Young Author's Showcase. For the past 5 years, teachers have helped children revise and edit their stories, bind them into books, and display them at a parent meeting.

Each child was awarded a certificate, and every child had an opportunity to read his or her story to an adult. Last year, over 300 beaming parents came to witness the joy on their children's faces as they shared their work.

CONCLUSIONS

Several major factors contributed to change in the Step Up Language Arts program. First, a need was evident. Second, school district administration considered the need and took appropriate action to support the change. Without this continued support, effective change would not have been possible. Third, research from many disciplines acted as the catalytic agent to alter teacher behavior.

Planned change cannot occur without staff development. In this case, it was the vehicle used to disseminate research information, to translate this information into successful classroom practice, and to establish a support network for encouraging further professional growth. Evidence of change in teacher behavior was monitored in a number of ways:

- Teacher lesson plans, completed daily, were submitted to program assistants for review.
- New activities, change in use of materials, and integration of skills were noted as they occurred.
- Classroom observations provided additional feedback and were a source of information for an on-going needs assessment.
- Teacher questionnaires furnished opportunities for evaluating on-site support, for stating needs and for requesting teaching materials. These questionnaires reflected a positive attitude and provided evidence of a growing sophistication both in expressed needs and in the type of instructional materials requested.

Within 4 years, SULA teachers were serving on summer curriculum committees and were using their knowledge of research to help develop district-wide curriculum in reading and writing.

Has the new instructional program met its goals? A coordinated plan of instruction now exists for students in the SULA program. SULA teachers support the classroom basal program, reinforcing the classroom and district curriculum objectives, and students must no longer deal with a number of unrelated or even contradictory reading strategies. Surveys of classroom teachers indicate that 99% feel the program helps students function better in the classroom. Students are motivated to become independent learners and to develop some of the self-monitoring strategies used by their more successful peers. Annual surveys reflect principals' enthusiasm about program results

(98.76%). Parent involvement has increased over the years, and data from annual questionnaires indicate they are extremely satisfied with the program because they see improvement in their child's reading and writing performance.

Evaluation, completed each year, shows program impact to be consistently positive for each of the last 5 years. Longitudinal data are being gathered to determine sustained effects. However, it is sometimes difficult to complete long-term studies because of the extreme mobility of the student population. Perhaps more significant than statistical data are the numerous letters and calls received from classroom teachers and parents at the close of each year to ascertain whether the program will be continued in their school.

If success can be measured by the influence of philosophy and techniques on the mainstream curriculum, then the SULA program is indeed successful, for it has served as a prototype for the writing-reading program in Fairfax County Schools. This year, the writing section of the Step Up Language Arts Activity Guide was expanded by a team of county curriculum specialists and used as part of a planned curriculum change to integrate the teaching of reading and writing in all the elementary schools. SULA teachers were used as models to demonstrate the teaching of writing and some of the strategies of integration they had already perfected. The Young Authors' Conference expanded into 39 additional schools and indeed became writing celebrations. Although this program is only in its infancy, it has already met with success, and classroom teachers in those schools where it has been implemented are extremely enthusiastic about the results.

Research findings coupled with dedicated, hardworking teachers have made SULA successful. This growing partnership between researcher and practitioner may be part of that long-awaited solution to improving instruction. From this partnership, the SULA program evolved a measurement device that encourages testing of research-based teaching strategies in the real world of the classroom, with the reasonable expectation that objective assessment is possible. At this point, there is ample evidence that continued application of the techniques described in this chapter will extend the ability to use what is effective from the growing body of research, provide new questions for researchers to answer, and thus progressively develop a more fruitful learning environment.

17　Rethinking Reading and Listening in a Large Public School System: A Case History

R. T. Schuder
Montgomery County Public Schools, Maryland

BACKGROUND: THE CONTEXT OF CHANGE[1]

The Setting

Demographics and Achievement.　Comprising part of the Washington, D.C. metropolitan area, Montgomery County, Maryland covers a geographical expanse of nearly 500 square miles. Its sub-populations are urban, suburban, and rural, with suburbanites dominant in numbers. Although the majority of the population is white, there are significant numbers of ethnic and racial minorities and non-native English speakers. In 1975, the year before planning on this project began, the median income in the county was $26,100. At that time, Montgomery County Public Schools served 125,439 students in 205 schools, spending $1,568 per student. Achievement on standardized tests was well above national norms. High percentages of students graduated from high school and went on to college. The school system prided itself on the number of National Merit Scholarships its students won each year.

Local Autonomy and Inconsistency in Programs.　With affluence and success on standardized tests and other measures of achievement came considerable self-esteem, a fertile environment for innovation, and a tolerance for diversity in reading programs, management, and teaching practices. State and

---

[1] The point of view expressed in this chapter is that of its author. The paper is written in retrospect and has all the liabilities and advantages associated with that perspective. The intention is to throw some light on the actual process of using research to improve curriculum and instruction in a large public school system.

269

county-mandated reading curricula were sufficiently general or minimal-achievement oriented to pose no threat to any reading program in individual schools. Reading programs ranged from highly structured commercial instructional management systems to locally developed programs without specific objectives or textbooks. Schools and classrooms were largely autonomous.

Local autonomy is both a strength and a weakness. It often allows schools and teachers to better serve diverse populations, and it allows a strong, dedicated staff to be innovative. It protects schools from constantly shifting priorities and projects too. But local autonomy also assures inconsistency across and within schools. Issues of equity inevitably arise. Variations in the quality of programs are bound to occur.

Comparisons of reading programs across schools, however, were difficult to make. Beyond standardized tests, there were no systemwide measures, and there was no consistent record keeping in reading programs across schools. It was difficult to hold anyone accountable for the quality of school programs or for student achievement. Standardized test scores seemed to reflect socioeconomic status rather than school programs.

In spite of generally high achievement levels, the district had (and has) a sizable population of low-achieving students. In 1976, 2,442 students in 19 schools qualified for Title I assistance. The Head Start program served 800 students in 53 classes. Although low-achieving students have the highest need for systematic, consistent, appropriate instruction, they are often the most geographically mobile. Given significant differences in reading programs, students transferring from one school to another or moving in and out of the county were essentially changing programs every time they moved. Even within the school, pull-out programs for students with special needs often had the same effect. Moreover, without consistent assessment measures and record keeping, students carried no useful record of performance with them as they moved. Students with the most need for systematic, consistent, appropriate instruction often got the least.

The Basal Reader Movement. Two movements in the school system in the 1970s attempted to bring more consistency to reading programs. The first focused on inconsistencies in programs within schools. Beginning in the early 1970s, curriculum specialists and supervisors encouraged each school to purchase one of the many basal reader programs sold nationally. They felt that adoption of a basal reader at least assured an identifiable and reputable reading program within a school. The school's (if not the classroom's) autonomy was protected by allowing staffs in individual schools to select their basal reader.

By 1976, considerable money and staff prestige had been committed to basal readers. A 1977 survey revealed that more than 24 basal reader programs were in use in the system. Virtually every major basal reader sold in the nation was represented. Basal readers formed the core of the reading program for 81%

of the teachers in 1976–77. At present, every elementary school has at least one basal reader program and often two—one for low- or average- and one for average- or high-achieving students. Some schools have also purchased the accompanying management systems in an effort to keep track of student progress.

Basal readers became a powerful new presence in the schools. Local reading programs became indistinguishable from publishers' national programs. Commercial programs swallowed up local innovations. The most creative and successful teachers were often the most unhappy with basal readers. Basal reading programs leave little room or need for teacher or principal initiative. They engulf reading time so thoroughly that the school reading program becomes the basal reader no matter what the local school needs or the state- or district-mandated curriculum. Moreover, proliferating basal readers did not solve the problem of inconsistencies across schools, a special problem for low-achieving and high-mobility students.

Instructional Management Systems. In 1975, the Montgomery County Board of Education became increasingly concerned about the school system's inability to keep individual students or low-achieving subpopulations from "falling between the cracks." In essence, the problem was how to get student achievement to reflect something other than socioeconomic status. The Board responded in two ways. First, they established a new office to consolidate services to low-achieving students and students with special needs. Second, they established a policy for developing and implementing "learner-centered management support systems" for grades K-8 in mathematics, reading and language arts, science and social studies. Their resolution contained a 5-year plan for developing, implementing, and evaluating the four instructional management systems in academic subjects. Each system was to be comprised of instructional, evaluation, and reporting components, and each component was to reflect the popular notions of the times, e.g., performance objective hierarchies, criterion-referenced mastery measures, and computer-generated classroom and summary reports for instructional and management decision making.

The Board had come full circle in about a decade from what appeared to be a laissez faire approach to a consistent, systemwide, mandated curriculum with consistent assessments and reports. The change was initiated on a grand scale—four major curricular areas, all at once—and the change took place in the midst of a complete administrative reorganization.

The First Proposal: A Cloze Achievement Monitor

Two proposals for a reading management system were generated. The first, from the fledgling Department of Research and Evaluation, was hatched full blown with little or no input or support from curriculum specialists, supervisors, or school staffs. The proposal emphasized assessment with multiple-choice cloze[2] tests and achievement reports generated by computer terminals located in schools. There was no mention of a reading curriculum or specific provision for reading instruction. Essentially, it was a literal comprehension achievement monitoring procedure with sophisticated report-generation capacities. The project was funded by an ESEA Title IV-C grant in February of 1977, and work began on item writing.

But administrative and supervisory staff and curriculum specialists objected to the project, and the tests were never administered. By the fall of 1977, the cloze testing program was replaced by a design for a complete instructional management system, the Instructional System in Reading/Language Arts (ISR/LA), which had been under development concurrently in the Department of Curriculum and Instruction. Cloze tests were gradually phased out of that design. The cloze project was a classic case of failure in innovation because it had neither grass roots nor high-level support.

The Second Proposal: The ISR/LA

Reviewing the Literature. Curriculum specialists and coordinators in the Department of Curriculum and Instruction set out to develop an explicit conceptual framework for the new reading and language arts management system. In the winter and spring of 1977, five staff members reviewed on a full-time basis the research literature and current reading programs. They enlisted curriculum specialists, supervisors, principals, and reading teachers on a part-time basis. More than 40 staff members participated in this effort.

Central office staff recruited specialists, supervisors, school-based staff, and consultants in the review to build a local knowledge base and grass roots support, and to weigh the implications for practice in theory and research against the knowledge, experience, intuitions, and common sense of successful teachers and administrators. There were no preconceptions about the final system.

These review sessions functioned like graduate seminars. Subcommittees reviewed the research literature on a topic across several disciplines over a period of at least several decades. The intent was to gain historical and interdisciplinary perspective; to discover consistent directions in which the knowledge base was moving across time, theoretical biases, and methodological limitations; and to avoid the pendulum effect, those hasty applications of the latest findings to current practice which so plague education. Each subcommittee had to derive implications for instruction and assessment from consistent, interdisciplinary research findings and theory.

---

[2] Cloze tests are passages with words deleted systematically. Students have to fill in missing words or, in the case of multiple-choice cloze, choose the missing word from a set of responses.

It was an unprecedented beginning for a public school system. Morale was high among participating staff. Discussion was open and spirited. Large numbers of representative school-based, area-office-based, and central-office-based educators joined together in support of a research- and theory-based reading/language arts system for grades K-8.

The First Draft of the Conceptual Framework.   In March of 1977, administrators accepted the tentative findings of the subcommittee on comprehension as a first draft of a conceptual framework for reading and language arts K-8. In brief, the subcommittee recommended that:

1. Language learning in school ought to simulate natural language learning and use in order to build bridges between school and home.
2. The communicative functions of language ought to be emphasized in every way at every level in reading/language arts programs.
3. The core concept for language learning and instruction at every grade level K-8 ought to be meaning in whole discourse, the natural unit of meaning.
4. Comprehension ought to be the centerpiece of the reading and listening program at every grade level K-8 (rather than beginning belatedly at grade 3 or 4).
5. Listening, speaking, reading, writing, and thinking instruction ought to be integrated and governed by a single conceptual framework and integrated, whenever possible, with the aesthetic arts and content area subjects.
6. There should be a single reading/language arts curriculum for all personnel involved in language teaching, including classroom, reading, and special education teachers.

Staffing.   The comprehension subcommittee took responsibility for the design and development of the instructional management system. The group included the staff from the Title IV-C project mentioned above: one coordinator with experience in curriculum and test development in reading/language arts, one assessment specialist with a reading research background, one secretary, and two clerk-typists. To these five full-time staff members supported by federal funds, the school system contributed five full-time curriculum specialists: one elementary reading specialist, one elementary language arts specialist, one junior high school English teacher, one sociolinguist, and one language and literature specialist. In addition, an evaluation specialist from another department with experience and training in test development and program evaluation worked nearly full-time with the curriculum and instruction team. Finally, another department contributed half of the time of a media specialist to the project.

The coordinator, the assessment specialist, the sociolinguist, and the language and literature specialist were all recruited from outside the system especially for this project. Each was trained in research and knowledgeable about current theory and research. They formed a balanced team with the three specialists who were thoroughly experienced in classrooms and who had spent most if not all of their careers in the school system.

Planning.   The major problem confronting the team was the 24 basal reader programs firmly in place throughout the system. Not only were they in seeming conflict with the Board's intention to mandate a consistent, countywide curriculum, but, compared with the implications for instruction and assessment in the tentative conceptual framework, they emphasized discrete skill development to the detriment of comprehension. The short-range strategy was to superimpose the new curriculum on existing school programs and to require school staffs to supplement basal readers as necessary to teach that new curriculum, in effect setting up standards for basal reader programs. The long-range strategy was to teach teachers to use basal readers selectively and to encourage them to use richer texts and instructional activities.

The project staff, however, had little time to work on such plans. In May of 1977, with only a tentative draft of a conceptual framework in hand, the design and development team was charged with developing performance objectives and instructional activities in reading and language arts for grades K through 8 and pilot testing them that September in 15 elementary and 2 junior high schools. The entire curriculum had to be developed during the summer!

The Original Generic Objectives.   During the traditional county summer curriculum development workshops in 1977, 40 teachers and curriculum specialists were employed under the leadership of the design and development team to write objectives and instructional activites. Given the time constraints, they developed instead a set of "generic objectives" and associated activities which preserved some of the rethinking of the tentative conceptual framework and which could be used as organizing principles for performance objectives and activities. The categories for the generic objectives were:

1. Semantics
2. Syntax
3. Cohesion (e.g., pronoun reference)
4. Discourse structure (discourse type and coherence)
5. Extending discourse
6. Effective communication (pragmatic context)

The generic objectives were organized conceptually rather than in sequence for instruction. The intent was to stimulate thinking about reading and listening. While 17 pilot schools fretted with or ignored these objectives and activities, design and development of the ISR/LA began in earnest in the fall of 1977. The generic objectives allowed the staff to buy some critical time.

DESCRIPTION OF THE NEW READING/LISTENING PROGRAM

Summary Description of the Reading/Listening Program

The reading/listening program is embedded in an integrated listening, speaking, reading, writing, and thinking program. Only the reading/listening portion is discussed in this paper.

The reading and listening program is comprised of six major components: (1) a conceptual framework and (2) curriculum design; (3) instructional, (4) evaluation, and (5) reporting components; (6) in-service training and implementation, materials and procedures. These components are outlined in Fig. 17.1. The genesis and characteristics of the program are described below.

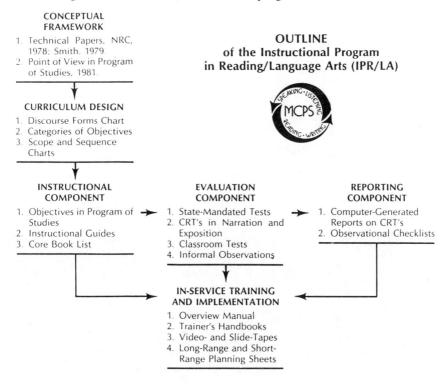

FIG. 17.1.   Summary outline of the components of the reading/language arts program.

Rethinking Reading and Listening

A major design decision made in the fall of 1977 was to organize the new reading and listening program around the types of discourse that students were expected to understand in school, on the job, and in the community. Organization by type of discourse was a radical departure from traditional reading programs which assumed that a single hierarchy of skills was equally applicable to, say, a novel or a Jell-O recipe. Organization by discourse assumes, on the contrary, that text variance is significant enough to require different reading strategies and to warrant different instructional treatments.

This design decision was the result of considerable work by the design and development team. Between the fall of 1977 and the fall of 1978, they wrestled simultaneously with conceptual, design, development, implementation, and in-service training issues. Area-office based curriculum specialists and supervisors in reading and language arts contributed up to 50 percent of their time to these efforts. Attempts to translate implications for instruction from the draft conceptual framework into practice led to refinements in the notion of practice or suspicions about feasibility and hence refinements in conceptualization. Conceptualization and curriculum design evolved together.

Each time a particularly difficult conceptual, design, or development issue was identified, a consultant with nationally recognized expertise was invited in to discuss the issue with staff and to review their proposed solution. On problems with ramifications throughout the program, staff consulted at least two experts, usually from different academic disciplines. This practice continued through 1982, by which time 26 different experts had been consulted.

The conceptual framework was articulated in a set of papers written by the design and development team members in the fall of 1978. Titled "Bridging Theory and Practice: An Instructional System in Reading/Language Arts K-8" (see Smith, 1979), it included the following sections:

1. Introduction: The Importance of an Explicit Conceptualization (Schuder, 1978)
2. Conceptual Framework for Interactive Processes in Effective Communication (Greene, 1978)
3. Framework for Curriculum: Types and Forms of Discourse (Jackson, 1978)
4. Framework for Instructional Objectives: Comprehension (Smith, 1978)
5. Framework for Instructional Objectives: Contextual Decoding (Mathias, 1978)
6. Framework for Instructional Activities (Englar, 1978)
7. Framework for Evaluation (Marshall, 1978)

Objectives in Reading and Listening Comprehension

Organization. There are four sets of instructional and performance objectives in the reading and listening program: Prereading (K-1), Decoding/Word Structure/Sight Vocabulary (1-8), Language Experience (K-2), and Comprehension (K-8). The categories appear traditional enough, but the radical revision comes in the comprehension objectives. In terms of the number of objectives and the amount of time devoted to teaching them, comprehension dominates the program at every level K-8.

The comprehension objectives are organized by type and form of discourse: narration, exposition, persuasion, procedure, drama, lyric, and additional forms. The emphasis is on the first four. "Additional forms" refers to a miscellany of state-mandated forms (e.g., telephone directories). Within each discourse category, specific forms or genre (e.g., fables) are identified for instructional emphasis, and a set of objectives is written for that form. The number of forms emphasized in each category is balanced carefully at each grade level. Fig. 17.2 shows the discourse forms chart as it was approved by the Board in June of 1981.

Five criteria were used to distribute discourse forms and hence objectives across grade levels:

1. Student interest in the form and its characteristic content.
2. Importance of the form and its characteristic content in school, on the job, in the community, and in private life.
3. Inherent difficulty of the form and its characteristic content.
4. Availability and cost of good texts in that form at an appropriate level of comprehensibility.
5. Opportunities for interface with other subject areas.

Level of Specificity and Content. The primary difficulty in developing comprehension objectives was determining the appropriate level of specificity for objectives. The Board charge to develop performance objectives and criterion-referenced measures implied a level of specificity that would have made the task meaningless for students and further atomized their experience with language beyond what was already happening in basal readers. At the other extreme, "global" or "generic" objectives are difficult to assess and therefore easily ignored. And the level of specificity had to take into account the nature of the status quo—basal readers.

The development team tried to write comprehension objectives that were, above all else, meaningful tasks for students. The objective had to *promote* understanding by engaging students in actively constructing an interpretation of the text, evaluating or extending that interpretation, or simply playing with

■   Will receive instructional emphasis

□   Will be included in reading/listening program

(blank)   May be included in reading/listening program **when appropriate**

NARRATIVE FORMS CHART

NARRATIVE PROSE	K	1	2	3	4	5	6	7	8
1. Experience Stories	■	■	■	□					
2. Short Narratives	■	■	■	■	■	■	■		
3. Folk Tales	■	■	■	■	□	□	■	■	□
4. Fables		□	□	□	■			■	
5. Novels				□	■	■	■	■	■
6. Biographies/Autobiographies				□	□	■	□	■	■
7. Legends					□	■	■	■	■
8. Myths						□	■		■
9. Short Stories							□	■	■
NARRATIVE VERSE	■	■	■	■	■	■	■	■	■

EXPOSITORY AND PERSUASIVE FORMS CHART

EXPOSITION	K	1	2	3	4	5	6	7	8
1. Experience Reports	■	■	■	□	□	□	□	□	□
2. Introductory Exposition	□	■	■	□					
3. Textbook Prose				■	■	■	■	■	■
4. Tradebook Prose				■	■	■	■	■	■
5. Reference Articles					□	■	■	■	■
6. News Articles					□	□	□	■	■
7. Feature Articles			□	■	■	■	■	■	■

PERSUASION	K	1	2	3	4	5	6	7	8
1. Advertisements					■	□	■	■	□
2. Reviews/Critiques								□	■
3. Editorials					□	□	□	□	■

PROCEDURAL FORMS CHART

PROCEDURE	K	1	2	3	4	5	6	7	8
1. Signs and Warnings	■	■				■			
2. Directions for Getting to a Location			■						■
3. Game Directions			■				■		
4. Science Investigations				■		■		■	
5. Test and Assignment Directions				■		■		■	
6. Recipes and Cooking Directions					■		■		
7. Construction and Assembly Directions					■				■
8. Directions for Filling out Forms							■		■
9. Operating Directions								■	
10. First Aid Directions								■	
11. *Additional Essential Forms	□	□	□	□	□	□	□	□	□

* A miscellany of state-mandated forms (e.g., telephone book).

FIG. 17.2.   Discourse forms chart for reading and listening.

278

important features of the text that affect understanding. In addition, objectives had to be good *indicators* of understanding, if possible. But good learning tasks were never excluded from the curriculum simply because no convenient, reliable measure of the attainment of that objective was available. Staff would not reduce the program to what was currently measurable.

Finally, the objectives were written as a teaching tool. Just by reading the objectives, teachers should reach a better understanding of reading and listening comprehension. Objectives for each discourse form at each grade level were written as a lesson plan; they always included the categories indicated in Fig. 17.3.

The arrows in Fig. 17.3 indicate a general sequence for instruction. In practice, however, the categories of objectives are interactive; it is difficult to teach any of them without encroaching on the domain of others. The arrows reflect iterative processes. That is, once an objective enters a sequence of instruction, it should remain active throughout the lesson. For example, one should not develop background knowledge and experience in prereading activities and ignore it thereafter.

In essence, Fig. 17.3 is an encapsulated version of the entire K-8 reading and listening curriculum. Every instructional and performance objective at every level is simply an elaboration of this generic set. The elaboration can be extensive or limited, depending on needs.

But Fig. 17.3 represents more than a complete K-8 or K-12 curriculum. It also represents the essence of the conceptual framework that engendered the

Outline of a
GENERIC TEACHING LESSON
Instructional Program in Reading/Language Arts (IPR/LA)

I.   Developing and using background knowledge and experience

II.   Setting a purpose for reading or listening

III. Understanding the gist of the discourse

IV.   Understanding the structure of the discourse

V.   Developing concepts and language and vocabulary skills

VI.   Developing critical thinking skills

VII. Developing interest and confidence in reading/listening

VIII. Interpreting creatively or applying new information

FIG. 17.3.   Generic categories of objectives/lesson plan.

curriculum. Every essential learning principle in the program can be read out of this generic set. For example, the crucial principle that one can only learn in relation to what one already knows is represented in the objective, "developing and using background knowledge and experience." "Setting a purpose for reading and listening" represents the principles that learners are active, not passive; that readers and listeners must actively construct an interpretation of a text; and that reading and listening processes vary dramatically with readers'/listeners' purpose(s). Principals and teachers have been enthusiastic about the simplicity and explanatory power of this generic curriculum/lesson plan.

Status of the Objective in a New Setting.   The objectives were pilot tested in 17 schools, including seven Title I schools, for 2 years and an additional 15 schools in the third year. In February of 1981, the new curriculum in reading and listening gained the unanimous approval of the Council on Instruction, a representative body of teachers, principals, specialists and administrators. In June of 1981, the Board of Education unanimously approved the reading and listening curriculum.

Meanwhile, the setting had changed radically. The Board that had initiated this project had been replaced by a new Board with a very different agenda— back to basics. When the program appeared before the new Board in 1981, it had been transformed from an "instructional management system" into an "instructional program" or a "revised curriculum" in an effort to keep it alive in a rapidly changing environment. The management system (accountability) apparatus was mostly gone or dormant, but the core language learning concepts survived in a new guise.

Meaningful and constructive change in a public school system is a longterm effort. To maintain such an effort in an arena with constantly shifting priorities and leaders required flexibility on superficial aspects of the project and tenacity on important project goals. The project also required support from outside the system. Without federal funding and a dedicated group of parents, this project probably would not have survived in any recognizable form.

Instructional Guides in Reading and Listening Comprehension

Every summer since 1977, the development team has led an average of 50 school-based teachers in full-time curriculum development workshops for 20 days. In each of these workshops, teachers working in grade level teams write illustrative instructional units, indicating how the objectives should be taught. All these units are assembled in grade level instructional guides. The intention is to provide teachers with a bridge from traditional practices to the new curriculum.

Narration.   There are four kinds of illustrative units for narration objectives at each grade level:

1. *Instructional plans* demonstrate how to get from a basal reader into the new curriculum and books outside of the basal reader.
2. *Thematic units* demonstrate how to use the new curriculum to organize instruction around themes of interest to students.
3. *Mini-units* focus on one of the instructional objectives (e.g., understanding characterization) that governs from 5 to 15 performance objectives at a grade level. The mini-units illustrate how to teach this cluster of objectives across forms of narration (e.g., fables, folk tales, and short narratives) and individual titles, including selections from basal readers.
4. *Form units* illustrate how to teach whole discourse in one of the forms (e.g., novel) emphasized in the program.

The first three kinds of units use basal readers as anthologies whenever possible and illustrate how to use the wealth of instructional materials available in classrooms and media centers. In all these units, teachers are being weaned away from dependence on basal readers. The intention was to refine, refocus, and reduce instruction in narration to make room for instruction in exposition, persuasion, and procedure.

Exposition.   Teachers have much more difficulty dealing with expository texts than with narration. In comparison with the highly evolved narrative form, exposition appears to be a loose conglomerate of evolving forms. Generalizations regarding the structure of exposition are usually derived from adult or prototypic texts and poorly fit the social studies and science textbooks used in grades 1–6. Available expository text was simply inferior to texts in narration. Therefore, the strategy in exposition was to teach teachers and students to deal with less-than-perfect text, to use textbooks selectively for clearly defined purposes, taking into account text characteristics.

At a curriculum development workshop in the summer of 1981, teachers were trained to analyze the textbook characteristics which affect their comprehensibility (Clewell & Clifton, 1983). Using five descriptive categories (textual aids, content, type of discourse, coherence, language and style), teachers and curriculum specialists reviewed the most widely used science textbooks in grades 1–8. Teachers then worked out instructional strategies for science textbooks by individual title.

The instructional guides in exposition also contain form units (social studies), report units, and thematic units. The form units teach students how to read popular social studies textbooks by providing intensive reading instruction on one chapter of the book. These units are intended to be taught early in the year. The report units provide students with intensive instruction in researching and writing a report on a topic in social studies or science. In thematic units, students learn to gain information on a social studies or science topic by reading widely across types of discourse and media. The research and thematic units are for use late in the instructional year.

Parent Involvement Activities.   Parents were involved in the design, development, and survival of this project from the beginning. They participated in design decisions, reviewed curricular material as it was developed, and co-authored a companion project proposal in 1980. Most important, they imbued the project with a sense of the primacy of learning and the child, and supported the need for program improvements in the face of considerable inertia in the system.

In the fall of 1980, a Parent Involvement in Basic Skills Project was funded for 2 years by the Department of Education under a Title II grant. Parents wrote informal home learning activities in mathematics and reading/language arts for grades K-3. Each set of activities complements an instructional unit in reading/language arts or an objective in mathematics. The activities serve two purposes: (1) they tell parents what students are learning in basic skills and why it is important, and (2) they suggest what parents can do informally at home to support this kind of learning. Teachers send the activities home with students when they are actually covering the unit. The informal home learning activities were pilot tested in nine schools in 1981–82. Informal feedback and responses to questionnaires were enthusiastic. The project was expanded to 56 volunteer schools in 1982–83.

Textbooks for Reading and Listening Instruction

The instructional units in the teacher's guides were often written on selected basal reader stories. But the units were only illustrative. Teachers had to be able to teach as many of the objectives as possible with already familiar and accessible basal readers. Units on selected stories were not enough to promote use of the new curriculum.

Curriculum specialists coded every selection in major basal reader series against the required discourse forms chart. Teachers could then quickly find the required forms in their basal readers, if there at all. Curriculum specialists became familiar with the formal contents of the basal readers they were recommending. The coding amounted to a readily interpretable content analysis. Most basal readers were embarrassingly short of discourse variety. Exposition, persuasion, and procedure were almost always underrepresented. Most of the selections were narration of a limited variety. Those basal readers that looked best against the discourse forms chart began to sell well in the county.

But basal reader selections were ultimately and inherently insufficient. The revised *Program of Studies* states that the reading and literature programs are combined because students ought to learn to read with the best and most interesting texts available. Unfortunately, those texts were often found gathering dust in media centers.

Transporting a handful of books back and forth from the media center, however, could not compete with the convenience of a basal reader and the textbook funds available for its purchase. Beginning in the fall of 1979, the development team began to apply the textbook approval process to child and adolescent literature books ("tradebooks" or "library books") featured in the popular mini-units and form units. These were published as a list of approved textbooks for the school system. Given the new Board's emphasis on textbooks in the budget, supplemental textbook funds were readily available. Sales of good children's books in the county went up astronomically as a consequence. In some cases, every available copy in the nation of a title was purchased. Classrooms began to sprout "real" books, and students began reading them. Many of them had never read a real book before.

Evaluation of Student Achievement

The Array of Measures. The conceptual framework stressed the inadequacy of any single instrument administered on any single occasion as a measure of reading comprehension. The new reading and listening program features a carefully balanced, minimal array of instruments and procedures in a minimal administration design, using as many existing tools as possible. No attempt was made to compete with or ignore state-mandated standardized or minimal competency tests. Besides those state-mandated tests, there are four sources of information for instructional decision making in the reading and listening program, beginning with the undervalued good sense of most teachers:

1. Informal teacher observations during instruction.
2. Summary teacher observations of performance on the generic categories of objectives (Fig. 17.3) recorded yearly on a checklist.
3. Classroom tests (e.g., for novel units emphasized at grades 4–8) administered at teacher discretion following instruction or independent reading.
4. Criterion-referenced reading comprehension tests (CRTs) in narration (grades 1–8) and exposition (grades 4–8).

Of all these measures and procedures, the most expensive, time consuming, controversial, and valuable were the CRTs. From the beginning, they were suspect as an accountability instrument, given the setting in which they were developed and validated. Procedures had to be thoroughly open and defensible, and the tests had to be able to withstand the most biased scrutiny. The development team recruited key principals and supervisors and nationally known consultants for advice.

CRTs in Narration.   The first item-writing workshop on the tests in narration was run in the spring of 1978. Classroom teachers and reading teachers wrote the items. The best consultants available were brought in to help plan and run the workshop, to review the item specifications and the Item-Writer's Handbook, and to review the items. Items were also reviewed by measurement and evaluation specialists from the new Department of Educational Accountability and by reading/language arts specialists in area offices. The development team served as group leaders during the workshop. The CRTs in narration were field-tested in 1978–79 using a pre- and post-test design, revised, and field-tested again in 1979–80.

CRTs in narration measure achievement of selected performance objectives. The 40-item tests are usually administered in two sittings and take approximately 45 minutes per administration. The tests are not timed. Each item represents a different narrative excerpt, carefully sampled from narrative texts widely used in local schools and in the nation.

Many teachers and principals quickly discovered the utility of the achievement data for diagnosis and instructional planning. In 1982–83, over 80% of the schools were voluntarily administering the tests. Reliability and other statistical properties of the tests are exceptionally good (Flach & Berk, 1980; Schuder & Flach, 1983).

CRTs in Exposition.   These tests were developed in the spring and summer of 1979, using the same procedures as those for narration. They were field-tested in 1981–82 and are currently being revised. In general, students showed much higher achievement levels in narration than in exposition. This is due to the inherent difficulty of expository discourse, limited experience reading texts with those characteristics, the poor quality of much published exposition for grades 4–8, and the lack of instruction in reading exposition, especially in basal reader programs.

Reports and Record Keeping

Computer-generated grade level reports for the CRTs in narration and exposition indicate the number of items each student got correct for each objective. Scores below criterion are asterisked. Summary reports are also available.

The observational checklist is the only record-keeping form that comes with the program. It is a heavy manila folder that stays with each student from kindergarten through eighth grade. Teachers record summary observations of performance on the generic categories of objectives (Fig. 17.3), and there is a place to enter criterion-referenced test results. Summary comments regarding strengths and weaknesses are recorded each year by each teacher. Achievement levels in basal readers and books read are also noted. The checklists involve minimal paperwork and maximum useful information. CRTs and the observational checklists provide the school system with consistent assessment data and record-keeping forms across all schools in the county.

IMPLEMENTATION

Moving into the Beleaguered Schools

By the time the Board approved the curriculum as the official *Program of Studies* for reading and listening K-8 in June of 1981, it had been pilot-tested in 32 schools over a period of 4 years. Subsequently, area administrative offices made plans to phase the new program into the remaining 96 schools over the next 3 years. At the same time, however, schools were attempting to implement revised curricula in mathematics, social studies, and science. Needless to say, that was not an optimum environment for making substantive changes of the sort outlined in the new reading and listening program. Human and material resources were stretched to the extreme.

Nonetheless, by September of 1983, all 126 K-8 schools were implementing the program, to some extent. That is a testament both to the willingness of staff to take on Herculean tasks and to the quality of the new program. Staff usually recognized the value of the curriculum, even in the worst of circumstances. Such a massive, sustained effort in development and implementation is also a testament to the dedication of the Board to continuous improvement in instruction and learning in Montgomery County Public Schools. Three successive Board majorities, elected over a period of 6 years with very different political and educational agendas, supported the new program with near unanimity.

Training and Resources for Implementation

Over the 6 years of pilot testing and implementation, resources have been radically reduced as the school system faced a declining student population, school closures, and a shrinking budget for program improvement. Original pilot school staffs received between 1 1/2 and 6 days of in-service training per year, depending on local administrative priorities. By 1982, no extra funds were available for in-service training. Training in reading and language arts had to compete with other priorities. Between 1978 and 1982, curriculum specialist support in reading and language arts fell from 20 to 6 full-time positions countywide. In the beginning, the 32 pilot schools received many extra dollars to purchase literature books to support instruction in narration. By 1982, few extra funds were available. Money for literature books had to come from regular textbook accounts where it competed with other school priorities.

Not only did the extent of in-service training vary with available funds and administrative styles and priorities, but the content also varied considerably, depending on trainers. In general, training tended to focus on management aspects of the program rather than generic ideas or core learning principles that made sense of the pieces of the program. Consequently, questionnaires, interviews, and observations revealed a low level of understanding of the program by teachers and principals in 1982 and 1983. Given the opportunity, individual teachers and principals made rapid progress toward full implementation. By and large, however, substantive changes in practice have been slow to appear. Even with consistent curriculum, assessments, reports, and record keeping, local autonomy remains dominant.

Toward Full Implementation

In a large school system, implementation is a long, slow, complex process in the best of circumstances. What is most significant at this point is signs of progress toward the declared intention of full implementation. Even with severe budgetary strictures, a large school system has immense resources that can be redeployed. Successful implementation depends on the ability to make choices and to marshal existing resources in support of declared priorities over a sufficient period of time to effect significant changes.

Signs of substantive change are beginning to appear. Teachers and principals are becoming more critical and selective in using basal readers; teachers and students have been touched by the excitement of meaningful tasks and good books. The ante is up. Title I/Chapter I staff adopted and supported the new curriculum for low-achieving students from its inception. Special and alternative education teachers are receiving in-service training in the new program and are beginning to report success with students.

In 1982, the Department of Educational Accountability launched a 3-year study of elementary reading programs in the county and implementation of the new curriculum. The study is a clear sign that the school system is serious about implementation. The results will provide administrators with instruments, procedures, and a data base to monitor implementation.

Finally, and perhaps most significantly, one of the area administrative offices, on its own initiative, has begun a systematic and objective effort to monitor implementation in its schools (using the Concerns Based Adoption Model, CBAM; see Hulig et al., 1983) and to provide principals and teachers with in-service training that meets their assessed needs. All these signs of substantive change augur well for the future of language learning in Montgomery County Public Schools.

18 Collaboration for School Improvement: A Case Study of a School District and a College

Donna Ogle
National College of Education

INTRODUCTION

The following is an account of a collaborative leadership training program in reading and writing. Based in an elementary school setting, it is described from the perspective of its director.

One of the most consistent characteristics of an effective school is a principal who functions as an instructional leader (Brookover & Lezotte, 1979; Kean et al., 1979; Rutter et al., 1979; Sweeney, 1982; Weber, 1971). Principals set the tone for the school, establish goals, facilitate change, support, encourage, and evaluate teaching efforts, and monitor achievement. Yet many principals feel they lack knowledge of basic curriculum areas, and few programs exist to help them develop instructional leadership.

This case study confirms the importance of school leadership and the need to translate sound theory into practice. Our efforts were designed to develop and implement an instructional leadership training program that would effectively:

- Increase principal and teacher knowledge of the learning processes
- Expand the principals' instructional leadership
- Change teaching practices
- Improve the working climate of the schools
- Increase student achievement

Our project came about through shared interests of the National College of Education faculty and the administration of the small school district of Zion,

Illinois. Because the Curriculum Supervisor position in that district had been eliminated through budget cuts, the Zion Superintendent of Schools was eager to increase the responsibilities of his principals in curriculum and instruction. The district had not had a focused program of staff development for a few years, and this was a high priority.

Zion School District, located between Chicago and Milwaukee, is in a stable, small community which has recently experienced an influx of short-term transient population. One third of the district's students are minority, and 25% are from low-income families. Four of five elementary schools operate Title I programs in reading.

A student-needs assessment and a check of principals' interests revealed that writing, reading, math, and oral language were high priorities, in that order. Yet none of the schools had contemplated or initiated a writing development project to enhance the curriculum, and no principal had professional preparation in that subject. They also had little formal training in the teaching of reading, and were interested in upgrading their knowledge.

At the National College of Education (NCE), a small, private single-purpose institution, the faculty was keenly interested in bridging theory and practice and was oriented toward school-based research. For instance, Trafton was developing and conducting research on a Title I math project; Ogle had completed a cooperative project with a school district on reading curriculum; and Wagner was co-directing the Chicago Area Writing Project.

Additionally, National College reading faculty were interested in change process research. In particular, Stallings' research on developing effective teaching practices in secondary classrooms, Hall and Loucks' (1978) Concerns Based Adoption Model, and Kean's (1979) *What Works in Reading* provided useful models of change which underscored the importance of the principal's leadership.

The need for administrative staff development was further substantiated by requests from two principals' organizations to NCE staff. With funding from the U.S. Office of Education, we were able to launch our project in leadership development in the summer of 1980. Donna Ogle served as project director; B.J. Wagner was the first skills area coordinator.

DESIGNING THE PROJECT

Project Goals

Our basic vision for the project was the creation of a setting in which teams of principals and teachers would learn about the latest research findings in reading and writing and then be assisted in implementing changes consistent with those findings. As we created this model for leadership development, we were aware that we would need to allow ample time for change to occur and to provide the additional support personnel needed to facilitate those changes.

The 4-year time frame of our basic skills project seemed ideal. We would be able to establish a good working relationship with administrators and teachers during the initial phase and build with them toward fulfillment of our shared goals.The principals would participate for the duration, but teachers would rotate each year, depending on their strengths in the designated area and their role as leaders in the school. At the end, there would be a common theoretical and instructional base across the district in the basic skills area and a strong cadre of leadership personnel in all the schools. Principals would have built a strong background of knowledge and practice in instruction, while expanding their repertoire of instructional leadership behaviors.

Operation Plan

To implement our goals, we decided on a process that is repeated on a yearly basis. One skill is addressed each year so that over the 4-year project periods all of the areas, writing, reading, oral language and math, are addressed. The yearly cycle is divided into two parts: planning and implementation. During the planning phase each principal is interviewed about specific interests and concerns. This interview introduces principals to the theoretical orientation of the project. Each principal then selects three teachers to join in the project for that year. These teachers are potential leaders in that skill area, who will implement the project goals. Based on input from principals and other data from the schools, a summer institute is planned by the skills coordinator, an NCE faculty member expert in the particular area of focus.

The summer institute, conducted over a 2-week span, 4 hours each day, focuses on current research and theory. Teaching practices are introduced and modeled. On the first day, principals meet with NCE staff to discuss ways of working collaboratively to build leadership teams. For the rest of the institute, teachers and principals learn together. Because the latest research in each field is presented, the material is generally new to both.

During the school year teachers implement the newly learned techniques, and principals expand their instructional leadership behaviors. This phase includes three major elements: monthly in-service workshops, weekly contacts with a project intern, and periodic meetings of the principals and project director. Workshops focus on applications of concepts introduced in the summer institute. The skills area experts lead the workshops, help participants to adapt research ideas to their particular settings, and promote sharing of teaching ideas.

Periodic meetings between the principal and project director focus on the expansion of the principal's instructional leadership. The initial proposal contained two particular objectives: (a) improvement of observational skills and (b) development of a strategy to expand the project ideas to the other teachers in each building. This in-service training is conducted by the principal and teachers, rather than by NCE staff. Each year, these two objectives and additional concerns are reviewed. The NCE faculty are interested in exploring with the administrators their perceptions of their own instructional leadership roles and supporting their efforts to expand those roles.

Thus, the model provides for summer learning of new content and theory, a group process for application and support during the process of changing teaching, meetings for administrators on applications of their leadership to the particular skill area being developed, and one-to-one weekly meetings between teachers and the intern.

Staffing

Project staff includes three people from the National College of Education: the project director, a skills area coordinator, and an intern. The project director remains constant over the term of the project and oversees the general implementation of each phase. This person also works directly with the administrators in facilitating their instructional leadership development. Each year a different skills area coordinator, expert in the area of focus, develops and leads the skills training. The coordinator also directs the work of the intern. The project intern, either an advanced student from the college or someone from the school district who has been through the NCE master's level program in the area of focus, serves an important linking role. Interns have the major responsibility for ensuring that the monthly targeted teaching strategies actually get implemented. To encourage teachers to try the new ideas, the interns demonstrate the strategies in each location and encourage teachers to try the same. Following a monthly observation with each teacher, the interns give feedback on these efforts. Interns also provide support for teachers and principals. Change is not easy and having someone to encourage change is extremely valuable. They provide new materials, help teachers plan new approaches, make suggestions when teachers seem "stuck," and, very importantly, provide positive feedback. In some cases they serve as the catalysts for teachers' opening their doors to other adults. By having regular visits in classrooms as a structural part of the program, teachers come to accept a more "open door" policy essential for change.

BUILDING THE KNOWLEDGE BASE FOR THE PROJECT

In its first year the project focused on writing; in its second, reading.

Writing

The theoretical base for the writing project came from the process models of Murray at the University of New Hampshire and the Bay Area Writing Project. The works of Graves (1982), Calkins (1980), Bissex (1980) and Clay (1975) have clearly established that children can, at very young ages, engage in productive writing experiences and that writing taught in elementary schools is both possible and valuable. Their efforts provided guidance and incentive for our own project.

From the Bay Area model we learned that engaging teachers and principals in actual writing experiences would be a valuable way of increasing their understanding of the writing process. Rather than just providing them with articles and talking about writing, we used actual writing events to broaden and in many cases develop a totally new concept of writing for our participants. These activities helped them learn that writing does not happen in one class period; rather, it takes several days for most writing to evolve. Initially, we helped them find topics, often asking them to generate lists of possible ones and having them try out a few before settling on the "right" one. During this prewriting phase, ideas and experiences took time to develop. Past experiences needed to be recalled and reconstructed; new formulations needed to be mulled over before being committed to paper. Once actual writing began, time was needed for jotting down ideas, drafting, and revising. Writing did not occur in a final form with the first effort. We encouraged them to share their drafts with others and get feedback. They learned that writers are often so close to their own experiences that they forget what elaborations audiences need to make sense of another's writing. Conferencing did help these writers become more clear in communication. We also helped them clarify the place for their interest in correct punctuation and grammar. Final editing was done on pieces to be shared with a broader audience.

Their own writing experiences and input from other sources challenged participants to rethink their assumptions about young children's abilities to write and about how writing could be taught. They began to see ways to translate into classrooms more real writing experiences. We talked about the need to reorder some classroom priorities, to make writing part of the ongoing school curriculum. And they began to see the need to withhold "red marks" on every form of error in children's writing. They began to understand the teacher's role in modeling and encouraging children's own efforts and own voice in their writing. Children's questions about spelling and punctuation, about ways to express feelings and ideas serve as initiation points for teaching. Children's low points of creativity provide opportunities for the exploration of new kinds of writing, perhaps an informative piece on some animal or natural phenomenon in which the child has shown interest.

Hearing about school writing projects initiated by others (Graves, Calkins, and Wagner) was valuable. Even more important initially, however, was the opportunity to watch videotapes of actual lessons so some shared concrete base was established for what a classroom engaged in this kind of writing looked like. In addition, seeing samples of children's writing, particularly the Grosse Pointe, Michigan, models of development in writing, was very useful.

Throughout this process we kept a focus on the development and communication of thinking. As children learn to write they first clarify their own thinking. Then they learn to balance their ideas and the needs of their readers. Their major audience is not the teacher, but classroom peers, and they test their writing frequently. Other audiences are also important and teachers can do a great deal to find real audiences for children's work. Many classes write to other schools, to people in the community, and for school newspapers and magazines. Young author contests and celebrations are popular vehicles for sharing finished writing efforts.

Our goals were for teachers and principals to understand the writing process and to provide time for writing weekly. We wanted them to build conferencing into their writing programs, to find real audiences for their children's writing, and to have clear and authentic communication as the hallmark of their programs.

Reading

The theoretical perspective guiding our reading priorities emphasized the interactive, constructive nature of the reading process. In this view, the success of comprehension depends on the reader's relevant prior knowledge and strategies for achieving his/her reading purposes. Good readers anticipate and predict what a text is likely to contain, focus their attention, and test what they read against their own knowledge.

Work being done at the Center for the Study of Reading was especially important in establishing this perspective. Anderson's work on prior knowledge and schema activation (1977), Pearson, Hansen, and Gordon's studies of inference and prediction (1979), Tierney and LaZansky's explorations of the author-reader transaction (1980), and Brown's work on metacognitive strategies and anticipation "set" (1982) provided compelling evidence. The importance of understanding how readers use structures, both narrative and expository, and the responsibility authors have to write well were underscored by Stein's work in story grammar (1979) and Anderson, Armbruster, and Kantor's work with expository text (1980). More applied studies of comprehension instruction by Durkin (1979) and of materials used to teach reading (Durkin, 1981) established the importance of our efforts to build a better understanding of reading.

Research on beginning reading also was included in the summer institute. We used the work of the Goodmans (1976b), Smith (1978), and Durkin (1966) to explain how children learn to read. The relations between reading and writing were introduced through the research of Henderson and Beers (1980), Clay (1975), and Graves (1982).

The intent of our project was for teachers to shift from testing students' reading by questioning to teaching strategies that actively involve students in reading and thinking. These strategies engage students prior to, during, and after reading. Before reading, students need to assess what they already know about the topic and form of literature, make predictions, and set reading goals. During reading they should be actively thinking ahead, reconstructing ideas, focusing on important concepts and information. Active readers think about why particular pieces are written, for whom, and from what perspectives. They also evaluate what they have accomplished after reading.

Two group teaching strategies were selected to develop a more interactive approach to reading: one for narrative (DR-TA) and one for expository material (K-W-L). The Directed Reading-Thinking Approach or DR-TA (Stauffer, 1969a) has children predict what will happen in a story based on information given in the text and their prior knowledge. After predicting, children read to confirm or alter those predictions. The teacher discusses their predictions and asks for proof. Initial predictions come from general clues available in title, picture, or author information and from the nature of the story itself. After reading some of the text and finding out more about the character, setting, and context, readers are able to make much more informed predictions and read intently with clear purpose.

In the K-W-L "reading to learn" process developed by Ogle, elementary children learn how to learn from texts. The teacher uses a three-part worksheet that includes columns for "What We *Know*," "What We *Want* to Find Out," and "What We *Learned*." Through a process of brainstorming, children call up all they know about the topic. Questions are raised as children disagree and these are recorded. The teacher may ask students to find general categories of information by charting what they already know and by predicting how they think the article will be organized. After reading, students record what was learned and discuss questions that remain unanswered.

Attention was also given to many excellent books and magazines, with demonstrations of ways to use them in classrooms to increase students' interest in reading and writing. Choral reading, readers' theater, and radio reading were modeled and ideas for relating reading and writing provided. For example, teachers were shown how to have students write endings to stories, rewrite textbook sections, and turn one form of literature into another; e.g., rewriting a scene from a novel into a play.

To familiarize teachers and principals with key issues in instructional organization, time allocation, and leadership, we included in our Summer Institute a summary of the research on effective schools and teacher effectiveness.

Based on feedback from teachers and principals during the summer institute, five objectives were identified for the application phase:

- Integrating reading and writing instruction
- Teaching the DR-TA in fiction
- Using the K-W-L with nonfiction

- Evaluating classroom organization
- Providing oral reading and motivational activities

EVALUATION DESIGN

Our initial evaluation design included both formative and summative measures. Because a major goal was the creation of an effective staff development model, we wanted each component evaluated by participants. Appropriate forced-choice and open-ended questionnaires were developed. Informal discussion and feedback were also useful sources of input in determining how adequately our design met the school personnel's needs.

To measure the impact of the project on the knowledge and behaviors of principals and teachers, we administered three instruments at the beginning and end of each project year. The first was a test of knowledge constructed to parallel the content of our project. The second, the Teacher Assessment of Writing Program or TAWP (in year 2 the Teacher Assessment of Reading Program or TARP), measured the working climate defined by the relation between perceptions of the actual and the ideal. The Levels of Use structured interview, part of the Concerns Based Adoption Model or CBAM (Hall, Loucks, Rutherford, & Newlove, 1975), also was conducted with each participant by an outside evaluator to determine the degree of utilization.

Measures of student achievement also were needed. Because achievement had not been the major target of this project, and time and money were limited, our attention to this need was minimal. Therefore, the National Assessment evaluation process was used to measure student writing on a pre-post basis, and the Gates-MacGinitie Reading Test was administered.

During each year, three additional measures were used to evaluate impact. First, the Levels of Concern Questionnaire part of the CBAM was administered to monitor teacher concerns and to help plan workshops. Second, the principals, the project director, and the intern observed project teachers to determine the implementation of what was taught. The intern and the director kept logs of these observations, pertinent events, and discussions.

IMPLEMENTING THE PROJECT

Working with a small group of principals and teachers, it was possible for us to follow the impact of our project in the schools and make needed alterations. By the end of the 2 years, there were significant changes in the language arts and reading instruction in the Zion schools. Teachers were implementing and adapting strategies they had learned. They were asking more of children and listening in new ways to what children contributed. Principals were utilizing their knowledge to support teachers and make decisions about their schools' instructional programs. Some were adapting their leadership behaviors to become more actively involved in the instructional program.

Year One

Teachers' Classroom Activities.   The first year had begun slowly and was a period of adjustment and trust building. Although the principals and teachers had wanted to learn about writing, they knew little about the process approach and thought in very traditional terms. Some teachers and principals were resistant to our approach; they did not want to write and had no thought of sharing their own writing.

During that first year three factors helped convince participants of the worth of the writing process approach with elementary children. We provided concrete examples of what children could accomplish and how to teach writing. We worked with teachers in their own classrooms, helping them adapt new ideas to their teaching styles and organization. Finally, they had positive experiences, which helped them become increasingly comfortable with writing.

Videotapes of children in school writing projects were introduced in the fall in-services to provide concrete examples. Many participants did not have background experiences to help them understand our input and were frustrated. They wanted more examples of children's writing and what could be expected at different grade levels. As they watched several videotapes and saw many writing samples, they formed a clearer idea of what the implementation of writing would be, and participants became more committed to applying these ideas.

The intern's regular visits to classrooms were important to our experimentation efforts in two ways. She modeled demonstration writing lessons for teachers and helped us understand some of the problems teachers faced as they tried writing activities. From her observations, we learned of conflicts between teachers' classroom organization and management structures and those modeled in our videotapes and demonstrations. Small-group work and freedom for children to move around for conferencing and peer efforts were all assumed in the processes we demonstrated, but some of our teachers did not encourage those behaviors. Therefore, we helped those teachers modify writing process activities to their classroom rules. We also showed them how to teach children new participation behaviors so that more small-group activity would be possible without their losing control of classroom discipline.

As the year progressed, teachers began to bring samples of their children's writing to the intern and, with encouragement, some shared their writing assignments and projects at the workshops. They also began to ask for more ways to engage children in writing and wanted assistance in purchasing materials to support their efforts. Principals demonstrated their understanding of the process and its importance in a variety of ways. These included willingness to purchase materials, to send teachers to writing workshops, and to publicize efforts to parents. One principal even exchanged letters with a fourth-grade class over a school controversy.

Principals' Leadership Development.   The aspect of our original design needing the most rethinking was our plan to support the development of the principals' instructional leadership. We quickly learned that the in-service sessions designed to develop their skills in observing writing lessons and working with teachers were not appropriate. Principals were unaccustomed to providing this kind of supervision and support. We should have taken more time with the principals—initially assessing their leadership styles and preferred behaviors and then exploring ways to extend their leadership in instructional areas. We had made some unfortunate assumptions that needed to be revised. However, there was a good working relationship between the principals and teachers on which to build. Rather than push our original plan, we decided to learn from them and present a variety of suggestions that would be compatible with their leadership styles. For example, one principal presented new ideas to his staff through memos and professional articles and never visited classrooms, so we provided him well-written articles supporting the project goals that could be shared with his teachers.

The principals recognized the inappropriateness of our assumptions about their leadership training and expertise but were interested in developing some of the skills basic to implementing our objectives. They decided to take a series of administrative workshops that dealt with clinical supervision and leadership styles during the second year of the project. The superintendent and principals asked that our project and this workshop series be coordinated. Fortunately, the leader was one of our faculty members also interested in integrating administration more directly with curriculum efforts. We decided that the project director would attend the sessions on clinical supervision and teach the Stallings (1981) Classroom Observation Snapshot to the principals. She would also present guidelines for observing writing and reading lessons. We hoped this would encourage principals to practice their clinical supervision in those areas. This plan worked well, and during year 2 some of the principals more actively observed and conferred with teachers about their instructional strategies.

Postscript.   By the end of the first year, principals and teachers had learned a great deal about the writing process and were familiar with prewriting, drafting, revising, and editing. Teachers had used writing activities in their classrooms and had enabled children to conference with them about their writing ideas and to edit pieces with their peers. Writing folders reflected the children's growth, and teachers had been freed of their fears that every paper needed a thorough teacher editing for errors.

In his end-of-the-year evaluation using the Levels of Use structured interview, Dane Manis, our external evaluator from CEMREL, wrote:

> One theme that came through strongly in the comments of teachers and principals at the end of the first year is that there existed a group of 12–15 individuals in the district who shared commitment to providing instruction in writing of the type promoted by the project. They felt they had made a good start and reported plans for continuing or even expanding. Still, along with their reports of enthusiasm and plans, there seemed to be a clear call for additional support for their efforts in the second year.

Year Two

The second year of the project went more smoothly than the first. We had established a good working relationship and could develop both the process and our objectives for the second year. In addition, both principals and teachers considered reading a priority area and were interested in learning all they could.

Our experiences throughout the year reinforced the value of being flexible and open when serving as change agents. We listened to the teachers and principals as we developed the workshops and in-service sessions and worked in the building. We learned to adjust our expectations for how long it would take to implement newly introduced strategies as we worked with individual teacher and school constraints. Finally, we found that our project was heavily influenced by external events—some unanticipated and all beyond our control.

The summer institute gave us a good opportunity to determine the areas that we should expand during the school application phase and which ones were of less priority to teachers. The most unexpected teacher reactions came near the end of the institute when we brought in some recent books and suggested these would be good to read to children in the fall. Many teachers were surprised that we were advocating oral reading. They thought that spending time that way was considered wasteful by professionals and had been adhering strictly to materials and skills in their basal programs, although they enjoyed reading to children and knew that children loved to hear them read. As a result, we introduced more recent books and demonstrated ways to expand oral reading and literary appreciation activities during the monthly workshops.

We also received mixed and somewhat surprising responses to our suggestions that teachers teach nonfiction reading strategies. Many of the teachers were in departmentalized settings and did not teach subjects other than reading and language arts. They had not used much nonfiction and did not place priority on the retention of new content. However, we did not want them to overlook this important area and so modeled reading to learn with nonfiction articles in magazines like "Ranger Rick" and "National Geographic World." This introduced several teachers to the possibility of using varied types of materials during their reading period and of not relying solely on basal stories. A few teachers implemented Ogle's three-part reading-to-learn strategy in social studies and science and became convinced of the value of the approach beyond reading lessons.

The necessity of a process perspective on implementing change with time and support for change behaviors was underscored as we helped teachers utilize new group reading strategies (DR-TA, K-W-L and ReQuest). Our experiences with the DR-TA are illustrative. We introduced this interactive, prediction-based strategy during the summer institute. We led a group DR-TA with participants and explained how teachers could plan stories utilizing this technique. We then had teachers work in groups to develop and execute their own DR-TA lessons. From their first experiences, teachers liked it. However, this did not mean they would begin to use the idea in their own teaching; most needed more encouragement. They asked us to model the technique in their classrooms. We did so and spent more workshop time reviewing the process. Finally, we issued an edict that the intern would observe all teachers trying a DR-TA during November. Only with this strong mandate were some of the teachers ready to risk implementing a new technique.

As we continued to work with teachers on classroom strategy, we again found how easily conflicts between classroom organization and our instructions undermined our efforts. We needed to help teachers find ways to adapt a strategy and make it work for them. Several of the teachers in departmentalized intermediate programs wanted to continue teaching to the whole group, although we had cautioned against more than 12 students in any interactive discussion group. For these teachers, we developed a way to involve half of the class in writing out their responses to predictive questions while the teacher worked orally with others.

It took until spring before most of the teachers were using the DR-TA strategy easily. By that time, some were confident enough that they were willing to demonstrate it in other classrooms and videotape lessons for future projects. One principal became so convinced of its value that he conducted demonstrations in all nonproject classrooms and has made it an objective for teachers each year. Another principal chose this as the focus for an in-service. However, as late as May some still were not convinced. One principal came to me asking that I again explain the power of the DR-TA. He had just observed a first-grade teacher using the strategy and could not believe how it excited and involved the children.

During the second year, we also experienced several intrusions that affected the project. Such unexpected events always provide opportunities for learning, but they can substantially thwart objectives and distort project effectiveness. We lived with both types of intrusions. Several enhanced our project efforts.

The junior high principal wanted to have his reading staff included in the workshops. This added to the meetings some strong well-informed reading teachers who contributed many of the ideas they had found helpful in their teaching. For the first time this provided direct communication between elementary and junior high schools. Teachers appreciated learning more about each other's programs. By incorporating the administrative workshops into our project, the principals had expanded their basic understanding of supervision and leadership styles and were exploring new ways of exerting instructional leadership. Another positive addition to our schedule was attendance by teachers and principals at an IRA convention in Chicago. Workshop time was spent preparing for the conference and sharing learning afterwards. This experience was for most an exciting and confirming one. They heard talks by researchers they had learned about earlier, and took pride in what they knew and in being part of a much larger professional world. Taking advantage of these opportunities certainly strengthened the project.

Other events were less constructive and weakened our efforts. Midway through the year, the superintendent was reported to be ready to leave for a better job. Almost immediately, this diverted energies and left participants less eager to make changes in curriculum, particularly to institute more writing. A new person might reorder priorities. Even later in the spring of the second year, the administration, school board, and teachers came to loggerheads over contract negotiations. This tense situation had a very visible effect on the teachers. Even more debilitating was the news that a significant portion of the tax base for the district was being reclassified by court order. Consequently, the administration tabled plans to continue the project for the third year. Only late in the summer, due to strong teacher and principal interest, was the project reinstated. It became clear that both enhancing and debilitating external influences must be accounted for in describing field-based projects.

By the end of just 2 years a great deal had been accomplished. Principals and teachers knew a great deal more about writing and reading. In teaching, they relied more on what they knew instead of depending on a basal manual. As one veteran teacher put it:

> This project was like a shot in the arm. After teaching 20 years I needed to be stimulated to do new things. I had learned the DR-TA quite some time ago and then got away from it when we got a new reading series. I was spending so much time on just phonics and cueing systems that I lost sight of good stories. This year has brought me back to an interest in stories. Instead of ignoring our basal I began to look further to find additional stories by authors in our book. This was a real reawakening for me, and my students love it. It helped me integrate and try things I didn't seem to have the energy to do on my own.

In summarizing the end-of-year interviews with principals, the evaluator concluded that, for at least three of the principals, the reading in-service provided confidence, information, and skills to meet and talk with teachers not previously experienced.

EVALUATING THE PROJECT

Had we been able to develop an effective instructional leadership training model? Our own perceptions, feedback from participants and others in the district, and formative measures administered throughout the project indicated we were making an impact in the district. These impressions were confirmed by the independent evaluation conducted by a trained CBAM evaluator using the Levels of Use interviews. Given the nature of the changes we had asked teachers and principals to make, the interview data certainly indicated the project objectives were being applied.

Was principal and teacher knowledge increased? Comparison of the pretest and posttest scores for participants each year indicated a substantial knowledge-of-content increase.

Did the principals expand their instructional leadership behaviors? Our own observations, meetings with principals, and the Levels of Use interviews confirm that principals were implementing the project and using their knowledge and leadership skills. The additional leadership workshops conducted during the school year had also affected their general leadership self-perceptions. Data from the LEAD instrument indicated that the work was paying off. Teachers in four of the five schools perceived their principals as more effective leaders on the posttest as compared to the pretest.

Did we improve the working climate in the schools? We have no way beyond our informal observations to answer this question. We learned that we could not use the TAWP/TARP in the way we had planned. It proved as sensitive to teachers' changing perceptions of what ought to be as it was to their evaluations of what was in place. As we expanded their knowledge about what could be done in writing and reading instruction, they wanted more. We plan to continue to work with this instrument, especially as a tool for formative evaluation for both teachers and principals.

Did the teachers implement the project in their classrooms? Indications of teacher implementation came from three sources: Levels of Use interview, Stages of Concern questionnaires, and classroom observations. All confirmed a high level of application of the project ideas and specific teaching strategies.

Did student achievement improve? The impact on student learning was difficult to measure since we did not devise specific measures to assess the impact of the particular strategies. Results of the writing evaluations indicated that students did show more growth in writing than the nonproject controls, but it was not statistically significant. The same trend was true of the reading evaluation.

WHAT ABOUT THE FUTURE?

Perhaps the best indication of the effectiveness of a project is what happens after federal or foundation dollars are removed. In our case, federal withdrawal was coupled with the loss of thousands of tax dollars because of an industrial tax-base decision and contract negotiations in the district. Both principals and teachers had indicated that they very much wanted to continue, but we had to wait until late in the summer before the final affirmative decision was made.

The project also is being implemented in one of the Chicago school districts. Both the superintendent and the associate superintendent are eager to provide a vehicle for their principals to grow as instructional leaders. The recent research on effective schools is being disseminated to school leaders, and they are responding.

We plan to continue to refine the project model, especially in two areas. The principals' component needs to include a more careful initial diagnosis, followed by adaptation of objectives to the particular district needs. In addition, we want to explore ways to incorporate more use of existing school personnel to maintain the momentum of project innovations over time.

The time seems right for school implementation projects. There is much good research that needs to be made available to practitioners so they can improve their efforts. Instruments and technology exist to make both current behaviors and change efforts concrete for practitioners and researchers. In addition, tools are available to help us monitor the impact of change efforts with principals and teachers. Most importantly, there are practitioners who want to learn and grow with us.

19 Content Reading in Secondary Schools

Carol Minnick Santa
School District 5 Kalispell, Montana

Secondary teachers are usually sensitive to the content demands of their subject areas, but often fail to address problems related to reading comprehension and general study skills. Secondary teachers feel their job is to impart particular content information. All too often they forget that their fundamental role is to teach the process of learning. From the students' perspective this means they will either flounder, or devise their own strategies for reading and studying. Those who succeed are ingenious enough to derive an efficient system. Most, however, are not such successful detectives and need explicit instruction in how to learn.

With these concerns in mind, we have developed a content reading program designed to increase secondary teachers' ability to teach students *how* to read and learn. Our project, Content Reading in Secondary Schools (CRISS), is based on the premise that teaching reading, studying, and writing is within the province of all teachers.

The CRISS project was developed in the junior high and high school of Kalispell, Montana. Kalispell is a small isolated community of approximately 16,000 people tucked among the Rocky Mountains in the northwestern part of the state. The district draws largely from low- to middle-income families. Many students are bussed to the junior high and high school from isolated mountainous areas and are often products of one- and two-room rural elementary schools.

Our project arose from teacher frustration. The high school English and social studies teachers were vocal about students' inability to learn from reading assignments. Teachers would assign a reading selection only to find that students gained practically no information. The chagrined teacher would then be forced to review the material in class, which left little time to expand upon the information. Student passivity became the rule. The more teachers would assign and review, the more passive students became. Teachers began to avoid reading assignments as a medium of instruction. It was much easier simply to lecture.

Given the student apathy and teacher frustration, our curriculum director wrote an ESEA Title IV-C Innovative Grant to develop a content reading and writing program, and hired me to direct the project. During the first year, eight high school teachers from the areas of science, social studies, mathematics, and language arts volunteered to help develop the content reading program.

DEVELOPING THE PROGRAM

Year One: Planning, Development and Research

As an initial step the teachers, the curriculum director, and I spent one week at the University of Northern Colorado with Bob Pavlik and Thomas Estes at an intensive in-service about practical approaches to content reading. During this time we examined current programs and discussed the kind of program we wished to develop. Next, to provide some exposure to more abstract and theoretical views of comprehension and the reading process, we arranged a visit by several members of the Center for the Study of Reading located at the University of Illinois, Champagne-Urbana. David Pearson, Rand Spiro, Andrew Ortony, and Tom Anderson provided the teachers with an overview of reading comprehension.

We decided that our content reading program must include three elements. First, it must incorporate the practical and theoretical ideas regarding the impact of text organization. Second, it must be designed to involve the student as an active learner capable of using her/his existing knowledge for comprehension. Finally, it should emphasize the importance of learning strategies and current notions of metacognition.

Textbook Organization. None of the teachers had really thought about how the organization of text might influence its comprehensibility. Textbooks were typically chosen on the basis of their content and on standard readability formulas. Learning about the importance of text structure made teachers aware of the significance of how a textbook is written, and helped them see the limitations of traditional readability assessments.

In fact, the first thing we did was to create a system for evaluating textbooks in science, social studies, language arts, and mathematics. In each content area teachers itemized qualities of well-written textbooks and combined these into a checklist for textbook evaluation.

In many cases the teachers learned that their books were poorly structured. One science teacher discovered that the organization and clarity of his text varied dramatically by chapter. Other teachers found the readability level to be perfectly adequate for the students, but the material poorly conceptualized and written. Becoming aware of the well and poorly written chapters was beneficial for instruction.

Background Knowledge and Active Learning.   The research on background knowledge and schema (Beck & Mckeown, this volume; Wilson & Anderson, this volume) provided our teachers with the empirical substantiation needed for emphasizing relations between background knowledge and reading comprehension. Such questions as, How can I find out what students know about a topic? How can I use this knowledge to guide comprehension? and What knowledge should be developed before my students read? became important. Such questions led teachers to change their instructional emphasis from postreading to prereading activities involving the development of relevant concepts and vocabulary before students read a selection.

An equally important shift in philosophy occurred with teachers' conceptions of comprehension. During in-service sessions with Pearson and Spiro, we learned that comprehension involved a change in one's schema. To teach comprehension as schema change means the student must become a very active participant in learning. It takes considerable energy to take in new information and integrate it into one's own frame of reference. Real comprehension, then, is an accommodation or change in one's existing knowledge structures to include new material from the text. Teachers began to see a need for using instructional strategies to help students move from being passive to being more active participants in learning.

Metacognition and Learning Strategies.   An understanding of metacognition helped us reevaluate our roles as teachers. Deluging students with content to get through the book by semester end was replaced by creating effective students. Effective students know when they do not understand and have a variety of deliberate strategies they use to obtain meaning. These vary depending on the learner's purpose for reading, the nature of the materials, and the criterial task (Brown, 1982; Brown, Armbruster, & Baker, this volume). For students to become effective, self-regulating learners, they must know the available options so they can choose the most appropriate one for the learning task. In addition, students need assistance in determining whether or not their choice has led to the desired end.

Basically, our teachers began to understand how to help students become competent in a variety of studying and self-monitoring strategies. They began to teach directly a variety of learning strategies. After students gained some competence, teachers allowed them to choose their strategy for a particular learning situation. One way teachers helped their students determine strategy effectiveness was through class discussion that focused student awareness on their performance. When a student performed well the teacher would ask questions about the strategies that led to success. The means became as important as the end.

Evolution in teaching philosophy and consequent changes in instruction came slowly. However, such an evolution would not have occurred had it not been for recent research. Research provided an overriding framework that guided the project's development. When thinking of ways to help our students better understand and remember content information, we would evaluate our ideas in terms of whether or not they would generate student activity. For example, does a particular strategy help students link what they know with what they are about to learn, or help students monitor whether or not the strategy was personally effective? An instructional philosophy created from an understanding of some basic research tenets was the first step toward program change.

Teachers As Research Collaborators.   Once we had worked out basic ideas about the program, we felt it was important to develop specific applications and to evaluate these ideas in classrooms. These experiments evolved into a very sensitive and successful way to change teaching behavior. Involving teachers in planning and carrying out experiments preserved ownership and provided convincing evidence to motivate change.

During the first year each of the eight teachers had six release days to work with me in developing the project. Initially these sessions began with a discussion of a theoretical issue and evolved into plans for some specific classroom practice the teachers wanted to investigate.

The first area we investigated, and the area most drastically in need of change, was the persistent practice of assigning reading without any instructional provisions. Typically the teacher would say, "I want you to read pages 25–30 for tomorrow," without any thought to what students knew or needed to know about the topic before reading. Although the teachers understood the relation between background knowledge and reading comprehension, they remained skeptical about its relevance for learning and were unsure about specific strategies to ensure its use. Classroom-based experiments laid the groundwork for change.

Our research began by posing the question, "Is it important to elicit and develop appropriate background knowledge before students read in mathematics and social studies?" We set up two classroom experiments, in geometry and history. In geometry two classes participated, both with the same teacher. The class that typically did better on chapter tests became the control, with the lower achieving group as the experimental class. The reading materials, a chapter on indirect proofs, and time on task, one class period, were kept constant across conditions. For the control group, the teacher assigned students to read the chapter and study the sample proofs. The students were free to ask questions during and after reading. Following the reading the teacher presented a short explanation about indirect proofs and went over the example problems.

For the experimental group the teacher taught basically the same lesson, but the emphasis was different. Before assigning the reading, the teacher put key vocabulary on the board and had students brainstorm about what the words might mean. Student comments were summarized on the board. Next, the teacher clarified any misconceptions and added any needed information. Then the students listed two or three ideas they hoped to gain from the selection, and read the material silently. Following discussion and rereading, the teacher went over the example problems. Both the experimental and control classes were assigned the problems at the end of the chapter as a test. The experimental procedure was basically a directed-reading activity, which included five general steps: establishment of background knowledge, development of purpose for reading, guided silent reading, discussion and rereading, and extension activities.

As predicted, applying a directed-reading model led to better performance on chapter tests. Data from this geometry study and from a similar study in history helped convince the teachers of the importance of background knowledge and student involvement in comprehension.

Subsequent to these experiments, the mathematics and history teachers began using directed-reading activities in their classes. To help change the behaviors of other teachers involved in the project, both teachers presented their data during brown bag lunches.

Learning Guides.   A second series of experiments with learning guides not only convinced teachers of their benefits, but helped them understand the effects of active learning and self-monitoring tasks. In the project, we use a two-column note-taking procedure. The format is simple. Students divide their paper lengthwise into two columns. In the left column they include questions or key words (triggers) describing an essential concept or main idea presented in the reading selection. In the right column students record information elaborating the main points. Upon completing their notes, they use them as a study guide. Covering the information on the right, the students test themselves using the questions in the left column.

Even though the format is simple, teachers spend considerable time teaching students how to construct the guides. At first, teachers are very directive to the point of supplying students with model guides. Gradually these models become more and more incomplete until students create their own guides. Instruction occurs as part of the directed-reading activity where background knowledge, purposes for reading, and vocabulary developed in the prereading activity become lead questions. Discussion follows on how the author developed main ideas and how to construct questions to extract key points from text. In addition, considerable discussion occurs about what goes into creating higher level questions tapping critical and evaluative thinking.

Classroom-based research played an essential role in convincing teachers of the merits of guides and in modifying instructional strategies for classroom delivery. We first did an experiment to determine whether or not learning guides helped students with course content in biology and American history. For the American history class we used two junior level classes. Again we biased the conditions so that the experimental class was the one that initially performed less well on tests than the control class. The history teacher introduced the experimental class to learning guides as part of a directed-reading activity. He provided model guides over part of the chapter and incomplete guides over the remaining selections. They discussed the types of questions that should be incorporated into the guide. The teacher covered the same material with the control group, but did not introduce these students to learning guides. The experiment began on Monday and ended on Friday with a chapter test. As predicted, the experimental group did better on the test than the control group. However, much of the tested information was contained in the teacher-supplied guides.

A much clearer evaluation of study guides occurred the following week when the teacher merely told the experimental class to develop their own guides. He instructed both classes following steps of a directed-reading activity during the same amount of class time. The experimental group received explicit instructions to construct a two-column study guide and the controls were told to study the material any way they chose. Again the experiment began on Monday and ended on Friday with a chapter test. The experimental class did significantly better than the control class on the chapter test. A similar result also occurred in two biology classes where the same procedure was repeated. These experiments helped convince the teachers that learning guides are useful instructional tools.

We then conducted several other experiments dealing with the use of learning guides. Two teachers in the project persisted in supplying students with teacher-made guides. Apparently they feared their students would miss something if allowed to construct their own guides, but these guides were contributing to continued student dependence and passivity. Again the approach to changing teacher behavior was to involve them in an experiment.

We used two American history classes taught by the same teacher; both classes had received similar exposure to learning guides. In one class, the teacher distributed a pre-made learning guide; in the other, students were instructed to create their own. The average chapter test performance of students who used teacher-make guides was 75%, compared to 89% for students who had constructed their own guides. These data convinced teachers to change their instructional strategies by putting the responsibility for guide construction on the students.

Another experiment designed by a teacher addressed students' reluctance to use the learning guides for self-testing. The teacher created pairs of students in the experimental class and told them to test one another for the last 5 minutes of the period. Testing came from the questions on their learning guides. The control class used the same class time for undirected study. This class had also written guides, but most chose not to use them. On the weekly chapter test, students who used the learning guides for self-testing scored an average of 93%, whereas those who did not scored 72%. The teacher shared these data with his students. As a result more students began to use the guides for self-monitoring of performance. It is interesting to note that the teacher used the experimental approach to convince students, much as I used it to convince teachers.

Year Two: Implementing and Disseminating the Program

Classroom experimentation turned out to be a sensitive and successful way to integrate basic theoretical notions into classroom practice. All of these experiments and discussions led to the development of a specific program for teaching reading in the content areas, including strategies for teaching vocabulary, main ideas, conceptual mapping, and writing. By the end of the first year we had developed materials and examples for social studies, English, and geometry. Our next task was to disseminate the materials to other teachers, at first within the district, and later throughout the state of Montana.

During the second year, 16 additional junior high and high school teachers from various content areas (home economics, social studies, science, mathematics, and language arts) joined us. We grouped the participants according to content areas so they could learn how the project had been specifically tailored to their own disciplines. The eight original teachers provided the in-service training because the best teacher trainers are successful teachers whose strategies are demonstrable. Their enthusiasm for what they had accomplished during our first year successfully kindled their colleagues' curiosity and made much more of an impression than if outside experts had presented the same message.

During the second year, the teachers continued to experiment with a variety of instructional strategies. Much of the work from the first year was reevaluated within different classroom settings by a variety of teachers. We continued our "research chats" during brown bag lunches and in brief after school meetings. In addition, project newsletters describing successful instructional strategies used by various teachers were distributed to teachers' lounges throughout the district. Finally, several teachers and I organized and taught a graduate course in content reading for district teachers not yet formally exposed to the project. As one course requirement, teachers implemented key components of the program and reported student performance.

Our hidden agenda was to create a project based on teacher participation and suggestion. Nothing was ever imposed. Instead, we let the ripples spread as they would. We realized we would never reach everyone because there are always those who resist change or are set in their ways. Yet, most have participated, and we can now say that all students who graduate from our high school have learned how to learn with a variety of methods from a variety of teachers.

At the end of the second year our project was validated as a state demonstration project for Montana. This evaluation, conducted by outside observers, was based on student achievement data and interviews with parents, teachers, administrators, and school board members. With this stamp of approval we are now providing workshops for other districts throughout the Northwest.

INSTRUCTIONAL COMPONENTS OF THE CONTENT READING PROGRAM

Our program can be divided into six components: text assessment, student assessment, main ideas, strategic learning processes, vocabulary, and directed-reading activities. For each we have written "how to" manuals for science, social studies, language arts, and mathematics. These manuals are support materials distributed to out-of-district teachers and are part of our workshops.

Text Assessment

We always include text assessment first because an awareness of text characteristics is a precursor to understanding how best to use the text for instruction. For each of the four major content areas, we have developed a system of evaluation summarized in checklists that teachers apply to their texts. Although the checklists vary according to content, the general areas of evaluation have some similarities: readability, overall organization, chapter organization, paragraph structure, vocabulary development, and visual aids.

The first part of the checklist requires that teachers apply several readability formulas to a number of random selections. Even though such formulas have received much criticism, we feel they have some use in text evaluation. However, it is important to be aware of the limitations of readability formulas (see Anderson & Armbruster, this volume).

To assess the overall organization and structure of a text, teachers first look for structural features such as table of contents, glossary, appendices, and studying aids such as chapter questions. Next they do an evaluation of two or more representative chapters, focusing on whether or not the chapters are divided into topics and subtopics that reflect the content. We have found many texts that appear well organized on the surface, but then discover that bold face topics do not reflect essential points of the written messages. Teachers then examine the representative chapters for well-written introductory and summary paragraphs reflecting the key concepts.

We next evaluate paragraph structure. Does the author explicitly state main points? Are there any patterns of main idea development such as simple listing, comparisons, or problem-solution formats? It is at the paragraph and multi-paragraph level that teachers have encountered the most difficulty. The text may have seemed appropriate according to a readability formula, but is actually ineffective because of poor organization. Another common problem is that main ideas are implicit rather than explicit. Such organization is often lost on poorer readers.

The next section of the checklist focuses on how authors develop new vocabulary through context. For each of the four content areas, we itemized the prevalent types of contextual information authors used for developing vocabulary: direct definitions, restatements, comparisons, inferences, and examples. In the ideal situation, new vocabulary should be defined directly, and then followed with elucidating examples or discussion. To determine the type of vocabulary development, we take several thousand word selections from a text and assess the specific ways vocabulary is presented. In many situations, teachers find that the authors have supplied few, if any contextual aids. This evaluation provides teachers with an index they can use to determine the amount of classroom time they must spend on background vocabulary development.

Finally, teachers focus on the visual information. They examine whether visual presentations (charts, graphs, pictures) are relevant to the written text and determine if the authors have provided verbal cues within the text to focus the reader's attention on specific visual information. They also examine the location of visual information within the text. Ideally, graphs, charts and pictures should be located on the same page, or at least within one or two pages of the written material to which they refer. If students have to flip pages back and forth, the information probably will not be used.

After teachers have become familiar with the various features of their text, they can begin thinking about ways to help their students attain the same familiarity. Students need to understand how information is presented so they can be more strategic in their use of text structure for comprehension.

A critical component is to have teachers develop a strategy for helping students become aware of text structure. Time is provided in our workshops for teachers to create an initial teaching plan. They typically have students analyze their own textbooks using checklists similar to those used by the teacher.

Student Assessment

The next component of the project provides a system for teachers to determine whether or not their students can read their textbooks adequately. We instruct teachers in the use of standardized reading tests as well as less formal, but more individualized methods for assessing reading comprehension. For example, we demonstrate the use of teacher-constructed group informal reading inventories and cloze procedures (Pikulski & Shanahan, 1982; Shepherd, 1978). This test information helps teachers become aware of their students' varying reading abilities and can be used to plan appropriate instructional strategies.

Given an understanding of text and an awareness of student reading abilities, teachers are now ready to begin instructional implementation as described in the next four sections.

Main Ideas

Understanding and remembering main points from text is crucial for mastering content information. Thus, teachers expend considerable effort helping students develop strategies for extracting main points. The goal is to have students become competent in a variety of methods so they can choose the best strategy given the constraints of the selection and learning requirements.

Main idea instruction is intimately intertwined with the particular structure of the material students are assigned. The teachers therefore help students analyze stylistic variables. Discussion addresses where main ideas are located in paragraphs and whether this development occurs explicitly or implicitly.

Students learn to underline selectively. Using old texts or pages copied from books, students develop specific underlining notation systems. They are discouraged from underlining complete sentences, but rather note key words and ideas that capture the essence of the material.

Summarizing also plays a central role in main idea instruction. Instruction typically begins by having students write one-sentence summaries of text sections. As students read they jot down key words, which they then combine into a one- or two-sentence summary. These brief summaries can then be expanded into longer paragraphs. An alternative to summarizing, which inspires students to get to the heart of the content, is telegrams. Students write telegrams to one another describing essential content of their text.

Conceptual mapping is another approach to getting main ideas. Teachers give their students large sheets of butcher paper and colored markers. The assignment is to read and visually diagram the main idea relationships within the text. Students who may work in pairs, then explain their maps to the class. Most maps are in the form of hierarchical networks, but students are free to unleash their creativity and use pictorial representations as well. The final task is to write a verbal description of the map, which is nothing more than a written summary of the material.

Learning Guides

Learning guides have become the strongest component of the project, since teachers can see immediate student improvement. Learning guides are basically note-taking and writing strategies that help students to organize text information. In addition, the guides provide students a system for monitoring whether or not they are understanding and remembering information from their text. For each type of guide they learn to test themselves over the content of the guide as well as learn procedures for going back to fix up their comprehension of the material.

Although we promote a wide variety of learning guides, the basic instructional progression for each is the same. At first, teachers are very directive, to the point of supplying model guides. During this modeling stage, teachers and students create guides together, jointly determining the form and content of the notes. When a teacher feels the students understand a particular guide, he/she will begin to put more responsibility on the students. This can be done by supplying students with incomplete guides to finish during reading. This transition period varies according to content and student abilities. The goal is to move students to the point of independence, both in constructing their own guides and in using the guide for self-testing.

Our most popular guide is the two-column format described earlier in this chapter. However, we emphasize that learning guides should take many forms depending on the material and the instructional goals of a particular lesson. Also, students should receive constant encouragement to develop their own guides.

Our science teachers, for example, favor three-column formats to encourage students to integrate class notes with notes from the text. (See Fig. 19.1). In mathematics teachers have had success with four-column guides. In the geometry example (Fig. 19.2) students read the selection, write down key terms, define these terms in their own words, create a diagram to demonstrate their understanding of terminology, and then come up with their own problem demonstrating how the term is used mathematically.

We have used a similar guide in high school algebra classes. It, too, is a four-column format, with formulae replacing diagrams, and a question column in which students record any questions they have about the information. The algebra teachers found the question column helped students think more critically about presented information.

In literature, teachers have found guides helpful for focusing students' attention on specific literary aspects such as character development, plot, and conflict. As students read, they jot down reactions in the specified columns—

	Explanation from book	Class discussion
CHAPTER 5 "WATER IN THE SEA"		
1. On the drawing of the water cycle label the processes and features; indicate at each feature the time out of 100 years a water molecule would spend there.		
2. How do salts and other particles get into the oceans?		

FIG. 19.1   Three-Column Learning Guide in Science

Term	Definition	Diagram	Problem
1. Quadrilateral	1. Union of 4 line segments that join 4 coplanar pts., no 3 of which are coll. Each inter-sects exactly 2 others, one at each end pt.		Note exercises p. 293. Choose one of these and make one of your own. Set 1, #1, 3, 4 2-4

2. Vertices
  a. Consecutive
  b. Opposite
	2. End points of the line segments
	  a. Angles that share a side
	  b. Angles that don't share a side
		2. A, B, C, D
		  a. A and B
		  b. A and C
			2. Name the vertices
			  a. Consecutive
			  b. Opposite

FIG. 19.2   Learning Guide: Geometry

Character, Actions, Problem, and Solution. These comments become the focus of discussion and serve as prewriting guides to help students organize compositions.

Another form of a learning guide is the framed paragraph from the Individualized Language Arts Project (Alder, 1971). The framed paragraph is in prose rather than table form. The teacher provides structure by supplying phrases to guide and constrain student responses. Again, the frame is only supplied as long as students need help in constructing well-organized and meaningful written responses. As soon as students are competent, frames are no longer provided. An example of a framed paragraph followed by a complete student example is as follows:

FRAMED PARAGRAPH

"_____, a character from the classic
novel by _____, seems to have been a
_____ person. An example
of this was when _____.
Another example was when _____
_____. Finally _____
_____
_____. This character _____
_____ always _____
_____.

STUDENT RESPONSE

"Huck Finn, a character from the classic novel, *The Adventures of Huckleberry Finn* by Mark Twain, seems to have been an adventurous boy. An example of this was when he decided to run away from the widow's house where he was staying. Another example was when he and his friend Jim rode a homemade raft down the Mississippi River by themselves. Finally, Huck decided to adventure back to the widow's by himself. This character, Huck Finn, always dared to do exciting things."

FIG. 19.3   Framed Paragraph and Student Response

Vocabulary

After content teachers understand the magnitude of the vocabulary burden facing secondary students, they begin to provide more instruction. Most of the instructional strategies focus on analysis of the author's context, and the use of technical and nontechnical terminology in student writing about course content.

One very simple strategy is to have students write logs of technical vocabulary. After discussing key words in class, students incorporate words into sentences using specific types of context clues to explain the meaning of the word. For example, teachers might ask students to use clues of contrast or example to explain the word. Having students write their own context clues makes them more sensitive to how authors use context to impart meaning.

Another practical approach is to have students combine four or five key terms into one or two sentences. Such synthesis provides an excellent review of course content and is a good way to incorporate brief writing activities as part of content instruction. We have conducted several experiments that provide clear evidence of the positive effect of writing on vocabulary learning. The more students incorporate new words in their writing, the better the long-term retention of these words.

Directed Reading Activity

The Directed Reading Activity (DRA), as mentioned earlier, is an instructional model we use to integrate specific reading strategies into reading lessons applied to the content areas. All of the instructional components of our project fit within one or more of the five steps of DRA: preparation for reading, purpose setting, guided silent reading, discussion and rereading, and extension activities. All of the activities we have discussed, such as summarizing and vocabulary synthesis, should be taught as part of an integrated DRA approach to reading.

When disseminating our project to other content teachers, the culmination is to have the participating teachers build a complete DRA over a selection in their text. For this, they piece together activities to provide background knowledge, develop main ideas, create learning guides, and introduce vocabulary as components of a general reading program. With the overview, teachers begin to see how students can learn to use a variety of activities to promote comprehension of text.

PROJECT DISSEMINATION

Since completing our project in Kalispell, we have made efforts to disseminate our approach and materials beyond our local school district. Our efforts have been enhanced by being designated a state demonstraton project and being partially funded by an ESEA Title II basic skills grant. Our designation as a state demonstration project has resulted in adoption and in-service programs for over 55 school districts throughout the state of Montana. To date, 650 teachers have been exposed to our project. This number might not seem large in comparison to urban projects, but one must remember that these 650 teachers are spread over 147,000 square miles.

Our in-service session is a 1- or 3-day workshop presented by history, science, and language arts teachers from Kalispell. It covers the project's six components along with a theoretical rationale for each component. After we have presented and modeled strategies, participating teachers have opportunities to develop specific instructional strategies using their own texts. At the conclusion of the workshop, teachers have evaluated their texts, written a student assessment, and developed main idea strategies, learning guides, and vocabulary activities for their textbooks. Finally, they develop a model for integrating the various components of teaching comprehension. Teachers return to their schools with a better theoretical understanding of how students learn from text, so they can continue to evolve instructional procedures to complement their revised instructional philosophies.

The teachers and administrators who attend the workshop are now responsible for disseminating the project throughout their own district. Their first task is to try out new techniques within their own classes, and collect some classroom based data assessing how well the techniques improve student performance. Next, administrators are responsible for finding time for teachers to "brag" about their successes. After about 2 months the teachers should begin plans for training the remaining staff.

This "Amway" model, in which we set up district-based trainer hierarchies, works almost as well for CRISS as it does for laundry detergent. Our role becomes one of contact with our distributors in each district. The newsletters about CRISS activities, which I write for our own staff, are sent to these key people. They in turn send me similar "brag" sheets from their districts. We also make periodic visits to adopting districts to provide them with consulting help.

These visits provide an endless stream of ideas for improving our own project. Teachers are infinitely creative in the way they adapt the program to their unique learning situations. This constant interaction with teachers has made CRISS an ever-changing and evolving project. Ultimately, I cannot help but think that one of the important contributions of a project like ours is that it stimulates all of us, students, teachers, and even administrators, to think critically about the learning process. Such thought and effort are bound to be rewarding for everyone.

Effective Literacy Training Programs for Adults in Business and Municipal Employment

Larry Mikulecky
Rebecca L. Strange
Indiana University, Bloomington

The gap is wide between school literacy training and what is called for in a growing number of jobs. This chapter examines job literacy training in two effective training programs developed as cooperative ventures involving business, local government, and private consulting firms.

AN OVERVIEW

Many leaders in business, industry, and government are concerned about workers with insufficient reading and writing skills. In the *Wall Street Journal* (Hymowitz, 1981), William Barnes of J.L.G. Industries reports having spent over $1 million to correct worker literacy mistakes. Mutual of New York reports an "estimated 70% of the Insurance firm's correspondence must be corrected and retyped at least once." In addition, workers' abilities to read safety warnings and written directions have been issues in recent litigation.

In reaction to these concerns, educators, consulting firms, businesses, and municipalities are developing literacy programs to train workers to read effectively and utilize job-related materials. These training programs are used both before and during employment for occupation upgrading. Nearly all programs must demonstrate success while being cost-effective. This usually means that trainees must be screened and time expended for training must be efficiently utilized. Goals are specific and directly related to job competency.

As the technological revolution gains momentum, the demand for technical literacy programs is also likely to increase. The available jobs require ability to *learn* the technical language and competencies of new fields. A secretary who simply types is in less demand than a word processor operator who can operate new equipment, edit, and handle material coming from several different technical departments. Assembly line workers are being phased out, but openings exist for electronics technicians and data processing specialists. Even existing jobs that previously called for little training and few literacy abilities are being changed by the new technology.

This chapter briefly examines what is known about occupational literacy, then highlights two existing programs that teach occupational literacy—a CETA program to train word processing equipment operators and a retraining program for wastewater treatment plant operators.

LITERACY IN THE WORKPLACE

Literacy at work is a ubiquitous, time-consuming activity. In a survey of a hundred workers reflecting a cross-section of occupations, Diehl and Mikulecky (1980) found that nearly 99% of workers participated in some form of reading each day. This was usually in blocks of under 5 minutes per episode, but averaged nearly 2 hours daily. In a later study, Mikulecky compared high school reading to work reading and found students to be reading less for school than most workers do for work. Students spend about the same time reading daily as blue-collar workers (98 min vs 97 min). In addition, workers read considerably more often for application or to make judgments than do students who mainly read to gather facts (Mikulecky, 1982). Several studies have found that difficulty levels of job-related materials average 11th-grade level, ranging from 9th grade to college level (Diehl & Mikulecky, 1980; Mikulecky, 1982; Moe, Rush, & Storlie, 1980).

In order to complete job tasks, workers frequently move from one print format to another, so that mastery of a variety of formats is called for. Types of materials workers read include directions, diagrams, manuals, forms, flyers, computer print-outs, and textbooks. Since 95% of high school reading is from textbooks (Mikulecky, 1982), there is little in the school experience to prepare new workers for the range of literacy strategies called for in the workplace.

Successful workers make use of a variety of extra-linguistic strategies to handle the literacy demands they face. By moving back and forth between print and a piece of equipment, workers make comparisons and relate words to the real world (Diehl & Mikulecky, 1980). In addition, workers use other workers to help them solve problems. Brice-Heath (1980) found that adults cooperate in examining print, sharing relevant experience, and making suggestions about solutions. Mikulecky (1982) found that workers talk to each other and ask questions about twice as often as high school students. These strategies may, in part, explain why workers perform one to two grade levels higher on work material than on general newspaper reading.

The workplace calls for a wider range of literacy strategies than do typical tasks. Middle-level workers and professionals divide their reading time between reading for application, reading to assess, and reading to learn new information. Most school reading is to learn factual information. Workers employ problem-solving strategies, relate what they read to known information, and focus their attention with personal note-taking systems. Students mainly re-read to retain information, rarely relate information to known ideas, and even more rarely read to solve problems or accomplish tasks.

The literacy competency of employees, on the average, is quite high. Blue-collar workers average between 10th- and 11th-grade level in ability, though the range is wide. Professional and middle-level workers average somewhat higher with more readers on the upper end of the ability range. Mikulecky (1982) found 5% of workers experiencing extreme difficulty with a 9th-grade newspaper-like passage, whereas 16% of high school juniors experienced difficulty with the same passage. Research in the military (Sacher & Duffy, 1978) indicates that workers' overall job performance suffers if they read more than two grade levels below job demands. It appears that many individuals with low literacy abilities are not being allowed to enter or remain in the work force.

Transfer of Training

In the past, much schooling and many literacy training programs were built on the assumption that general training would generalize to the specific literacy tasks encountered on the job. Educators have assumed that reading consists of one vast, generalizable literacy ability. This assumption was based on research that showed various literacy abilities or subskills to be highly intercorrelated.

Research of the last few years suggests that this assumption is not fully warranted. Carroll (1981) pointed out that these correlations among subskills could reflect attendance patterns, with good students attending school more regularly and mastering many subskills and poor students being absent a great deal and failing to master all the necessary subskills. The assumption of transfer from one subskill to another or from one type of reading to another is not necessarily supported by the correlational data.

There is growing evidence to suggest that whatever transfer exists may be minimal in nature. Among the Vai people in Liberia (Scribner & Cole, 1978a), literacy acquisition is often separate from schooling. Schooling trains one to function in society, but training in reading and writing comes later if at all. Literacy learning is individual and often on the job as it is needed. School attendance patterns do not cloud the degree of correlation between one skill and another. Scribner and Cole conclude that "the effects of literacy and perhaps of schooling as well are restricted . . . generalized only to closely related practices" (1978a, p. 457).

Sticht (1980) has also observed low transferability of general reading skills to specific literacy tasks in the military. He states: "Job reading gains were much larger than general reading. This is important because it indicates that people are learning what they are being taught. Clearly the present results show that reading is not altogether a generic skill assessable by any test of general reading'' (p. 303).

The military has paid heed to its research findings. The army has discontinued general literacy training, focusing instead on specific job literacy demands of over 120 major military jobs (Begland, 1981). This program does not assume that general training will transfer to particular job demands.

Legal Aspects of Using Literacy for Screening

Several industries and institutions, concerned about workers' literacy abilities, have considered using literacy ability as a consideration for employment decisions. This is a complicated issue on which courts have ruled repeatedly. The end product of several different decisions is that job literacy screening must be validated as job related (e g., Griggs v. Duke Power Company). In Davis v. Ameripol, Inc., the court found that special reading and writing tests were justified in selecting oilers and forklift drivers since oilers were required to read labels on oil drums and forklift operators had to read warning signs. Other cases such as EEOC Decision 72-0691 have ruled that general standarized reading ability tests may not be acceptable since they may discriminate against minorities and are not directly job related (Mikulecky & Diehl, 1979).

CASE STUDY I: WORD PROCESSOR OPERATORS

A current employment problem is the inability to find properly trained employees, even though thousands of unemployed workers are available. In Chicago in 1981–1982, the local Private Industry Council faced such a problem with word processor operators for major industries and businesses. Positions paying over $20,000 per year were going unfilled.

Being a word processor operator involves a good deal more than being a traditional secretary who knows how to operate the new machinery. The operator must be able to edit for spelling, verb/subject agreement, and a number of other flaws. The operator must also be able to produce copy rapidly with few mistakes and to correct errors quickly.

A Cooperative Program

Technical Assistance Training Corporation (TATC), a private consulting firm in the Chicago area, has had extensive experience working nationally with CETA training programs. TATC saw in Chicago the opportunity to bring together business and governmental efforts.

A survey of businesses involved with the Chicago area Private Industry Council revealed the need for trained word processor operators. Administrators of the CETA program were interested in training CETA eligible individuals for such jobs, but did not have a history of cooperative efforts with business. A survey of existing high school and vocational school training programs revealed that training courses were not coordinated to produce effective word processor operators and used out-of-date word processing equipment.

In addition, business personnel and CETA program officials were suspicious of each other. Business was reluctant to be trapped into accepting CETA trained workers who might be undertrained. Businessmen also had concerns about unnecessary red tape. Government agencies believed that the problems in getting business support made cooperative programs difficult or impossible to implement. Also, government officials were reluctant to invest CETA funds in programs that differed from existing schooling, especially programs designed by private consulting firms.

To overcome mutual suspicions, TATC saw its role to be a facilitator between government and business. The initial problem was to get business and local governmental agencies to communicate and cooperate. TATC chose developing solid business support as its first objective. Private Industry Council members were visited, word processor operators were observed, standards of proficiency were established, and industry trainers were asked to help establish training guidelines. TATC spent several months enlisting support and planning training goals and procedures. Business personnel were assured that training would not be "like school." Business was involved in planning at each step along the way.

A proposal was finally submitted to CETA after over a year of planning. It involved businesses contributing furniture and equipment, as well as the promise of hiring trainees who met industry criteria *if positions were available*. CETA was to pay trainees and TATC training personnel.

Once facilities were ready, potential employers were brought to TATC offices to see that the training area looked like a business, not a school. Business equipment was clearly visible; training materials included forms and print material from cooperating businesses. Careful task analyses of on-the-job word processing were used to develop a curriculum based on realistic goals and expectations. Every attempt was made to assure employers that high standards would be met. The fact that a private business was doing the training seemed to help convince employers that trainers were sensitive to their needs.

The time and effort expended in gaining business support was invaluable in convincing CETA officials to support the program. At several points during the 6-month process of gaining governmental approval, business support made the difference between continued progress and having the proposed program stall in bureaucratic red tape.

Recruiting and Screening Applicants for Training

Announcements describing the TATC word processing program and its goals were distributed to social agencies in contact with CETA eligible candidates. These agencies disseminated information about the program and steered interested applicants to an assessment center for interviews. During interviews, applicants received information about the program and job characteristics. Applicants' educational, personal, and work backgrounds were explored. Applicants and counselors then jointly decided whether applicants should attend a special Exploration Day at the word processing center.

Exploration Day.   During Exploration Day, groups of 15 received information on word processing careers and information about the training program. Applicants had the opportunity to try out equipment and get some "hands-on" experience with what work might be like. If an applicant was still interested in the program, he or she was asked to take a battery of tests to assess reading comprehension with business-related material.

Job Literacy Screening.   The literacy level required to do well as a word processor operator is quite high. A sustantial proportion of business correspondence read and sometimes edited by word processor operators is above the 10th-grade level in reading difficulty. Therefore, success in the training program depended, in part, on trainees being able to attain those literacy abilities in a relatively short period of time (14 to 20 weeks). To select trainees most likely to succeed from among the thousands of potential applicants, a series of literacy screening exercises was developed from actual job materials. Employed secretaries and word processor operators took the screening exercises so performance levels could be set.

The first-level screening exercise was a cloze test constructed from business correspondence and word processing manuals used on the job. Trainees who scored more than two reading grade levels below the average practicing operator were likely to be screened out of the program.

A second level of screening involved spotting and correcting errors on actual job correspondence, invoice forms, and business reports. Norms were set on these problem-solving tasks by establishing how well the average secretary or word processor operator performed. Potential trainees were given two chances with each type of problem. First, they would attempt to identify and correct errors on a piece of print material. When they had done their best, the tester would point out what they had missed and show them how to make additional corrections. Following this, an extremely similar task would be given to determine if the potential trainee learned quickly. Acceptance into the training program was based on performance slightly below that of employed secretaries *or* on the ability to learn quickly.

Population Selected For the Word Processing Program

All trainees selected for the program were CETA eligible (i.e., economically disadvantaged, unemployed or underemployed, and identified as having particular difficulties in entering or advancing in private sector employment). One hundred trainees were selected to enter the program in three waves of 30 students. Approximately 30% of the trainees were male, 70% female; 80% were between the ages of 22 and 44. The racial distribution was 79% black, 15% Hispanic, 5% Caucasian, and 1% Asian. Although about half of the applicants had some secretarial or clerical experience, a few trainees had no work or clerical experience at all.

The screening procedures had selected individuals who were CETA eligible, but who were also likely to succeed. Applicants scoring significantly below the job literacy performance level of actual workers were not accepted because it seemed unlikely they would gain more than two or three grade levels in job literacy abilities during the half-year program. Experience with the first wave suggested that literacy levels needed to be even more stringent for applicants without some clerical experience. Such applicants needed more time mastering typing and machinery. The extra time usually came from language training.

The Training Program

Classes of 30 to 35 trainees were accepted into the program. These individuals were paid to attend training 40 hours per week. Each day was divided amongst language training, typing and word processing training, work habits training, and individual study time. Three full-time teachers (a reading specialist, a word processing specialist, and a business specialist) worked with students.

The amount of time a trainee spent in any given area depended on his or her needs. Some trainees needed more emphasis on language improvement and others on machine skills. On the average, 20% of time was spent attending classroom presentations and 80% working independently or in student work groups to master information presented in classes (unlike traditional schools where figures are reversed).

Assignments were planned to integrate language and machine skills. Much of the classwork simulated actual job demands. Students would compose business communications which other students would edit and produce in final form on word processing equipment. The work involved using actual business communications which were hand written in rough draft form with editing notations. The job simulation training, which integrated language and machine experience, ranged from about 5% of assignments the first week to nearly 100% in the final weeks. Class assignments replicated the time constraints in business performance. Though much of the work was done on an individual level, some work made use of worker teams, again replicating workplace conditions.

Major instructor classroom efforts to improve student reading ability involved introducing classes to major concepts and vocabulary before reading and occasional modeling of methods to determine meanings from context and the dictionary. Instructors provided more individual attention and modeling when students encountered difficulties with material. The emphasis in reading instruction, editing instruction, and grammatical awareness was on producing flawless copy.

Trainee time on task ranged from 80% to 90% during any given work day, compared to public school figures of 30% to 50%. Instructors met on a weekly basis to determine how each student's time might be most wisely allocated. Individual conferences informed students of their progress. Feedback was also provided by wall charts that showed the average class performance on a wide selection of language and machine competencies. Individual trainee performance listed by number provided individual feedback relative to other students and employed word processor operators.

The most clear-cut differences between this program and school programs had to do with application and integration of training. TATC trainees actually used up-to-date word processing equipment and were aware of industry standards. Their training in language, work habits, and machine use was integrated so they received focused practice to meet those standards. This contrasted with programs in public schools and community colleges, which offer fragmented classes with little integration and feedback. In addition, most in-school training programs assume transfer of general competencies to actual job application. The cooperative program assumed no such transfer and consistently used job simulation as a major training device.

Program Results

The time needed for trainees to reach job level competence varied. The earliest trainees were able to find employment after 14 weeks of training. The average time needed for the screened applicants to reach the pre-set standards was 20 weeks, with a few trainees taking nearly 28 weeks. During the approximately 20 weeks of training time, trainees improved in ability to read business material by an average of a full grade level. Reading ability was measured using cloze tests developed from actual business correspondence and reading material (Bormuth, 1975). Many trainees improved considerably more than one grade level. Even more spectacular gains were made in proofreading and editing skills.

In 1981–1982 the economy entered a recession, which limited the ability of cooperating industries to hire acceptably trained word processors. A third of the cooperating companies stopped all hiring. Several additional companies raised their hiring standards for accurate word processing speed from 55 words per minute to 65 or 70 words per minute. In the face of these economic difficulties, slightly over one third of trainees found word processing employment within a few weeks of program completion. Other trainees used the training facilities as a base for a "job search club." Within 3 months of program completion, 70% of trainees had found employment. Several other trainees were encouraged with the offer of jobs "as soon as the economy improved."

In summary, the word processing program is an excellent example of how trainers can integrate language training with on-the-job training while employing insights from current research. The authors attribute program success to the following factors:

- Careful screening of program applicants.
- Integration of training to simulate job conditions.
- Extremely high trainee time-on-task.
- Daily individual attention and criterion-related feedback.
- High trainee motivation to succeed.

CASE STUDY II: UPGRADING TRAINING FOR WASTEWATER TREATMENT WORKERS

A second cooperative venture involves the retraining of workers for the new literacy and technical demands of a job that is changing. An urban municipality had recently opened a new wastewater treatment plant and incorporated several technological innovations. Workers who needed little technical training to work in the old treatment plant faced an entirely different situation in the new plant. Newer, more effective treatment units called for the use of sophisticated instrumentation, working around potentially dangerous gases, and operating and maintaining complex mechanical equipment.

Before workers could be transferred from the old to the new plant they had to be retrained. This retraining involved (1) learning how the new process and equipment functioned, (2) learning safety precautions when working with a variety of dangerous gases, and (3) learning how to operate and maintain essential equipment. Mistakes made through ignorance could be costly in terms of personal injury, plant shut-downs, and equipment repair or replacement. The unstated implication of the training program was that workers unable to be adequately retrained could not be transferred. Unemployment or job demotion seemed the only alternatives.

The Retraining Program

The municipality initially contracted with an engineering firm to provide technical retraining for workers. The firm was experienced in retraining engineers and gathering the best technical expertise available to upgrade the training of technicians. They developed a technical curriculum and arranged for workers to attend full-day classes at a centrally located facility. They were working under the pressures of accomplishing retraining goals with a minimum loss of worker time on the job. The learning format was 2 full weeks of classes followed by 2 weeks of on-the-job training. This procedure alternated until the employee had attended each of the 10 two-week training modules. The class modules resembled high-powered science courses stressing how the new plant worked, how micro-organisms were used and could be injured, and how to maintain safety in the newer and potentially more dangerous plant.

It soon became apparent that the usual technical retraining procedures would not be sufficient for a large percentage of the workers. Many read below an 8th-grade level and several read below a 3rd-grade level. Classroom training materials ranged in difficulty from 11th grade to college level and included many graphs, charts, and schematics. Actual on-the-job explanatory material was nearly as difficult. In addition, many of the workers had little or no familiarity with concepts covered in the brief, high-powered technical classes.

The engineering consulting firm attempted to establish a cooperative relationship with area technical schools, but school personnel were unwilling to set up special classes for wastewater treatment trainees or to assign technical school instructors to the training facility. Eventually the engineering consulting firm set up a cooperative relationship with a university reading consultant and hired a trained reading specialist to develop a job-literacy component. They also introduced microcomputers to provide more individual practice and feedback.

Technical classes were scheduled for mornings. Reinforcing quizzes and exercises on microcomputers were scheduled for afternoons. Workers identified as having difficulties with literacy spent three afternoons a week with a reading specialist, concentrating on job literacy demands.

The efforts of the reading specialist were divided among working directly with trainees, working with instructors of technical classes, and redesigning training materials and tests to lower reading difficulty levels. Literacy and language training were not integrated into technical training in initial planning. In the classes of some technical instructors, such integration did tend to evolve, however.

Working with Students.   A typical training day involved 4 hours of technical training classes in the morning—2 hours of lecture or films, an hour of questions and class discussion, and an hour of in-class reading and study tasks. After lunch, trainees would spend 2 or more hours working with specially designed microcomputer learning programs or with worksheets and film-loops. Workers assigned to the reading specialist would spend an additional hour and a half receiving individualized help.

Developing rapport and trust was of primary importance when working with trainees directed to the reading specialist. She estimated that nearly 80% of referred trainees were extremely worried about appearing ignorant or retarded. Most had experienced difficulty in public school and over a quarter had negative experiences in Adult Basic Education classes. Initial attempts to diagnose reading difficulties in an efficient, clinic-like manner resulted in trainees refusing to return. Diagnostic information was more accessible through careful observation of performance during learning sessions.

The major academic goal was to help trainees master technical vocabulary, concepts, and materials. The reading specialist set up special study guides to break down reading assignments into manageable tasks. Special help was given in interpreting graphs and schematic diagrams. About half of each 90-minute session was allocated to oral feedback and questioning of trainees on what they had read from manuals or work material. The remainder was spent in focused reading for which the specialist had provided a clearly understood reading purpose.

In some cases, the reading specialist was able to rewrite training materials to lower readability levels. Students were asked to read these at home. In addition, students were asked to read regularly material at a difficulty level they could handle independently. The reading specialist helped in the selection of this material, taught trainees how to self-select appropriately difficult material, and asked trainees to discuss orally and summarize what they had read. Some used simple newspaper articles, some read books to their children, one read from the Bible, but many did little or no outside reading at all.

Working with Instructors.   The reading specialist had mixed success in working with the technical training instructors. Some had never worked with a nonengineering population and could see no justification for simplifying their approaches. Most agreed to let the reading specialist rewrite materials to a lower level, if she checked with them to see that accuracy had been maintained. As training progressed, about one third of the instructors began to use study guides with their entire classes and began the preteaching of technical vocabulary. Attempts to get instructors to design summaries of key ideas or advance organizers met with complete failure. Many instructors saw themselves as technical experts and resented having to deal with students who could not follow traditional methods of lecture teaching. Two instructors who were exceptions to this pattern rewrote tests and handouts to lower difficulty levels. The average mastery level of their students improved significantly over those of other instructors.

Working with Materials.   The reading specialist developed study guides and rewrote a good deal of classroom material to the 8th-grade level. She also designed simplified graphs and schematics to teach students to interpret these materials. Questions used in microcomputer programs were also rewritten.

Nearly all material developed by technical instructors was of 11th-grade difficulty or higher. In many cases, rewriting lowered the difficulty level by 40% without noticeably losing content. Reducing the difficulty levels of materials below the 6th-grade level was counterproductive. Students at that level did not understand the essential concepts unaided.

Trainee Time on Task.   Trainee time on task during a typical day ranged from 30% to 50% (comparable to an average high school). During lectures some trainees would be engaged while others would not. A good deal of socializing and trips outside for a cigarette or drink of water occurred during practice time on the microcomputer or during classroom application sessions. Time on task for students referred to the reading specialist was somewhat higher since they were in structured learning situations during their sessions.

Selecting the Population for Literacy Training

All workers had been administered the TABE reading test. Workers scoring below an 8th-grade level were referred to the reading specialist for further diagnosis. The diagnosis was based on an extensive interview about previous educational and literacy experiences and two other procedures: a cloze test constructed from job and training materials, and informal assessments of ability to read various job and training material. The reading specialist avoided conventional testing and limited herself to asking the trainee what he found difficult or how he went about reading various types of material. Comprehension was checked by asking the trainee to restate the message. Additional diagnostic data were gathered from responses to a pretest of technical knowledge and vocabulary. A majority of identified workers were asked to volunteer for special literacy training three afternoons a week.

During the first few days of classes, technical instructors identified students experiencing extreme learning difficulties. These students were also referred to the reading specialist for further diagnosis and treatment. The amount of special literacy training varied depending on need and the demands of the particular technical class they were attending. Twenty percent of the workers received some form of special literacy help.

Implementation of Research

The wastewater treatment retraining program was able to implement some research findings. Workers were trained using as much actual job material as possible. This included graphs, charts, manuals, and color-coded safety information. Trainees who worked with the reading specialist were able to receive specific instruction on the various strategies needed to use information successfully in each of these formats.

Alternating classroom training with on-the-job training can be seen as an attempt at building application and problem solving into the training. This attempt has been crucial, since the majority of classroom technical training was of the traditional lecture/listen variety. This traditional approach is clearly revealed in the low trainee time on task and heavy reliance on teacher activity. Afternoon work on microcomputers increased the potential for trainee activity, but trainees' time on task varied greatly since time was not structured and feedback was minimal.

Time spent by some trainees with the reading specialist was well spent. The specialists created application situations for trainees to solve as she set purposes for reading. Time on task for trainees increased while they were with the specialist and to a certain extent at home if they chose to follow outside reading suggestions.

Program Results

The literacy component of the retraining program can be judged a success by several standards. Nearly half the students who took special job literacy training passed technical class posttests. It was the consensus of both technical instructors and the reading specialist that fewer than 5% of these students would have passed without the special attention. Of the students who attended, 70% were able to summarize materials by the end of training. Retention of students receiving special literacy training was actually higher than that of students who only attended technical classes. Gains in general reading ability were less encouraging. Only about 10% of the students taking special literacy training made noticeable gains in their ability to read general or new material for which they had received no direction or teacher-provided purpose. According to the reading specialist, students making the most significant gains in job and general reading ability invested 5 or more hours per week in outside reading practice.

There were also some successes in efforts to modify classroom teaching and materials. The reading specialist estimated a 30% to 40% change in the way reading assignments were handled in technical classes. A third of the technical instructors regularly employed content area reading techniques and a few others would occasionally provide study guides or purpose-setting questions. Nearly every instructor made some use of the material the reading specialist had rewritten. Most instructors introduced key vocabulary before assigning readings. One third of the technical instructors went on to simplify their own hand-outs and one instructor rewrote test items with considerable success.

Areas of greatest program weakness are similar to weaknesses in traditional schooling. Since literacy training was not integrated with technical training from the beginning, the effectiveness of such training was severely limited. The reading specialist could provide some remedial attention to referred trainees, but follow-up reinforcement depended on the reading specialist's success in convincing technical instructors to modify teaching techniques. Instruction was often fragmented. Classroom instructors could voluntarily meet with the reading specialist and the microcomputer lab director, but most did not. Student feedback was usually limited to tests and short-term feedback provided by computers. Nobody took responsibility for regularly informing trainees of gains and weak areas or for adjusting their learning schedules.

An outgrowth of this style of teaching is very low student time on task—much like typically public school training. Since trainees were passive for a large percentage of their training time, time on task depended on self-discipline and interest. These same factors were at play during unstructured individual learning time with computers and video-learning packages. Some trainees attended to learning a good deal of the time and others did not.

OBSERVATIONS AND CONCLUSIONS

The two progrmas discussed in this chapter were both successful to some degree. An examination of program similarities and differences serves to highlight reasons for both success and difficulty.

Program Similarities

Both programs were successful with literacy training of their target populations. In terms of actual percentages of successful trainees, the word processing program was somewhat more successful. Both programs addressed the specific job literacy demands of the target occupations and improved the ability of trainees to handle those demands. Little transfer to general reading ability was apparent in either program, with the exception of wastewater treatment workers who did a good deal of general reading at home under instructor guidance. The instructor to trainee ratio in each program was high compared to public schools. The ratio for the word processing program was 1 to 10. The wastewater treatment program had a higher program ratio of 1 to 20, but referred trainees received several hours of one-to-one attention from the reading specialist.

Program Differences

Several differences between programs were apparent. Language training was integrated with technical training from the beginning of the word processing program. Such language training was added on after the wastewater treatment program had begun. Integration of language and technical instruction was beginning to emerge in the wastewater treatment program, but still was fragmented. Other program differences in structure also were apparent. The engineering-based program was much like a typical high school: Student time on task was low; learning experiences were fragmented; and there was little coordination among instructors. The word processing program built in instructor cooperation. As a result, everyone was responsible for aiding all trainees. This contrasted to the reading specialist being mainly responsible for literacy concerns in the wastewater treatment program. Outgrowths of this difference were clearly noted in differences in feedback to trainees and flexibility in individual programs. Lest the criticism of the wastewater treatment program appear too harsh, it should be noted that the individual feedback provided by the microcomputers and reading specialist was superior to anything most trainees had previously experienced.

Though both programs trained for application, each used a different route. One program built job simulations into assignments and encouraged work teams. The other alternated classroom training with on-the-job training. Though both were effective, the daily integration appeared somewhat more effective. It seemed to produce the welcome by-product of more trainee time engaged in "doing" the job and less time daydreaming and socializing.

A final set of differences resides in the trainee populations themselves. The word processing population was carefully screened with potential success in mind. Though some trainees had literacy difficulties, these were not extreme. The wastewater treatment program, on the other hand, dealt with all employees who volunteered for retraining. The word processing group was motivated positively by the opportunity to get a high-paying job. The wastewater treatment group was motivated negatively by the prospect of losing a job.

Conclusions

There are several conclusions suggested by these two case studies. It does appear possible to make fairly rapid gains in the ability to comprehend technical material if training is focused on that material. General literacy improvement is not a noticeable by-product, but can occur with sufficient time on task (here 5 hours per week) with an appropriate variety of general materials. Best results seemed to occur when literacy training was integrated with technical training. Job simulations and applications of literacy increased trainee time on task. Actively involved students received up to three times more practice per paid day than traditionally trained students. The integrated program, therefore, is more cost-effective.

Both programs were successful with a large percentage of trainees. It is difficult to compare systematically the cost-effectiveness of the two programs. The word processing program spent less time training workers (20 weeks vs.

40 weeks). It was able to screen trainees, however. Wastewater treatment workers received on-the-job training for half their 40 weeks, during which they did some productive work, adding to overall cost-effectiveness. Instructor salaries differed greatly, with engineers being paid more highly than the others. The teacher-student ratio for word processors was higher, however, so cost per trainee may have averaged out.

Probably the most significant conclusion to be drawn is that successful technical literacy training programs are beginning to emerge, filling the vacuum left by traditional schooling. Where schools are unwilling or unable to match literacy training to specific occupational needs, private consulting firms are successfully filling the gap. They are successful to the degree that they do not assume transfer from general literacy training to specific job literacy training. Matching training to the application required on the job appears to be the key.

References

Abelson, H., & diSessa, A. A. (1981). *Turtle geometry: The computer as a medium for exploring mathematics.* Cambridge, MA: MIT Press.

Ackerman, B. P. (1982). Children's recall of contextually integrable and nonintegrable episodic events. *Journal of Experimental Child Psychology, 33,* 429–438.

Adams, M. J. (1980a). Failures to comprehend and levels of processing in reading. In R. J. Spiro, B. C. Bruce, & W. F. Brewer (Eds.), *Theoretical issues in reading comprehension.* Hillsdale, NJ: Lawrence Erlbaum Associates.

Adams, M. J. (1980b). What good is orthographic redundancy? In O. J. L. Tzeng & H. Singer (Eds.), *Perception of print: Reading research in experimental psychology.* Hillsdale, NJ: Lawrence Erlbaum Associates.

Adams, M. J., & Collins, A. (1979). A schema-theoretic view of reading. In R. Freedle (Ed.), *Discourse processing: A multidisciplinary perspective.* Norwood, NJ: Ablex.

Ainsworth, N. (1981). *Oral narratives of bilingual Mexican-American adults enrolled in adult basic education* (Research Project, NIE). East Lansing: Michigan State University, Department of English.

Alder, J. (1971). *Individualized language arts.* Unpublished manuscript. (Available from Woodrow Wilson School, Hauxhurst Avenue, Weehauken, NJ).

Alessi, S. M., Anderson, T. H., & Goetz, E. T. (1979). An investigation of lookbacks during studying. *Discourse Processes, 2,* 197–212.

Allington, R. L. (1980). Poor readers don't get to read much. *Language Arts, 57,* 872–876.

Anderson, I. H. (1937). Eye movements of good and poor readers. *Psychological Monographs, 48,* 1–35.

Anderson, L. (1984). The environment of instruction: Classrooms using standard curricula. In G. Duffy, L. Roehler, & J. Mason (Eds.), *Comprehension instruction.* New York: Longman.

Anderson, R. C. (1977, July). *Schema-directed processes in language comprehension* (Tech. Rep. No. 50). Urbana: University of Illinois, Center for the Study of Reading.

Anderson, R. C. (1982). Allocation of attention during reading. In A. Flammer & W. Kintsch (Eds.), *Discourse processing.* Amsterdam: North Holland.

Anderson, R. C. (1983). Role of the reader's schema during comprehension, learning, and memory. In R. C. Anderson, J. Osborn, & R. Tierney (Eds.), *Learning to read in American schools.* Hillsdale, NJ: Lawrence Erlbaum Associates.

Anderson, R. C., & Biddle, W. B. (1975). On asking people questions about what they are reading. In G. H. Bower (Ed.), *The psychology of learning and motivation, (Vol. 9).* New York: Academic Press.

Anderson, R. C., & Freebody, P. (1981). Vocabulary knowledge. In J. T. Guthrie (Ed.), *Comprehension and teaching: Research review.* Newark, DE: International Reading Association.

Anderson, R. C., & Freebody, P. (1982). *Reading comprehension and the assessment and acquisition of word knowledge* (Tech. Rep. No. 249). Urbana: University of Illinois, Center for the study of Reading.

Anderson, R. C., Mason, J. M., & Shirey, L. L. (1983, February). *The reading group: An experimental investigation of a labyrinth* (Tech. Rep. No. 271). Urbana: University of Illinois, Center for the Study of Reading.

Anderson, R. C., & Pichert, J. W. (1978). Recall of previously unrecallable information following a shift in perspective. *Journal of Verbal Learning and Verbal Behavior, 17*, 1–12.

Anderson, R. C., Pichert, J., & Shirey, L. L. (1983). Role of the reader's schema at different points in time. *Journal of Educational Psychology, 75*, 271–279.

Anderson, R. C., Reynolds, R. E., Schallert, D. L., & Goetz, E. T. (1977). Frameworks for comprehending discourse. *American Educational Research Journal, 14*, 367–381.

Anderson, R. C., & Shifrin, Z. (1980). The meaning of words in context. In R. J. Spiro, B. C. Bruce, & W. F. Brewer (Eds.), *Theoretical issues in reading comprehension*. Hillsdale, NJ: Lawrence Erlbaum Associates.

Anderson, R. C., Spiro, R. J., & Anderson, M. C. (1978). Schemata as scaffolding for the representation of information in connected discourse. *American Educational Research Journal, 15*, 433–440.

Anderson, R. C., Spiro, R. J., & Montague, W. E. (1977). *Schooling and the acquisition of knowledge*. Hillsdale, NJ: Lawrence Erlbaum Associates.

Anderson, R. C., Stevens, K. C., Shifrin, Z., & Osborn, J. (1978). Instantiation of word meanings in children. *Journal of Reading Behavior, 10*, 145–157.

Anderson, T. H. (1978). *Study skills and learning strategies* (Tech. Rep. No. 104). Urbana: University of Illinois, Center for the Study of Reading. (ERIC Document Reproduction Service No. ED 161 000).

Anderson, T. H. (1980). Study strategies and adjunct aids. In R. J. Spiro, B. C. Bruce, & W. F. Brewer (Eds.), *Theoretical issues in reading comprehension*. Hillsdale, NJ: Lawrence Erlbaum Associates.

Anderson, T. H., & Armbruster, B. B. (1978–1979). Studying. *Reading Research Quarterly, 14*, 605–623.

Anderson, T. H., & Armbruster, B. B. (1982). Reader and text studying strategies. In W. Otto & S. White (Eds.), *Reading expository material*. New York: Academic Press.

Anderson, T. H., & Armbruster, B. B. (1984a). Content area textbooks. In R. C. Anderson, J. Osborn, & R. J. Tierney (Eds.), *Learning to Read in American Schools*. Hillsdale, NJ: Lawrence Erlbaum Associates.

Anderson, T. H., & Armbruster, B. B. (1984b). Studying. In P. D. Pearson (Ed.), *Handbook of reading research*. New York: Longman.

Anderson, T. H., Armbruster, B. B., & Kantor, R. N. (1980, August). *How clearly written are children's textbooks? Or, Of bladderworts and alfa* (Reading Education Rep. No. 16). Urbana: University of Illinois, Center for the Study of Reading. (ERIC Document Reproduction Service No. ED 192 275).

Anderson, T. H., Wardrop, J. L., Hively, W., Muller, K. D., Anderson, R. I., Hastings, C. N., & Frederiksen, J. (1978). *Development and trial of a model for developing domain referenced tests of reading comprehension* (Tech. Rep. No. 85). Urbana: University of Illinois, Center for the Study of Reading.

Andre, M. E. D. A., & Anderson, T. H. (1978–1979). The development and evaluation of a self-questioning study technique. *Reading Research Quarterly, 14*, 605–623.

Anglin, J. M. (1977). *Word, object, and conceptual development*. New York: Norton.

Applebee, A. (1981). *Writing in the secondary school*. Urbana, IL: National Council of Teachers of English.

Applebee, A. (1978). *The child's concept of story*. Chicago: University of Chicago Press.

Armbruster, B. B., & Anderson, T. H. (1980). *The effect of mapping on the free recall of expository text* (Tech. Rep. No. 160). Urbana: University of Illinois, Center for the Study of Reading.

Armbruster, B. B., & Anderson, T. H. (1981a). *Content-area textbooks* (Reading Education Rep. No. 23). Urbana: University of Illinois, Center for the Study of Reading.

Armbruster, B. B., & Anderson, T. H. (1981b). Research synthesis on study skills. *Educational Leadership, 39,* 154–156.

Armbruster, B. B., & Anderson, T. H. (1982a). *Structures for explanations in history textbooks, or So what if Governor Stanford missed the spike and hit the rail?* (Tech. Rep. No. 252). Urbana: University of Illinois, Center for the Study of Reading.

Armbruster, B. B., & Anderson, T. H. (1982b). *Idea-mapping: The technique and its use in the classroom, or simulating the "ups" and "downs" of reading comprehension* (Reading Education Rep. No. 36). Urbana: University of Illinois, Center for the Study of Reading.

Armbruster, B. B., Echols, C. H., & Brown, A. L. (1982). The role of metacognition in reading to learn: A developmental perspective. *Volta Review, 84* (5), 45–56.

Arnold, H. F. (1942). The comparative effectiveness of certain study techniques in the field of history. *Journal of Educational Psychology, 33,* 449–457.

Aronoff, M. (1976). *Word formation in generative grammar.* Cambridge, MA: MIT Press.

Artley, A. (1980). Psycholinguistics applied to reading instruction. *Reading Horizons, 20*(2), 106–111.

Au, K. H. (1979). Using the experience-text-relationship method with minority children. *Reading Teacher, 32,* 677–679.

Au, K. H. (1981). *The essential features list of the KEEP reading program* (Language Arts Series No. 3). Honolulu: Kamehameha Early Education Program.

Au, K. H., & Jordan, C. (1981). Teaching reading to Hawaiian children: Finding a culturally appropriate solution. In H. T. Trueba, G. P. Guthrie, & K. H. Au (Eds.), *Culture in the bilingual classroom: Studies in classroom ethnography.* Rowley, MA: Newbury House.

Au, K. H. & Mason, J. M. (1981). Social organization factors in learning to read: The balance of rights hypothesis. *Reading Research Quarterly, 17,* 115–152.

Austin, J. L. (1962). *How to do things with words.* Cambridge, MA: Harvard University Press.

Ausubel, D. P. (1963). *The psychology of meaningful verbal learning.* New York: Grune & Stratton.

Ausubel, D. P. (1968). *Educational psychology: A cognitive view.* New York: Holt, Rinehart & Winston.

Bailey, P. (1979). The adolescent writer's developing sense of audience: Implications for teaching (Doctoral dissertation. Purdue University, 1979). *Dissertation Abstracts International, 40,* 3274A–3277A. (University Microfilms No. 7926348).

Baker, L. (1979). Comprehension monitoring: Identifying and coping with text confusions. *Journal of Reading Behavior, 11,* 363–374.

Baker, L. (1979, July). *Do I understand or do I not understand: That is the question* (Reading Education Rep. No. 10). Urbana: University of Illinois, Center for the Study of Reading.

Baker, L. (1983). *Children's effective use of multiple standards for evaluating their comprehension.* Unpublished manuscript, University of Maryland, Baltimore County.

Baker, L. (in press). How do we know when we don't understand? Standards for evaluating text comprehension. In D. L. Forrest, G. E. Mackinnon, & T. G. Waller (Eds.), *Metacognition, cognition and human performance.* New York: Academic Press.

Baker, L., & Anderson, R. I. (1982). Effects of inconsistent information on text processing: Evidence for comprehension monitoring. *Reading Research Quarterly, 17,* 281–294.

Baker, L., & Brown, A. L. (1984a). Metacognitive skills and reading. In P. D. Pearson (Ed.), *Handbook of reading research.* New York: Longman.

Baker, L., & Brown, A. L. (1984b). Cognitive monitoring in reading. In J. Flood (Ed.), *Understanding reading comprehension.* Newark, DE: International Reading Association.

Banks, W. P., Oka, E., & Sugarman, C. (1981). Recoding of printed words to internal speech:

Does reading come before lexical access? In O. J. L. Teng & H. Singer (Eds.), *Perception of print: Reading research in experimental psychology.* Hillsdale, NJ: Lawrence Erlbaum Associates.

Baratz, J., & Stewart, W. (1969). *Ollie and friends (Experimental readers).* Washington, DC: Education Study Center.

Barnitz, J. (1980). Syntactic effects on the reading comprehension of pronoun-referent structures by children in grades two, four, and six. *Reading Research Quarterly, 15,* 268–289.

Baron, J. (1977). Mechanisms for pronouncing printed words: Use and acquisition. In D. LaBerge & S. J. Samuels (Eds.), *Basic processes in reading: Perception and comprehension.* Hillsdale, NJ: Lawrence Erlbaum Associates.

Baron, J., & Thurston, I. (1973). An analysis of the word superiority effect. *Cognitive Psychology, 4,* 207–228.

Bartlett, B. J. (1978). *Top-level structure as an organizational strategy for recall of classroom text.* Unpublished doctoral dissertation, Arizona State University, Tempe.

Bartlett, F. C. (1932). *Remembering: A study in experimental and social psychology.* Cambridge, England: Cambridge University Press.

Barton, W. A. (1930). *Outlining as a study procedure.* New York: Teachers College Press.

Bates, M., Beinashowitz, J., Ingria, R., & Wilson, K. (1981). *Generative tutorial systems.* Paper presented at the Association for the Development of Computer-based Instructional Systems, Western Washington University, Bellingham, WA.

Beck, I. L. (1985). Comprehension instruction in the primary grades. In J. Osborn, P. Wilson, & R. C. Anderson (Eds.), *Reading education: Foundations for a literate America.* Lexington, MA: Lexington Books.

Beck, I. L., McKeown, M. G., McCaslin, E. S., & Burkes, A. (1979). *Instructional dimensions that may affect reading comprehension: Examples from two commercial reading programs* (LRDC Publication 1979/20). Pittsburgh: University of Pittsburgh, Learning Research and Development Center.

Beck, I. L., Omanson, R. C., & McKeown, M. G. (1982). An instructional redesign of reading lessons: Effects on comprehension. *Reading Research Quarterly, 17,* 462–481.

Beck, I. L., Perfetti, C. A., & McKeown, M. G. (1982). The effects of long-term vocabulary instruction on lexical access and reading comprehension. *Journal of Educational Psychology, 74,* 506–521.

Beebe, M. J. (1980). The effect of different types of substitution miscues on reading. *Reading Research Quarterly, 15,* 324–336.

Begland, R. R. (1981, April). *A multi-faceted approach for the development of the Army's functional basic skills program (BESEP).* Paper presented at the meeting of the American Educational Research Association. (Document Reproduction Service No. ED 200 643).

Benedict, H. (1979). Early lexical development: comprehension and production. *Journal of Child Language, 6,* 183–200.

Benson, N. (1979). The effects of peer feedback during the writing process on writing performance, revision behavior and attitude toward writing. *Dissertation Abstracts International, 40,* 1989A.

Benton, A. L., & Pearl, D. P. (Eds.) (1978). *Dyslexia: An appraisal of current knowledge.* New York: Oxford University Press.

Berkey, S. C. (1967). A successful high school developmental reading program. *Journal of Reading, 10,* 442–447.

Berko, J. (1958). The child's learning of English morphology. *Word, 14,* 150–177.

Betts, E. A. (1946). *Foundations of reading instruction.* New York: American Book Co.

Binet, A. (1909). *Les idees modernes sur les infants.* Paris: Ernest Flammarion.

Binet, A., & Henri, V. (1978). La memoire des phrases (memoire des indees). In T. J. Thiemann & W. F. Brewer (Eds. and Trans.), Alfred Binet on memory for ideas. *Genetic Psychology Monographs, 97,* 243–264. (Original work published 1894)

Birch, H. G. (1962). Dyslexia and maturation of visual function. In J. Money (Ed.), *Read-*

ing disability: Progress and research needs in dyslexia. Baltimore: Johns Hopkins Press.

Bird, M. (1980). *Reading comprehension strategies: A direct teaching approach.* Unpublished doctoral dissertation, University of Toronto, Ontario, Canada.

Bishop, C. H. (1964). Transfer effects of word and letter training in reading. *Journal of Verbal Learning and Verbal Behavior, 3,* 215–221.

Bissex, G. (1980). *Gyns at wrk: A child learns to write and read.* Cambridge, MA: Harvard University Press.

Black, J. B. (1977). *Story memory structure.* Unpublished doctoral dissertation, Stanford University, Stanford, CA.

Black, J. B., & Bower, G. H. (1980). Story understanding as problem solving. *Poetics, 9,* 223–250.

Blewitt, P. (1982). Word meaning acquisition in young children: a review of theory and research. In H. W. Reese & L. P. Lipsitt (Eds.), *Advances in child development and behavior* (Vol. 17). New York: Academic Press, 1982.

Bliesmer, E. P. & Yarborough, B. H. (1965). A comparison of ten different beginning reading programs in first grade. *Phi Delta Kappan, 46,* 500–504.

Bloom, L. (1974). *Form and function in emerging grammars.* Cambridge, MA: MIT Press.

Bobrow, D. G., & Norman, D. A. (1975). Some principles of memory schemata. In D. G. Bobrow & A. M. Collins (Eds.), *Representation and understanding: Studies in cognitive science.* New York: Academic Press.

Boggs, S. T. (1983). *Discourse analysis of classroom narrative and speech play of island children.* (Final Report, NIE). University of Hawaii, Honolulu. (ERIC Document Reproduction Service No. ED 228 851).

Bond, G. L., & Dykstra, R. (1967). The cooperative research program in first–grade reading instruction. *Reading Research Quarterly, 24,* 5–142.

Bond, G. L., & Tinker, M. A. (1973). *Reading difficulties: Their diagnosis and correction* (3rd ed.). New York: Appleton-Century-Crofts.

Booth, W. C. (1961). *The rhetoric of fiction.* Chicago: University of Chicago Press.

Bork, A. (1981). *Learning with computers.* Bedford, MA: Digital Press.

Bormuth, J. R. (1966). Readability: A new approach. *Reading Research Quarterly, 1,* 79–132.

Bormuth, J. R. (1970). *On the theory of achievement test items.* Chicago: University of Chicago Press.

Bormuth, J. R. (1975). Literacy in the classroom. In W. Page (Ed.), *Help for the reading teacher: New directions in research.* Urbana, IL: National Council of Teachers of English.

Bower, J. A. (1982). Memory limitations in the oral reading comprehension of fourth-grade children. *Journal of Experimental Child Psychology, 34,* 200–216.

Bowerman, M. (1979). The acquisition of complex sentences. In P. Fletcher & M. Garman (Eds.), *Language Acquisition.* New York: Cambridge University Press.

Bowerman, M. (1981). Language development. In H. C. Triandis & A. Heron (Eds.) *Handbook of cross-cultural psychology: Developmental psychology.* Boston, MA: Allyn & Bacon.

Bradshaw, J. L. (1975). Three interrelated problems in reading: A review. *Memory and Cognition, 3,* 123–134.

Brady, S., Shankweiler, D., & Mann, V. (1983). Speech perception and memory coding in relation to reading ability. *Journal of Experimental Child Psychology, 35,* 345–367.

Bransford, J. D. (1979). *Human cognition: Learning, understanding and remembering.* Belmont, CA: Wadsworth.

Bransford, J. D. (1984). Schema activation and schema acquisition: Comments on Richard C. Anderson's remarks. In R. C. Anderson, J. Osborn, & R. J. Tierney (Eds.), *Learning to read in American schools: Basal readers and content texts.* Hillsdale, NJ: Lawrence Erlbaum Associates.

Bransford, J. D., Barclay, J., & Franks, J. J. (1972). Sentence memory: Constructive vs. interpretive approach. *Cognitive Psychology, 3,* 193–209.

Bransford, J. D., & Johnson, M. K. (1972). Contextual prerequisites for understanding: Some investigations of comprehension and recall. *Journal of Verbal Learning and Verbal Behavior, 11,* 717–726.

Bransford, J. D., & Johnson, M. K. (1973). Considerations of some problems of comprehension. In W. G. Chase (Ed.), *Visual information processing.* New York: Academic Press.

Bransford, J., Nitsch, K., & Franks, J. (1977). Schooling and the facilitation of knowing. In R. Anderson, R. Spiro, & W. Montague (Eds.), *Schooling and the acquisition of knowledge.* Hillsdale, NJ: Lawrence Erlbaum Associates.

Bransford, J. D., Stein, B. S., Arbitman–Smith, R., & Vye, N. J. (1985). Three approaches to improving thinking and learning skills. In J. Segal, S. Chipman, & R. Glaser (Eds.), *Thinking and learning skills: Relating instruction to basic research* (Vol. 1). Hillsdale, NJ: Lawrence Erlbaum Associates.

Bransford, J. D., Stein, B. S., Shelton, T. S., & Owings, R. A. (1980). Cognition and adaptation: The importance of learning to learn. In J. Harvey (Ed.), *Cognition, social behavior and the environment.* Hillsdale, NJ: Lawrence Erlbaum Associates.

Brause, H., & Bruno, R. (1980). *Assessing school language competence of bilingual students.* Washington, D.C.: National Institute of Education.

Brewer, W. F. (1977, July). *Two types of convention in indirect speech* (Tech. Rep. No. 52). Urbana: University of Illinois, Center for the Study of Reading.

Brewer, W. F., & Lichtenstein, E. H. (1981). Event schemas, story schemas, and story grammars. In A. D. Baddely & J. D. Long (Eds.), *Attention and performance IX.* Hillsdale, NJ: Lawrence Erlbaum Associates, 1981.

Brewer, W. F., & Lichtenstein, E. H. (1982). Stories are to entertain: A structural-affect theory of stories. *Journal of Pragmatics, 6,* 473–486.

Briggs, P., & Underwood, G. (1982). Phonological coding in good and poor readers. *Journal of Experimental Child Psychology, 34,* 93–112.

Brookover, W., & Lezotte, L. (1979, May). *Changes in school characteristics coincident with changes in student achievement* (Occasional Paper No. 17). East Lansing: Michigan State University, Institute for Research on Teaching.

Brown, A. L. (1975). The development of memory: Knowing, knowing about knowing, and knowing how to know. In H. W. Reese (Ed.), *Advances in child development and behavior* (Vol. 10). New York: Academic Press.

Brown, A. L. (1978). Knowing when, where, and how to remember: A problem of metacognition. In R. Glaser (Ed.), *Advances in instructional psychology.* Hillsdale, NJ: Lawrence Erlbaum Associates.

Brown, A. L. (1980). Metacognitive development and reading. In R. J. Spiro, B. C. Bruce, & W. F. Brewer (Eds.), *Theoretical issues in reading comprehension.* Hillsdale, NJ: Lawrence Erlbaum Associates.

Brown, A. (1982). Learning how to learn from reading. In J. Langer & M. Smith–Burke, *Reader meets author/bridging the gap.* Newark, DE: International Reading Association.

Brown, A. L., Bransford, J. D., Ferrara, R. A., & Campione, J. C. (1983). Learning, remembering, and understanding. In J. H. Flavell & E. M. Markman (Eds.), *Carmichael's handbook of child psychology* (Vol. 3). New York: Wiley.

Brown, A., & Campione, J. (1978a). The effects of knowledge and experience on the formation of retrieval plans for studying from text. In M. Gruneberg, P. Morris, & R. Syhes, (Eds.) *Practical aspects of memory.* New York: Academic Press.

Brown, A. L., & Campione, J. C. (1978b). Permissible inferences from the outcome of training studies in cognitive development research. *Quarterly Newsletter of the Institute for Comparative Human Development, 2,* 46–53.

Brown, A. L., & Campione, J. C. (1981). Inducing flexible thinking: A problem of access. In M. Freidman, J. P. Das, & N. O'Connor (Eds.), *Intelligence and learning.* New York: Plenum Press.

Brown, A. L., Campione, J. C., & Barclay, C. R. (1979). Training self-checking routines for estimating test readiness: Generalization from list learning to prose recall. *Child Development, 50*, 501–512.

Brown, A. L., Campione, J. C., & Day, J. D. (1981). Learning to learn: On training students to learn from texts. *Educational Researcher, 10*, 14–21.

Brown, A. L., & Day, J. D. (1983). Macrorules for summarizing texts: The development of expertise. *Journal of Verbal Learning and Verbal Behavior, 22*, 1–16.

Brown, A. L., & Smiley, S. S. (1977). Rating the importance of structural units of prose passages: A problem of metacognitive development. *Child Development, 48*, 1–8.

Brown, A. L., & Smiley, S. S. (1978). The development of strategies for studying texts. *Child Development, 49*, 1076–1088.

Brown, A. L., Smiley, S. S., & Lawton, S. C. (1978). The effects of experience on the selection of suitable retrieval cues for studying texts. *Child Development, 49*, 829–835.

Brown, J. (1979). Language acquisition: Linguistic structure and rule-governed behavior. In G. J. Whitehurst & B. J. Zimmerman (Eds.), *The functions of language and cognition*. New York: Academic Press.

Brown, J. S., & Burton, R. R. (1979). A computer coach for "How the West Was Won." *International Journal of Man-Machine Studies, 11*, 3–43.

Brown, R. (1958). *Words and things*. New York: Free Press.

Bruce, B. C. (1977, April). *Plans and social actions* (Tech. Rep. No. 34). Urbana: University of Illinois, Center for the Study of Reading. (ERIC Document Reproduction Service No. ED 149 328).

Bruce, B. C. (1978, June). What makes a good story? (Reading Education Rep. No. 5). Urbana: University of Illinois, Center for the Study of Reading. (ERIC Document Reproduction Service No. ED 158 222).

Bruce, B. C. (1981a). *A new point of view on children's stories* (Reading Education Rep. No. 25). Urbana: University of Illinois, Center for the Study of Reading.

Bruce, B. C. (1981b). *Stones within stones* (Reading Education Rep. No. 29). Urbana: University of Illinois, Center for the Study of Reading.

Bruce, B. C. (1981c). A social interaction model of reading. *Discourse Processes, 4*, 273–311.

Bruce, B. C., Collins, A., Rubin, A., & Gentner, D. (1978). *A cognitive science approach to writing* (Tech. Rep. No. 89). Urbana: University of Illinois, Center for the Study of Reading.

Bruce, B. C., & Newman, D. (1978). Interacting plans. *Cognitive Science, 2*, 195–233.

Bruce, B. C., & Rubin, A. D. (1984, Sept.). *The utility of technology in the development of basic skill instruction: Written communications*. BBN Report #5766, Cambridge, MA: Bolt Beranek & Newman.

Bruce, B. C., Rubin, A. D., & Starr, K. (1981). *Why readability formulas fail* (Reading Ed. Rep. No. 28). Urbana: University of Illinois, Center for the Study of Reading.

Bruce, D. (1964). Analysis of word sounds by young children. *British Journal of Educational Psychology, 34*, 158–169.

Bruner, J. S. (1957). Going beyond the information given. In H. Gruber et al. (Eds.), *Contemporary approaches to cognition*. Cambridge, MA: Harvard University Press.

Bruner, J. S. (1960). *The process of education*. Cambridge, MA: Harvard University Press.

Bruner, J. S., Olver, R. R., & Greenfield, P. M. (1966). *Studies in cognitive growth*. New York: Wiley.

Bryant, N. (1968). Some principles of remedial instruction for dyslexia. In G. Natchez (Ed.), *Children with reading problems*. New York: Basic Books.

Byers, R., & Byers, H. (1972). Nonverbal communication and the education of children. In C. B. Cazden, V. P. John, & D. Hymes. (Eds.), *Functions of language in the classroom*. New York: Teachers College Press.

Byrne, B. (1981). Deficient syntactic control in poor readers: Is a weak phonetic memory code responsible? *Applied Psycholinguistics, 2*, 201–212.

Calfee, R. C., & Piontkowski, D. C. (1981). The reading diary: Acquisition of decoding. *Reading Research Quarterly, 16,* 346–373.

Calkins, L. (1980). Children learn the writer's craft. *Language Arts, 57,* 207–213.

Canney, G., & Winograd, P. (1979, April). *Schemata for reading and reading comprehension performance* (Tech. Rep. No. 120). Urbana: University of Illinois, Center for the Study of Reading.

Capelli, C. A., & Markman, E. M. (1980). *Children's sensitivity to incomprehensible material in written texts.* Unpublished manuscript. Stanford University, Stanford, CA.

Carpenter, P. A., & Daneman, M. (1981). Lexical retrieval and error recovery in reading: A model based on eye fixations. *Journal of Verbal Learning and Verbal Behavior, 20,* 137–160.

Carpenter, P. A., & Just, M. A. (1977). Integrative processes in comprehension. In D. LaBerge and S. J. Samuels (Eds.), *Basic processes in reading: Perception and comprehension.* Hillsdale, NJ: Lawrence Erlbaum Associates.

Carpenter, P. A., & Just, M. A. (1983). What your eyes do while your mind reads. In K. Rayner (Ed.), *Eye movements and reading: perceptual and language processes.* New York: Academic Press.

Carroll, J. B., Davies, P., & Richman, B. (1971). *The American Heritage word frequency book.* Boston: Houghton Mifflin.

Carroll, J. B., & Freedle, R. O. (1972). *Language comprehension and the acquisition of knowledge.* Washington, DC: Winston.

Carver, R. P., & Hoffman, J. V. (1981). The effect of practice through repeated reading on gain in reading ability using a computer-based instructional system. *Reading Research Quarterly, 16,* 374–390.

Cazden, C. B. (1972). *Child Language and Education.* New York: Holt, Rinehart, and Winston.

Chabot, R. J., Petros, T. V., & McCord, G. (1983). Developmental and reading ability differences in accessing information from semantic memory. *Journal of Experimental Child Psychology, 35,* 128–142.

Chafe, W. L. (1970). *Meaning and the structure of language.* Chicago: University of Chicago Press.

Chafe, W. L. (1982). *Features differentiating written from spoken language and their relation to the writing process* (Research Project, NIE). Berkeley: University of California, Department of Linguistics.

Chafe, W. L. (1983). Integration and involvement: Speaking, writing and oral literature. In D. Tannen (Ed.), *Spoken and written language.* Norwood, NJ: Ablex.

Chall, J. (1967). *Learning to read: The great debate.* New York: McGraw-Hill.

Charniak, E. (1972). *Toward a model of children's story comprehension* (Tech. Rep. No. 266). Cambridge, MA: MIT Artificial Intelligence Laboratory.

Chiesi, H. L., Spilich, G. J., & Voss, J. F. (1979). Acquisition of domain–related information in relation to high and low domain knowledge. *Journal of Verbal Learning and Verbal Behavior, 18,* 257–274.

Chipman, S., Segal, J., & Glaser, R. (Eds.) (1985). *Thinking and learning skills: Current research and open questions (Vol. 2).* Hillsdale, NJ: Lawrence Erlbaum Associates.

Chomsky, C. (1969). *The acquisition of syntax in children from 5 to 10.* Cambridge, MA: MIT Press.

Chomsky, C. (1970). Reading, writing and phonology. *Harvard Educational Review, 40,* 287–309.

Chomsky, C. (1978). When you still can't read in third grade: After decoding, what? In S. J. Samuels (Ed.), *What research has to say about reading instruction.* Newark, DE: International Reading Association.

Chomsky, N. (1957). *Syntactic structures.* The Hague: Mouton.

Chomsky, N. (1959). Review of *Verbal Behavior* by B. F. Skinner. *Language, 35,* 26–58.

Cirilo, R. K. (1981). Referential coherence and text structure in story comprehension. *Journal of Verbal Learning and Verbal Behavior, 20,* 358–367.

Cirilo, R. K., & Foss, D. J. (1980). Text structure and reading time for sentences. *Journal of Verbal Learning and Verbal Behavior, 19,* 96–109.

Cirrin, F. M. (1983). Lexical access in children and adults. *Developmental Psychology, 19,* 452–460.

Clark, E. V. (1973). What's in a word? On the child's acquisition of semantics in his first language. In T. E. Moore (Ed.), *Cognitive development and the acquisition of language.* New York: Academic Press.

Clark, H. H. (1977). Inferences in comprehension. In D. LaBerge & S. J. Samuels (Eds.), *Basic processing in reading: Perception and comprehension.* Hillsdale, NJ: Lawrence Erlbaum Associates.

Clark, H. H., & Clark, E. V. (1977). *Psychology and language: An introduction to psycholinguistics.* New York: Harcourt, Brace, Jovanovich.

Clark, H. H., & Haviland, S. E. (1977). Comprehension and the given-new contract. In R. O. Freedle (Ed.), *Discourse production and comprehension.* Norwood, NJ: Ablex.

Clay, M. (1973). *Reading: The patterning of complex behavior.* Auckland, New Zealand: Heinemann.

Clay, M. (1975). *What did I write?* Auckland, New Zealand: Heinemann.

Clay, M., & Imlach, R. (1971). Juncture, pitch and stress as reading behavior variables. *Journal of Verbal Behavior and Verbal Learning, 10,*133–139.

Clewell, S. F., & Clifton, A. N. (1983). Examining your textbook for comprehensibility. *Journal of Reading. 27* (3): 219–224

Cohen, R. (1979, September). *Elements of a plan-based theory of speech acts* (Tech. Rep. No. 141). Urbana: University of Illinois, Center for the Study of Reading.

Cohen, S. A. (1974). *High intensity learning systems*™. New York: Random House.

Collins, A., Brown, J. S., & Larkin, K. M. (1980). Inference in text understanding. In R. J. Spiro, B. C. Bruce, & W. F. Brewer (Eds.), *Theoretical issues in reading comprehension.* Hillsdale, NJ: Lawrence Erlbaum Associates.

Collins, A., Bruce, B. C., & Rubin, A. (1982, February). Microcomputer–based writing activities for the upper elementary grades. In *Proceedings of the Fourth International Congress and Exposition of the Society for Applied Learning Technology,* Orlando, FL.

Collins, A., & Smith, E. E. (1982). Teaching the process of reading comprehension. In D. K. Detterman & R. J. Sternberg (Eds.), *How and how much can intelligence be increased.* Norwood, NJ: Ablex.

Collins, A., Warnock, E. H., & Passafiume, J. J. (1975). Analysis and synthesis of tutorial dialogues. In G. H. Bower (Ed.), *The psychology of learning and motivation* (Vol. 9). New York: Academic Press.

Collins, J. (1979). Teaching writing: An interactionist approach to alleviated and idiosyncratic language in the writing of secondary students. *Dissertation Abstracts International, 40,* 1425–A.

Collins, J. (1980). Differential treatment in reading instruction. Unpublished paper, University of California, Language Behavior Research Laboratory, Berkeley.

Collins, W. A. (Ed.) (1979). Children's language and communication, *The Minnesota Symposium on Child Psychology,* (Vol. 12). Hillsdale, NJ: Lawrence Erlbaum Associates.

Cook–Gumperz, J., & Corsaro, W. (1976). *Social-ecological constraints on children's communicative strategies* (Working Paper No. 46). Berkeley: Berkeley Language Behavior Research Lab.

Cooper, C., & Petrosky, A. (1976). A psycholinguistic view of the fluent reading process. *Journal of Reading, 20,* 184–207.

Crisucuolo, N., & Rossman, J. (1977). A fresh look at secondary reading. *Clearing House, 50,* 336–368.

Cross, T. G. (1977). Mother's speech adjustments: The contributions of selected child listener variables. In C. Ferguson & C. Snow (Eds.), *Talking to children: Language input and acquisition.* Cambridge: Cambridge University Press.

Crowell, D. C. (1981). *Kamehameha Reading Objective System (KROS).* Honolulu: Kamehameha Early Education Program.

Crowell, D. C. & Au, K. H. (1981). Developing children's comprehension in listening, reading and television viewing. *Elementary School Journal, 82,* 51–57.

Cuff, N. B. (1930). Vocabulary tests. *Journal of Educational Psychology, 21,* 212–220.

Curtis, M. E. (1980). Development of components of reading skill. *Journal of Educational Psychology. 72,* 656–669.

Cushenberry, D. (1977). The reading problem and what you can do about it. *The High School Journal, 61,* 34–43.

Daiute, C. (1982). Word processing. Can it make even good writers better? *Electronic Learning,* March/April, 29–31.

Dale, E., & Chall, J. S. (1948). A formula for predicting readability. *Educational Research Bulletin, 27,* 11–20, 37–54.

Dale, P. S. (1976). *Language development.* New York: Holt, Rinehart & Winston.

Daneman, M., & Carpenter, P. A. (1980). Individual differences in working memory and reading. *Journal of Verbal Learning and Verbal Behavior, 19,* 450–466.

Danner, F. W. (1976). Children's understanding of intersentence organization in the recall of short descriptive passages. *Journal of Educational Psychology, 68,* 174–183.

Dansereau, D. F. (1978). The development of a learning strategy curriculum. In H. F. O'Neil, Jr. (Ed.), *Learning strategies.* New York: Academic Press.

Dansereau, D. F. (1985). Learning strategy research. In J. Segal, S. Chipman, & R. Glaser (Eds.), *Thinking and learning skills,* Vol. 1. Hillsdale, NJ: Lawrence Erlbaum Associates.

Davis, F. B. (1972). Psychometric research on comprehension in reading. *Reading Research Quarterly, 7,* 628–678.

Davison, A. (1980). *Linguistics and the measurement of syntactic complexity: The case of raising* (Tech. Rep. No. 173). Urbana: University of Illinois, Center for the Study of Reading.

Davison, A. (1984). Readability-appraising text difficulty. In R. C. Anderson, J. Osborn, & R. J. Tierney (Eds.), *Learning to read in American schools: Basal Readers and Content Texts.* Hillsdale, NJ: Lawrence Erlbaum Associates.

Day, J. D. (1980). *Training summarization skills: A comparison of teaching methods.* Unpublished doctoral dissertation, University of Illinois, Urbana.

Day, J., Stein, N. L., Trabasso, T., & Shirey, L. L. (1979, March). *A study of inferential comprehension: The use of a story schema to remember pictures.* Paper presented at the meeting of the Society for Research in Child Development, San Francisco.

de Beaugrande, R., & Dressler, W. (1982). *Introduction to textlinguistics.* London: Longman.

Dearman, N., & Plisko, V. (1981). Test scores and attainment rates. *American Education, 17,* 15–20.

Deese, J. (1983). *Thought into speech: The psychology of language.* Englewood Cliffs, NJ: Prentice-Hall.

DeFord, D. (1980). Learning to write: An expression of language. *Theory into Practice, 19,* 157–162.

Denckla, M. B., & Rudel, R. (1976a). Naming of object drawings by dyslexic and other learning disabled children. *Brain and Language, 3,* 1–15.

Denckla, M. B., & Rudel, R. (1976b). Rapid "automized" naming (R.A.N.): Dyslexia differentiated from other learning disabilities. *Neuropsychologia, 14,* 471–479.

Denney, T., & Weintraub, S. (1963). Exploring first graders' concepts of reading. *The Reading Teacher, 16,* 363–365.

Denney, T., & Weintraub, S. (1966). First-graders' responses to three questions about reading. *Elementary School Journal, 66,* 441–448.

de Villiers, P. A. (1974). Imagery and theme in recall of connected discourse. *Journal of Experimental Psychology, 103,* 263–268.

Dewey, J. (1933). *How we think* (second ed.). Boston: Heath. (Original work published 1910).

Diederich, P. B. (1973). *Educating those who teach reading* (TM Report No. 23). Princeton, NJ: Educational Testing Service.

Diehl, W., & Mikulecky, L. (1980). The nature of literacy at work. *Journal of Reading, 24,* 221–227.

Dolch, E. W. (1928). Vocabulary burden. *Journal of Educational Research, 17,* 170–183.

Dolch, E. W. (1948). Grading reading difficulty. In E. W. Dolch (Ed.), *Problems in reading.* Champaign, IL: Garrard Press.

Dooling, D. J., & Mullet, R. L. (1973). Locus of thematic effects in retention of prose. *Journal of Experimental Psychology, 97,* 404–406.

Dore, J. (1979). What's so conceptual about the acquisition of linguistic structures? *Journal of Child Language, 6,* 129–137.

Dowhower–Vuyk, S., & Speidel, G. E. (1982). The process of language and reading instruction. In *Oral language: A successful reading program for Hawaiian children* (Tech. Rep. No. 105). Honolulu: The Kamehameha School, Kamehameha Early Education Program.

Dreher, M. J., & Singer, H. (1980). Story grammar instruction unnecessary for intermediate grade students. *The Reading Teacher, 34,* 261–268.

Duffy, G. G. (1982). Fighting off the alligators: What research in real classrooms has to say about reading instruction. *Journal of Reading Behavior, 14,* 357–373.

Dugdale, S., & Kibbee, D. (1975). *The fractions curriculum.* Champaign-Urbana: University of Illinois, Plato Elementary School Mathematics Project.

Durkin, D. (1966). The achievement of preschool readers: Two longitudinal studies, *Reading Research Quarterly. 1,* 5–36.

Durkin, D. (1978–1979). What classroom observations reveal about reading comprehension instruction. *Reading Research Quarterly, 14,* 481–533.

Durkin, D. (1981). Reading comprehension instruction in five basal reader series. *Reading Research Quarterly, 16,* 515–544.

Durkin, D. (1985). Materials for the teaching of reading: Teacher's manuals. In J. Osborn, P. Wilson, & R. C. Anderson (Eds.), *Reading education: Foundations for a literate America.* Lexington, MA: Lexington Books.

Earle, R. A. (1969). Reading and mathematics: Research in the classroom. In H. A. Robinson & E. L. Thomas (Eds.), *Fusing reading skills and content.* Newark, DE: International Reading Association.

Early, M. (1973). Taking stock: Secondary school reading in the '70s. *Journal of Reading, 16,* 364–373.

Ehri, L. C. (1975). Word consciousness in readers and pre-readers. *Journal of Educational Psychology, 67,* 204–212.

Emig, J. (1971). *The composing processes of twelfth graders.* Urbana, IL: National Council of Teachers of English.

Englar, M. A. (1978, November). *Framework for instructional activities.* Paper presented at National Reading Conference, St. Petersburg, FL.

Entwisle, D. R., & Frasure, N. E. (1974). A contradiction resolved: Children's processing of syntactic cues. *Developmental Psychology, 10,* 852–857.

Estes, T. H., & Wetmore, M. E. (1983). Assessing the comprehensibility of text. *Reading Psychology, 4*(1), 37–51.

Fairbanks, G. (1937). The relation between eye-movements and voice in oral reading of good and poor readers. *Psychological Monographs, 48,* 78–107.

Farr, R. C. (1978). *Reading survey tests: Metropolitan Achievement Tests.* New York: The Psychological Corporation.

Fasold, R. (1972). *Tense marking in Black English: A linguistic and social analysis.* Washington, DC: Center for Applied Linguistics.

Feigenbaum, E. A. & Feldman, J. (1963). *Computers and thought*. New York: McGraw-Hill.

Feldman, K. V., & Klausmeier, H. J. (1974). Effects of two kinds of definition on the concept attainment of fourth and eighth graders. *The Journal of Education Research, 67*, 219–223.

Fillmore, C. J., & Kay, P. (1983). *Text semantic analysis of reading comprehension tests* (Final report, NIE). Berkeley: University of California, Institute of Human Learning.

Fisher, D. L. (1978). *Functional literacy and the schools*. Washington, DC: U.S. Department of Health, Education and Welfare and the National Institute of Education.

Flach, E. G., & Berk, R. A. (1980). *A methodology for identifying sex- and ethnic-biased achievement test items*. Paper presented at the meeting of the American Educational Research Association.

Flavell, J. H. (1981). Cognitive monitoring. In W. P. Dickson (Ed.), *Children's oral communication skills*. New York: Academic Press.

Flavell, J. H., Speer, J. R., Green, F. L., & August, D. L. (1981). *The development of comprehension monitoring and knowledge about communication* (Whole No. 192). Monographs of the Society for Research in Child Development, 46.

Flavell, J. H., & Wellman, H. M. (1977). Metamemory. In R. V. Kail, Jr. & J. W. Hagen (Eds.), *Perspectives on the development of memory and cognition*. Hillsdale, NJ: Lawrence Erlbaum Associates.

Fleisher, L. S., Jenkins, J. R., & Pany, D. (1979). Effects on poor readers' comprehension of training in rapid decoding. *Reading Research Quarterly, 15*, 30–48.

Fletcher, P., & Garman, M. (1979). *Language acquisition*. Cambridge: Cambridge University Press.

Florio, S., & Clark, C. (1979). *Schooling and the acquisition of written literacy: A descriptive case study*. Pittsburgh: Carnegie–Mellon University, Psychology Dept. & National Institute of Education.

Flower, L. S., & Hayes, J. R. (1980). The dynamics of composing: Making plans and juggling constraints. In L. W. Gregg & E. R. Steinberg (Eds.), *Cognitive processes in writing*. Hillsdale, NJ: Lawrence Erlbaum Associates.

Flower, L. S., & Hayes, J. R. (1981). A cognitive process theory of writing. *College Composition and Communication, 4*, 365–387.

Fodor, J. A., Bever, T. G., and Garrett, M. F. (1974). *The psychology of language*. New York: McGraw-Hill.

Forrest, D. L., & Waller, T. G. (1979, March). *Cognitive and metacognitive aspects of reading*. Paper presented at the meeting of the Society for Research in Child Development, San Francisco.

Fowler, R. L., & Barker, A. S. (1974). Effectiveness of highlighting for retention of text material. *Journal of Applied Psychology, 59*, 358–364.

Franks, J. J., Vye, N. J., Auble, P. N., Mezynski, K. J., Perfetto, G. A., Bransford, J. D., Stein, B. S., & Littlefield, J. (1982). *Learning from explicit vs. implicit text*. Unpublished manuscript, Vanderbilt University, Nashville, TN.

Frederiksen, C. H., (1975). Representing logical and semantic structure of knowledge acquired from discourse. *Cognitive Psychology, 7*, 371–458.

Frederiksen, C. H. (1977a). *Discourse comprehension and early reading*. Hillsdale, NJ: Lawrence Erlbaum Associates.

Frederiksen, C. H. (1977b). Semantic processing units in understanding text. In R. O. Freedle (Ed.), *Discourse production and comprehension*. Norwood, NJ: Ablex.

Frederiksen, C. H. (1981). Inference in preschool children's conversation—a cognitive perspective. In J. Green & C. Wallat (Eds.), *Ethnography and language in educational settings*. Norwood, NJ: Ablex Publishing.

Frederiksen, C. H., & Dominic, J. (Eds.). (1981). *Writing: Process development and communication*. Hillsdale, NJ: Lawrence Erlbaum Associates.

Frederiksen, J. R. (1981). Sources of process interactions in reading. In A. M. Lesgold & C. A.

Perfetti (Eds.), *Interactive processes in reading*. Hillsdale, NJ: Lawrence Erlbaum Associates.

Frederiksen, J. R., Warren, B. M., Gillotte, H. P., & Weaver, P. A. (1982). The name of the game is literacy. *Classroom Computer News, 2*, 23–24, 26–27.

Frederiksen, N. (1979). Some emerging trends in testing. In R. W. Tyler & S. H. White (Chairmen), *Testing, Teaching and Learning: Report of a conference on Research in Testing*. Washington, DC: National Institute of Education.

Freebody, P., & Anderson, R. C. (1983). Effects of vocabulary difficulty, text cohesion, and schema availability on reading comprehension. *Reading Research Quarterly, 18*, 277–294.

Freeman, C. (1981). A study of the degrees of reading power test. *Final report to the Ford Foundation*, Washington, DC: Center for Applied Linguistics.

Fremgen, A., & Fay, D. (1980). Overextensions in production and comprehension: A methodological clarification. *Journal of Child Language, 7*, 205–211.

Fries, C. (1966). *Linguistics and Reading*. New York: Holt, Rinehart, & Winston.

Fry, E. B. (1968). A readability formula that saves time. *The Journal of Reading, 11*, 513–516, 575–578.

Fry, E. B. (1977). *Elementary reading instruction*. New York: McGraw-Hill.

Gagne, E. D. (1978). Long–term retention of information following learning from prose. *Review of Educational Research, 48*, 629–665.

Gallimore, R., Boggs, J. W., & Jordan, C. (1974). *Culture, behavior and education: A study of Hawaiian-Americans*. Beverly Hills: Sage Publications.

Gallimore, R., Tharp, R. G., Klein, T., & Sloat, K. C. M. (1982). *Analysis of reading achievement test results for the Kamehameha Early Education Program, 1972–1979* Technical Report #95). Honolulu: Kamehameha Early Education Program.

Garner, R. (1981). Monitoring of passage inconsistency among poor comprehenders: A preliminary test of the "piecemeal processing" explanation. *Journal of Educational Research, 67*, 628–635.

Garner, R., & Kraus, C. (1981–1982). Good and poor comprehender differences in knowing and regulating reading behaviors. *Educational Research Quarterly, 6*, 5–12.

Garner, R., & Reis, R. (1981). Monitoring and resolving comprehension obstacles: An investigation of spontaneous text lookbacks among upper-grade good and poor comprehenders. *Reading Research Quarterly, 16*, 569–582.

Garner, R., & Taylor, N. (1982). Monitoring of understanding: An investigation of attentional assistance needs at different grade and reading proficiency levels. *Journal of Reading Behavior, 12*, 55–63.

Garner, R., Wagoner, S., & Smith, T. (1982). *Externalizing question–answering strategies of good and poor comprehenders*. Unpublished manuscript, University of Maryland, College Park, MD.

Gearhart, M., & Hall, W. S. (1979, February). *Internal state words: Cultural and situational variation in vocabulary usage* (Tech. Rep. No. 115). Urbana: University of Ilinois, Center for the Study of Reading.

Gentner, D. (1975). Evidence for the psychological reality of semantic components: The verbs of possession. In D. A. Norman & D. E. Rumelhart (Eds.), *Explorations in cognition*. San Francisco: Freeman.

Gibson, E., & Levin, H. (1975). *The psychology of reading*. Cambridge, MA: MIT Press.

Gitomer, D. H., Pellegrino, J. W., & Bisanz, J. (1983). Developmental change and invariance in semantic processing. *Journal of Experimental Child Psychology, 35*, 56–80.

Glaser, R. (Ed.). (1978). *Advances in instructional psychology*. Hillsdale, NJ: Lawrence Erlbaum Associates.

Goetz, E., & Armbruster, B. B. (1980). Psychological correlates of text structure. In R. Spiro, B. Bruce, & W. Brewer (Eds.), *Theoretical issues in reading comprehension*. Hillsdale, NJ: Lawrence Erlbaum Associates.

Goldberg, A., & Robson, D. (1980). *A metaphor for user interface design*. Palo Alto, CA: Xerox Palo Alto Research Center, Learning Research Group.

Goldman, S. R. (1976). Reading skill and the minimum distance principle: A comparison of listening and reading comprehension. *Journal of Experimental Child Psychology, 22,* 123–142.

Goodman, K. S. (Ed.) (1968). *The psycholinguistic nature of the reading process*. Detroit: Wayne State University Press.

Goodman, K. S. (1969). Analysis of oral reading miscues: Applied psycholinguistics. *Reading Research Quarterly, 5,* 9–30.

Goodman, K. S. (1976a) Behind the eye: What happens in reading. In H. S. Singer & R. B. Ruddell (Eds.), *Theoretical models and processes of reading* (2nd ed.). Newark, DE: International Reading Association.

Goodman, K. S. (1976b). Reading: A psycholinguistic guessing game. In H. S. Singer & R. B. Ruddell (Eds.), *Theoretical models and processes of reading*. Newark, DE: International Reading Association.

Goodman, Y. M., & Burke, C. L. (1972). *Reading miscue inventory manual*. New York: Macmillan. Reprinted by Richard C. Owen Publisher, NY, 1982.

Gordon, C. J. (1980). *The effects of instruction in metacomprehension and inferencing on children's comprehension abilities*. Unpublished doctoral dissertation, University of Minnesota, Minneapolis.

Gordon, C. J., & Braun, C. (1983). Story schemata: Metatextual aid to reading and writing. In J. A. Niles, & L. A. Harris (Eds.), *New inquiries in reading research and instruction*. National Reading Conference: 31st yearbook. Rochester, NY: National Reading Conference, Inc.

Gould, S. M., Haas, L. W., & Marino, J. L. (1982). *Writing as schema-building: The effects of writing as a pre-reading activity on a delayed recall of narrative text*. Unpublished manuscript.

Graves, D. H. (1975). An examination of the writing process of seven-year old children. *Research in the Teaching of English, 9,* 227–241.

Graves, D. H. (1982). *Writing: Teachers and children at work*. Exeter, NH: Heineman.

Graves, D. H., & Hansen, J. (1983). The author's chair. *Language Arts, 60,* 176–183.

Graves, M. F., & Cooke, C. L. (1980). Effects of previewing difficult short stories for high school students. *Research on Reading in Secondary Schools, 6,* 38–54.

Graves, M. F., & Cooke, C. L. (1981). *Effects of previewing difficult short stories on low ability junior high school students' comprehension, recall, and attitudes*. Manuscript submitted for publication.

Graves, M. F., & Palmer, R. J. (1981). Validating previewing as a method of improving fifth and sixth grade students' comprehension of short stories. *Michigan Reading Journal, 15,* 1–3.

Gray, W. S., & Leary, B. E. (1935). *What makes a book readable?* Chicago: University of Chicago Press.

Gray, W. S., & Rogers, B. (1956). *Maturity in reading: Its nature and appraisal*. Chicago: University of Chicago Press.

Green, G. M. (1978, July). *Discourse functions of inversion construction* (Tech. Rep. No. 98). Urbana: University of Illinois, Center for the Study of Reading.

Green, G. M. (1980, August). *Linguistics and the pragmatics of language use: What you know when you know a language . . . and what else you know* (Tech. Rep. No. 179). Urbana: University of Illinois, Center for the Study of Reading.

Green, G. M., & Laff, M. O. (1980, September). *Five–year–olds' recognition of authorship by literary style* (Tech. Rep. No. 181). Urbana: University of Illinois, Center for the Study of Reading.

Green, J. (1978, November). *Conceptual framework for interactive processes in effective communication*. Paper presented at the National Reading Conference, St. Petersburg, FL.

Green-Morgan, G. (1984). On the appropriateness of adaptation in primary-level basal readers: Reaction to remarks by Bertram Bruce. In R. C. Anderson, J. Osborn & R. J. Tierney,

(Eds.), *Learning to read in American schools: Basal readers and content texts*. Hillsdale, NJ: Lawrence Erlbaum Associates.

Greenberg, J., & Kuczaj, S. A. (1982). Towards a theory of substantive word-meaning acquisition. In S. A. Kuczaj (Ed.), *Language development (Vol. 1): Syntax and semantics*. Hillsdale, NJ: Lawrence Erlbaum Associates.

Grice, H. P. (1975). Logic and conversation. In P. Cole & J. L. Morgan (Eds.), *Syntax and semantics: Vol. 3. Speech acts*. New York: Academic Press.

Griffin, P. (1977). Reading and pragmatics. In R. Shuy (Ed.), *Linguistic theory: What can it say about reading*. Newark, DE: International Reading Association.

Grimm, H. (1982). *On the interrelation of internal and external factors in the development of language structures in normal and dysphasic preschoolers: A longitudinal study.* Occasional paper #5, The Kamehameha Early Education Program, The Kamehameha Schools, Honolulu.

Gumperz, J. (1964). Linguistics and social interaction in two communities (In J. Gumperz & D. Hymes [Eds.], *The Ethnography of Communication*). *American Anthropology, 66*(6), Pt. 2, 137–153.

Gumperz, J., & Herasimchuck, E. (1975). The conversation analysis of social meaning: A study of classroom interaction. In M. Sanches & B. Blount (Eds.), *Sociocultural dimensions of language use*. New York: Academic Press.

Gumperz, J., Simons, H., & Cook–Gumperz, J. (1981). *School-Home Ethnography Project,* Washington, DC: National Institute of Education. Document Reproduction Service (ERIC No. ED 233 915).

Gunning, R. (1952). *The technique of clear writing*. New York: McGraw-Hill.

Haberlandt, K., Berian, C., & Sandson, J. (1980). The episode schema in story processing. *Journal of Verbal Learning and Verbal Behavior, 19,* 635–650.

Haertel, E. (1980). *A study of domain heterogeneity and content acquisition*. Evanston, IL: Cemrel.

Hall, G., Loucks, S., Rutherford, W. L., & Newlove, B. W. (1975). Levels of use of the innovation: A framework for analyzing innovation adaptation. *Journal of Teacher Education, 29,* 52–56.

Hall, M. A. (1976). *Teaching reading as a language experience* (second ed.). Columbus, OH: Charles E. Merrill.

Hall, W. S., & Guthrie, L. F. (1979, May). *On the dialect question and reading* (Tech. Rep. No. 121). Urbana: University of Illinois, Center for the Study of Reading.

Hall, W. S., Nagy, W. E., & Linn, R. (1984). *Spoken words: The effect of situation and social group on the use and frequency of words*. Hillsdale, NJ: Lawrence Erlbaum Associates.

Halliday, M. A. K., & Hasan, R. (1976). *Cohesion in English*. London: Longman.

Hansen, J. (1983a). First-grade writers who pursue reading. In P. Stock (Ed.), *Forum revisited*. Upper Montclair, NJ: Boynton/Cook.

Hansen, J. (1983b). The writer as meaning maker. In J. L. Collins (Ed.), *Teaching all the children to write*. Liverpool, NY: New York State English Council.

Hansen, J., & Pearson, P. D. (1983). An instructional study: Improving the inferential comprehension of 4th grade and poor readers. *Journal of Educational Psychology, 75,* 821–829.

Harker, W. (1975). Materials for problem readers: Why aren't they working? *Journal of Reading, 18,* 451–454.

Harker, W. (1979). Implications from psycholinguistics for secondary reading. *Reading Horizons, 19,* 217–221.

Harris, P. L., Kruithof, A., Terwogt, M., & Visser, T. (1981). Children's detection and awareness of textual anomaly. *Journal of Experimental Child Psychology, 31,* 212–230.

Harris, A. J., & Sipay, E. R. (1975). *How to increase reading ability* (6th ed.). New York: David McKay.

Harste, J. C., Burke, C. L., & Woodward, V. A. (1982). *Children, their language and world: Initial encounters with print* (Final Report). Bloomington: Indiana University, Department of Reading, School of Education.

Haviland, S. E., & Clark, H. H. (1974). What's new? Acquiring new information as a process in comprehension. *Journal of Verbal Learning and Verbal Behavior, 13,* 512–521.

Hayes, D., & Tierney, R. J. (1982). Developing readers' knowledge through analogy. *Reading Research Quarterly, 17,* 256–280.

Henderson, E. & Beers, J. (1980). *Developmental and cognitive aspects of learning to spell: A reflection of word knowledge.* Newark, DE: International Reading Association.

Hennings, D. G. (1982). *Communication in action: Teaching the language arts.* Boston: Houghton Mifflin.

Herber, H. L. (1978). *Teaching reading in content areas.* Englewood Cliffs, NJ: Prentice-Hall.

Herman, M. (1979, September). *On the discourse structure of direct quotations* (Tech. Rep. No. 143). Urbana: University of Illinois, Center for the Study of Reading.

Hittleman, D. R. (1978). *Developmental reading: A psycholinguistic perspective.* Chicago: Rand McNally.

Hoff–Ginsberg, E., & Shatz, M. (1982). Linguistic input and the child's acquisition of language. *Psychological Bulletin, 92,* 3–26.

Holden, M., & MacGinitie, W. (1972). Children's conceptions of word boundaries in speech and print. *Journal of Educational Psychology, 63,* 551–557.

Holland, N. (1975). *Five readers reading.* New Haven: Yale University Press.

Holland, V. M., & Redish, J. C. (1981). *Strategies for understanding forms and other public documents.* Washington, DC: American Institute for Research, Document Design Project.

Hoon, P. W. (1974). Efficacy of three common study methods. *Psychology Reports, 35,* 1057–1058.

Hoskisson, K., & Krohm, B. (1974). Reading by immersion: Assisted reading. *Elementary English, 51,* 832–836.

Howie, S. (1979). A study: The effects of sentence combining practice on the writing ability and reading level of ninth grade students. *Dissertation Abstracts International, 40,* 1980–A.

Huey, E. B. (1968). *The psychology and pedagogy of reading.* Cambridge, MA: MIT Press. (Original work published 1908).

Huggins, A. W. F., & Adams, M. J. (1980). Syntactic aspects of reading comprehension. In R. J. Spiro, B. C. Bruce, & W. F. Brewer (Eds.), *Theoretical issues in reading comprehension.* Hillsdale, NJ: Lawrence Erlbaum Associates.

Hulig, L. L., Hall, J. E., Hoard, S. M., & Rutherford, W. L. (1983). *A multidimensional approach for assessing implementation success.* Paper presented at the meeting of the American Educational Research Association.

Hunt, E., Lunneborg, C., & Lewis, J. (1975). What does it mean to be high verbal? *Cognitive Psychology, 7,* 194–226.

Huttenlocher, J. (1964). Children's language: Word-phrase relationship. *Science, 143,* 264–265.

Hymes, D. (1972). Models of the interaction of language and social life. In J. Grumperz & D. Hymes (Eds.), *Directions in sociolinguistics.* New York: Holt, Rinehart, & Winston.

Hymes, D. (1978). *Ethno–linguistic study of classroom discourse.* Washington, DC: National Institute of Education.

Hymowitz, L. J. (1981, January 22). Employers take over where school failed to teach the basics. *Wall Street Journal, LXI*(65), 11.

Idstein, P., & Jenkins, J. R. (1972). Underlining versus repetitive reading. *Journal of Educational Research, 65,* 321–323.

Isakson, R. L., & Miller, J. W. (1976). Sensitivity to syntactic and semantic cues in good and poor comprehenders. *Journal of Educational Psychology, 68,* 787–792.

Jackson, M. D., & McClelland, J. L. (1979). Processing determinants of reading speed. *Journal of Experimental Psychology: General, 108,* 151–181.

Jackson, N. A. (1978, November). *Framework for curriculum: Types and forms of discourse.* Paper presented at National Reading Conference, St. Petersberg, FL.

Jeffrey, W. E., & Samuels, S. J. (1967). Effect of method of reading training on initial learning and transfer. *Journal of Verbal Learning and Verbal Behavior, 6,* 354–358.

Johns, J., & Ellis, D. (1976). Reading: Children tell it like it is. *Reading World, 16,* 115–128.

Johnston, P. (1981). *Implications of basic research for the assessment of reading comprehension* (Tech. Rep. No. 206). Urbana: University of Illinois, Center for the Study of Reading.

Jordan, C. (1976). Maternal teaching modes and school adaptation (Kamehameha Early Education Program Tech. Rep. No. 61). Honolulu: The Kamehameha Schools.

Jordan, C. (1978a). *Peer relationships among Hawaiian children and their educational implications.* Paper presented at the annual meetings of the American Anthropological Association, Los Angeles.

Jordan, C. (1978b). Teaching/learning interactions and school adaptation: The Hawaiian case. In C. Jordan, T. S. Weisner, R. G. Tharp, R. Gallimore, & K. H. Au. *A multidisciplinary approach to research in education: The Kamehameha early education program* (Kamehameha Early Education Program Tech. Rep. No. 81). Honolulu: The Kamehameha Schools.

Jordan, C. (1981a). *Educationally effective ethnology: A study of the contributions of cultural knowledge to effective education for minority children.* Unpublished doctoral dissertation, University Microfilms Library Services, Xerox Corporation, Ann Arbor, MI.

Jordan, C. (1981b). The selection of culturally compatible classroom practices. *Educational Perspectives, 20,* 16–19.

Jordan, C., & Tharp, R. G. (1979). Culture and education. In A. Marsella, R. G. Tharp, & T. Cibrowski (Eds.), *Perspectives in cross-cultural psychology.* New York: Academic Press.

Just, M. A., & Carpenter, P. A. (1978). Inference processes during reading: Reflections from eye fixations. In J. W. Sendes, D. F. Fisher, & R. A. Monty (Eds.), *Eye movements and the higher psychological functions.* Hillsdale, NJ: Lawrence Erlbaum Associates.

Just, M. A., & Carpenter, P. A. (1980). A theory of reading: From eye fixations to comprehension. *Psychological Review, 87,* 329–354.

Katz, E., & Brent, S. (1968). Understanding connections. *Journal of Verbal Learning and Verbal Behavior, 1,* 501–509.

Katz, L., & Baldasare, J. (1983). Syllable coding in printed-word recognition by children and adults. *Journal of Educational Psychology, 75,* 245–256.

Kavale, K., & Schreiner, R. (1979). The reading processes of above average and average readers: A comparison of the use of reasoning strategies in responding to standardized comprehension measures. *Reading Research Quarterly, 15,* 102–128.

Kay, A. (1977, September). Microelectronics and the personal computer. *Scientific American,* 230–244.

Kean, M., Sommers, A., Raivetz, M. J., & Farber, I. P. J. (1979). *What works in reading?* Philadelphia: Office of Research and Evaluation, School District of Philadelphia.

Kennedy, B. A., & Miller, D. J. (1976). Persistent use of verbal rehearsal as a function of information about its value. *Child Development, 47,* 566–569.

Kern, R. P. (1980). *Usefulness of readability formulas for achieving Army readability objectives: Research and state–of–the–art applied to the Army's problem.* Fort Benjamin Harrison, IN: U. S. Army Research Institute, Technical Advisory Service.

Kieras, D. E. (1981). The role of major referents and sentence topics in the construction of passage macrostructures. *Discourse Processes, 4,* 1–15.

Kimball, J. P. (1973). Seven principles of surface structure parsing in natural language. *Cognition, 2,* 15–47.

King, M. (1979). *Children's planning cohesion in three modes of discourse: Interactive speech, dictation and writing.* Washington, DC: National Institute of Education.

Kintsch, W. (1974). *The representation of meaning in memory.* Hillsdale, NJ: Lawrence Erlbaum Associates.

Kintsch, W., & Keenan, J. M. (1973). Reading rate as a function of the number of propositions in the base structure of sentences. *Cognitive Psychology, 5,* 257–274.

Kintsch, W., Kozminsky, E., Streby, W. J., McKoon, G., & Keenan, J. M. (1975). Comprehension and recall of text as a function of content variables. *Journal of Verbal Learning and Verbal Behavior, 14,* 196–214.

Kintsch, W., Mandel, T. S., & Kozminzky, E. (1977). Summarizing scrambled stories. *Memory and Cognition, 5,* 547–552.

Kintsch, W., & vanDijk, T. A. (1978). Toward a model of text comprehension and production. *Psychological Review, 85,* 363–394.

Kintsch, W., & Vipond, D. (1979). Reading comprehension and readability in educational practice and psychological theory. In L. G. Nilsson (Ed.), *Perspectives on memory research.* Hillsdale, NJ: Lawrence Erlbaum Associates.

Klare, G. R. (1984). Readability. In P. D. Pearson (Ed.), *Handbook of reading research.* New York: Longman.

Kleiman, G. M. (1975). Speech recoding in reading. *Journal of Verbal Learning and Verbal Behavior, 14,* 323–339.

Kleiman, G. M. (1982). Comparing good and poor readers: A critique of research. In K. E. Nelson (Ed.), *Children's language,* Vol. 3. Hillsdale, NJ: Lawrence Erlbaum Associates.

Klein, T. W. (1981). Results of the reading program. *Educational Perspectives, 20,* 8–9.

Knott, G. (1979). Developing reading potential in black remedial high school freshmen. *Reading Improvement, 16,* 262–269.

Kobasigawa, A., Ransom, C. C., & Holland, C. J. (1980). Children's knowledge about skimming. *Alberta Journal of Educational Research, 26,* 169–182.

Koch, K. (1970). *Wishes, lies, and dreams.* New York: Random House.

Koslin, B. L., Koslin, S., & Zeno, S. (1979). Towards an effectiveness measure in reading. In R. W. Tyler & S. H. White (Chairmen), *Testing, teaching and learning: Report of a conference on research in testing,* August 17–26, 1978. Washington, DC: National Institute of Education.

Krashen, S. (1978). The monitor model for second language acquisition. In R. Gingras (Ed.), *Second language acquisition and foreign language teaching.* Washington, DC: Center for Applied Linguistics.

Kreider, K. (1981). The effect of topic sentences and their placement on the reading comprehension of groups of achieving eleventh grade male readers. *Dissertation Abstracts International, 42,* 631–A.

Kroch, A., & Hindle, D. (1978). *A quantitative study of the syntax of speech and writing.* Washington, DC: National Institute of Education.

Kuczaj, S. A. (1982). Syntax and semantics. In S. A. Kuczaj (Ed.), *Language development* (Vol. 1). Hillsdale, NJ: Lawrence Erlbaum Associates.

Kulhavy, R. W., Dyer, J. W., & Silver, L. (1975). The effects of note taking and test expectancy on the learning of text material. *Journal of Educational Research, 68,* 363–365.

Labov, W. (1966). *The social stratification of English in New York City.* Washington, DC: Center for Applied Linguistics.

Labov, W. (1972). *Language in the inner city.* Philadelphia: University of Pennsylvania Press.

Langer, J. A. (1978). An idiosyncratic model of cognitive and affective silent reading strategies. *Dissertation Abstracts International, 39,* 3425 (University Microfilm No. 78, 21251).

Langer, J. A. (1981). Pre-reading plan (PRep): Facilitating text comprehension. In J. Chapman (Ed.), *The reader and the text.* London: Heineman.

Langer, J. (1982a). Facilitating text processing: The elaboration of prior knowledge. In J. Langer & M. Smith–Burke (Eds.) *Reader meets author/bridging the gap: A psycholinguistic and sociolinguistic perspective* (pp 149–162). Newark, DE: International Reading Association.

Langer, J. (1982b). What research in reading reveals about the reading process. In A. Berger & H. A. Robinson (Eds.), *Secondary school reading: What research reveals for classroom practice.* Urbana, IL: National Council of Teachers of English.

Langer, J. A. (1983). How readers construct meaning: An analysis of reader performance on standardized test items. In R. Freedle (Ed.), *Cognitive and linguistic analyses of test performance*. Norwood, NJ: Ablex.

Langer, J. (1984). Examining background knowledge and text comprehension. *Reading Research Quarterly, 19*, 468–481.

Langer, J. A., & Nicolich, M. (1980, November). Effect of altered prior knowledge on passage recall. Paper presented at National Reading Conference. (ERIC Document Reproduction Service No. E9 197 282).

Langer, J., & Nicolich, M. (1981). Prior knowledge and its relationship to comprehension. *Journal of Reading Behavior, 13*, 373–379.

Lawler, R. W., & Papert, S. ((1982). *The unreachable word*. Cambridge, MA: Massachusetts Institute of Technology, Logo Project.

Leaverton, L., Gladney, M., & Davis, O. (1969). *The psycholinguistics reading series: A bidialectical approach*. Chicago: Board of Education.

Lee, D. M., & Allen, R. V. (1963). *Learning to read through experience* (2nd edition). NY: Appleton-Century-Crofts.

Lesgold, A. M., & Resnick, L. B. (1983). How reading differences develop: Perspectives from a longitudinal study. In J. P. Das, R. Mulcahy, & A. E. Wall (Eds.), *Theory and research in learning disabilities*. New York: Plenum Press.

Lesgold, A. M., Roth, S. F., & Curtis, M. E. (1979). Foregrounding effects in discourse comprehension. *Journal of Verbal Learning and Verbal Behavior, 18*, 291–308.

Levin, J. A. (1982a). Microcomputers as interactive communication media: An interactive text interpreter. *The Quarterly Newsletter of the Laboratory of Comparative Human Cognition*, No. 2(4).

Levin, J. A. (1982b). Microcomputer communication networks for education. *The Quarterly Newsletter of the Laboratory of Comparative Human Cognition*, No. 2(4).

Levin, J. A., Boruta, M. J., & Vasconcellos, M. T. (1983). Microcomputer-based environments for writing: A writer's assistant. In A. C. Wilkinson (Ed.), *Classroom computers and cognitive science*. New York: Academic Press.

Liberman, I. Y., Shankweiler, D., Fischer, F., & Carter, B. (1974). Explicit syllable and phoneme segmentation in the young child. *Journal of Experimental Child Psychology, 18*, 201–212.

Liberman, I. Y., Shankweiler, D., Orlando, C., Harris, K. S., & Berti, F. B. (1971). Letter confusion and reversals of sequence in the beginning reader: Implications for Orton's theory of developmental dyslexia. *Cortex, 7*, 127–142.

Loban, W. (1976). *Language development: Kindergarten through grade 12*. Urbana, IL: National Council of Teachers of English.

Lunzer, E., Davies, F., & Greene, T. (1980). *Reading for learning in science* (Schools Council Project Report). Nottingham, England: University of Nottingham, School of Education.

MacDonald, N. H., Frase, L. T., Gingrich, P. S., & Keenan, S. A. (1982). The Writer's Workbench: Computer aids for text analysis. *IEEE Transactions on Communication, 20*, 1–14.

Magoon, J. (1977). Constructivist approach in educational research. *Review of Education Research, 47*, 651–693.

Mandler, J. M. (1978). A code in the node: The use of a story schema in retrieval. *Discourse Processes, 1*, 14–35.

Mandler, J. M., & Johnson, N. S. (1977). Remembrance of things parsed: Story structure and recall. *Cognitive Psychology, 9*, 111–151.

Manelis, L., & Yekovich, F. R. (1976). Repetitions of propositional arguments in sentences. *Journal of Verbal learning and Verbal Behavior, 15*, 301–312.

Maratosos, M. P. (1974). How preschool children understand missing complement sentences. *Child Development, 45*, 446–455.

Markman, E. M. (1977). Realizing that you don't understand: A preliminary investigation. *Child Development, 46*, 986–992.

Markman, E. M. (1979). Realizing you don't understand: Elementary school children's awareness of inconsistencies. *Child Development, 50*, 643–655.

Markman, E. M. (1981). Comprehension monitoring. In W. P. Dickson (Ed.), *Children's oral communication skills*. New York: Academic Press.

Markman, E. M., & Gorin, L. (1981). Children's ability to adjust their standards for evaluating comprehension. *Journal of Educational Psychology, 83*, 320–325.

Marr, M. B., & Kamil, M. L. (1981). Single word decoding and comprehension: A constructive replication. *Journal of Reading Behavior, 13*, 81–86.

Marshalek, B. (1981). *Trait and process aspects of vocabulary knowledge and verbal ability* (Tech. Rep. No. 15). Stanford: Stanford University.

Marshall, N. (1978, November). *Framework for evaluation*. Paper presented at National Reading Conference. St. Petersburg, FL.

Marshall, N., & Glock, M. D. (1978–1979). Comprehension of connected discourse: A study into the relationship between the structure of text and information recalled. *Reading Research Quarterly, 16*, 10–56.

Mason, J. M. (1983). An examination of reading instruction for third and fourth grades. *The Reading Teacher, 36*, 906–913.

Mason, J. M. (1984). Prereading: A developmental perspective. In P. D. Pearson (Ed.), *Handbook of research in reading*. New York: Longman.

Masur, E. F., McIntyre, C. W., & Flavell, J. H. (1973). Developmental changes in apportionment of study time among items in a multitrial free recall task. *Journal of Experimental Child Psychology, 15*, 237–246.

Mathews, M. M. (1966). *Teaching to read historically considered*. Chicago: University of Chicago Press.

Mathias, A. R. (1978, November). *Framework for instructional objectives: Contextual decoding*. Paper presented at National Reading Conference, St. Petersburg, FL.

McCraig, R. A. (1972). *The writing of elementary school children: A model for evaluation*. Grosse Pointe, MI: Grosse Pointe Public School System.

Mc Carthy, D. (1954). Language development in children. In L. Carmichael (Ed.), *Manual of Child Psychology* (pp. 492–630). New York: Wiley.

McClelland, J. L., & Rumelhart, D. E. (1981). An interactive activation model of context effects in letter perception: Part I. An account of basic findings. *Psychological Review, 88*, 375–407.

McClure, E., Mason, J. M., & Barnitz, J. (1979). Story structure and age effects on children's ability to sequence stories. *Discourse Processes, 2*, 213–249.

McConkie, G. W. (1983). Eye movements and perception during reading. In K. Rayner (Ed.), *Eye movements in reading: Perceptual and language processes*. New York: Academic Press.

McConkie, G. W., & Rayner, K. (1974). *Identifying the span of the effective stimulus in reading* (Tech. Rep. 3). Ithaca, NY: Cornell University.

McDermott, R. (1974). Achieving school failure: An anthropological approach to illiteracy and school stratification. In G. Spindler (Ed.), *Education and cultural process*. New York: Holt, Rinehart, & Winston.

McDermott, R. (1978). Relating and learning: An analysis of two classroom reading groups. In R. Shuy (Ed.). *Linguistics and reading*. Rowley, MA: Newbury House.

McDonell, G. (1978). *Effects of instruction in the use of an abstract structural schema as an aid to comprehension and recall of written discourse*. Unpublished doctoral dissertation, Virginia Polytechnic Institute, Blacksburg.

Meichenbaum, D. (1985). Cognitive behavior modification. In S. Chipman, J. Segal, & R. Glaser (Eds.), *Thinking and learning skills: Current research and open questions* (Vol. 2). Hillsdale, NJ: Lawrence Erlbaum Associates.

Melmed, J. P. (1971). *Black English phonology: The question of reading interference.* Monographs of the Language Behavior Research Lab., No. 1. Berkeley: University of California.

Messer, S. (1967). Implicit phonology in children. *Journal of Verbal Learning and Verbal Behaviour, 6,* 609–613.

Meyer, B. J. F. (1975). *The organization of prose and its effect on recall.* Amsterdam: North Holland.

Meyer, B. J. F. (1977). The structure of prose: Effects on learning and memory and implications for educational practice. In R. C. Anderson, R. Spiro, & W. Montague (Eds.), *Schooling and the acquisition of knowledge.* Hillsdale, NJ: Lawrence Erlbaum Associates.

Meyer, B. J. F. (1979). Organizational patterns in prose and their use in reading. In M. L. Kamil & A. J. Moe (Eds.), *Reading research: Studies and applications* (109–117). 28th Yearbook of the National Reading Conference.

Meyer, B. J. F. (1982). *Prose analysis: Purposes, procedures, and problems* (Research Rep. No. 11, Prose Learning Series). Tempe: Arizona State University, Dept. of Educational Psychology.

Meyer, B. J. F. (1984). Text structure and text comprehension. In H. Mandl, N. Stein, & T. Trabasso (Eds.), *Learning and comprehension of text.* Hillsdale, NJ: Lawrence Erlbaum Associates.

Meyer, B. J. F., Brandt, D. M., & Bluth, G. J. (1980). Use of top-level structure in text: Key for reading comprehension of ninth-grade students. *Reading Research Quarterly, 16,* 72–103.

Meyer, B. J. F. & Freedle, R. O. (1979). *Effects of discourse type on recall.* Princeton, NJ: Educational Testing Service.

Meyer, B. J. F., & Freedle, R. O. (1984). Effects of discourse type on recall. *American Educational Research Journal, 21,* 121–143.

Meyer, D. E., & Schvaneveldt, R. W. (1971). Facilitation in recognizing pairs of words: Evidence of a dependence between retrieval operations. *Journal of Experimental Psychology, 90,* 227–234.

Mikulecky, L. J. (1982). Job literacy: The relationship between school preparation and work place actuality. *Reading Research Quarterly, 17,* 400–419.

Mikulecky, L. J. & Diehl, W. (1979). Literacy requirements in business and industry. Bloomington: Indiana University School of Education, Reading Research Center.

Mikulecky, L. J., Diehl, W. (1980). *Job literacy: A study of literacy demands, attitudes, and strategies in a cross-section of occupations.* Bloomington, IN: Indiana University, Reading Research Center.

Miller, G. A. (1956). The magical number seven plus or minus two: Some limits on our capacity to process information. *Psychological Review. 63,* 81–97.

Miller G. A. (1965). Some preliminaries to psycholinguistics. *American Psychologist. 20,* 15–20.

Miller, G. A. (Ed.). (1973). *Linguistic communication: Perspectives for research.* Newark, DE: International Reading Association.

Miller, G. A. (1977). *Spontaneous apprentices.* New York: Seabury Press.

Miller, G. A. (1978). The acquisition of word meaning. *Child Development, 59,* 999–1004.

Miller, G. A. (1979, October). *Automated dictionaries: Testing, teaching and learning.* Washington, DC: The National Institute of Education.

Miller, G. A., & Selfridge, J. (1950). Verbal context and the recall of meaningful materials. *American Journal of Psychology. 63,* 176–185.

Miller, J. R., & Kintsch, W. (1980). Readability and recall of short prose passages: A theoretical analysis. *Journal of Experimental Psychology: Human Learning and Memory, 6,* 335–354.

Moe, J., Rush, R., & Storlie, R. L. (1980, January). *The literacy requirements of ten occupations on the job and in a vocational training program* (Project No. FY-80-8075-T). Lafayette, IN: Purdue University Dept. of Education, Indiana Dept. of Public Instruction.

Moerk, E. L. (1983). *The mother of Eve: As a first language teacher.* Norwood, NJ: Ablex.

Morgan, J. (1977, July). *Two types of convention in indirect speech acts* (Tech. Rep.No. 52). Urbana: University of Illinois, Center for the Study of Reading.

Myers, M., & Paris, S. G. (1978). Children's metacognitive knowledge about reading. *Journal of Educational Psychology, 70,* 680–690.

Nagy, W. E., & Anderson, R. C. (1982). *The number of words in printed school English* (Tech. Rep. No. 253), Urbana: University of Illinois, Center for the Study of Reading.

Nelson, J., & Herber, H. L. (1982). Organization and management of programs. In A. Berger & H. Robinson (Eds.), *Secondary school reading: What research reveals for classroom practice.* Urbana: National Council of Teachers of English.

Nelson, K. (1973). Structure and strategy in learning to talk. *Monographs of the Society for Research in Child Development, 38*(1–2 Serial No. 149).

Nelson, K. E. (Ed.). (1978). *Children's language* (Vol. 1). Hillsdale, NJ: Lawrence Erlbaum Associates.

Nelson, K. E. (Ed.). (1980). *Children's language* (Vol. 2). Hillsdale, NJ: Lawrence Erlbaum Associates.

Nelson, K. E. (1982). Experimental gambits in the service of language acquisition theory: From the fiffin project to operation input swap. In S. A. Kuczaj (Ed.), *Language Development (Vol. 1): Syntax and semantics.* Hillsdale, NJ: Lawrence Erlbaum Associates.

Nezworski, M. T., Stein, N. L. & Trabasso, T. (1979, June). *Story structures versus content effects on children's recall of evaluative inferences* (Tech. Rep. No. 129). Urbana: University of Illinois, Center for the Study of Reading. (ERIC Document Reproduction Service No. ED 172 187).

Norman, D. A. (1980). Twelve issues for cognitive science. *Cognitive Science, 4,* 1–32.

Northcutt, N. (1975). *Adult functional competency: a summary.* Austin: University of Texas at Austin.

Odell, L. (1980). Business writing, Observations and implications for teaching composition. *Theory into Practice, 19,* 725–731.

Olshavsky, J. (1976–1977). Reading as problem solving: An investigation of strategies. *Reading Research Quarterly, 12,* 654–674.

Olson, D. (1977). From utterance to text: The bias of language in speech and writing. *Harvard Educational Review, 47,* 257–281.

Omanson, R. C. (1979). *The narrative analysis.* Unpublished doctoral dissertation, University of Minnesota, Minneapolis.

Omanson, R. C. (1982a). An analysis of narratives: Identifying central, supportive, and distracting content. *Discourse Processes, 5,* 195–224.

Omanson, R. C. (1982b). The relation between centrality and story grammar categories. *Journal of Verbal Learning and Verbal Behavior, 21,* 326–337.

Ortony, A. (1976, February). *Names, descriptions, and pragmatics* (Tech. Rep. No. 7). Urbana: University of Illinois, Center for the Study of Reading.

Owens, J., Bower, G. H., & Black, J. B. (1979). The "soap-opera" effect in story recall. *Memory & Cognition, 7,* 185–191.

Owings, R. A., Petersen, G. A., Bransford, J. D., Morris, C. D., & Stein, B. S. (1980). Spontaneous monitoring and regulation of learning: A comparison of successful and less successful fifth graders. *Journal of Educational Psychology, 72,* 250–256.

Palermo, D. S., & Molfese, D. L. (1972). Language acquisition from age five onward. *Psychological Bulletin, 78,* 408–428.

Palincsar, A. S., & Brown, A. L. (1982). *Reciprocal teaching of comprehension–monitoring activities.* Unpublished manuscript, University of Illinois, Urbana.

Palincsar, A. S., & Brown, A. L. (1985). Reciprocal teaching of comprehension monitoring activities. In J. Osborn, P. Wilson, & R. C. Anderson (Eds.), *Reading education: Foundations for a literate America.* Lexington, MA: Lexington Books.

Papert, S. (1980). *Mindstorms: Children, computers, and powerful ideas.* New York: Basic Books.

Paris, S. G., & Lindauer, B. K. (1976). The role of inference in children's comprehension and memory. *Cognitive Psychology, 8,* 217–227.

Paris, S. G., Lipson, M. Y., Jacobs, J., Oka, E., Debritto, A. M., & Cross, D. (1982, April). *Metacognition and reading comprehension.* A symposium presented at the International Reading Association meeting, Chicago.

Paris, S. G., & Myers, M. (1981). Comprehension monitoring, memory, and study strategies of good and poor readers. *Journal of Reading Behavior, 8,* 5–22.

Paris, S. G., Newman, R. S., & McVey, K. A. (1982). Learning the functional significance of mnemonic actions: A microgenetic study of strategy acquisition. *Journal of Experimental Child Psychology, 34,* 490–509.

Pearson, P. D. (1974–1975). The effects of grammatical complexity on children's comprehension, recall, and conception of certain semantic relations. *Reading Research Quarterly, 10,* 155–192.

Pearson, P. D., & Camperell, K. (1981). Comprehension of text structures. In J. Guthrie (Ed.), *Comprehension and teaching: Research reviews.* Newark, DE: International Reading Association.

Pearson, P. D., Hansen, J., & Gordon, C. (1979). The effect of background knowledge on young children's comprehension of explicit and implicit information. *Journal of Reading Behavior, 11*(3), 201–209.

Pearson, P. D., & Johnson, D. C. (1978). *Teaching reading comprehension.* New York: Holt, Rinehart, & Winston.

Perfetti, C. A., & Hogaboam, T. W. (1975). The relationship between single word decoding and reading comprehension skill. *Journal of Educational Psychology, 67,* 461–469.

Perfetti, C. A., & Lesgold, A. M. (1977). Discourse comprehension and sources of individual differences. In M. A. Just & P. A. Carpenter (Eds.), *Cognitive Processes in Comprehension.* Hillsdale, NJ: Lawrence Erlbaum Associates.

Perfetti, C. A., & Lesgold, A. M. (1979). Coding and comprehension in skilled reading and implications for reading instruction. In L. B. Resnick & P. A. Weaver (Eds.). *Theory and practice of early reading* (Vol. 1). Hillsdale, NJ: Lawrence Erlbaum Associates.

Perfetti, C. A., & Roth, S. F. (1981). Some of the interactive processes in reading and their role in reading skill. In A. M. Lesgold & C. A. Perfetti (Eds.), *Interactive processes in reading.* Hillsdale, NJ: Lawrence Erlbaum Associates.

Petrosky, A. (1982). From story to essay: Reading and writing. *College Composition and Communication, 33,* 4.

Petty, W. T., & Jensen, J. M. (1980). *Developing children's language.* Boston: Allyn & Bacon.

Piaget, J. (1972). Intellectual development from adolescence to adulthood. *Human Development, 15,* 1–11.

Pichert, J. W. (1978). *Sensitivity to what is important in prose: A developmental study.* Unpublished doctoral dissertation, University of Illinois, Urbana.

Pichert, J. W., & Anderson, R. C. (1977). Taking different perspectives on a story. *Journal of Educational Psychology, 69,* 309–315.

Pikulski, J. E., & Shanahan, T. (Eds.). (1982). *Approaches to the informal evaluation of reading.* Newark, DE: International Reading Association.

Raphael, T. E. (1980). *Question–answering strategies of good and poor readers.* Unpublished doctoral dissertation, University of Illinois, Urbana.

Rayner, K. (1975). The perceptual span and peripheral cues in reading. *Cognitive Psychology, 7,* 65–81.

Rayner, K. (1978). Eye movements in reading and information processing. *Psychological Bulletin, 85,* 618–660.

Read, C. (1971). Preschool children's knowledge of English phonology. *Harvard Educational Review, 41*, 1–34.

Reder, L. M. (1980). The role of elaboration in the comprehension and retention of prose: A critical review. *Review of Educational Research, 50*, 5–53.

Reichman, G. (1978, July). *Conversational coherency* (Tech. Rep. No. 95). Urbana: University of Illinois, Center for the Study of Reading.

Rental, V., & Kennedy, J. (1972). Effects of pattern drills on the phonology, syntax and reading achievement of Applachian children. *American Education Research Journal, 9*, 87–100.

Rescorla, L. (1980). Overextension in early language development. *Journal of Child Language, 7*, 321–335.

Resnick, L. B., & Weaver, P. A. (Eds.). (1979). *Theory and practice of early reading* (Vol. 1). Hillsdale, NJ: Lawrence Erlbaum Associates.

Reynolds, R. E., Taylor, M. A., Steffensen, M. S., Shirey, L. L., & Anderson, R. C. (1982) Cultural schemata and reading comprehension. *Reading Research Quarterly, 17*, 353–366.

Richards, J. P., & August, G. J. (1975). Generative underlining strategies in prose recall. *Journal of Educational Psychology, 67*, 860–865.

Richards, M. M. (1979). Sorting out what's in a word from what's not: Evaluating Clark's semantic features acquisition theory. *Journal of Experimental Child Psychology, 27*, 1–47.

Richgels, D. J. (1983, December). *Second, third, and fourth graders' comprehension of spoken and written complex sentences—with and without training.* Paper presented at the National Reading Conference, Austin, TX.

Ringel, B. A., & Springer, C. (1980). On knowing how well one is remembering: The persistence of strategy use during transfer. *Journal of Experimental Child Psychology, 29*, 322–333.

Ringler, L. H. (1982). *Personal materials,* Workshop Presentation.

Ringler, L. H., & Weber, C. K. (1984). *A language–thinking approach to reading: Diagnosis and teaching.* New York: Harcourt, Brace, Jovanovich.

Roberts, P. (1970). *An evaluation of statistical tests as tools for measuring language development* (Language Research Rep. No. 1). Cambridge, MA: Language Research Foundation.

Robinson, H. A. (1978a). *Facilitating successful reading strategies.* Paper presented at the meeting of the International Reading Association, Houston, TX.

Robinson, H. A. (1978b). *Teaching reading and study strategies: The content areas* (2nd ed.) Boston: Allyn & Bacon.

Robinson, R. P. (1941). *Effective study.* New York: Harper & Row.

Rosenblatt, L. M. (1978). *The reader, the text, the poem.* Carbondale: Southern Illinois University Press.

Rosenshine, B. V. (1980). Skill hierarchies in reading comprehension. In R. J. Spiro, B. C. Bruce, & W. F. Brewer (Eds.). *Theoretical issues in reading comprehension.* Hillsdale, NJ: Lawrence Erlbaum Associates.

Royer, J. M., & Cable, G. W. (1976). Illustrations, analogies, and facilitative transfer in prose learning. *Journal of Educational Psychology. 68*, 205–209.

Royer, J. M., & Cunningham, D. J. (1978). *On the theory and measurement of reading comprehension* (Tech. Rep. No. 91). Urbana: University of Illinois, Center for the Study of Reading.

Royer, J. M., Hastings, C. N., & Hook, C. (1979). *A sentence verification technique for measuring reading comprehension* (Tech. Rep. No. 137). Urbana: University of Illinois, Center for the Study of Reading.

Rubin, A. D. (1980a). Making stories, making sense. *Language Arts, 57*, 285–298.

Rubin, A. D. (1980b). A theoretical taxonomy of the differences between oral and written language. In R. J. Spiro, B. C. Bruce, & W. F. Brewer (Eds.), *Theoretical issues in reading comprehension.* Hillsdale, NJ: Lawrence Erlbaum Associates.

Rubin, A. D. (1983). The computer confronts language arts: Cans and shoulds for education. In A. C. Wilkinson (Ed.), *Classroom computers and cognitive science*. New York: Academic Press.

Rubin, A. D., & Bruce, B. C. (1983). QUILL: Reading and writing with a microcomputer. In B. A. Hutson (Ed.), *Advances in reading and language research*. Greenwich, CT: JAI Press.

Rumelhart, D. E. (1975). Notes on a schema for stories. In D. G. Brown & A. Collins (Eds.), *Representation and understanding: Studies in cognitive science*. New York: Academic Press.

Rumelhart, D. E. (1977a). Toward an interactive model of reading. In S. Dornic (Ed.), *Attention and performance VI*. Hillsdale, NJ: Lawrence Erlbaum Associates.

Rumelhart, D. E. (1977b). Understanding and summarizing brief stories. In D. LaBerge & J. Samuels (Eds.), *Basic processes in reading: Perception and comprehension*. Hillsdale, NJ: Lawrence Erlbaum Associates.

Rumelhart, D. E. (1980). Schemata: The building blocks of cognition. In R. J. Spiro, B. C. Bruce, & W. F. Brewer (Eds.), *Theoretical issues in reading comprehension*. Hillsdale, NJ: Lawrence Erlbaum Associates.

Rumelhart, D. E., & Ortony, A. (1977). The representation of knowledge in memory. In R. C. Anderson, R. J. Spiro, & W. E. Montague (Eds.), *Schooling and the acquisition of knowledge*. Hillsdale, NJ: Lawrence Erlbaum Associates.

Rutter, M. (1978). Prevalence and types of dyslexia. In A. L. Benton & D. Pearl (Eds.), *Dyslexia*. New York: Oxford University Press.

Rutter, M., Mayghan, B., Mortimore, P., Ouston, J. & Smith, A. (1979). *Fifteen Thousand Hours*. Cambridge, MA: Harvard University Press.

Ryan, M. P. (1982). *Monitoring text comprehension: Individual differences in epistemological standards*. Unpublished manuscript, University of Texas, San Antonio.

Rystrom, R. (1970). Dialect training and reading: A further look. *Reading Research Quarterly, 5*, 581–599.

Sacher, J., & Duffy, T. (1978, March). *Reading skill and military effectiveness*. Paper presented at American Educational Research Association, Toronto, Ontario, Canada. (ERIC Document Reproduction Serv. ED 151 745).

Saddock, J. M. (1974). *Toward a linguistic theory of speech acts*. New York: Academic Press.

Sajavaara, K. (1978). The monitor model and monitoring in foreign language speech communication. In R. Gingras (Ed.), *Second language acquisition and foreign language teaching*. Washington, DC: Center for Applied Linguistics.

Salisbury, R. (1935). Some effects of training in outlining. *The English Journal, 24*, 11–116.

Samuels, S. J. (1979). The method of repeated readings. *The Reading Teacher, 32*, 403–408.

Samuels, S. J. (1981). Characteristics of exemplary reading programs. In J. T. Guthrie (Ed.) *Comprehension and teaching: Research reviews*. Newark, DE: International Reading Association.

Scardamalia, M., & Bereiter, C. (1981, October). *Development of dialectical processes in composition*. Paper presented at Conference on the Nature and Consequences of Literacy, Ontario Institute for Studies in Education, Toronto, Ontario, Canada.

Scardamalia, M., & Bereiter, C. (1983). Child as coinvestigator: Helping children gain insight into their own mental processes. In S. Paris, G. Olson, & H. Stevenson (Eds.), *Learning and motivation in the classroom*. Hillsdale, NJ: Lawrence Erlbaum Associates.

Schallert, D. L., Kleiman, G. M., & Rubin, A. D. (1977). *Analyses of differences between written and oral language* (Tech. Rep. No. 29). Urbana: University of Illinois, Center for the Study of Reading.

Schallert, D. L., & Tierney, R. J. (1982). *Learning from expository text: The interaction of text structure with reader characteristics*. Washington, DC: National Institute of Education. (ERIC Document Reproduction Service No. ED 221 833).

Schank, R. C. (1975). The structure of episodes in memory. In D. G. Bobrow & A. Collins (Eds.), *Representation and understanding: studies in cognitive science*. NY: Academic Press.

Schank, R. C., & Abelson, R. P. (1977). *Scripts, plans, goals, and understanding: An inquiry into human knowledge structures*. Hillsdale, NJ: Lawrence Erlbaum Associates.

Schnell, T. R., & Rocchio, D. (1975). A comparison of underlining strategies for improving reading comprehension and retention. In G. H. McNick & W. D. Miller (Eds.), *Reading: Convention and inquiry*. 24th Yearbook of the National Reading Conference.

Schuder, R. T. (1978, November). *Introduction: The importance of an explicit conceptualization*. Paper presented at National Reading Conference, St. Petersburg, FL.

Schuder, R. T., & Flach, E. G. (1983). *Report on the reliability and validity of the criterion-referenced reading comprehension tests in narration for the Instructional Program in Reading/Language Arts*. Rockville, MD: The Montgomery County Public Schools, 1983.

Schumann, J. (1978). The acculturation model for second language acquisition. In R. Gingras (Ed.), *Second language acquisition and foreign language teaching*. Washington, DC: Center for Applied Linguistics.

Scollen, R. (1976). *Conversations with a one-year-old*. Honolulu: University of Hawaii Press.

Scribner, S., & Cole, M. (1978a). Literacy without schooling: Testing for intellectual effects. *Harvard Education Review, 48*, 448–461.

Scribner, S., & Cole, M. (1978b). Unpackaging literacy. *Social Science Information, 17*, 19–40.

Scribner, S., & Cole, M. (1981). *The psychology of literacy*. Cambridge, MA: Harvard University Press.

Searle, J. (1969). *Speech Acts*. Cambridge: Cambridge University Press.

Searle, J. (1975). A taxonomy of illocutionary acts. In K. Gunderson (Ed.), *The philosophy of science: VII. 1 Language, mind and society*. Minneapolis: University of Minnesota Press.

Seifert, M. (1978–1979). High schools where scores haven't declined. *Journal of Reading, 22*, 164–166.

Selden, R. (1981, August). On the validation of the original readability formulas. In A. Davison, R. Lutz, & A. Roalef (Eds.), *Text Readability: Proceedings of the March 1980 Conference* (Tech. Rep. No. 213). Urbana: University of Illinois, Center for the Study of Reading.

Shafer, R. (1978). Will psycholinguistics change reading in the secondary schools? *Journal of Reading, 21*, 305–316.

Shanklin, N. (1981). *Relating reading and writing: Developing a transactional theory of the writing process*. Bloomington: Indiana University Monograph in Language and Reading Studies.

Sharples, M. (1980). *A computer written language lab* (DAI Working Paper No. 134). Edinburgh: University of Edinburgh, Scotland, Artificial Intelligence Department.

Sheingold, K., Kane, J., Endreweit, M., Billings, K. (1981, July). *Study of issues related to implementation of computer technology in schools* (Final report). Washington, DC: National Institute of Education. (ERIC Document Reproduction Serv. No. ED 210 034).

Shepherd, D. (1978). *Comprehensive high school reading methods*. (2nd ed.) Columbus, OH: Charles E. Merrill.

Sherzer, J. (1974). Introduction. In R. Bauman & J. Sherzer (Eds.), *Explorations in the ethnography of speaking*. New York: Cambridge University Press.

Shimron, J., & Navon, D. (1981). *The dependence on graphemes and on their translation to phonemes in reading: A developmental perspective* (Tech. Rep. No. 208). Urbana: University of Illinois, Center for the Study of Reading.

Shuy, R. W. (1968). A linguistic background for developing reading materials for Black children. In J. Baratz & R. Shuy (Eds.), *Teaching black children to read*. Washington, DC: Center for Applied Linguistics.

Shuy, R. W. (1979). The mismatch of child language to school language: Implications for beginning reading instruction. In L. Resnick & P. Weaver (Eds.), *Theory and practice of early reading*. Hillsdale, NJ: Lawrence Erlbaum Associates.

Shuy, R. W., Wolfram, W. A., & Riley, W. K. (1967). Linguistic correlates of social stratification in Detroit speech. Cooperative Research Project No. 6-1347, East Lansing, MI.

Simons, H. (1973). *Black dialect and reading interference: A review and analysis of the research evidence*. Unpublished manuscript, University of California, Berkeley.

Simpson, G. B., Lorsbach, T. C., & Whitehouse, D. (1983). Encoding and contextual components of word recognition in good and poor readers. *Journal of Experimental Child Psychology, 35*, 161–171.

Skinner, B. F. (1957). *Verbal behavior*. New York: Appleton, Century, Crofts.

Smiley, S. S., Oakley, D. D., Worthen, D., Campione, J. C., & Brown, A. L. (1977). Recall of thematically relevant material by adolescent good and poor readers as a function of written versus oral presentation. *Journal of Educational Psychology, 69*, 381–387.

Smith, E. E., & Kleiman, G. M. (1979). Word recognition: Theoretical issues and instructional hints. In L. B. Resnick & P. A. Weaver (Eds.), *Theory and practice in early reading* (Vol. 2). Hillsdale, NJ: Lawrence Erlbaum Associates.

Smith, F. (1971). *Understanding reading*. New York: Holt, Rinehart, & Winston.

Smith, F. (1975). *Comprehension and learning: A conceptual framework for teachers*. New York: Holt, Rinehart, & Winston.

Smith, H. K. (1967). The responses of good and poor readers when asked to read for different purposes. *Reading Research Quarterly, 3*, 53–84.

Smith, J. D. (1978, November). *Framework for instructional objectives: Comprehension*. Paper presented at the National Reading Conference, St. Petersburg, FL.

Smith, J. D. (1979). Bridging theory and practice: An instructional system in reading/language arts (K-8). In M. Kamil & A. Moe (Eds.), *28th Yearbook of the National Reading Conference*. Clemson University: The National Reading Conference.

Smith, M. E. (1926). An investigation of the development of the sentence and the extent of vocabulary in young children. *University of Iowa Studies in Child Welfare, 3*.

Smith, M. K. (1941). Measurement of the size of general English vocabulary through the elementary grades and high school. *General Psychological Monographs, 24*, 311–345.

Smith, N. B. (1963). *Reading instruction for today's children*. Englewood Cliffs, NJ: Prentice-Hall.

Smith-Burke, M. T. (1979). *Content area teaching: Problems and strategies*. CBS Television Sunrise Semester.

Smith-Burke, M. T. (1982). Comprehension in proficient and less proficient readers: Implications for teaching. In Y. Taylor (Ed.), *Special education and regular education: A partnership for the 80's*. Proceedings of a conference, Boca Raton, FL: Florida Atlantic University, Department of Exceptional Student Education.

Snow, C. E. (1983). Literacy and language: Relationships during the preschool years. *Harvard Educational Review, 53*, 165–189.

Spache, G. (1953). A new readability formula for primary grade reading materials. *Elementary School Journal, 53*, 410–413.

Spache, G. D., & Spache, E. B. (1977). *Reading in the elementary school* (4th ed.). Boston: Allyn and Bacon.

Speidel, G. E. (1979). *The relationship between psycholinguistic abilities and reading achievement in dialect-speaking children*. Paper presented at the annual meeting of the American Educational Research Association, San Francisco.

Speidel, G. E. (1981a). Bridging the language difference for children who speak Hawaiian English. *Education Perspectives, 20,* 23–30.

Speidel, G. E. (1981b). *Psycholinguistic abilities and reading achievement in children speaking nonstandard English* (Tech. Rep. No. 91). Honolulu: The Kamehameha Schools, Kamehameha Early Education Program.

Speidel, G. E. (1982). Creole and Standard English in Hawaii: A comparison of two approaches to language development in Hawaiian Creole-speaking children. In K. Li and J. Lum (Eds.), *Research on Asian and Pacific bilingual education.* National Dissemination and Assessment Center, Los Angeles.

Speidel, G. E., & Dowhower–Vuyk, S. (1982). *Developing children's discourse skills* (Tech. Rep. No. 104). Honolulu: The Kamehameha Schools, Kamehameha Early Education Program.

Speidel, G. E., Tharp, R. G., & Kobayashi, L. (1982). *Is there a comprehension problem for children who speak Hawaiian English? Study with children who speak Hawaiian English.* Manuscript submitted for publication. Honolulu: Kamehameha Early Education Project.

Spiegal, D. L., & Whaley, J. F. (1980, December). *Elevating comprehension skills by sensitizing students to structural aspects of narratives.* Paper presented at National Reading Conference, San Diego.

Spilich, G. J., Vesonder, G. T., Chiesi, H. I.., & Voss, J. F. (1979). Text processing of domain-related information for individuals with high and low domain knowledge. *Journal of Verbal Learning and Verbal Behavior, 18,* 275–290.

Spiro, R. J. (1977). Remembering information from text: The state of schema approach. In R. J. Spiro, R. C. Anderson, & W. Montague (Eds.), *Schooling and the acquisition of knowledge.* Hillsdale, NJ: Lawrence Erlbaum Associates.

Spiro, R. J. (1980). *Schema theory and reading comprehension: new directions* (Tech. Rep. No. 191). Urbana: University of Illinois, Center for the Study of Reading.

Spiro, R. J. (1980). Constructive processes in prose comprehension and recall. In R. J. Spiro, B. C. Bruce, & W. F. Brewer (Eds.). *Theoretical issues in reading comprehension.* Hillsdale, NJ: Lawrence Erlbaum Associates.

Spiro, R. J., Bruce, B. C., & Brewer, W. F. (1980). *Theoretical issues in reading comprehension.* Hillsdale, NJ: Lawrence Erlbaum Associates.

Spiro, R. J., & Taylor, R. (1980, December). *On investigating children's transition from narrative to expository discourse: The multidimensional nature of psychological text classification* (Tech. Rep. No. 195). Urbana: University of Illinois, Center for the Study of Reading.

Stallings, J. (1980, December). *The process of teaching basic reading skills in secondary schools.* Washington, DC: National Institute of Education. (ERIC Document Reproduction Serv. Nos. ED 210, 669, p. 186; ED210 670, p. 279; ED210 671, p. 30).

Stallings, J. (1981, April). *Changing teacher behavior: A challenge for the 1980s.* Paper presented to American Educational Research Association, Los Angeles.

Stanovich, K. E. (1980). Toward an interactive compensatory model of individual differences in the development of reading fluency. *Reading Research Quarterly, 16,* 32–71.

Stanovich, K. E., Cunningham, A. E., & West, R. F. (1981). A longitudinal study of the development of automatic recognition skills in first graders. *Journal of Reading Behavior, 13,* 57–74.

Stanovich, K. E., West, R. F., & Freeman, D. J. (1981). A longitudinal study of sentence context effects in second-grade children: Test of an interactive-compensatory model. *Journal of Experimental Child Psychology, 32,* 185–199.

Staton, J. (1979). *The value of literacy: Cross cultural research on the cognitive effects of learning to use a written language.* Unpublished manuscript, University of California, Los Angeles.

Staton, J. (1980a). *Getting things done with words: Teacher's guide and model lessons.* Los Angeles: Los Angeles Unified School District.

Staton, J. (1980b). Writing and counseling: Using a dialogue journal. *Language Arts, 57,* 5.

Staton, J., Shuy, R. W., & Kreeft, J. (1982). Analysis of dialogue writing as a communicative event (Final Report No. G-NO-80-0122). Washington, DC: Center for Applied Linguistics.

Stauffer, R. G. (1969a). *Directing reading maturity as a cognitive process.* New York: Harper & Row.

Stauffer, R. G. (1969b). *Teaching reading as a thinking process.* New York: Harper & Row.

Stauffer, R. G. (1970). *The language experience approach to the teaching of reading.* New York: Harper & Row.

Stauffer, R. G. (1975). *Directing the reading-thinking process.* New York: Harper & Row.

Steffensen, M. S. (1978, March). *Bereiter and Engelman reconsidered: The evidence from children acquiring Black English vernacular* (Tech. Rep. No. 82). Urbana: University of Illinois, Center for the Study of Reading.

Steffensen, M. S., & Guthrie, L. F. (1980). *Effects of situation on the verbalization of black inner-city children* (Tech. Rep. No. 180). Urbana: University of Illinois, Center for the Study of Reading.

Steffensen, M. S., Joag–dev, C., & Anderson, R. C. (1979). A cross-cultural perspective on reading comprehension. *Reading Research Quarterly, 15,* 10–29.

Stein, N. L. (1976, November). *The effects of increasing temporal disorganization on children's recall of stories.* Paper presented at the Psychonomic Society Meeting, St. Louis.

Stein, N. L. (1978). The comprehension and appreciation of stories: A developmental analysis. In S. Madeja (Ed.), *The arts, cognition, and basic skills.* St. Louis: Cemrel.

Stein, N. (1979). An analysis of story comprehension in elementary school children. In R. O. Freedle (Ed.), *New directions in discourse processing.* Norwood, NJ: Ablex.

Stein, N. L., & Glenn, C. G. (1978, March). *The role of temporal organization in story comprehension* (Tech. Rep. No. 71). Urbana: University of Illinois, Center for the Study of Reading.

Stein, N. L., & Glenn, C. G. (1979). An analysis of story comprehension in elementary school children. In R. O. Freedle (Ed.), *New directions in discourse processing.* Norwood, NJ: Ablex.

Stein, N. L., & Nezworski, M. T. (1978). The effect of organization and instructional set on story memory. *Discourse Processes, 1,* 177–193.

Stein, N. L., & Trabasso, T. (1982). What's in a story: Critical issues in comprehension and instruction. In R. Glaser (Ed.), *Advances in the psychology of instruction* (Vol. 2). Hillsdale, NJ: Lawrence Erlbaum Associates.

Stein, N. L., Trabasso, T., & Garfin, D. (1979, Sept.). *Comprehension and memory for moral dilemmas.* Paper presented at the annual meeting of the American Psychological Association, New York.

Stevens, K. (1980). The effect of background knowledge on the reading comprehension of ninth graders. *Journal of Reading Behavior, 12,* 151–154.

Stewart, C. M., & Hamilton, M. L. (1976). Imitation as a learning strategy in the acquisition of vocabulary. *Journal of Experimental Child Psychology, 21,* 380–392.

Sticht, T. G. (1972). Learning by listening. In J. Carroll & R. Freedle (Eds.), *Language comprehension and the acquisition of knowledge.* Washington, DC: V. H. Winston.

Sticht, T. G. (Ed.). (1975). *Reading for working.* Alexandria, VA: Human Resources Research Organization.

Sticht, T. G. (1980, April). *Literacy and vocational competence* (Columbus, OH: National Center for Research on Vocational Education, Rep. 2, No. 12). Washington, DC: Dept. of Labor.

Sticht, T. G., & Caylor, J. S. (1972). Development and evaluation of job reading task tests. *Journal of Reading Behavior, 4,* 29–50.

Sticht, T. G., Caylor, J. S., Hern, R. P., & Fox, L. C. (1973). Project REALISTIC: determination of adult functional literacy skill levels. *Reading Research Quarterly, 7,* 424–465.

Sticht, T. G., & McFann, H. H. (1975). Reading requirements for career entry. In D. M. Nielsen and H. F. Hjelm (Eds.), *Reading and career education.* Newark, DE: International Reading Association.

Stotsky, S. (1983). The politics of literacy teaching in the 1980's. *Harvard Educational Review, 53,* 60–68.

Stordahl, K. E., & Christensen, C. M. (1956). The effect of study techniques on comprehension and retention. *Journal of Education Research, 49,* 561–570.

Strickland, D. S. (1985). Building children's knowledge of stories. In J. Osborn, P. Wilson, & R. C. Anderson (Eds.), *Reading education: Foundations for a literate America.* Lexington, MA: Lexington Books.

Svensson, L. (1977). On qualitative differences in learning: III. Study skill and learning. *British Journal of Educational Psychology, 47,* 233–243.

Sweeney, J. (1982). Research synthesis on effective school leadership. *Educational Leadership, 39,* 346–352.

Tannen, D. (1981, June). *Oral and literate strategies in spoken and written discourse.* Paper presented at Literacy in the 1980's Conference held at the University of Michigan, Ann Arbor.

Tannen, D. (Ed.). (1982). *Spoken and written language.* Norwood, NJ: Ablex.

Templin, M. C. (1957). *Certain language skills in children: Their development and interrelationships.* Minneapolis: University of Minnesota Press.

Tennenberg, M., & Morine–Dershimer, G. (1978). Participant perspectives of a classroom discourse. National Institute of Education. (ERIC Document Reproduction Serv. No. ED 210 102–7).

Tharp, R. G. (1982). The effective instruction of comprehension: Results and description of the Kamehameha Early Education Program. *Reading Research Quarterly, 17,* 503–527.

Thibadeau, R., Just, M. A., & Carpenter, P. A. (1982). A model of the time course and content of reading. *Cognitive Science, 6,* 157–203.

Thompson, M., & Hannahs, N. (1979, November). *Testimony prepared for the Native Hawaiian Education Act.* Presented to a joint committee on elementary, secondary, and vocational educational and post-secondary education of the United States House of Representatives. Honolulu: Kamehameha Schools.

Thorndike, E. L. (1917). Reading as reasoning: A study of mistakes in paragraph reading. *Journal of Educational Psychology, 8,* 323–332.

Thorndike, E.L. (1921). *A teacher's word book of 10,000 words.* New York: Teacher's College, Columbia University.

Thorndyke, P. W. (1977). Cognitive structures in comprehension and memory of narrative discourse. *Cognitive Psychology, 9,* 77–110.

Thorndyke, P. W., & Yekovich, F. R. (1980). A critique of schemata as a theory of human story memory. *Poetics, 9,* 23–49.

Tierney, R. J., & LaZansky, J. (1980). The rights and responsibilities of readers and writers: A contractual agreement. *Language Arts, 57,* 606–613.

Tierney, R. J., & Mosenthal, P. J. (1982). Discourse comprehension and production: Analyzing text structure and cohesion. In J. Langer & M. Smith-Burke (Eds.), *Reader meets author/*

bridging the gap: A psycholinguistic and sociolinguistic perspective. Newark, DE: International Reading Association. (Also, 1980, Tech. Rep. No. 152, Urbana: University of Illinois, Center for the Study of Reading).

Tierney, R. J., Readence, J. E., & Dishner, E. K. (1980). *Reading strategies and practices: A guide for improving instruction.* Boston: Allyn & Bacon.

Tiernery, R., & Spiro, R. (1979, October). Some basic notions about reading comprehension. In J. Carey & R. Carey (Eds.), *New perspectives on comprehension* (Monographs in Teaching and Learning, No. 3). Bloomington: Indiana University.

Todd, W., & Kessler, C. C. (1971). Influence of response mode, sex, reading ability and level of difficulty on four measures of recall of meaningfully written material. *Journal of Educational Psychology, 62,* 229–234.

Trabasso, T. (1981). On the making of inferences during reading and their assessment. In J. T. Guthrie (Ed.), *Comprehension and teaching: Research reviews.* Newark, DE: International Reading Association.

Tuinman, J. J. (1973–1974). Determining the passage depencency of comprehension questions in 5 major tests. *Reading Research Quarterly, 9,* 206–223.

Tuinman, J. J., & Brady, M. (1973, December). *How does vocabulary account for variance on reading comprehension tests? A preliminary to an instructional analysis.* Paper presented at the National Reading Conference, Houston.

Tyler, R. W., & White, S. H. (1979, October) *Testing, teaching and learning.* Report of a Conference on Research on Testing, August 17–26, 1978. Washington, DC: National Institute of Education.

Veatch, J., Sawicki, F., Elliot, G., Barnette, E., & Blakey, J. (1973). *Keys to reading: The language experience approach begins.* Columbus, OH: Charles E. Merrill.

Vellutino, F. R. (1979). *Dyslexia: Theory and research.* Cambridge, MA: MIT Press.

Vellutino, F. R., & Scanlon, D. M. (1982). Verbal processing in poor and normal readers. In C. J. Brainerd & M. Pressley (Eds.), *Verbal processes in children: Progress in cognitive development research.* New York: Springer-Verlag.

Vellutino, F. R., Smith, H., Steger, J. A., & Kamin, M. (1975). Reading disability: Age differences and the perceptual-deficit hypothesis. *Child Development, 46,* 487–493.

Venezky, R. L. (1970). *Non-standard language and reading* (Working Paper No. 43). Madison: University of Wisconsin, Wisconsin Research and Development Center for Cognitive Learning.

Vogel, M. (1981). A comparison of basic concept formation performance and verbal concept formation performances of ninth graders grouped according to reading ability. *Dissertation Abstracts International, 42,* 637–A.

Vygotsky, L. S. (1978). *Mind in Society.* Cambridge, MA: Harvard University Press.

Waller, T. G., & MacKinnon, G. E. (Eds.). (1979). *Advances in reading research* (Vol 1.). New York: Academic Press.

Warder, D. (1981). Children's understanding of *ask* and *tell. Journal of Child Lanaguage, 8,* 139–149.

Warren, W. H., Nicholas, D. N., & Trabasso, T. (1979). Event chains and inferences in understanding narratives. In R. O. Freedle (Ed.), *New directions in discourse processing: Advances in discourse processes* (Vol. 2). Norwood, NJ: Ablex.

Watson-Gegeo, K. A., & Boggs, S. T. (1977). From verbal play to talk story: The role of routines in speech events among Hawaiian children. In S. Ervin-Tripp & C. Mitchell-Kernan (Eds.), *Child discourse.* New York: Academic Press.

Weaver, P. A., Frederiksen, J. R., Warren, B. M., Gillotte, H. P., Freeman, B., & Goodman, L. (1982, March). *Perceptual units training for improving word analysis* (Tech. Rep. No. 1). Harvard University, Cambridge, MA.

Webber, B. L. (1980). Syntax beyond the sentence: Anaphora. In R. J. Spiro, B. C. Bruce, & W. F. Brewer (Eds.), *Theoretical issues in reading comprehension.* Hillsdale, NJ: Lawrence Erlbaum Associates.

Weber, G. (1971). *Inner-city children can be taught to read: Four successful schools.* Washington, DC: Council for Basic Education.

Weber, R. M. (1970). A linguistic analysis of first-grade reading errors. *Reading Research Quarterly, 5,* 427–451.

Werner, H., & Kaplan, E. (1952). The acquisition of word meanings: A developmental study. *Monographs of the Society for Research in Child Development, 15* (Serial No. 51).

Weyer, S. A. (1982). The design of a dynamic book for information search. *International Journal of Man-Machine Studies, 17,* 87–107.

Whaley, J. F. (1981). Readers' expectations for story structure *Reading Research Quarterly, 17,* 90–114.

Wheeler, D. (1970). Processes in word recognition. *Cognitive Psychology, 1,* 59–85.

White, T. G. (1982). Naming practices, typicality, and underextension in child language. *Journal of Experimental Child Psychology, 33,* 324–326.

Whitehurst, G. J. (1979). Meaning and semantics. In G. J. Whitehurst & B. J. Zimmerman (Eds.), *The functions of language and cognition.* New York: Academic Press.

Whitehurst, G. J. (1982). Language development. In B. B. Wolman (Ed.), *Handbook of developmental psychology.* Englewood Cliffs, NJ: Prentice–Hall.

Whitehurst, G. J., & Vasta, R. (1975). Is language acquired through imitation? *Journal of Psycholinguistic Research, 4,* 37–59.

Whitehurst, G. J., & Vasta, R. (1977). *Child Behavior.* Boston: Houghton Mifflin.

Whitehurst, G. J., Kedesdy, J., & White, T. G. (1982). A functional analysis of meaning. In S. A. Kuczaj (Ed.), *Language development: Vol. 1. Syntax and semantics.* Hillsdale, NJ: Lawrence Erlbaum Associates.

Whiteman, M. (1980). What we can learn from writing research. *Theory into Practice, 19.*

Whiteman, M. (Ed.). (1981a). *Variation in writing: Functional and linguistic-cultural differences.* Hillsdale, NJ: Lawrence Erlbaum Associates.

Whiteman, M. (1981b). Dialect influence in writing. In M. Whiteman (Ed.), *Writing: The nature, development and teaching of written communication: Vol. 1. Variation in writing.* Hillsdale, NJ: Lawrence Erlbaum Associates.

Willows, D. M., & Ryan, E. B. (1981). Differential utilization of syntactic and semantic information by skilled and less skilled readers in the intermediate grades. *Journal of Educational Psychology, 73,* 607–615.

Wilmore, D. J. (1966). *A comparison of four methods of studying a textbook.* Unpublished doctoral dissertation, University of Minnesota.

Winograd, T. (1972). A program for understanding natural language. *Cognitive Psychology, 3,* 1–191.

Wittrock, M. C., Marks, C., & Doctorow, M. (1975). Reading as a generative process. *Journal of Educational Psychology, 67,* 484–489.

Wolfram, W. A. (1969). *A sociolinguistic description of Detroit Negro speech.* Washington, DC: The Center for Applied Linguistics.

Wolfram, W. A. (1971). *Overlapping influence in the English of second generation Puerto Rican teenagers in Harlem.* Final Report, U.S.O.E. 3-70-0033(508), Washington, DC (mimeo).

Wong, B., & Jones, W. (1981). Increasing metacomprehension in L. D. normally-achieving students through self-questioning training. Unpublished manuscript, Simon Fraser University, Vancouver, BC, Canada.

Yussen, S. R., Mathews, S. R., Buss, R. R., & Kane, P. T. (1980). Developmental changes in judging important and critical elements of stories. *Developmental Psychology, 16,* 213–217.

Zacchei, D. (1982). The adventures and exploits of the dynamic Story Maker and Textman. *Classroom Computer News, 2,* 28–30, 76–77.

Author Index

Subject Index